MASKED GODS

BOOKS BY FRANK WATERS

Midas of the Rockies (1937)
People of the Valley (1941)
The Man Who Killed the Deer (1942)
The Colorado (1946)
The Yogi of Cockroach Court (1947, 1972)
Masked Gods: Navaho and Pueblo Ceremonialism (1950)
The Earp Brothers of Tombstone (1960)
Book of the Hopi (1963)
Leon Gaspard (1964)
The Woman at Otowi Crossing (1966)
Pumpkin Seed Point (1969)
Pike's Peak (1971)
To Possess the Land (1973)
Mexico Mystique: The Coming Sixth World of Consciousness (1975)
Mountain Dialogues (1981)
Flight from Fiesta (1987)

ALSO AVAILABLE

Frank Waters: A Retrospective Anthology, ed. Charles L. Adams (1985)
A Sunrise Brighter Still: The Visionary Novels of Frank Waters, by Alexander Blackburn (1991)
Frank Waters: Man and Mystic, ed. Vine Deloria, Jr. (1993)

MASKED GODS
NAVAHO AND PUEBLO CEREMONIALISM

FRANK WATERS

SWALLOW PRESS
Athens

Printed in the United States of America
Second Edition
First Swallow Press / Ohio University Press edition 1984
97 96 95 94 7 6 5 4

Swallow Press / Ohio University Press Books are
printed on acid-free paper ∞

Illustrations and calligraphy by Ralph Douglas

Library of Congress Cataloging-in-Publication Data

Waters, Frank, 1902-
Masked gods.
1. Navajo Indians–Rites and ceremonies. 2. Pueblo Indians–Rites and ceremonies. 3. Indians of North America–Southwest. New–Rites and ceremonies. I. Title.
E99.N3W287 1984 299'.78 73-1799
ISBN 0-8040-0641-5 (pbk.)

TO JANEY

Table of Contents

Mr. Waters has written a book which is as powerful as it is interesting. He has synthesized in an altogether new way an amazing amount of material, adding new data based on his own experience and on his own research into primary sources. His organizing conception is certainly the prime problem of our times: the question of values or of philosophy of life.

The academic anthropologist will inevitably wince many times as he reads this book. He will challenge a number of the author's "facts" and disagree violently with some bold and unconventional interpretations. I confess that I myself was unhappy more than a few times as I read the manuscript. Nevertheless I found the reading both stirring and rewarding. I found myself seeing implications and relationships that had not been pointed out before nor occurred to me directly but which appeared rich in meaning. I found myself questioning familiar assumptions and, more important still, realizing for the first time some of the hidden premises in my habitual thinking about the cultures of the Southwest. These are healthy processes.

Just how seriously the professional reader should take his technical objections to details and broad generalizations in this book is itself a provocative query of a philosophic order. Professor Hartley Burr Alexander used to say that Plato was a wiser man than Aristotle because Plato realized the essentially dynamic nature of events and therefore utilized the myth and other dramatic modes, whereas Aristotle looked upon experience as something almost static, something which could be described adequately by an architect's drawing. Mr.

Waters approaches his materials at the mythic and symbolic levels. He is concerned primarily with the inner drama that lies beneath the surface of ethnological documentation. Perhaps he points to a deeper truth.

Although I am personally more comfortable with conclusions that can be reached independently by different observers using the same explicit methods, I recognize the profound usefulness of the warmth and imagination of Mr. Waters' approach. His picture may—I believe it does—require correction in details of color, size, shading, and perspective but it is at least a painting with depth and color. The lay reader will get a wealth of acceptable fact and an intuitive understanding of peoples and cultures that he is not likely to obtain from our rather cold ethnographies. Let us hope the appetites of many will be whetted sufficiently so that they will balance the breadth and sweep of this canvas with the scrupulous workmanship in detail of such scholars as Father Berard Haile, Fred Eggan, and W. W. Hill.

This is a heady wine. It is not, however, old wine in a new bottle. It is a new vintage from a rare soil. The roots are deep in the writer's personal life. He has not just assembled a congeries of curious facts pilfering the storehouses of other workers in the vineyard. No, these materials have been thought through *and* felt through. Mr. Waters practices what he preaches. One may well question, in my opinion, this or that aspect of his integration, but there is no doubt of the integration and no doubt that it is the author's own. This is much to say for any book.

CLYDE KLUCKHOHN,
Harvard University,
Department of Anthropology

Introduction

It was a brilliant winter day, and the boy, wrapped in a smelly horse-blanket, sat on the cliffs shivering with excitement.

Around him the rocks and the snow-swept roofs of the pueblo were crowded with people. Dark, broad-faced Pueblos swathed to the chin in bright blankets. Arrogant, lean Navahos huddled in sheepskins. A few Whites in muddy boots and battered Stetsons. A trader, chewing the stem of his pipe. A new missionary dressed in rusty black . . . all petrified by cold and silence, listening to the low beat of a drum. Waiting with loose-jointed patience. For what?

The boy knew better than to ask questions. He sat shivering with expectation.

Below him, at the foot of the cliffs, stood a clump of shaggy Indian ponies, the missionary's grey nag, a scrubby team munching hay out of the box-wagon he himself had come in. Its tracks wound back across the empty, snowy plain as far as he could see.

Then suddenly they came. Out of the wide, white universe, out of myth and legend, out of the depths of America itself.

They came filing into the open plaza, shaking their gourd rattles, uttering their strange cries. A line of figures part man, part beast, part bird. Bare bodies splotched with paint, sinuously bending at the waist. Wearing ceremonial kirtles, a ruff of spruce around the neck, and dancing in moccasined feet. But glaring with bulging eyes from great wooden heads—heads with long bird beaks and toothed snouts, square heads, round heads, cloud-terraced heads bearing the symbols of lightning and rain, and hung with tufts of eagle feathers.

How brilliant their clear colors against the snow! Beautiful, so beautiful. But so horrible and frightening too.

They began dancing. Shaking their rattles at the cringing children. Glaring at the stolid missionary. Crying at the pipe-chewing trader. Dancing back and forth before the rapt boy seeing them for the first time. No longer man nor beast nor bird, but embodied forces of earth and sky swirling across the sea of snow from the blue mountains on the horizon, shaking this remote and rocky island, stirring awake the archaic wonder and mystery and pristine purity of man's apperception of his cosmic role. Dancing as gods have always danced before their people. Masked by the grotesque, but commanding that comprehension of the heart which alone recognizes the beauty within.

Suddenly it was over.

"Humph!" muttered Bruce, the trader. "Let's go."

The boy silently followed him down the trail to the wagon. The missionary mounted his grey nag. They plodded homeward to the trading post and Bruce put on a pot of coffee. The missionary stood in front of a shelf looking at a row of small figures carved out of cottonwood and painted to resemble the dancers.

"Idols," he said disapprovingly, new to the country.

"Dolls!" muttered Bruce tersely.

The boy still held his tongue. This was the first time he had ever seen a kachina dance, and it still held him in a strange spell he could not shake off.

"You say these carved wooden idols or dolls are called kachinas," persisted the missionary. "But you called those masked dancers kachinas too. Now I can understand that all these images represent a pagan anthropomorphic god called Kachina. But when an ethnologist tells me the spirits of the dead, of mountains, clouds, trees, and animals are all kachina, I'm confused. I simply don't understand."

"Why the hell should you?" demanded Bruce, gruffly. "I don't know anything about Indians, even after forty years."

The remarks about the kachinas were confusing to the boy. It did not matter. For, as years of comprehension slowly crept upon him, he began to understand. Life is a mystery play. Its players are cosmic principles wearing the mortal masks of mountain and man. We have only to lift the masks which cloak us to find at last the immortal gods who walk in our image across the stage.

The following interpretation of the history and ceremonialism of the Pueblo and Navaho Indians is based on this subtle and profound symbol of Indian thought, the kachina.

Part One, "The Masks," consists of a brief history of the Pueblos and Navahos within a "frame of reference" which includes the Spanish conquest of Mexico and the Anglo conquest of the United States.

Part Two, "The Gods," is an interpretative analysis of Indian ceremonialism. Navaho sings, Rio Grande Pueblo dances, Zuñi kachina ceremonies, and Hopi ritualism are synthesized within a common pattern which included those of the Aztecs, Mayas, and Incas. The meaning of this pattern is compared with that of the Eastern philosophies of Taoism and Buddhism. And it is reconciled in turn with the tenets of modern Western science, as expressed in biology, geology, psychology, and atomic physics.

Part Three, "Man: Mask and God," investigates the reflection of this religious ideology in the secular life and character of the Indians, and our relation to them as a rational people opposed to a people predominantly intuitive by nature, which has its counterparts in our relationships to Latin America and the Far East on a larger scale.

Hence this exploration into the life and ceremonialism of the Pueblos and Navahos must also be a probing of our own contrasting life, our own religious, social, and scientific ceremonialism—our own kachina cults . . . To find, at the core of both, that the development of racial groups, of civilizations themselves, follows the same stages of psychological evolution inherent in the individual; a process whose end can be glimpsed through the coinciding symbols of their transcending faith.

This then is another book about Indians. But not in the romantic or academic tradition. Whatever its faults it is a testament to that mother earth which has borne this flesh from her own, a tribute to those people who have molded so largely the shape of its thought. If there resides in it any portion of the immeasurable and boundless truth, let it be said simply: It comes from the east, the south, the west, the north. It puts out its face, its belly before you, because it has no evil in it. It speaks straight. It is kachina . . . .

Part One: The Masks

To refuse to perceive the unique face of man under the masks that cover it, is no longer a sign of force but rather of senility . . . .

ELIE FAURE

CONTENTS OF PART ONE

1 The Four Corners

If there exists such a thing as a spirit-of-place, imbuing each of the continental masses of the world with its own unique and ineradicable sense of rhythm, mood, and character, and if there exists an indigenous form of faith deriving from it, then it is to the Indian we must look for that expression of life's meaning which alone differentiates America from Europe, Africa, and Asia.

The Indian-American has never been separated from his land. Unlike us immigrant Euro-Americans, his traditions stem back to its prehistoric past. And he has doggedly clung to them, preferring to die out as an ever-dwindling racial minority rather than to adapt himself and assimilate others. Whatever he is, whatever he believes, stems from the very soil of his ancient homeland. He is inseparable from the earth itself.

But what this earth is, and what the Indian is, we now have little means of knowing. Before the resistless tide of conquest the very earth has vanished under axe and plow, steel and concrete. So has the Indian vanished—not alone whole tribes but practically the race itself. And this obliteration has been accomplished too swiftly to record fully.

The Algonquin, Dakotan, Muskhogean, and Shoshonean families have almost vanished, most of the tribes on the Atlantic shore. Of the Chippewas, Menominees, and Winnebagos there remains scarcely a memory. The Mohicans, Delawares, and Objibwas, Erie, Huron, and Conestoga, are gone without trace. The Six Nations of the Iroquois—Mohawks, Oneidas, Cayugas, Onondagas, Senecas, and Tuscaroras—have left of their alliance only the pattern of the Constitution of the United States itself. The Five Civilized Tribes—the Choctaws, Chickasaws, Cherokees, Seminoles, and Creeks—herded into new "Indian Territory," lasted just long enough to name it "Oklahoma." The Four Nations alliance of Cheyennes, Arapahoes, Kiowas, and Comanches vanished with the thundering herds of buffalo. The Caddoes are forgotten in the swamps of the South. The Mission tribes of the Pacific Coast, the Osages, Pawnees, Mandans, and Potowatomis of the prairies, the desert Cocopahs, Mohaves, Pimas, and Maricopas, are dying out. Of the hard-riding tribes of the northern plains, the Sioux, the Brules, the Miniconjous and the Crows, the San Arcs and the Hunkpapas, only a handful of Ogalalas and Blackfeet remain . . . Uprooted from their tribal homeland almost all have withered away.

The only Indians left as integral groups today exist within the immemorial boundaries of their ancient homeland. The village Pueblos and semi-nomadic Navahos, fringed by the mountain Utes and desert Apaches—these today are the last homogenous remnants of what we call the Vanishing American. And they all live within the one last wilderness of what they may well call Vanishing America.

We today call it the Four Corners, because here in this upland wilderness exists the only point where four states touch: Utah, Colorado, New Mexico, and Arizona. Yet its geographical boundaries and the legendary significance of its name stem back to a prehistoric tradition that immemorially antedates the discovery of the continent by Europeans.

Physically and metaphysically the Four Corners is indeed the heartland of America. Squared astronomically to space and time by the sacred peaks of the directions, it is still rigidly defined by legend and nature alike.

To the north it is walled by the high male Rockies. Out of them well the two great rivers that divide and curve south to mark its eastern and western boundaries: the Rio Grande, on the east, which cuts a deep trough between the Sangre de Cristo and Jemez mountains; and the San Juan, which joins the Colorado to cut the sublime gorge of the Grand Canyon to the west. To the south the plateaus give way to a broken desert through which meander the Zuñi river and the Little Colorado, also tributary to the Colorado.

Surrounded by high mountain ranges, abysmal gorges, and rivers, the Four Corners is a vast, high, desert plateau; the center of gravity of the continental Colorado Pyramid; the hinterland heart of America. Paradoxically it is the oldest habitation of known life in America—both animal and human, and the least populated today. No train whistles across its far expanse. Only along its southern boundary runs a railroad and a transcontinental highway marked by the lonely little towns grown up from government forts, trading posts, and water-stops. No cities bestride its crawling rivers, which are for the most part sluggish, red creeks and dry washes. Its place-names are Indian pueblos, solitary trading posts, government agencies and missions, an occasional ranch, archeological sites and small villages. Few green fields break the monotonous miles of desert. Under sun and stars the sage slopes emptily down the canyons. The low dark hills of cedar and piñon appear no more than shadows of clouds in the sunshine. Mesa and butte stand visible upon the horizon sixty, seventy miles away. Rock-ribbed and empty the land stretches out interminably, long as time, wide as the imagination.

This is Indian country. But where are they? A pueblo atop a mesa, almost indistinguishable from the rocky escarpment. A lone and ragged Navaho horseman riding out of a wash. All lost in time, dwarfed by space, transient and inconsequential. These are its only signs of occupancy.

A lifelong search would not reveal any more than what is endlessly repeated in every square mile of the whole. A sunken blue canyon, an uplifted rock glowing red on the horizon, and rolling between them the tawny pelagic plain. Yet by their constant mutations, the interplay of light and shade, their shifting drama of color, the ecstatic leap and lift of rock, the vibratory quality of the land itself, no earth seems so dynamic with life and change. It is as if by some strange integration they express, like the kachinas they are, the meaning of the invisible forces that created them.

The Rock and the Canyon

In the middle of a vast unknown continent there stood a great Rock in a weary land. It was oriented to the four directions, its sides glowing with their corresponding colors—white on the east, blue on the south, red on the west, black on the north.

To the farthermost limits of the land surrounding it there rose on the horizon four lesser mountains: that to the east made of white shell, that to the south of blue-green turquoise, that to the west of yellow-red sand and abalone, and that to the north of black jet.

From these far points on the four horizons the land rolled in upon the great Rock like the waves of a turbulent sea. It was a land in the travail of birth. It shook and was rent asunder. New mountains rose belching fire and smoke. Rivers of molten rock flowed across the land. Slowly the earth cooled and cracked. Whole forests petrified into stone. Huge monsters left their footprints and finally their skeletons in the cooling rock. Then the forces of snow and frost, of wind and dust and rain began to warp and twist and change the land still more.

Far below it on all sides the seas swept in. The vast unknown continent itself sank under water and rose again. New steaming jungles gave way to sheets of glacial ice, to grassy plains and barren deserts. Again the land suffered the travail of birth . . . A land in perpetual movement, dramatic with constant change.

But against all these cataclysmic changes the great axial Rock stood firm. Eternity gnawed at it with the teeth of time. Nature loosed upon it the apocalyptic fury of the four elements, fire, air, water, earth. The heavens smote it with thunderbolts from above. The underworlds shook it from below. And the land kept rolling in upon it in turbulent waves of molten rock, and storms of cutting sand and dust. Still the Rock stood inviolate, like the core of the universe, rooted in time and space.

There was something else besides this land and the rock. It belonged to neither, yet it embraced the qualities of both. In many respects it even resembled them without looking like either.

It too was a mighty rock, as long as a mountain range, as high as its highest peak. But upside down. A deep cleft in the earth, a monstrous chasm. Like the Rock, this great canyon was impervious to time and change. It had lain here since time began; and paradoxically enough, the more it was assaulted by change the more it grew. Its spires and pinnacles lengthened, its clefts and crannies deepened, its buttes and mesas broadened. Until it seemed as stupendous and indestructible and mysterious as the Rock itself.

At the same time, the canyon was cleft in and out of the land and thus reflected all its changes. The centuries-slow submersion and uplift of the whole continent it recorded with the seashells imbedded in its stones. The presence of tropical jungles with the ferns impressed into its sands. The advance and retreat of glacial ice with the scoring on its cliffs . . . The canyon, even more than the land, was a phenomenon of perpetual change. With every quick storm, with every hour, it changed shape, size, pattern, and color. Never static, never still, it perpetually recapitulated the land's whole drama of constant change.

Such was the canyon, whose depth balanced the height of the rock, whose length measured the wide land. Inconstant as the passing moment and yet endurable as time itself, it seemed carven out of the rock's serenity by the fury of the land's change. Into a passionless calm beyond both, an incomprehensible paradox, a sublime mystery.

Thus do we know it today, this domain of the rock and the canyon. A vast hinterland plateau oriented to the four directions, still retaining the salient characteristics of its immortal past.

Little wonder that, like nature, man himself has worn the kachina masks of its dual forces.

The Cliff Dwellers

Created by the same immutable forces that had made the land, and drifting on the sea of change washing over the new unknown continent, the first people grasped at the Rock.

Shuddering with fear they looked back down at the dangers lurking below—at the mountains smoking on the far horizon; the camels and lumbering mammoths, the thundering herds of bison and wild horses, and the savage beasts which preyed upon them; the sudden violent storms; and, above all, the mysterious fears to which they could give no shape or name. The world was dark, as yet unlit by human reason. But instinct pointed out clefts and crannies and caves in the great Rock that offered security.

When and where did these people appear in America?

Until recently it seemed definitely settled that man first appeared in America about 2,000 years ago. Divine revelation had assured the Mormon Church, at least, that the Indians of America were one of the lost ten tribes of Israel. In 1926, a Negro cowpoke turned up some stone dart points associated with the skeletal remains of a post-glacial species of bison near Folsom, New Mexico.

Folsom Man of 10,000 years ago was discovered, and a trail of similar points has since been followed north through Canada. Then, in 1941, the University of New Mexico excavated earlier, pre-glacial remains in a cave in the Sandía Mountains, near Albuquerque, and Sandía Man was credited with having existed 25,000 years ago.

Where did they come from? When?

The most commonly accepted view is that the Indians of all the Americas are Mongoloid, and that they crossed Bering Strait from Asia to America. The distance from East Cape, Siberia, to Cape Prince of Wales, Alaska, is only fifty-four miles. Some 25,000 years ago, when the last glacial advance was at its height, Bering Strait was a land bridge. Today the "Mongolian spot," a bluish patch near the base of the spine, is found on Navahos and Mayas as well as on Asiatics.

Or were some of the earliest long-headed, non-Mongoloid types related to the European-African, Negroid, and Mediterranean types, as some authorities maintain? If so, what was their bridge to the west—a submerging, yet unverified but certainly sometime existent continent that lay in the Atlantic?

Dr. Daniel Wilson, in his *Prehistoric Man,* some years ago offered the hypothesis of a peopling of America from the Polynesian Islands. Were these the mountain tips of another vast submerging continent in the Pacific, whose population had spread both west and east to new lands?

The Indians might as well have been indigenous to America. Villamil de Rada, a Bolivian etymologist, states that the name of Mt. Olympus is a corruption of Mt. Illiampu, the great 23,000-foot-high peak of the Andes; and that the ancient Greeks were Aymara Indians who crossed to the Eastern hemisphere via the continent or islands of the lost Atlantis.

Dr. Stacy-Judd, eminent English architect and archaeologist, asserts that the Maya civilization of Yucatán and Guatemala was the seminary of the human race and the Maya tongue the mother language of mankind.

What the Indians were, where they came from, when, how, why—we do not know. It is all a contradictory jigsaw puzzle, an academic quarrel conducted in the jargon of a dozen different sciences. Archaeologists forget that stones, cities, and civilizations may fall, but the soul of a people endures.

But here they were. What were they like?

What do we know of the character of a man when the smile and frown have left his face, when the light has faded from his eyes? What do we know of the spirit which piled these dead stones atop one another, that motivated this desiccated flesh? We have yet to develop a science of living man which will use as mere tools the present sciences of dead matter; to find men seismologically sensitive to the earth and its psychic effect upon a people; to boldly admit the continuity and evolutionary development of mankind throughout a physical world in a corresponding state of flux; to sense behind both the same cosmological pattern, and awake to all its manifestations.

But from the dead stones and broken pottery, the dried corn and skulls, archaeologists, anthropologists, and ethnologists have pieced together a crude chronology of their outward development: Basketmaker I, II, III, Pueblo I, II, III, IV. This is far less important than their inner evolution through the psychological stages of development from primitive consciousness and instinctive impulses to the ego stage of rational consciousness; and then to that consciousness of self which is both personal and non-personal, transcending both the conscious and unconscious. Of this they have a complete record in their ceremonialism, as we shall see in Part Two.

By 11 A.D., one of the earliest dates of the Southwestern ruins established by dendrochronology, the Indians were using an *atlatl* or spear thrower, and dressing themselves in the skins of the animals they killed. They had learned to make sandals from yucca fibers, to weave baskets and to fashion twine-woven bags and snares.

About this time the miracle of corn occurred. The people began to plant and to store surplus grain, digging circular pits in the floors of their caves, and lining them with stones and covering the tops with brush and mud. Later, at times, they buried their dead in the cists.

Settlements began when many families at a time gathered in larger caves, and expanded the storage pits into stone pit houses built in the shelter of overhanging cliffs, rectangular pit houses, as those along the Verde River, in Arizona, or still circular in form as those at Juniper Cove, near Kayenta. The people made pottery now, strings of clay coiled round and round like the yucca fibers of their coiled baskets. They replaced the *atlatl* with the bow and arrow. To their robes of fur they added robes of turkey feathers. And with tiny *milpas* of corn they began to grow squash and beans.

The security of the rock had made man a farmer, given him a home. Now he began to develop a society.

The people erected rectangular buildings with walls of stone, plastered with mud, prototypes of the great cave pueblos like Betatakin, with 130 rooms built on the sloping floor of a huge cave in Laguna Canyon, northeastern Arizona, and Keet Seel, on the opposite side of the canyon with 150 rooms arranged so as to leave courts and passages.

From caves these pueblos climbed up the faces of the cliffs, wherever a horizontal ledge provided support, and the overhanging lip a roof. Southward from the Rocky Mountains of Colorado, westward from the Jemez Mountains of New Mexico, across all Arizona to the Grand Canyon—everywhere, these high, almost inaccessible cliff cities looked down the canyons over valley and desert.

In the labyrinthian canyons of Mesa Verde there were 350 of these miniature cities, reached only by tiny hand and toe holes cut in the rock. Cliff Palace alone was 300 feet long, containing 150 rooms. Spruce Tree House was nearly as large with 114 rooms. In the walls of the three deep gorges slashing the Defiance Plateau—Cañon de Chelly, Cañon del Muerto and Monument Canyon—were 134 other major sites. Casa Blanca, the most spectacular, was built five stories high in the eight hundred-foot cliffs. Farther south, in Walnut Canyon, there were 350 more cliff dwellings in small groups of five or six rooms. Montezuma's Castle, on Beaver Creek, was lodged seventy-five feet up the side of its perpendicular cliff.

Nor did the people confine themselves to the faces of the cliffs. They built great communal houses on top. On the Pajarito Plateau were Návawi, Ótowi, Tshirége, with six hundred rooms, and Tsaukawi, in three stories with two hundred rooms. Puyé, to the north, was still larger, a great quadrangle of four terraced community houses surrounding a court and containing perhaps sixteen hundred rooms.

How beautiful they all were. Whole little sky cities perched almost indistinguishably on top of butte and mesa. Or seemingly carved in the walls, their smooth hewn stones glowing pink in the sun, their square or round towers and open terraces looking down upon the fields of corn and squash and beans below. The people were beginning to plant cotton too, which they wove, like yucca fibers, into cloth. The wild turkeys they had domesticated. Their pottery had improved. It was decorative as well as useful, containing a white slip over the surface on which they drew designs.

Yet, for all the people's increasing use of the land below, it was the rock to which they clung. Up its steep sides they swiftly climbed at the first approach of darkness and of danger. For the turbulent sea of change below could still, in an instant, menace the whole population.

Katzimo, the Enchanted Mesa, was such a rock: 431 feet high and forty acres in area, with only one narrow trail to the top. Down this precarious Ladder Rock the people climbed to till their fields. One day while they were harvesting their crops a sudden storm came up. The people raced back toward safety. It was too late. The rain was beating against the butte, the water had risen and undermined the talus approach to their rock ladder. Adrift again, they went to another lofty mesa three miles away. This rock of Acuco was a stone island nearly a mile long, seventy acres in area, and rising 357 feet above the wind-swept plain. Up this they climbed, cutting toe and finger holds into a trail. On top they dug reservoirs for holding rain and snow water, and built three blocks of terraced houses, each one thousand feet long and three stories high. In this new pueblo of Ácoma, perhaps now the oldest continuously occupied town in America, their descendants are still living today.

But with the development of all these new, rectangular pueblos built on top and in the sides of the cliffs, the people did not forsake the old, circular form of their early storage pits and pit houses. These pits had stored the grain which gave them life, and in them they had buried their dead. Now they were used for the sacred rites and ceremonies by which the people bridged life and death in the enduring continuity. They had become kivas. Built in the open terraces in front of each house group, the kiva was subterranean, round in shape. In it man was developing a religion whose ritualistic form corresponded to its symbolism, and whose faith corresponded to his physical security in the Rock. There were twenty-three of these kivas in Cliff Palace alone, and on top of the mesa they matured into the great Sun Temple. Man had climbed the Rock as high as he could go.

Strong of faith, physically self-reliant, the people now

descended. Gradually at first, building talus pueblos at the bottom, close against the walls of the cliffs, and still utilizing the caves above. In the Rito de los Frijoles Canyon there were thirteen groups of houses, each containing some twenty rooms, and standing from one to four stories high. The house walls were built of lava blocks and coated with gypsum plaster.

And now, at last, the great pueblos took shape alone on the plain, walled cities more compact than those of China, ancient city-states that rivalled those of Greece, certainly the greatest communal dwellings known. All rising out of the dark prehistoric past and standing in the sunlit desert hinterland of a vast, unknown continent.

A huge, round honeycomb covering ten acres like Tyuoni, on the floor of the Frijoles Canyon; an immense terraced tenement house, its first terrace rising one story high from the inner circular court, the second terrace one room back and two stories high, to a height of six stories with the outside wall solid and unbroken. Or semicircular in form like Pueblo Bonito, in Chaco Canyon, its back wall forty-eight feet high, and containing more than 800 terraced rooms surrounding its inner court. Or rectangular, E-shaped, like Chetro Ketl, covering an area as large as a modern city block, terraced to a height of five stories, and walled in front with a rampart of one-story rooms used as a passage-way between wings in times of attack. Pueblo del Arroyo, Pecos, to the south, with its vast tenements of 517 and 585 rooms, Aztec, to the north—they were all essentially alike. All standing alone on the sea of change, the open plain, but built in the semblance of the ancient Rock.

In Europe, the stones of Westminster Abbey had not been hewn. In Asia, Marco Polo had not yet journeyed to the court of Kublai Khan. The Church still proscribed as "heretical and unscriptural" the belief that the earth was round. But here, in the high hinterland of a vast undiscovered America, the people had planted in stone the roots of a civilization.

The walls of their immense pueblos were composed of stones hewn, smoothed, and set like mosaic; the ceilings timbered with huge vigas of pine and spruce. Inside they were decorated with paintings, in carbon and red ochre, of clouds, the sun, lightning, and masked dancers. In the shrines close to Tyuoni were sculptured life-size figures of mountain lions carved from lava, a frieze containing the figure of the great plumed serpent. The Chaco pottery, of tall cylindrical jars, pitchers, bowls, and ladles had become a fine art. The pottery was exquisitely shaped, carefully fired, and beautifully decorated with geometric patterns and stylized animal designs. Outside were fields of many kinds of corn, squash, beans, and cotton. The cotton was spun into cloth and elaborately patterned. Beyond the fields, trails led into the mountains, where trees were cut for wood and roof-beams, and stone was quarried. Turquoise was mined, traded for shells and feathers brought up from Mexico, and worked into ornaments. Pueblo Bonito was noted for its jewelry: turquoise bead and chunk necklaces, turquoise and shell pendants and mosaics, carved birds and insects, a frog of jet with turquoise eyes, and a superb necklace of 2,500 turquoise beads.

Here, a thousand years ago, the pueblos stood swarming with people. Great man-made rocks standing serene and firm on the sunlit plain. The immemorial Rock. That was the symbol of their lives as it was the shape of their vast complex cities. Their safety depended upon it. Their social structure derived from it. Their ritualistic religion was built upon it. And the sacred kivas reflected all this in their shape and ceremonials; the very heart of the Rock in which the people validated the strength of their faith and lives.

The Nomads

Throughout all these centuries, the Rock was constantly menaced. The pueblos were endangered not only by droughts and floods, disease and wild beasts; they were besieged by marauding neighbors.

At the first warning of the raiders' approach the Pueblos retreated into their dark caves, scurried up their steep cliffs or barricaded themselves behind their great walls. The newcomers were just as swift. They appeared as if rising out of the plain, attacking, killing, and looting; then vanished as suddenly without trace. It was this that set them apart from the dwellers on the rock. Restless and homeless as herds of antelope, they were nomads.

The Pueblos too had been adrift; their origin was unknown. Where the nomads came from was just as mysterious. They were a savage, rootless people, living in temporary brush shelters and moving on with no more than could be loaded on their own and their dogs' backs.

Coming to the high hinterland of the vast unknown continent, some of the nomads dropped out of the exodus. Groups settled in the Arizona deserts to the south, in the high Colorado mountains to the north, on the grassy plains of New Mexico, below the mountain wall to the east, and in the rugged plateaus of Nevada and Utah, around the great canyon to the west.

Gradually all converged upon the Four Corners. In small bands at first. Filing down through the dark forests. Crossing the baking sands at night, carrying water in greasy intestines slung over their shoulders. Threading the labyrinthian canyons with their eyes on the stars. Climbing up out of the grassy plains like stray bunches of buffalo and antelope . . . Slowly and wonderingly, on voyages of discovery. Swiftly and savagely, on sudden forays. Sometimes cautiously, to steal or trade.

From each of these invasions they brought back something new—the vision of a new land, sometimes only a glimpse of the high pink cities carven in the cliffs, then corn from the fields below, the loot of baskets and pottery, even the rich prize of a captured woman. On their lives too the rock had stamped its first mark.

But still they were a wild and rootless people. Raiding by day, sitting by night around a fire, beating on a drum. This was their life. The drum told it all. As far as the eye could see, the earth was round and flat as the drumhead. Over it rose the sun, upon it the sun fell—just as the rounded tip of the drumstick in their hand. So rhythmically both the people and the sun and earth beat out the days, marked the time in years and centuries. A people born of ceaseless change, but whose rhythmic mutations were constant too.

To the ravaging desert nomads the Zuñis are said to have given the simple general name "Apache," meaning "enemy." They were apparently composed of all the many diverse tribes of nomads. A parvenu people remarkably adaptable, their physical types embraced all tribes. Their speech was Athabascan. Their early basketry resembled that of the first Pueblos, while their later work duplicated that of the Uto-Aztecan-speaking tribes. And their drum-shaped earth-lodge dwellings resembled those of all Plains tribes.

Moving into northern New Mexico they centered between the curving San Juan and the mountains to the east. From a group of Pueblos settled in one of the valleys in the Pajarito Plateau they learned how to plant corn. From this they derived a new name, Apaches of Navahu, said to mean "planted fields" in the Tewa dialect of the Pueblos.

The nomads by now had learned from the Pueblos how to clear fields and plant corn, how to make baskets and pottery. They had congealed into tribes, established vast and ill-defined domains. The nomads had become semi-nomadic.

They were still far from being rooted like the Pueblos. Especially the Apaches of Navahu. To the north and east rose walls of mountains. But south and west stretched a vast grassy upland, which they were ambitious to make theirs. Swiftly they spread out. Attacking the great pueblos in Chaco Canyon, the cliff-dwellings in Cañon de Chelly and Cañon del Muerto, and spearheading those in Mesa Verde. But always moving west into the vast open plains, until Navahu became known no longer as a semi-permanent village but a province. An immense grassy sea containing the rocky island refuges of the Pueblos.

On the Pueblos, the Apaches of Navahu, the Navahus or Navahos, still preyed. Human waves beating against the Rock; but only outwardly. Inwardly they too had begun to grasp it.

They too developed a matrilineal social structure—always the sign of a people polarized to the intuitive, feminine side of man. They dressed in skins, but also in garments of cedar fiber, woven like the yucca fiber of the Pueblos. And their rich ceremonialism borrowed from the highly ritualized religion of the Pueblos.

More and more their drum-shaped earth and brush lodges began to take on meaning like that of kivas. These hogans were constructed of hewn logs chinked with earth; were octagonal in shape, oriented to the four cardinal directions and the points between, with the door always facing east. On the floor of these, during ceremonials, dry sand-paintings were laid, an art copied from the Pueblos. Different colored sands were used, the colors designating the directions, as in Pueblo ritualism. The stylized designs pictured the same four sacred plants: corn, squash, beans, and tobacco; and their sacred landmarks, springs, and shrines often coincided with those of the Pueblos.

"Dinneh"—"The People." This came to be their name in their own tongue, just as Apaches to the south called themselves "Inde" or "Tinde"—"The People." Here was the vast open land over which they roamed to raid and besiege the pueblos, and here was The People arising from it. It was as simple, as subtle, as arrogantly strong as that.

The Pueblos, high and safe on their rocky mesas in the center of this grassy sea, called themselves "Hopituh"—"The People of Peace."

This was the only real difference between them. For the nomads, ostensibly still a people of constant and turbulent change, had made the transition to the Rock. The land itself was their Rock. To it they were rooted as securely as the Cliff Dwellers to their cliffs.

Thus the centuries of a new people on an unknown continent, created by the same forces that made the land, and creating a civilization new to mankind. How wonderful it must have been. And how deeply, truly mysterious. A mystery masked only by its appalling simplicity of pure feeling; of a time when man, unguided by reason, maintained a direct intuitional relationship with the primal forces of a living universe.

Then suddenly, about seven hundred years ago, something happened. We believe it was a great drought beginning in 1276. Year after year for twenty-three years the rainfall lessened. The springs failed. The crops dried up. The game dwindled. One by one the great pueblos were abandoned, their populations wandering away on long hegiras seeking new homesites near water.

What we have left, washed up on today's beach, are hewn stones, fragments of pottery, ears of corn, and desiccated bodies perfectly preserved in the dry air, ruins of whole pueblos. All empty kachina masks of a vanished civilization.

But no post mortem is necessary; this ancient civilization still exists if we know where to look for it. From the sun temple of Mesa Verde its light flickered to the pyramid sun temples of Aztec Mexico, and was reflected from those of Inca Peru. In the modern Pueblo and Navaho ceremonials of today we find embodied the same ancient rituals. It is all one vast continuity spanning both time and space—an American Way still rooted in the soil and the soul of a continent.

The Wanderings

When the great pueblos were abandoned and their populations wandered away on long hegiras seeking new homesites, where did they go?

They may have migrated east as far as Ohio. Lewis H. Morgan, the "Father of American Ethnology," traced the Mound

Builders of the Scioto Valley directly to the "Village Indians" of New Mexico.

Morgan also evolved the theory that the Aztecs were people who had migrated south from the pueblos of New Mexico. His protege, the now famous Adolph Bandelier, adopted his views in principle, stating that "the key to aboriginal history of Mexico and Central America lies between the City of Mexico and the southern part of Colorado."

Many of the Pueblos must have migrated south into Mexico, along a line of march that long had been established. There is a striking coincidence between the growth of the similar pueblo-type architecture in the Four Corners and in Anahuac during 700–1000 A.D. Fragments of Toltec pottery of the period were found in Pueblo Bonito. More important, the Aztecs had a full tradition of their own and kindred migrations from the north.

Acosta, who was in Mexico early enough to reach original sources of information, published his findings at Seville in 1859.* He gives the name of "Chichemecas" to the first inhabitants. Of the second he states:

> These second peoples, Navatalcas, came from other far countries which lie towards the north, where they have discovered a kingdom which they call New Mexico . . . The Navatalcas paint their beginning and first territory in the figure of a cave, and say they came forth of seven caves to come and people the land of Mexico.

Acosta fixes the time of the migration of the first of the seven tribes at 720 A.D. and the length of time consumed in the movement at eighty years. Beginning with the Suchimilcos who settled upon Lake Xochimilco, he names these seven nations, their locations in the Valley of Mexico, and the order of their arrival: the Chalcas, Tepanecans, Culhuas, Tlatluicans, and Tlascaltecans.

> Three hundred and two years afterward (1022 A.D.) those of the seventh cave arrived, which is the Aztec (Mexican) nation; the which, like unto the rest, left Aztlan and Teaculhuacan a polite, cultivated, and warlike nation—these latter being the provinces in the kingdom of New Mexico.

Clavigero affirms the tradition, saying: †

> But of all the nations which peopled the region of Anahuac (Valley

* *Natural and Moral History of the East and West Indies,* London edition 1604, Grimstone's translation.

† *History of Mexico,* Philadelphia edition, 1817, Cullen's translation.

of Mexico), the most renowned . . . were those vulgarly called Nahuatlacas. This name was principally given to those seven nations, or rather those seven tribes of the same nation, who arrived after the Chichemecas . . . the Sochimilcas, the Chalchesc, Tepanecas, Colhuas, Tlahuicas, Tlascalans and Mexicans. The origin of all these tribes was the province of Aztlan . . . The Chichemecas, like the Toltecs who preceded them, and other nations which came after them, were originally from the north" . . .

Clavigero gives a complete timetable of the migration of the last tribe, saying that they left Aztlan in 1160, arriving at Tulla, north of the valley, in 1196, at Chapultepec in 1245, at Acoloco in 1262, were enslaved by the Cholulans during 1324, and in 1325 established the Aztec empire.

These are remarkable statements. They are based on original Aztec sources just after the Conquest, when the Spaniards destroyed the priceless codices. The period of migrations roughly corresponds to the so-called Classic Pueblo Era, the apogee of the great pueblos just before they were abandoned for those of the early historic era.

We now believe that Azteca (the Spanish form of Aztec), the name of the principal Nahua tribe migrating to Mexico, derives from Aztlan. The leader of the migration from Aztlan to Mexitli, or Tenochtitlan as it was later called, was named Mexi. Hence the people who followed him were also called Mexicas, from which Mexitli, Mexico and New Mexico derive their names.

In their name of Aztlan, a "place of herons," for their original homeland, we will later find another confirmation in the symbolism of the crane in Pueblo and Navaho ceremonialism.

The seven tribes, the seven womb-caves of the Aztecs, suggest immediately the legend of the Seven Cities of Cibola, which later inflamed the Spaniards. In reality they are something far different from this European fable. They parallel not only the traditional pueblo groupings, but the traditional seven kivas within a pueblo, and the symbolic seven worlds through which man climbs on his evolutionary journey.

When we compare Pueblo and Navaho ceremonialism with Buddhist and Taoist cosmography in light of modern psychology, later in this study, we will find exactly what these seven cavern-wombs were.

But not all the people wandered away; some of them

remained in the Four Corners. Wanderers from Chaco Canon and Mesa Verde built up the pueblo at Aztec, New Mexico. Inhabitants of Tyuoni, following their leader Cochití, founded Cochití. From Puyé stemmed Santa Clara; from Rito de los Frijoles, San Ildefonso. Oraibi, dating from 1200 A.D. and rivalling Ácoma in the claim of being the oldest occupied town in the United States, grew up. The thickly clustered pueblos along the Rio Grande, as well as innumerable others along the Little Colorado, the Puerco, Chama, and Galisteo later deserted and now forgotten, all sprang from this vast exodus. And all of them, mountain, mesa-top, and ground pueblo alike, were built in the ancestral pattern. Rocks of security built up anew from the turbulent sea of change.

During the next two hundred years the people developed variations in dress, customs, and handicraft. From their different dialects they eventually were classified into the language groups by which we distinguish them today. In the Tanoan group, the Tiwa-speaking pueblos of Taos, Picurís, Sandía, Isleta; the Tewa pueblos of San Juan, San Ildefonso, Santa Clara, Tesuque, Pojoaque, Nambé; and the Towa pueblo of Jemez; in the Keresan group, the pueblos of San Felipe, Santo Domingo, Santa Ana, Cochití, Zia, Ácoma, and Laguna; the Zuñian pueblo of Zuñi; and the Shoshonean Hopi pueblos.

Gradually they became identified by the Spanish names of their pueblos—just as Picurís, within the last few years is becoming known as San Lorenzo.

Yet, for all their non-essential differences, their lives conformed to a pattern outwardly simple and inwardly complex. In the fields they grew corn and cotton, squash and beans. The kernels they thrust into a hole in the ground made with a planting stick called the *coatl* by the Aztecs, who were also using it. The land was desert; they learned to plant deep so as to catch any underground flow of water; to retain moisture by tireless cultivation—they were the original dry farmers. The harvested corn they ground by hand between two stones called the *metate* and *mano* just as simple Spanish-Americans do today. Cotton was the main textile fiber. They wove it into blankets and clothing. The women wore cotton skirts, the men shirts. Over both were worn cotton blankets like cloaks, fastened at one shoulder and girded at the waist by sashes. All these were colored and embroidered with needles of bone, wood, or cactus spine. Baskets were woven, pottery was developed.

Isolate as they were, some contacts were made with the world beyond. The nomadic Navahus swept down from the north, carrying away women and corn and customs to root them firmer to the land. From the east, Plains tribes came to pillage and trade. Sea shells from the Pacific reached them through the hands of Mojave runners following the great intertribal highway paralleling the Gila River. And from Aztec Mexico, too, came rituals, trade stuffs, and the parrot feathers used in the ceremonial dances.

Outwardly a crude, difficult life, essentially the same life they live today. What enriched it and gave it its only meaning came from within. The certainty that they were not separate from the forces of the land and sky which bound them all into one living whole, in perfect balance. To preserve this precarious balance—which is the ultimate test of any life, civilized or savage, they clung to their traditions and perpetuated their ritualistic religion.

In this ceremonialism, the myth-language of the people, was perpetuated the record of their completely evolutionary past. But now something tremendous happened which forced its esoteric meanings underground. The unknown continent had been discovered by a new race. The tide was rising that was to sweep upon it, submerge the land and almost obliterate the Rock itself.

2 Tide from the South

The Black Kachina

THE FIRST JETSAM swept into the Four Corners was a giant black man.

He appeared alone, as if sprung from the depths of the black volcanic earth, striding boldly across the vast naked plain. Everything proclaimed him a kachina. His giant stature, his shining ebony skin. The beautiful pelts, feathers, and turquoise which adorned him. The respect and fear shown him by the Pimas, Papagos, Opatas, and Tarahumaras who followed behind. The gourd decorated with two bells, a red feather and a white, which he sent ahead to each village he approached . . . A great medicine man, a healer of the sick, a kachina certainly.

Coming to Hawikuh, the largest of the Zuñi pueblos, he was received with silent honor. The black kachina did not understand the silence nor the honor. He had no message of power, no healing for the sick. Instead, he reached forth a great greedy hand for all that pleased him—food, skins, blankets, necklaces of chunk turquoise. Imperiously, in a booming voice, he demanded women, many women, girls . . . He took off his kachina mask.

What happened no one knows. He simply vanished instantly and silently from sight. It is said that the Zuñis cut up his black body into small bits so as to leave no trace of him. All that remains is a legend among the Zuñis of a huge "black Mexican" who came their way long, long ago; and their stubborn refusal today, four hundred years later, to admit Spanish-Americans to the pueblo. Whites, Navahos, everybody else—but no "Mexicans."

The terrible Indian negation! The undying memory, the unbreakable secrecy that has outlasted the centuries! This was the result of their first betrayal, of the first visit of a stranger from another continent, of their first meeting with another race. There is no exaggerating its tremendous, lasting, psychological significance. On such obscure incidents pivots the history of mankind.

The black adventurer, the first "white man" to enter this vast hinterland of America, was, of course, the slave Estevan, Estevanico, or Black Stephen. No one knows whether he was a captive Moor brought from Spain or an African Negro slave. Indeed, little is known about him at all. But certainly he is one of the most fantastic figures ever thrown into relief against America's fantastic background.

Eight years before, in 1528, a vessel of the Narvaes expedition, from Spain, had been wrecked somewhere on the gulf coast of Florida or Texas. Among the survivors were Cabeza de Vaca, Castillo Maldonado, Andres Dorantes, and his black slave, Estevan. Passing from tribe to tribe, suffering thirst, starvation, and many privations, they wandered across the continent toward the Pacific, turned south into Mexico, and finally reached the outposts of Spanish conquest.

Brought before Cortéz, naked save for long matted hair and beards, with feverishly glowing eyes, they told what they had seen. Gleaming cities containing palaces ornamented with sapphires, rubies, and turquoise, gold without end. The legendary Seven Cities of Cíbola already reported by an Indian named Tejo, who had seen them while travelling north with his father to trade feathers. Now Cabeza de Vaca swore it was so. And the great black's eyes rolled confirmation.

Don Antonio de Mendoza, the first viceroy of New Spain, listened carefully. There seemed no doubt that the great black slave knew more than his masters. So as soon as Cortéz was out of the way, he sent Estevan back to the fabled north he pictured so glowingly. With him went Fray Marcos de Niza, a Franciscan monk, who had been with Pizarro in Peru. Mendoza's plan was simple. The slave would lead the way, and the friar would convert the inhabitants of the seven golden cities to the gentle creed of Christ. The viceroy could then readily obtain the gold.

In northern Sonora, Estevan pushed on ahead of the friar. He agreed to send back a small cross if reports indicated the seven cities to be "of medium importance." If "important," a cross "two spans in length" would be sent back; while a large cross was to be returned if the seven cities were indicated to be "more important than New Spain."

Four days later Estevan's Indian messengers staggered back to Fray Marcos' camp carrying a cross as "high as a man." The friar hurried forward.

But Estevan kept striding blithely ahead. His was every slave's dream come true. He was alone, free, a master. This was his empire—a land without limit, and he was its monarch. To the frantic messages of the priest commanding him in the name of the Lord to stop and wait, Estevan paid no heed. Mad with freedom and lust for wealth and power, a magnificent travesty of his Spanish masters, he strode on—to meet his fate as Spain was to meet hers, the irrevocable destiny of every race, every civilization grown mad with greed and power.

It is a wonderful, terrible story. It embodies the truth of two races, condenses the conflict of two civilizations, and prophecies the history of the continent for the next four hundred years.

The Fair Gods

In just such wise Cortéz and his conquerors had been received when they landed on the Aztec shore of the New World discovered by Columbus and decreed it the property of the Crown of Spain.

Native runners hastened to inform Moctezuma of their arrival. Their drawings and paintings on cotton cloth assured the Aztec ruler that the strangers were the white and bearded, maize-like but human likenesses of the Feathered Serpent Quetzalcoatl, long expected. He made haste to welcome them.

Four vassal kings carried his embassy to port. All four were garbed as gods. They took with them the masks of Quetzalcoatl with which they arrayed Cortéz, together with a gold symbol of the sun, a silver image of the moon, rich mantles, jewels, perfumes, and flowers.

Led by these emissaries, and swelled by hundreds of rival Tlaxcallan warriors, the little band of 633 Spanish invaders began their march inland to Tenochtitlan, capital of the Aztec empire.

On the way, writes Cortéz, "I burned more than ten towns, of more than three thousand houses . . . At dawn I fell upon a large town of more than twenty thousand dwellings. As I surprised them, they were unarmed. The women and children ran naked in the streets. And I fell upon them . . ."

They reached Cholula, sacred city of Quetzalcoatl. Received by priests and choruses of children singing and dancing, they were feasted for two days. On the third day Cortéz called all the inhabitants together. Priests, nobles, warriors, and populace crowded in the great courtyard of the Temple of Quetzalcoatl, unarmed, with eager and happy faces, to hear what the fair gods would say. The Spaniards attacked and killed them all.

Even so they were finally welcomed in Tenochtitlan by the patient, forgiving Moctezuma. Cortéz was suspicious. He promptly made hostage of the ruler, who graciously asked why the Spaniards had come. Cortéz replied with a classic answer.

"We are troubled with a disease of the heart for which gold is the only remedy."

Gold was forthcoming—treasures so fabulous that their value was beyond calculation. It was not enough to cure the Spaniards' disease. Moctezuma's son and fifteen nobles were put to death for refusing to order more from the provinces. Then Moctezuma. And when all the priests and nobles were called into the temple to celebrate the festival of Huitzilopochtli, the Spaniards set upon them. "And the first thing they did was to cut off the heads and hands of the musicians"—firing into unarmed throngs with cannon and musket, trampling the dead with their horses, slicing at the living with sword and spear. "So great was the flow of blood that streams ran in the courtyard . . . a muck of intestines and blood."

Too late the Aztecs realized that the fair gods were mortal men, that the fierce beasts they rode were but "animals like deer though fatter," that their "supposed lightnings were but ball-throwers better constructed than usual." The Conquest of Mexico had begun.

Despite Spanish reinforcements from the coast and the help of more than 150,000 Tlaxcalan allies, Cortéz' siege of the capital lasted sixty days. When it was over, Tenochtitlan, on its island, lay in ruins. The pyramids, temples, and palaces were razed, and their stones toppled into the canals. Fifty thousand corpses littered the causeways. The very bark of the trees had been gnawed off by the starving defenders. Fire, disease, and the putrid odor of death ran through the cluttered streets.

"Destroyed," wrote Cortéz to his king, "were the royal archives; all the chronicles of their ancient things; and also the other things which were like literature or stories"—the priceless codices recording the prehistoric past of America.

But the future was being written swiftly. Companies of Spaniards roamed over the land, laying waste the villages, enslaving men and women as serfs, branding the infants. To the south marched Pedro de Alvarado. And now another expedition was formed to march north.

It was more than a wild-goose chase, a mere gold rush. To be sure, there were the precedents of Pizarro's discovery of fabulous treasures in Peru, and the incalculable wealth found by Cortéz in Mexico. But behind it lay a compulsion not amenable to an analysis of rational fact, but which is psychologically significant.

In fifteenth-century Spain there was current an ancient fable of the island Antilla somewhere in the Western Ocean. It was called "Septe Citate" following the legend that in 734, the year when Spain was conquered by the Moors, seven fleeing Portuguese bishops and their flocks had founded on it seven cities.

Where the mysterious island was, no one knew. But Ferdinand Columbus, son of Christopher, reported that it was "not more than two hundred leagues due west from the Canaries and Azores." Further reports held that the sands of the island were "one-third" pure gold.

Discovery of America had substantiated the existence of the island. And now to the Spaniards in Mexico the seven cities seemed confirmed by the Aztec tradition of their seven caves or cavern-wombs in Aztlan, far to the north.

Estevan, the black slave, had vanished. But reports of the Indian, Tejo, and the friar who had accompanied Estevan substantiated the Aztec legend. Fray Marcos had returned with glowing descriptions of one of the fabled seven cities. From a nearby mountain he had seen it on the sandy plain. An immense city, large as Seville, with gates of gold, sapphire-studded doors, its walls shimmering in the sunlight . . . Hawikuh might well have answered his description. Four stories high, its pale-yellow adobe shimmered in the sun, turquoise studded the doorways; bits of straw and flecks of mica in the walls gleaming like jewels.

No time was lost in forming an expedition to conquer it. All noble families contributed to its expense; many members, unable to go, equipped servants in order to share in the gold. Pedro de Castañeda, its historian, described it as the most brilliant company ever assembled. There were 225 gallants in burnished armor riding horses whose ornate trappings hung to the ground, sixty-two foot soldiers and hundreds of Indian servants, followed by more than one thousand horses and mules carrying baggage, and several thousand sheep. The honor of command was held by young Francisco Vásquez de Coronado, who had contributed to the expense about one million dollars from his wife's estate.

In February, 1540, they started north to the Four Corners country.

On July 7, the company looked down upon the first of the golden cities—the fabulous Cíbola, ancient Hawikuh, near the present pueblo of Zuñi. It was merely a village of sun-baked mud, four stories high. "Such were the curses that some hurled at Friar Marcos," wrote Castañeda, "that I pray God may protect him from them."

The Pueblos had been equally disillusioned about Estevan. They gazed at Coronado and his company, not as white kachinas, but as men. When they refused to surrender, "the Spaniards then attacked the village, which was taken with not a little difficulty, since they held the narrow and crooked entrance." Even Coronado was knocked down with a large stone and almost killed.

The Spaniards continued on their way, hacking entrance into one pueblo after another, looting, raping, and spitting the inhabitants on lances. Tovar, with one force, marched northward to discover the Hopi villages in the so-called province of Tusayan; Cárdenas, with twelve men, westward to discover the Grand Canyon; Alvarado eastward to Ácoma on the lofty rock of Acuco in the "Kingdom of Hacus," and thence to Cicuyé or Pecos. Coronado, with the main force, pushed on eastward to the Rio Grande, then northward as far as the pueblos of Jemez and Taos.

Everywhere he found "food in abundance—corn, beans, fowls (turkeys), and fine white salt," but no gold. In desperation he then circled the trackless buffalo plains of the Texas Panhandle, Oklahoma, and Kansas.

Two years later, in April, the caravan began its straggling journey back to Mexico. Coronado had been injured by a kick in the head from a horse, and was carried in a litter. Devoid of gold and jewels, without honor, he was then subjected to an official inquiry into his epic "failure."

The Entradas

By 1542, then, the Four Corners had been discovered, explored, conquered, and abandoned by alien visitors. But Coronado's was only the first wave of the rising tide. One after another rolled up from the south.

The second of consequence was the entrada of Juan de Oñate in 1598. True, Chamuscado, Antonio de Espejo and others had entered the country with small parties. But it was the wealthy and influential Oñate who next secured official warrant to colonize the country, and the appointment as its supreme authority.

His train was impressive. It consisted of four hundred men, of whom 130 had brought their families, eighty-three carts loaded with baggage, and 7,000 head of stock. Reaching the pueblo of Caypa, on the Rio Grande, Oñate renamed it San Juan. A church was built, the colonists established, and eight Franciscan missionaries assigned to various other pueblos.

Ácoma, high on the rock of Acuco, refused allegiance. So, early in January, Zaldivar was sent to subdue it. After fighting for three days with high casualties, the Indians surrendered and offered corn, blankets, and turkeys as tokens of peace. Zaldivar refused the offerings and confined many of the warriors in a kiva. From here they were taken out, one by one, murdered and thrown over the cliffs. The remaining prisoners, some seventy warriors and five hundred women and children, were brought to trial at Santo Domingo pueblo. Finding them guilty of killing eleven Spaniards and two servants, Oñate pronounced sentence. All males of more than twenty-five years of age were condemned to have one foot cut off and to give twenty years of personal service; the males between twelve and twenty-five years of age, and all females were doomed to twenty years of servitude. Two Hopi Indians captured with them were condemned to have their right hand cut off and to be sent home as a warning. Villagrá, whose epic poem, "The History of New Mexico," published in Spain in 1610, celebrates the matter, himself transported sixty or seventy of the young captive girls to the viceroy in Mexico.

The province of New Mexico had been founded. Within two years it seemed well established. Fray Benavides, its *custodio*, reported that there were fifty friars, serving over sixty thousand Christianized Indians living in ninety pueblos, each with its own church. He also had founded a church at Santa Clara pueblo for the conversion of the nomadic Navahos, who had just caused the abandonment of Jemez pueblo by their frequent raids.

This Spanish colonization attempt lasted for eighty years. Every pueblo household was required to pay in yearly tribute to the Spanish authorities one vara (thirty-three inches) of cotton cloth. Men were imprisoned and flogged for all infringement of the laws. Land was appropriated. People were enslaved to labor for the crown and the Church. Their native worship was regarded as idolatry, and forty Indians who refused to give it up were hanged.

Meanwhile Popé, a medicine-man working from Taos pueblo, travelled quietly from pueblo to pueblo for fourteen years organizing revolt. On August 10, 1680, every pueblo rebelled.

The Indians killed nearly five hundred Spaniards, including twenty-one missionaries at their altars, tore down the churches, destroyed government and church records, "vented their fury on the hens, the sheep, the fruit trees of Castile, and even upon the wheat," and washed all baptised Indians with *amole* to cleanse them of the Spanish stain.

The surviving Spaniards fled back to Mexico, and again the Four Corners was abandoned by its alien masters.

And again, twelve years later, a new wave of conquest rolled in with Don Diego de Vargas on its crest. As before, there had been previous forays under Otermín, Cruzate, and Reneros to reconquer the realm, avenge the insult to Spanish pride and rededicate the errant souls of the savage Indians to the Catholic faith. The pueblo of Santa Ana had been leveled, Zia destroyed. But still the province remained obdurate and abandoned. A stronger motive was needed to win it back.

Quicksilver this time, in place of gold, supplied it.

Don Diego de Vargas, Zapata y Lujan Ponce de León, had gained the attention of the Crown as *justicia mayor* of the mining camp of Tlalpujohua. After being placed in charge of the royal supply of quicksilver, he was recommended to the viceroy. Conde de Galve promptly granted De Vargas the governorship of the deserted province and sent him a letter which read in part: "I understand that within the rebellious area of New Mexico lies a province called Moqui, and that twelve leagues from it in the direction of the Rio Grande is situated one of the most important of its ranges from which are extracted the minerals or vermilion-colored soil used by the Indians to daub themselves." This soft and butterlike substance was regarded as such a high-grade ore of quicksilver that it formed little pools of liquid mercury. De Vargas was requested to make a thorough investigation.

The viceroy did not state that the matter had already come to the attention of His Majesty, nor advise of the royal decree issued him that "without bringing about the subjection of New Mexico first, it was vain to discuss the advantages which might accrue from developing the quicksilver mines . . . between Zuñi and Moqui."

He did not have to. De Vargas was immediately inflamed by the news of the mythical mines in the mysterious north, that still haunted men's minds after a century and a half, and he was well aware of the advantages to the new governor who should find them. He promptly outfitted an expedition at his own expense and set forth.

Under him the Spaniards tried kindly measures. De Vargas appointed Indian leaders to positions of authority and promised forgiveness to all who would submit to Spanish rule. The Tewas of San Ildefonso fled to the top of steep-walled Black Mesa; the Zuñis to the rock of Kiakima, the mesa of Towayalane or Corn Mountain; the Keres of Ácoma were on the lofty rock of Acuco. The Indians of Jemez allied themselves with the Navahos . . . Nevertheless De Vargas, with much diplomacy and little bloodshed, won them over; he reported the subjection of seventy-three pueblos.

Despite his painstaking care, he was unable to find any trace of mercuric ores and turned back to Mexico on November 30, 1692, to write his report to Charles II, asking liberal honors for finally subduing the northern realm, and to prepare for another entrada.

The Spanish Mask

Thenceforth for 130 years the Four Corners was a province of Spain. Land and people were clothed in the raiment of a new civilization and knelt before the Holy Cross of their conquerors. But hidden beneath, their heart was still the impregnable Rock.

In the long perspective we see the secrecy and ironic humor, the implacable stubbornness and deceptive submission in their posture and attitude. The Spanish colonizers never did. They were too busy founding homes and towns in the wilderness.

The established route into it was El Camino Real, the Royal Highway. It led northward from El Paso del Norte up the Rio Grande, past the Piro pueblos of Socorro and Senecu to a new settlement named in honor of the Duke of Alburquerque, then viceroy in Mexico; curved east and north to the capital, La Villa Real de la Santa Fe de San Francisco; thence north to Don Fernando de Taos, founded near the old pueblo of San Geronimo de Taos. Here on the eastern boundary of the Four Corners, in the rich valley of the Rio Grande, stretched the thin line of Spanish settlements.

Westward lay the wild plateau of the Four Corners. If and when they entered it, it was from the southern boundary—west from Albuquerque to the pueblos of Laguna, Ácoma, and Zuñi, thence north and west to the isolated mesa-top pueblos of the Hopi, in the center of a vast empty plateau cut off on the west by the Grand Canyon and walled on the north by the high Rockies.

The pueblos along its eastern and southern boundaries first felt the Spanish influence. Many had been or were soon abandoned—Cieneguilla, Tziguma, Cuyamungue, Galisteo, Jacona, and Halona. The others in the Rio Grande Valley were renamed in honor of Catholic Saints like Santa Clara, San Ildefonso, Santo Domingo and San Juan. In each of them a church was built and dedicated to its patron saint, and their inhabitants allowed themselves to be duly baptised.

As small villages and great haciendas built up, more and more of the Indians' land was expropriated. More and more labor was required. Many of the Indians became serfs. The new language became common—the common tongue still used between pueblos of different tribes. To the Spaniards the sacred kivas resembled the outdoor ovens in which the Indians baked their bread; hence they were called estufas or stoves. Articles of clothing, handicraft, and household goods, as well as rivers and mountains, plants and animals all took on new names. So did the Indians themselves. New shiny Spanish names by which they were known to their masters and which they called each other in public, reserving their own Indian names for ceremonial and private use.

Thus the pueblos along the eastern and southern boundaries of the Four Corners. It was all a mask; adeptly worn, but still a mask under which the people preserved the integrity of their own belief.

It is a significant fact that in the whole province there was nothing comparable to the chain of Franciscan missions up the coast of California, the Jesuit missions extending through Lower California, and the missions established by Father Kino throughout Sonora and southern Arizona. The chapels and churches in the pueblos were not unified and closely knit, they had no protective presidios and settlements, and were not supported by docile congregations.

The Hopi Pueblos allowed no church or chapel at all. In 1700, Awatobi was destroyed by the other Pueblos for friendliness toward a Franciscan monk. And seventy-six years later, when the indomitable Franciscan padre, Garces, rode into Oraibi offering gifts and salvation in return for food and welcome, he was simply and quietly ordered to leave.

But if the Hopis were adamant about the religion, language and customs of the Spaniards, they adopted one Spanish tool which benefited them immeasurably—a new and strange "little black beast with wool and horns" which Coronado had brought into the country for the first time: European sheep. From the days of the prehistoric pueblos, the Hopis had been accomplished spinners and weavers. Now substituting wool for cotton, as they had previously substituted cotton for yucca and grass fiber—but without adopting the Spanish horizontal pedal loom in place of their own—they raised the craft to so high an art that today their ceremonial sashes and kirtles are being used in all pueblos. Sheep were easily grazed on the scanty desert forage, and provided mutton. The People of Peace continued with stubborn insistence their simple, hard lives, pastoral now as well as agricultural.

Coronado also had brought into the country another new strange beast—the horse. With it the Navahos now rose swiftly into prominence.

At the time of Coronado, the Spaniards made no mention of the Navahos; it is probable none were seen. But by 1785 it was reported that "the Navaho nation has 700 families more or less with 4 or 5 persons to each one in its five divisions of San Matheo, Zebolleta or Cañon, Chusca, Hozo, Chelli, with its thousand men of arms; that their possessions consist of 500 tame horses; 600 mares with their corresponding stallions and young; about 700 black ewes, 40 cows also with their bulls and calves, all looked after with the greatest care and diligence for their increase."

This report was carefully made by the commander-general of the Interior Provinces of New Spain, then in New Mexico on a military-diplomatic mission to break up an alliance between the Navahos and western Apaches. He could well be concerned with the safety of the thin line of Spanish settlements up the Rio Grande Valley. The Comanches of the Great Plains menaced the eastern boundary of the Four Corners; the desert Apaches the southern; the mountain Utes the northern. Inside, the Hopis, with their independence and stubborn, passive resistence, were a constant irritation. And now the Navahos were proving the most troublesome of all.

With horses they could move swiftly and widely. They raided Pueblo and Spanish communities impartially, advancing to the outskirts of the royal villa of Santa Fe itself. They kept the Apaches at bay to the south and the Utes to the north, and rode as far out on the Great Plains as eastern Colorado to trade and fight with the Pawnees.

From the Pueblos they learned the art of spinning and weaving wool. But whereas the men were the weavers in the pueblos, in accordance with their ceremonial conservatism, weaving among the Navahos was confined to the women, who soon proved versatile and imaginative. They supplemented moccasins, leggings, and breeches or breech-cloths with woolen shoulder blankets, worn like a poncho or serape, and frequently belted at the waist. Like the Arab's *burnous,* they used it to shield the face from sun and sand and cold, to carry firewood and babies, as a garment by day, a blanket at night. For their horses they wove saddle blankets, saddle throws and girths or cinches . . . So quickly and so well did the Navaho women adopt weaving that the Spanish governor reported "they work their wool with more delicacy and taste than the Spaniards. Men as well as women go decently clothed; and their Captains are rarely seen without silver jewelry"—indicating another craft The People were adopting.

But it was the horse that was making them masters of the Four Corners. A man's wealth was designated by the number of horses he owned; children learned to ride as soon or sooner than they learned to walk. The horse, too, made it possible to supply remote hogans and herders with food and water. Thus, paradoxically, it was the horse which finally rooted The People to the land.

The Navahos still shifted from their stout winter hogans to their flimsy summer shelters. For months at a time they followed their flocks of sheep. On swift forays they raided afar. But they were no longer truly nomadic. From their earliest location between the Chama and the San Juan they had expanded westward to claim the whole empty tableland of the Four Corners.

The Spaniards acknowledged it. On Escalante's map of 1776 the region was marked "Provincia de Nabajoo." At no time did the Spaniards feel equal to the task of "surrounding them and pressing upon them from all sides at once" although "there existed an almost constant condition of warfare with that powerful tribe." The Navahos, in turn, boasted that they let the Spaniards live on only because of their "usefulness as shepherds to the tribe," and their taunt was not exaggerated.

Such was the status of the Four Corners at the beginning of the nineteenth century, three hundred years after the first appearance of alien invaders. Over all, land and people, was spread the thin patina of a new civilization. It was like the whitewashed walls of the rooms in which Oñate and his officers once had been quartered. Underneath they could still distinguish the "fierce and terrible features of the demons" the Indians "worshipped as gods"—the kachina masks of their sacred personages. A patina of conquest soon to be erased.

3 Interregnum

DOWN IN MEXICO, in the obscure little village of Dolores, that morning of September 15, 1810, a simple parish priest began ringing the bell of his church.

Over *milpa* and *campo* the sound carried softly in the morning calm. Over all Mexico its mellow, silver tones carried a message of death and destruction, the old old message that he who lives by the sword shall perish by the sword. It echoed to Spain the ancient prophecy of Netzahualcoyotl, the Aztec poet, made when Tenochtitlan fell to the Spaniards:

Thy destiny shall snatch the sceptre from thy hand, thy moon shall wane, no longer wilt thou be strong and proud . . . The nobles of thy line, the province of thy might, children of noble parents, lacking thee as their lord, shall taste the bitterness of poverty . . . They shall call to mind how great was thy pomp, thy triumphs and victories, and bewailing the glory and majesty of the past, their tears will flow like the seas . . . These thy descendants who serve thy plume and crown, when thou art gone, shall forsake Culhuacan, and as exiles will increase their woes . . .

It kept ringing for twelve years. And when it stopped ringing, the glory and the power of Spain in the New World was gone, and the ancient Aztec empire of Moctezuma was again a free and independent nation.

The Dark Madonna

One night in a drab and murky *cantina* just off the Zocalo of Mexico City, Anita Brenner told us an amusing, significant story. A remote church in the rugged mountains of Michoacán was noted for years for the devout attention it received. From miles around, Indians trudged in over the steep trails to kneel at its altar, to bank it with flowers, and listen humbly to the simple young rural priest in charge. For such ignorant and obstinate Indians this was a baffling, most mysterious devotion . . . Until a slight earthquake overturned the altar, revealing a squat stone Aztec idol.

Three hundred years are nothing. The dark volcanic mountains are the same, the blinding sun, the slanting silver rain, the tender shoots of corn greening the steep *milpas* on the hillsides, the people, they are all the same—if you know Indians as did Father Miguel Hidalgo, the simple village priest, in rebellion against the government and against the church which frocked him, who announced the independence of Mexico. It was achieved, not surprisingly, in the name of Guadalupe, Dark Madonna of the Tepeyac, ancient Aztec mother of the gods.

We pushed back our benches and staggered out of the smoke-filled *cantina* to yell a little drunkenly, "*Toston!*"—("Taxi!")—under clear stars sparkling in the midnight black. One drew up at the curb. We climbed in and headed north to the suburb of Guadalupe Hidalgo. The *avenida* was already crowded with French limousines and American touring cars, other wild and cheap Mexican taxis, old *camiones* jammed with workers; wagons, carts, and plodding burros. Impossible! We got out and walked the rest of the twelve *kilometros.* Hour by hour the road became more jammed. Thousands of people trudging steadily through the night. Thousands more trickling in from the side streets, the *cantinas* and *pulquerias* on the corners. A dark river of people welling as if out of the earth and flowing steadily north, to crowd, near dawn, the base of Tepeyac Hill. To observe this, the four hundredth anniversary of the appearance of the Dark Madonna to an humble Indian.

Everywhere people jammed the cobblestone streets, the open courtyards, the drab *callejones.* Shivering tourists in overcoats, shop clerks in high celluloid collars, peons in tattered *serapes* and *rebozos. Cholos, mestizos, creoles, pelados,* and *gente de razon.* The shoeless, the lame, the deformed and diseased, the everpresent syphilitic, the people who had been carried burroback. Somewhere the *serape* weaver of Tetitlan del Valle who, after seven weeks of work, had asked for his labor only enough to bring him here. Our chambermaid who had saved for two years from her daily wage of twenty cents for this pilgrimage to La Virgin Morena. But mostly Indians—Zapotecs and Mixtecs from Oaxaca, Tarascans from Michoacan, rebellious Yaquis from Sonora, Huicholes, Mayos, Tarahumaras, Totonacs. All darkly massed like sheep awaiting dawn.

In its first drab greyishness, life and color emerged. Banners and colored streamers. The yellow and white of the Vatican. Guadalupe's pale blue and delicate rose-pink. We could see the myriad stalls and *puestos* lining the far adobe walls offering small corn cakes made of "*Maiz* de Cacahuazintla" from the valleys of Toluca and Tulancingo called "*gorditas de la Virgen*", "little fat ones of the Virgin"; papayos, *guayabas, jicamas de agua, tejocotes, tunas* from the nopal cactus, *granaditas;* decorated gourds and wooden plates; colored glassware and *bolsas* and *serapes* . . . The light of small cooking fires, the glow of charcoal braziers. The stench of open *mingitorios* before which stood lines of men and women waiting to urinate. The beat of a drum. A group of Indians dancing. But all subdued and muted, slow pulsed and curiously ominous, as if rooted in the darkness and the past.

Four hundred years ago that morning an humble Indian, named Cuauhtlactoatzin, of the village of Tolpectlac was proceeding to Tlaltelolco, when, crossing the slope of the barren hill of Tepeyac, he suddenly beheld the apparition of a dark Indian maiden clad like the Mexican sky in a "blue mantle dotted with stars like toasted maize grains." She commanded him to erect a church on the spot.

Cuauhtlactoatzin, lately baptised Juan Diego in the Catholic faith, hastened to inform Bishop Zumarraga. The bishop demanded a sign. Obediently Juan Diego returned to the barren cactus slope of Tepeyac. Again Guadalupe appeared. At her feet burst forth a small fountain; there appeared a garden of roses.

"Gather the roses in your *tilma* and carry them to the bishop," commanded Guadalupe. "That is your sign."

Juan Diego did so. And as he undid his mantle, letting the roses fall out, the bishop was amazed to see painted upon the cloth the image of the Virgin.

The miracle had been consummated, and it was accepted by the Catholic Church. A church was built on the spot. The miraculous *tilma*, protected by thick glass, was hung above the high altar. Our Lady of Guadalupe was proclaimed the patroness and protectoress of New Spain.

Such was the story of the Virgin of Guadalupe officially endorsed by the Catholic Church.

But Father Sahagún looked askance on Guadalupe's sudden popularity scarcely a decade after the conquest and only three years after the creation of the bishopric. With real genius he was making himself an authority on Aztec life, character, customs, and religious beliefs in a lifetime of futile endeavor. He wrote warningly of her lowly origin:

> Near the mountains there are three or four places where they used to offer most solemn sacrifices, and to which they came from distant lands. One of these is on a little hill they called Tepeyac, now named Our Lady of Guadalupe. In this place they had a temple dedicated to the mother of the gods whom they called Tonantzin, which means "our mother." Thither they came from far distant regions . . . men, women, boys and girls and brought many offerings . . . There were great assemblages and all said, "Let us go to the festival of Tonantzin." Now, the church built there is dedicated to Our Lady of Guadalupe whom they also call Tonantzin, imitating the prelates who called Our Lady the Mother of God (in Azetc), Tonantzin . . . And so they still come to visit this Tonantzin from afar, as much as before; a devotion which is suspicious because everywhere there are many churches for Our Lady and they do not go to them, but come from great distances here to their Tonantzin as before.

The dark-faced Madonna, *la Virgen Morena,* the ancient Tonantzin or Tinonantzin, mother of the Aztec gods. Goddess of the earth and corn, related to Tlaloc, god of rain. Clad in her mantle of sky-blue, dotted with stars like toasted maize grains. Reappearing on the site of her ancient temple. On the twelfth of December, the season just before the rains, when she was immemorially feted.

This was the idol behind the altar, the kachina within the mask, which the people still worshipped. Tonantzin's new Spanish name of Guadalupe did not deceive them. It only lent official and ecclesiastical sanctity to their forbidden pagan worship.

The local Church authorities made haste to take advantage of the miracle. By 1537, some 500,000 Indians had "received the faith" in Guadalupe's name. By 1539, more than a million in the City of Mexico and three million more in the provinces had been baptised. But not until 1667 did Pope Clement IX grant a concession for a plenary jubilee to be held each year on December 12. And not until 1754 did a Papal Bull recognize the Virgin of Guadalupe as the patroness and protectoress of New Spain—followed in 1756 by a brochure written by the celebrated painter, Miguel Cabrera, attesting that the venerated picture could not have been painted in water-color, nor in oil, nor in any artificial manner by human hands.

"Viva la Virgen Morena del Tepeyac!"—"Viva la Virgen Guadalupana!"—"Santisima Maria de Guadalupe!"

After four centuries we saw it now at dawn.

An iron picket fence six feet high, and hanging on the grillwork immense floral offerings as of old from the canals of Xochimilco, Ixtacalco, Mixuca, and Tlalpam. Behind it is the forecourt paved with stones. Then the church, the Basilica de Santa Maria de Guadalupe, just rebuilt and redecorated for the occasion. Behind it to the left a narrow lane of stone stairs winding up the hill to the Chapel of the Hill on top. And off to the right the Chapel of the Well, with its blue and white tiles ribbed in chrome yellow.

There it was. The shrine of the "brunette Virgin," the objective of more than half a million pilgrims from all of Mexico.

They stood as they had stood all night, massed before the fence in their thin white *pantalones, serapes,* and *rebozos.* A great brown river, viscuous as a lava flow oozing out of the earth. Patiently, silently waiting. But imperceptibly moving forward, an inch at a time, without lifting their feet.

Attendants with guns on hips reinforced the iron grill gates with ropes. Soldiers on horses tried to cut the crowd, and remained on the edges immobile as statues mounted on pedestals of stone. The people did not crowd. But they did not give. Imperceptibly they kept squeezing forward.

The pressure was becoming alarming. A woman fainted up front. Somehow she was got out. And immediately, like molasses, the crowd filled the gap. A breeze stirred; you realized it was winter, dawn, and cold. But you could not escape the suffocating heat of that volcanic flow pressing from all sides. And the sweat continued to roll, drop by drop, down the swarthy face of the man to the right.

Now you smelled the stench. The oddly familiar, acrid, spicy, racial smell of the Indian. And another, a cloying sickening odor you suddenly realized was that of the White, your own. Then still another—urine, as the stain darkened the white *pantalones* of the man to the left. And now you smelled nothing at all. It was too difficult to breathe.

But you kept hearing a faint ringing in your ears, conscious of a continuous dim commotion. The ringing of an ambulance bell and the removal of some four hundred persons to the hospital, we read in the next day's newspapers.

The imperceptible movement forward continued. With the silence, the slowness, and irresistible force of a lava flow. And suddenly you knew what it was. From a brown earth a wave of brown hands reaching up to a pair of brown feet. This was evolution and revolution, endlessly and forever repeated. What could stop it? Where else could it go but forward?

The iron gates before the atrium gave way like sluicegates. The cathedral doors swung open before the flood. Slowly it flowed inside, into a lofty chamber of green and gold. Faced with a new white altar of pure Carrara marble. A Guadalupe image in a new gold crown encrusted with rubies and emeralds, made in Paris, and worth a half million pesos. Attended by twenty-seven archbishops and two hundred priests. With flashlight photographs for the daily press. And all to the music of a new Wurlitzer organ, installed as advertised.

Another kachina mask for the simple faith that must again and forever tear it aside in the ceaseless search for the invisible and enduring truth that lies behind.

This is the meaning of all revolutions. Political, economic, and military reasons explain their effects, not their causes. They all are subterranean movements stemming from deep in the hearts of mankind. The Mexican revolution against Spain was not the result of Napoleon crossing the Pyrenees. It was a seed planted in 1531, flowering in 1810, and whose fruit has not yet been fully formed.

The Mestizos

With Mexican independence there came in swift succession a series of signs tacked on to the legendary Aztec province of Aztlan. From the northern Province of New Mexico of New Spain it became overnight the State of New Mexico of Mexico—a vast area which included Chihuahua and Durango, with the city of Chihuahua its capital. Durango, jealous of Chihuahua, objected; so the northern portion became a territory. Then in another political move it became a department, with neither eastern nor western limits to its extent.

These changes meant little to the Spanish Colonials settled along the eastern boundary of the Four Corners. It was a period of comparative obscurity; an era of huge *haciendas;* a "romantic" interlude of deceptive prosperity for the fortunate few.

Communication with the outside was infrequent and difficult. Trade goods were carted in by way of the old Camino Real—now the Chihuahua Trail, since kings were out of fashion. Only the rich could afford the luxuries brought in the creaking *carretas*—lace *mantillas* from Spain, carved chests and furniture, mirrors, muskets, silk shawls, and jewelry. And only the *ricos* could afford tutors to teach them to read and write; and by the unlearned they came to be called *gente de razon*, literally "people of reason." Their huge land grants supported whole villages of poorer families, dozens of servants, scores of *vaqueros,* and hundreds of Indian slaves. The *hacendado* was the undisputed master of his domain. He held his family in bondage like a sultan his harem. He ordered his servants flogged at his mood, sat in justice upon his peons, hanged offending Indians.

The worst of these offenders were, of course, the marauding Navahos. As the *hacendados* were the masters of the Rio Grande Valley, the Navahos were masters of the land westward to the Colorado. With herds of horses for swift forays, and flocks of sheep pastured in remote hidden canyons to fall back upon, they were at their raiding best. It was inevitable that the two should meet in even sharper conflict.

In vain the Mexican governors were induced to make frequent and official campaigns against them. Equally futile were the reprisal attacks made upon them by the *hacendados* themselves. Nothing could subdue them. But often Navahos were killed, their hogans burnt, and women and children brought back as captives. Slaves on the *haciendas,* they were gradually made household servants and mistresses, and absorbed into the population of the estates. An amalgamation of races, a new race itself, was being formed.

The pattern had been set in Mexico at the very beginning of the Conquest. Cortéz would probably have been killed had it not been for an Indian girl, Malintzi, who betrayed her own people to become his mistress and interpreter. She and twenty beautiful slaves presented to Cortéz by a Tabasco cacique became the mothers of a new mixed race on the American continent.

Martín Cortéz, son of the Conqueror and Malintzi or Malinche, was honored as a *comendador* of the order of St. Iago. Doña Isabel Tolosa Cortés Montezuma, the great-granddaughter of Moctezuma, granddaughter of Cortéz, became the wife of Juan de Oñate, the colonizer of New Mexico. The grandnephew of Moctezuma, Don Cristobal Becerra y Montezuma, married the daughter of Villagrá, who wrote the epic poem, "The History of New Mexico." It will thus be seen that, for all their antagonism, the Spaniards had no physical race prejudice against Indians. From the highest estates, interbreeding proceeded rapidly on all levels.

At the close of the colonial regime there were but fifteen thousand Spaniards, less than one-third of one per cent of the population of New Spain. Three centuries later, when independence was achieved, and after 300,000 more had come from Spain, there were but one million Spaniards, comprising less than one-fifth of the population. But there were two million *mestizos* (part Spanish, part Indian), over 38 per cent of the total.

On a lesser scale, the same thing was beginning to occur in the remote northern province. Many of the Pueblos and Navahos were being absorbed into the settlements along the upper Rio Grande, creating the nucleus of a new mixed race, the *mestizo.* And so it is today that Ranchos de Taos is so strongly impregnated with a strain of Navaho blood; and farther east the remote mountain village of El Alto de las Herreras shows racial vestiges of the almost abandoned Indian pueblo of Picurís.

Everywhere it was the same. A few great *haciendas* supporting noble families proud of their Castilian lineage. But dozens of small, growing villages of poor folk gradually adopting the life of the Indians. Growing corn, the primal foodstuff of all aboriginal America. Grinding the kernels on a concave stone, the *metate,* the Aztec *metatl.* Patting the dough into thin *tortillas,* the Aztec *tlaxcalli* "bread," and cooking them on a griddle, the *comal* (*comalli*). Or wrapping the hot cornmeal mush into the husk, flavoring it with meat or *chile* (*chilli*) to make the Aztec *tamalli* (*tamale*). Or serving it as a gruel, the *atole* (*atolli*) . . . Spinning and weaving cotton or wool, not with the Spanish horizontal pedal loom, but on the hip with the *malacatl* (*malacate*), into the *tzalape* (*zarape, serape*), and shoulder blanket. And coloring these with dyes made from native plants—chamisa for yellow, chokecherry for purple, cedar bark and urine for red, cedar roots for green . . . Doctoring themselves with *osha* and *yerba de manzo* for stomach troubles, *topalquin* to break a fever, *cota* for rheumatism, *yerba buena* to "warm the insides" of pregnant brides . . . Like the Pueblos about them they made their homes of sun-baked adobe bricks, conforming the lines to blend with the uneven horizon. *Popote* brooms to sweep them out were made of the tall wild grass. Roots of the *amole* were crushed into pulp for soap . . . Cooking, not in the *brassero,* a brick oven suitable only for charcoal fuel, as did the *hacendado,* but outside, as did the Pueblos, in an adobe oven, the *estufa,* resembling in miniature the pueblo *kiva.* And treasuring for cooking use the pottery of the Indians.

To what does the description of such a life belong—to the pre-Conquest Aztecs, the colonial period of Mexico and New Mexico, the present humble Spanish-American villages of the Rio Grande Valley or the Indian pueblos of today?

At night the *tecolote* hooted down the canyon its tidings of death: "When the owl cries, the Indian dies." That was the voice of Malintzi, the betrayed and the betrayer . . . In times of stress, when the thunder rolled over the hilltop, that was Malintzi casting thunderbolts at the Government . . . Always she mourned her betrayal by the rivers, she went wailing down the trails and the highways, Malintzi, the great *Llorona,* the weeping one . . .

What was happening? The terrible conflict of the two races was no longer conducted on the surface by force of arms, but continued underground—within the bloodstream. And the buffer, the stake, was the *mestizo*.

Which was winning? Let us peep a century into the future.

In 1810, when independence from Spain was begun, there were one million Whites in Mexico, comprising about one-fifth of the whole population. In 1910, there were but 1,150,000 comprising less than one-thirteenth. But the *mestizos* had increased from two million to eight million, forming 53 per cent of the population. And the Indians had almost trebled to reach 40 per cent.

The Whites were disappearing. The Indians, steadily claiming the *mestizos*, were winning back the land. Today, of Mexico's nineteen million population, fifteen million belong to Indian Mexico. It is the ancient motherland, the future sonland, of a new Amerindian race.

Such was the trend, already apparent in the Four Corners during its Mexican period. A time of flux, during which the Spaniards were beginning to dwindle, termited by the increasing *mestizos*. An ominous interregnum.

How long it would have continued, and with what result, it is useless to speculate. For now a new breed of men was appearing to herald the ever unpredictable future.

The Psychological Mestizos

They appeared in remote clearings noiselessly and alone, without source or destination, like ghosts. Dressed like men in greasy, bloodstained, buckskin shirts and leggings, wearing Indian moccasins. Carrying a rifle, a knife, a pinch of salt. Sleeping at night in a bearskin or buffalo robe. Then moving on in the shadows of the morning.

Eventually they wandered into one of the pueblos or one of the little villages along the Rio Grande. The Indians observed that they were white men, but not Spanish. The Spaniards identified them as French, French-Canadian, English, and American by their outlandish names—Ceran St. Vrain, Bautiste La Lande, Etienne Provot, and Antoine Rubidoux, Seth Grant, Ewing Young, William Wolfskill, Jedediah Strong, Bill Williams, George Yount, the Patties, Bent, Christopher Carson. By the beaver they brought, they were seen to be trappers.

But strangely enough there seemed no rhyme nor reason to their perilous lives. Solitary outcasts, they had made their way from the Far East across the Great Plains, through the hostile tribes of Osages, Pawnees, Comanches, Cheyennes, Arapahoes, and Kiowas. Surviving these, they had penetrated the Sangre de Cristo Mountains, heaving up on the east, the lofty, white-peaked Rockies to the north, the abysmal gorges of the Grand Canyon to the west. They had completely encircled the high tableland of the Four Corners, trapping in the almost inaccessible streams and rivers which flanked it—in the wild San Juan, the mysterious Colorado, Little Colorado, and the Puerco. And after a year or two, perhaps three, after surviving, with unbelievable endurance, the terrifying loneliness, the fabulous phantasmagoria of a land without limit, the Indians, the wild beasts, unspeakable privations—after all this they had returned to the outpost of civilization. For what? To cash in their bales of beaver and spend all their gold in one quick mad orgy before vanishing again in the heaving walls of mountains.

They cared nothing for conquest, for fortunes, homes, friends. The mountains! That was what held them with an incomprehensible, fatal, ever-mounting fascination. That was the only common denominator to all their lives. They were indeed "Mountain Men."

These men knew the mountains as perhaps no other single group of men ever would. From the Arctic Circle to the Mexican Border, from the western edge of the Great Plains to the Pacific Coast, from the bare peaks above timberline down to the bare deserts, there was not a canyon, not a ridge, that they did not know. And, in all this vast hinterland of a yet unmapped continent, Taos was the one place at which they came to make rendezvous.

There were many obvious reasons. Lying in the northeast corner of the Four Corners, it was the most accessible settlement to which they could bring furs from the flanking mountains without crossing the bare tableland held by the marauding Navahos. It was the northernmost Spanish settlement, and hence the most free of Spanish restrictions; nebulous restrictions which even here often served the authorities as excuses for confiscating their furs. As the easternmost settlement, it was also the most accessible to newcomers from the Great Plains. The Indian pueblo of Taos had long been a trading center for the Pueblos down river, the mountain Utes, the Kiowas and Comanches of the Great Plains, even the Navahos. Now the Mexican villages of Fernando de Taos and Ranchos de Taos supplied still other wants—not only salt, sugar, powder, and lead, but whiskey, "Taos Lightning," and women.

Beginning in 1824, and yearly thereafter for sixteen years, there was another "rendezvous" at Brown's Hole far to the north in the Green River Valley. Still later, beginning in 1832, they met at the great trading center of Bent's Fort, out on the Great Plains at the foot of the mountains. Yet Taos remained for the Mountain Men the primary rendezvous, the focal point of the vast wilderness of the Four Corners. Then again they scattered into the wilderness.

What was it that had made these Mountain Men seek escape from the civilization behind them? What kept them too independent to stay in the employ of the powerful companies growing up and dominating other areas—the Hudson's Bay Company, the American Fur Company, the Pacific Fur Company, the Missouri Fur Company, the Northwest Company, the Rocky Mountain Fur Company? What held them aloof from the Spaniards? What made them abjure all thought of conquest, of accumulating wealth, of gaining fame?

They killed Indians on sight as they killed animals, so coldly, impersonally, and dispassionately that they frightened even the Indians. And, in turn, perhaps three-fourths of them were eventually killed by Indians. But they had begun to act like Indians. They spoke the dialects of many of the tribes, knew a great deal about their ceremonialism, and followed many of their customs and traditions. They blew smoke to the sacred directions before starting out on a journey; observed taboos and avoided sacred spots, though it meant extra days of travelling. Believing, as the Indians, that matter has a spiritual essence as well as a material composition, that even mountains have a spirit form as well as a physical one, they refused to divulge the location of certain peaks in whose streams they had found gold nuggets.

Something of tremendous, psychic importance had happened to these men. They were growing wholly Indian in spirit and feeling.

Both the European Spaniards and these French and Anglo-Europeans had confronted here that great psychic entity which was the spirit-of-place, the heart of a new continent. The impact was tremendous. It shattered them completely. But each succumbed in a different way. The Spaniards gave in to it through miscegenation with the Indians, creating a new race, the *mestizo*, which was to absorb them as it, in turn, was to be slowly absorbed by the Indians. The French and Anglo-Europeans, few in number, gave themselves up to the invisible forces of the land. The first nonindigenous men to wholly and intuitively accept its values, they too created a new breed. Men European on the outside and Indian inside, men neither white nor wholly red—psychical *mestizos*.

What would have happened had they been followed by others of their kind during a century or two of slow migration and settlement, a long interregnum that would have rooted them to the land?

No one knows.

For a new sun was rising in the east, casting its pale rays into the darkest canyons. It was round and cold and white, in the shape of a silver dollar. The eagle stamped on it with upraised wings was screaming across the plains. It was the American Silver Dollar, the new light of conquest, the Great Kachina which was to change forever the history of the world.

4 The Rising Sun

I

The Puritan

IT WOULD ALWAYS BE for this boy a source of sentiment and pride that a Pueblo Indian showed him, for the first time, the capital of his country. Born and brought up in its high hinterland, he had never been east before. Now driving steadily toward the rising sun, they saw everywhere the strange and unbelievable, constant miracles of beauty. Prairies of wheat and lush, green meadows replaced the sere and sandy plains of withered bunch grass. Pines and cottonwoods gave way to hardwoods of maple, elm, and oak. Everywhere there was water. Water above ground. Clear sparkling streams and rushing rivers that bore no resemblance whatever to the turgid red rivers, so often dry, that he had always known. And the towns. No longer were they drab villages of squat adobe and weathered wood spaced fifty or a hundred miles apart. They leapt at him from every twist in the road, one after another without end, with houses of stone and brick, and tidy green lawns and shady trees. Then began the cities—the fabulous growths of steel and concrete, rumbling and roaring with traffic, spouting smoke like forest fires, that he had only known in books.

Tony gave up the wheel. "Too many peoples," he said briefly. Massive and imperturbed, he gathered his best red blanket around him, picked up the small drum on the seat beside him, and began singing the Eagle Song.

To its rhythm, and with the plume of white eagle-down fluttering on the windshield and the beaded rabbit's foot swaying on the dashboard, they drove into Washin'don.

Somehow they found a hotel and telephoned Tony's old friend, John Collier. A girl answered. The Honorable John Collier, United States Commissioner of Indian Affairs, would be busy all day. What was their business?

The Indians wanted their land back. Pueblo land. They had a paper. An old paper. From the King of Spain it was. It had been a long time but they had not forgotten it. Now they had found it in an old leather trunk. Now was the time to do something about it. About getting their land back as the Government had promised . . . Silence on one end. The undying elephant memory, that implacable Indian stubbornness on the other.

The young lady cut both short. "Mr. Collier will see you tomorrow morning at nine o'clock."

Tony lifted one hairless eyebrow. After a couple of hundred years the pueblo could wait a day longer. Unhurriedly he took a shower, washed his hair. He sat combing it dry. Long and black like a woman's, it hung over his great shoulders to the waist. He parted it in the middle, combed it, then braided it into two long pigtails with red and white tape. Then he put on his new suit and shined shoes.

Now the boy lay on the bed watching him play solitaire. The great, brown, hairless hands dealt the cards carefully. The smooth, brown, hairless face showed no impatience when he lost. His people were used to that.

After an hour he looked up. Both grinned. It was time for a drink. Where?

"Anyplace. The town's full of saloons, bars, and cocktail places," the boy was sure. But Tony was more cautious. Always, everywhere, somebody was coming up and tapping him on the shoulder. "No liquor sold to Indians!" In really the damndest places: tourist hotels, honky-tonks, dining rooms, cafes, dance halls.

"But not here!" the boy protested. "This is the Capitol. It's full of Chinese ambassadors, Peruvian ministers, French dukes, English lords, Siamese scholars, and Texas politicians. It's cosmopolitan, Tony! Why, anybody can buy a drink. Even an Indian."

"This place the Gover'ment make the law." His logic was unassailable.

Well then, they would order up a drink to the room.

No. Here was where the law had been made. Besides—"Mebbe they spill some of them drinks, mebbe we pay just the same."

As usual the boy went out for a bottle of Scotch. But no sooner had it been opened than the telephone rang. It was the manager speaking.

"See?" said Tony's plucked eyebrow.

But no. The manager merely wanted to know if the Chief would let a newspaper man talk to him a minute.

He came up, three of him. A reporter on the *Post,* a photographer, and an assistant. "Well, well, Chief! Come to see the Great White Father at Washington, eh? Set right here now in this big chair. Got any feathers to put on? No? Well this here red blanket will do right smart . . . Yessiree. A drink all around now and we'll give you a front page spread that'll knock your eyes out. Here's to you, Chief!"

When they went out the room was full of flashlight powder smoke, and the bottle was empty. Tony grinned. Hadn't it always been like that with his people?

Soon he vanished. The boy found him out front. He was cautiously looking over a row of taxis, kicking their tires, punching the cushions. Finding one to suit, he began inquiring of the driver the mileage and the price of gasoline, the cost of oil, the driver's familiarity with the region.

"What you figurin' on doin', Chief? Driving to hell and back or buyin' her outright?"

With quiet dignity Tony smiled at the boy. "Compadre, you have nothing to do. You see Washin'don. Everything. No?"

He settled his six feet two inches and two hundred odd pounds down in the back seat with a gentle air of paternal benevolence. He had been here before and with an infallible memory recognized many of the buildings. How proud he was to point them out. The United States Treasury Building—"mucho dinero, eh compadre!" The tall Washington Monument, almost two-thirds as high as the sheer sandstone cliffs in the Navahos' Monument Canyon. "La Casa Blanca!"—not the White House of the ancient cliff dwellers in Canon de Chelly but the gracious old residence "where the *Presidente* lives." For a long time they sat staring at a tall seated figure of a homely man with a mole. The man who had tried to emancipate the Negroes from abject slavery; who had presented the governor of each Indian pueblo with a silver-mounted cane in token of their inalienable right to govern themselves by their own immemorial laws—the staff of office they still proudly carry today; the one man of all America who embodies to all peoples of all time its imperishable ideals of a free humanity. There was a catch in the boy's throat. Tony jogged his arm. "Kachina!" The cab moved on. Up wide and noble avenues, beside gracious parks, past great white marble buildings, whose massive simplicity marked them as monuments of a country and a civilization built to endure. To the Capitol. The Capitol of their country, the United States of America.

How wonderful it all was, leaping to life from dreary schoolboy history books, stirring the heart and mind awake with a new pride, a new consciousness of what it meant to be an American, a citizen of the greatest democracy on earth! What a gift that afternoon ride had been—a gift that somehow, sometime, should be the heritage of every American youth.

"You ain't seen no art museums yet," drawled the cabdriver. "Now Bud, give the Chief a break. Show him them little bronze statues of Indians and horses and cowboys in there." He drew up at a gloomy building marked the Corcoran Art Gallery.

The cast bronzes were downstairs to the left all right. But for the rest, the place was filled with classical bric-a-brac, fusty Victorian portraits, and an air of repression and outmoded conservatism that stifled all feeling of life; in the interests of a progressive country somebody should have touched a match to it all.

Tony, the boy noticed, was standing in the doorway of a back room, facing left. Something had happened to him. His fiesta mood was gone. He had lost his genial air of paternal benevolence. His pride was shattered. His body had suddenly slumped with indescribable heaviness, like wet clay. Head raised, he was staring upward with a look of fear, horror, and contempt at a huge figure towering on a pedestal before him.

The boy hurried in to stare transfixed himself.

There he stood on his pedestal as he first had stood on Plymouth Rock three centuries before, just disembarked from the Mayflower. A massive, big-boned man anchored solidly in his heavy, square-toed, buckled shoes. Hand on his hip, Bible under arm, strong and indomitable in his implacable self-righteousness. In every line of his stiff and truculent figure, in all the features of his severe and square-jawed face he revealed his character.

He feared God and he felt it righteous to strike this fear into the hearts of others by imprisonment in public stocks and burning at the stake. As a member of an oppressed minority, he knew it his duty to oppress and enslave other minorities to prove that all men were equal. Poor, he hated wealth; and to make sure that no others would be tempted with false desire, he was to gut the continent of its riches. He knew the folly of leisure and play. He was suspicious of a smile, abhored laughter. To him beauty was a mask of evil. Tenderness and mercy an indication of weakness. The show of emotions superfluous. The natural inclinations of sex an abomination legally hid by night.

Deeply inhibited, muscle-bound by tradition, he stood there confidently clad in all the virtues known to man, embodying the unquestionable dictates of a destiny that was to freeze the hot blood of Spain, topple Napoleon from his French throne, strike terror into the colored skins of Africa, Asia, America, and Australia, and exact homage from every people on the face of the earth.

Here, by the grace of God, conceived and executed in His own image, stood the Englishman, the Puritan. Recarved by that compassionate hand of the sculptor, Augustus St. Gaudens, which also has given posterity his antithesis and its only hope, the Adams Memorial, in Rock Creek Cemetery, Washington, D.C.

"This—this I think the White Man," said Tony decisively. Like his voice, his body had changed. He too stood feet apart, well braced, as if rooted to the earth which begot him, clutching one pigtail in his hand. He had forgotten his pride in the noble marble halls outside, thrown off his mask as a loyal "American." He was again all Indian—and he had his back up.

"Now this John Collier. She never see no Indians till I show her. Now I think we call her at home and say she see us now. We wait long enough!"

Pilgrims' Progress

So the English Puritan stepped down off Plymouth Rock. And forever after, the American Indian knew him, the Anglo, rather than the Spaniard, the Portuguese, the French, Dutch, and the German, as the White Man.

It was 1620, and a new race had landed on the eastern shore of the new continent just as the Spaniards had arrived far to the south more than a century before.

There was a great difference between them. The Spaniards had been hot-blooded, avaricious adventurers seeking to extend the domains, the glory, and the wealth of their motherland. Always it was their dream to go back to her as honored, wealthy sons. Tied down to their vast estates, they still sent their grandsons back to nurse their culture at her breast. The umbilical cord which bound them was never broken. It was only the *mestizo,* part Indian, who finally remained in Mexico.

The English Puritans were their direct antithesis. They were cold, grim, unsuccessful, discontented, and thwarted people, who had uprooted themselves from their motherland. To break from the past. To strike off the shackles that bound them. To escape everything that thwarted them. To get away! That was the dominating impulse driving them to a new continent to begin life anew under any conditions. That was the nemesis which pursued them, the psychosis they carried with them. They were indeed Pilgrims.

It took Mexico three hundred years from the arrival of Cortéz to break free of Spain; and it was the *mestizos* and Indians, and not the Spanish Colonials, who achieved independence. It took the Pilgrims only 150 years to achieve freedom from England; and they did it alone, as well as defeating other rival European colonists. In Mexico, independence consisted of winning back the motherland. In the United States of America, as the new confederation of English colonies was named, economic independence was the primary object; they revolted against their motherland kingdom because of their excessive high taxes.

In his penetrative study, *The Meeting of East and West,* F. S. C. Northrop traces the political origin of the new commonwealth to the philosophy of John Locke, which held that the sole justification for the existence of any government, even a democratic one, was the preservation of private property. Consequently it was self-contradictory and hence unconstitutional for even a vote of the majority to place human rights above property rights. Thus the new nation, based on this Lockean democratic thesis, embodied all the strange paradoxes which composed the characters of its founders.

The Declaration of Independence was a magnificent statement of human rights crystallized under immense pressure into articulate form. Yet, in practice, the inalienable rights of freedom were guardedly restricted by laws, and these laws were drawn to defend property rights against human rights.

All the leading citizens were traditionally aristocratic; Washington, Madison, Monroe, Randolph, and Lee were described as "cavaliers pervaded by the Angelican sentiment." Great wealth and huge areas of land concentrated in the hands of the few. The great estates along the James River and the vast plantations in Virginia rivalled the huge *haciendas* and *encomiendas* of the Spaniards in Mexico. "The transmission of this property," wrote Thomas Jefferson, "from generation to generation, in the same name, raised up a distinct set of families, who, being privileged by law in the perpetuation of their wealth, were thus formed into a Patrician order, distinguished by the splendor and luxury of their establishments." To work these vast estates, Negroes from Africa were imported as slaves to this new land of freedom, where all men were proclaimed equal.

The Puritan Church, with its restrained and aristocratic social forms, still dominated heart and landscape. The English Protestant Church set in the village green. Dull grey or white, with a small, white steeple and without stained glass windows. So cold and neat and forbidding. So different from the great baroque cathedrals in Mexico, with their soaring towers, their color, pomp, and majesty. Just as, early in the 1600's, only church members could vote and in the New Haven Colony only sixteen out of 144 planters were free citizens, now a definite attempt was made to restrict freedom of religious belief to freedom of belief in this church. But two years after the new federation was established, the first amendment to the new constitution was added to declare: "Congress shall make no law respecting an establishment of religion, or prohibiting the free exercise thereof." Still the soul of the new federation was distinctly Anglo. "It was not an accident," writes Northrop, "that the Federalists were Episcopalians or that financial New York's Wall Street begins at Trinity Church."

Such was the shape and color of the new country as its population expanded swiftly westward. To strike off the ancestral shackles that still bound them. To break from the cold, penurious mold that encompassed them. To escape everything that thwarted them. To get away! That was the dominating impulse still driving them to begin life anew under any conditions. They were Pilgrims still. And they were still Puritans. Such were the Mountain Men who, less than twenty-five years after the formation of the new United States, entered the far wilderness of the Four Corners. Solitary pilgrims, fleeing the lusts and comforts of civilization, fleeing home, companionship, and women; puritans fleeing from themselves. That was the nemesis still pursuing them, the psychosis they still carried with them.

Behind them the new nation kept growing. Not by swift, bold *entradas* like those of the Spaniards, annexing new provinces by spear thrusts of conquest. But by a cold and dispassionate procedure far more effective. They bought the land. The precedent had been set by the Dutch, who had bought Manhattan Island from the Indians for seventeen dollars. The average price paid by the United States up to 1826 to Indian tribes was three cents an acre. The Louisiana Purchase, bought pig-in-a-poke, in 1803, from France, which had extorted it from Spain, doubled the size of the nation. It consisted of some 909,000 square miles acquired for about two and a half cents an acre. This was followed by the acquisition of more territory ceded by Spain in 1819, still more ceded by Mexico in 1848, and the Gadsden Purchase in 1853.

Once bought from whatever foreign rival claimed it—though no man knew of what the territory consisted or could define the exact boundaries of the purchase—there remained only the judicial process of taking possession of it. All intruders were evicted. The land was then resold to private enterprises which could "develop" its natural resources, and thrown open to settlers, who then petitioned for admittance as a new state in the federation, whose chief justification was to secure their property rights against "foreign" aggression.

This primary sanctity of property rights, then, was the economic, political, and philosophical basis of the new nation growing up on the eastern seaboard as the Spanish domination, to the south, began to wane.

The Trail of Tears

When the Spaniards arrived in the New World they found an indigenous civilization, the Aztec empire of Moctezuma. When the Anglos arrived, they found an indigenous democracy.

The Confederacy of the United Five Nations had been

established by the Iroquois Indians about fifty years before the Pilgrims landed at Plymouth Rock. This confederation was formed by five separate tribes, the Mohawk, Seneca, Oneida, Onondaga, and Cayuga, and joined later by the Tuscarora. Its primary object was to establish and maintain peace throughout these most powerful of the eastern tribes. Its structure was formed so that authority flowed upward, rather than being enforced downward from the top. At the bottom, forty-nine chiefs were selected by the mothers of lines of descent possessing hereditary chieftainship rights, subject to confirmation by popular vote. Each tribe, through the representative chiefs, cast a vote in the Council on all questions. One tribe, the Onondaga, refrained from voting in order to act in the capacity of moderator or chairman, which remanded subjects not unanimously agreed upon back to the other voting tribes.

The later United States of America was a confederacy of thirteen English colonics bound together by a representative central government. It was similar in organization to this Confederacy of the United Five (Six) Nations except for the functioning of women in it; it was significantly a social structure for males only.

It was inevitable that the two should come in conflict. What was the relationship of the Anglos to the Indians, as compared to that of the Spaniards? The Spanish Catholics destroyed the Indian culture and intermarried with the Indians to create the *mestizo*. The English Protestants destroyed both the Indian culture and the Indians themselves.

From the start it was a program of complete extermination. Of a Pequot massacre shortly after the Mayflower arrived, Dr. Cotton Mather wrote, "The woods were almost cleared of those pernicious creatures, to make room for a better growth." A century and a half later Benjamin Franklin echoed this opinion when he wrote of "the design of Providence to extirpate those savages in order to make room for the cultivators of the earth." Still later, in Lincoln's boyhood, the "natural and kindly fraternization of the Frenchmen with the Indians was a cause of wonder to the Americans. This friendly intercourse between them, and their occasional intermarriages, seemed little short of monstrous to the ferocious exclusiveness of the Anglo-Saxon." This self-righteous slaughtering and horror of miscegenation, was not a paradoxical behavior on the part of a people who had founded a new republic expressly to give all men freedom. It was a direct expression of their inherent Puritan character, a prejudice which soon included all dark races, an *idée fixe* which soon became a national psychosis.

The Cherokee Nation was the largest of the Iroquoian tribes. Its people had invented an alphabet and had written a constitution, establishing a legislature, a judiciary and executive branch. In 1794, it stopped fighting, in accordance with the terms of a treaty made with them by the United States, and was confined to seven million acres of mountain country in Georgia, North Carolina, and Tennessee. In 1828, gold was discovered on their land. The Georgia legislature passed an act confiscating all Cherokee lands, declaring all laws of the Cherokee Nation to be null and void, and forbidding Indians to testify in court against Whites. The confiscated lands were distributed by lottery to Whites.

The Cherokee Nation appealed to President Jackson, and the case came up before the Supreme Court. The Chief Justice rendered his decision:

"The Cherokee Nation, then, is a distinct community, occupying its own territory, with boundaries actually described, in which the laws of Georgia can have no force, and which the citizens of Georgia have no right to enter, but with the assent of the Cherokees themselves, or in conformity with treaties, and with the acts of Congress."

Retorted President Jackson, "John Marshall has rendered his decision; now let him enforce it."

What was enforced was a fictional treaty whereby the Cherokees agreed to give up their remaining seven million acres for $4,500,000 to be deposited to their credit in the United States treasury. Three years later General Winfield Scott with seven thousand troops enforced their removal west of the Mississippi.

Of the fourteen to seventeen thousand who started on the "trail of tears," some four thousand died on the way. The financial costs of their removal were promptly charged against the funds credited to them from the sale of their homeland. And, when it was over, President Van Buren, in December 1838, proudly informed Congress, "The measures authorized by Congress at its last session have had the happiest effects . . . The Cherokees have emigrated without any apparent reluctance."

But before leaving the people had made their answer. It was not addressed to the President of the United States, to the Supreme Court or to the new American people replacing them. It was a resolution passed for all posterity, the ultimate tribunal, and an epitaph written for every dispossessed people on the face of the earth.

The title of the Cherokee people to their lands is the most ancient, pure and absolute known to man; its date is beyond the reach of human record; its validity confirmed by possession and enjoyment antecedent to all pretense of claim by any portion of the human race.

The free consent of the Cherokee people is indispensable to a valid transfer of the Cherokee title. The Cherokee people have neither by themselves nor their representatives given such consent. It follows that the original title and ownership of lands still rests in the Cherokee Nation, unimpaired and absolute. The Cherokee people have existed as a distinct national community for a period extending into antiquity beyond the dates and records and memory of man. These attributes have never been relinquished by the Cherokee people, and cannot be dissolved by the expulsion of the Nation from its territory by the power of the United States government.

A new, cold, white sun was rising in the east. The old, familiar sun was sinking in the west, blood red. And straggling toward it was a perpetual file of ragged, destitute people uprooted from their homeland. The Vanishing Americans.

In their silhouette is told the future of the Confederacy of the United Six Nations of the Iroquois—the Mohawk, Seneca, Oneida, Onondaga, Tuscarora, and Cayuga; the Five Civilized Tribes—the Cherokees, Choctaws, Chickasaws, Creeks, and Seminoles; the Four Nations Alliance of Cheyennes, Arapahoes, Kiowas, and Comanches; the United Nations of the Sioux; the Oglalas, Brules, Miniconjous, Crows, San Arcs, and Hunkpapas; the Apaches—Jicarillas, Chiricahuas, Mescaleros, the Llaneros and Olleros; the Osages and Blackfeet; the Nez Perces and a dozen others; is told the history of the next century, the story of the death of one race and the psychosis of another, the tragedy of a continent.

The immemorial land was being swept again with change. Where was the rock to which they could cling now?

5 Tide from the East

IN SANTA FE, that spring of 1822, whistles were blowing, muskets were being fired, people were running out into the plaza. William Becknell, a Missouri trader, had arrived with a wagon train of merchandise. Two years later, the spring caravan brought in $30,000 worth of goods, returning with $190,000 worth of furs, gold, and silver. By 1844, the value of merchandise carried had increased to $450,000.

With this diversion of trade from the new republic of Mexico by way of the old Chihuahua Trail, to the new republic of the United States by way of the new Santa Fe Trail, a change in ownership of the wilderness province of the Four Corners was indicated. History no longer was being written on scrolls and parchment, but in ledgers; no longer by sword and cross, but by dollars, the greatest weapon for conquest and colonization, for religious conversion and cultural adaptation, ever known.

On May 13, 1846, President Polk announced the existence of a state of war between Mexico and the United States. General Stephen W. Kearney, commanding the Army of the West, was sent to invade New Mexico, Chihuahua, and California. At the same time, James Magoffin, a secret agent, was sent to the governors of these Mexican provinces, with ample credit to entertain and an "unlimited capacity for drinking wine and making friends."

On August 18, 1846, General Kearney entered Santa Fe. He was cordially received by Governor Vigil and given a salute of thirteen guns. The American flag was raised over the *palacio*, the people were absolved from allegiance to Mexico, and the area proclaimed a territory of the United States. Kearney immediately appointed Charles Bent as governor and Donaciano Vigil as secretary.

Charles Bent, of Taos, was a partner in the firm of Bent and Vrain, the largest fur-trading company in the Southwest; a man with excellent social connections among the Spanish Colonials, and with a remarkable background of experience with the Indians.

His brother, William Bent, Bent or Roman Nose as he was known, had established Bent's Fort, in 1828, as a rendezvous for the Mountain Men and a trading post for the Indians, at the base of the mountains in eastern Colorado. He was married to Owl Woman, a Cheyenne noted for her intelligence. With her help, in 1841, he induced the Cheyennes, Kiowas, Arapahoes, and Commanches to make peace and allocate hunting grounds for each tribe.

His partner, Ceran St. Vrain, was a gentleman of the aristocratic French-Spanish family of St. Louis, who had trapped all over the area before establishing a post at Taos. His brother in turn, Marcelline St. Vrain, established Fort St. Vrain, another trading post on the South Platte, near the site of Denver. He was married to a Pawnee woman named Spotted Fawn, six feet tall and famous for her corn, melons, and pumpkins.

Well satisfied that the new American governor with

these connections could control the area, General Kearney wrote to Washington, "the people of the Territory are now perfectly tranquil and can easily be kept so." He received submissive delegations from the Pueblo Indians and then set out for California.

Colonel Doniphan, left in charge, concluded a treaty with the Navahos, then marched down to Chihuahua. He was replaced by Colonel Price, who arrived with more troops.

The American occupation was complete; not a shot had been fired.

Taos Rebellion

The Anglo mask had replaced that of the Spanish. But underneath it the people were the same. The aristocratic *hacendados* looked down upon the swaggering Americans as crude barbarians. The poorer *mestizos* called the newcomers "Gringos," perhaps a perversion of the Greek word "griego" meaning "foreigner," or perhaps from their popular song "Green Grow the Lilacs," but more subtly expressed today in the children's game of Cops and Robbers, when the robbers are known as Gringos. The Americans in turn called the *mestizos* "Greasers"—peons fit only to grease the wheels of their wagons. The Indians were silent, and in this silence lurked a sullen animosity.

It was not surprising that the mask was suddenly ripped asunder in Taos—the home of the New American governor, and the birthplace of the Pueblo Revolt of 1680, when the Spaniards were driven from the country.

On the morning of January 19, 1847, a crowd of Spanish-Americans and Indians broke into Bent's house, shot him, and scalped him while he was still alive; killed the sheriff, circuit attorney, and the brother-in-law of Bent and Kit Carson; murdered seven men at Turley's mill, near Arroyo Hondo; and shot eight traders in the village of Mora.

Like the earlier Pueblo Revolt, the Taos Rebellion was part of a general uprising planned for Christmas Eve. As in the former case, the news leaked out and the conspirators had scattered. But now retribution swiftly followed. Colonel Price, with 353 men, marched up river from Santa Fe. The revolutionists gathered in Taos pueblo and barricaded themselves in the massive old church.

On the morning of February 4, Price attacked. A breach

was made in the thick walls; through it a six-pound howitzer poured grape and shell. The great doors were battered down. Storming parties, with ladders and axes, advanced over the pueblo walls; riflemen picked off the defenders as they ran.

Of the Americans, fifteen were killed and forty-seven wounded. Of the insurgents, one hundred and fifty were killed, fourteen taken prisoner and hanged, and an unknown number wounded. Among these latter there still lives today, near the ruins of the church, an old Pueblo Indian. As a child in arms he was blinded by a spurt of powdery adobe knocked off the wall by a musket ball while his mother was passing arrows to the defenders. He is a gentle neighbor with a miraculous memory and sense of hearing. His one hundred years of blindness is a pertinent commentary on the trite phrase "another redskin bit the dust," and attests how recent is the advent of those who coined it.

Who cares? Things are happening too fast to be recorded. Hurry! It is 1848 and gold has been discovered in California. The whole country is moving westward. Regular weekly stage lines are running in over the Santa Fe Trail. It is 1851; sixty thousand people are passing through the territory. It is 1853 and a feasible route for a transcontinental railroad is already being sought. It is 1861 and a part of New Mexico is knocked off to make part of Colorado. It is 1863; the western half is made Arizona. Still another part becomes the Mormon state of Deseret, then Utah. Hurry, hurry! Let's get these territories built up as proper states. There are fortunes to be dug out of the hills, more fortunes to be made out of cattle, timber, land. Hurry, hurry, hurry! People are pouring in, gold prospectors and timber cruisers, cattle barons and cattle rustlers, Indian fighters, Indian agents, land grabbers, surveyors, gamblers, politicians, squatters, homesteaders, settlers.

The whole land is washed by a sea of change, a tide that cannot be stopped.

The Long Walk

The dead center of this whirling maelstrom was the Four Corners. The Hopis sat on their rock and looked down upon the land. The dust green sage stretched away endlessly and emptily to all horizons. Slowly it grew violet, purple, black. The stars came out. A coyote howled. The people slept. Black night gave way to grey dawn. The cliffs turned salmon-pink, rose-red. The people rose and stood on the edge, offering handfuls of corn meal to the rising sun with their morning prayers. They went down to their tiny fields. They drew up the strength of the earth into the growing corn, they transposed the flesh of the corn into the flesh of their own bodies. The withered stalks died, their withered bodies died, and both returned to the earth which had made them. But each had left their seed. It was a cycle endlessly repeated. A life of tremendous inner meaning impacted with all the potencies of the sun and moon and stars and clouds. A ritual whose undying theme was the harmony of the universe. Of what importance were temporal surface changes compared to this?

Around them there was movement, but not much. Flocks of sheep moved over the land slowly and whitely and with the same infinite variations in shape as the clouds moving overhead. Herds of horses broke from the arroyos like deer and antelope. The Navaho shepherds moved back and forth with the seasons, from winter hogans to summer shelters. Occasionally they raided the Hopi pueblos, mostly for women to rejuvenate their stock, and always with a ritual blessing before and a ritual cleansing after. This was their traditional meaning of war, a definite procedure for their common good carried out by a ritual technique that gave it its only validity. A people whose main concern was maintaining harmony between man and the supernatural forces around him, they respected and feared those whose ritualistic power superseded theirs in fact and principle—that of maintaining the harmony of the universe.

But farther outside, on the edges of that vast wilderness pool as it were, rippling with slow and rhythmic life, and at whose center was the stillness of meditative calm, boiled and churned the maelstrom of perpetual turmoil.

And so it was the Navahos who were caught between. More than any other people of the Four Corners, theirs was the tragedy of the next century.

It began at once.

Within a few weeks of General Kearney's arrival, Colonel Doniphan sent a reconnaissance party through the Navaho country. Major Gilpin, with two hundred men, marched up the Chama to the mountains, down the San Juan, and up the Little Colorado. All Indians were told to send their chiefs to a council to be held at Ojo del Oso (Bear Spring) by November 21. Here they were met by Doniphan, who had marched down the Rio Grande and up the Rio Puerco. After two days of council between the American leaders and fourteen Navaho chiefs, a peace treaty was made.

The ink was hardly dry before the Navahos resumed their accustomed raiding and the Americans their habitual military sorties. In 1847, under Major Walker; in 1848, Colonel Newby; in 1849, Colonel Washington; in 1851, Colonel Sumner. During this period the Navahos were officially reported to have stolen 453,293 sheep, 12,887 mules, 7,050 horses and 31,581 cattle.

With Colonel Sumner in charge, the Americans established the first military post in the Navaho country, Fort Defiance, just below the sacred precincts of Canon de Chelly. Against this encroachment the Navahos settled down to incessant warfare. They attacked settlements, raided Santa Fe, attacked the fort itself. By 1861, they were reported to have killed nearly three hundred citizens within the previous eighteen months.

The inevitable could be postponed no longer. Elaborate plans were made for a decisive Navaho campaign to begin July 1, 1863. The men selected to direct it and to lead it were Brigadier General James H. Carleton, commander of the Headquarters Department of New Mexico, and Colonel Christopher Carson. Kit Carson had come west in 1826, as a young runaway saddler's apprentice, had hunted and trapped all through the country, been a guide for Fremont's three expeditions, guided Kearney to California, and married the sister of Pablo Jaramillo, a brother-in-law of Charles Bent, killed in Taos.

Together they had just subdued the Mescalero Apaches, imprisoning at Fort Sumner the surviving 350 members who had not been killed, run off into Mexico, or joined the Gila Apaches. With the same cold precision and relentless care they began preparations.

Fort Wingate was established near the site of the first peace treaty made with the Navahos at Ojo del Oso. It was garrisoned by some three hundred men of the First California Infantry, and all crops within seventy miles were destroyed. A new post, Fort Canby, near the prehistoric Pueblo Colorado, was built to serve as headquarters for Kit Carson, who commanded some seven hundred men of the First New Mexico Volunteers. Fort Craig and Fort

Defiance were strengthened, Fort Stanton made ready for more captives.

The Utes, traditional enemies of the Navahos, were impressed into service as scouts and guides. As payment, Carson requested that they be allowed to keep the women and children captured.

"As a general thing," he wrote, "the Utes dispose of the captives to Mexican families where they are fed and taken care of, and thus cease to require any further attention on the part of the government. Besides this, their being distributed as servants through the territory causes them to lose that collectiveness of interest as a tribe which they will retain if kept together."

This was refused; the Utes were to be allowed to keep only the livestock they could capture. The white volunteers, however, were to be given a bounty of twenty dollars for every sound horse and mule, and one dollar for every sheep taken.

Suspecting that the Zuñis and Hopis would attempt to aid the Navahos, Carson sent out their warriors with his scouting parties. Any attempt to aid the Navahos, he warned, would bring complete destruction of their pueblos, "as sure as the sun shines."

To add to the complete military resources of the territory and the Ute and Pueblo allies, so many private citizens joined the hunt that it was necessary for the governor to call them off by proclamation.

By summer all was ready. The Navahos were given until July 20 to surrender themselves and join the surviving Mescalero Apaches captive at Fort Summer. After that date every Navaho then living was to be killed or made prisoner.

The hunt began. From the start there was no doubt of the issue. Carson advanced slowly westward, destroying small patches of corn, running in sheep and horses, relentlessly tracking down every family, every individual, with his Indian scouts. He fought no battles, stormed no cliffs. He could afford to be patient; winter was coming.

The deep snows came, driving the fugitives down from the high mountains. There was no corn in the desert fields. They could not gather piñons on the lower hills. They could not hunt game, tracking was so easy. They could not light fires to keep warm. There were no more sheep and horses.

Carson knew the country and the Navahos. On January

6, 1864, in the dead of winter and with unfailing instinct, he led some four hundred men to the mouth of Cañon de Chelly, their most secure stronghold. There are three deep gorges—Cañon del Muerto, Cañon de Chelly, and Monument Canyon—slashed nearly a thousand feet deep and thirty miles long into the plateau, spreading fanwise from their convergence on the west. Carson divided his force, sending parties to patrol the rims while a third detachment sent direct from Fort Canby blocked the entrance. He destroyed some two thousand peach trees planted in the cañons, depriving the Navahos of even the bark for food, and closed the trap.

Huddling in the icy caves of the ancient cliff-dwellers, the Navahos faced starvation, death, or capture. Their surrender marked the defeat of the people. Nowhere on earth, however formidable or inaccessible, could they escape the relentless power of the white men. One after another small, destitute, and starving bands began to straggle in.

On March 6, 1864, The Long Walk began: 2,400 people with thirty wagons loaded with the aged and maimed trudging over another "trail of tears" to captivity in the Bosque Redondo, 180 miles southeast of Santa Fe.

Still they kept coming: 3,500 more through April. Wise old men, proud young warriors, women, children, a few spavined horses, some sheep and scrawny goats. Trudging past Fort Canby, Fort Defiance, Fort Wingate, Fort Sumner, past crowds of their jeering conquerors.

And still they kept coming; a total of 8,491 Navahos, including the small band of Manuelito, their last great chief, all that was left save a few scattered groups hiding like animals in the Grand Canyon and in the unexplored basin of the lower San Juan.

The Long Walk was over. As a free and independent nation they had ceased to exist. They were Navaho Israelites held in bondage in a Mescalero Egypt.

How long, Lord, how long?

Bosque Redondo

. . . And the children of Israel sighed by reason of their bondage, and they cried, and their cry came up unto God. . . . And the nation to whom they shall be in bondage will I judge, said God: after that shall they come forth. . . .

Not until we know the cosmography of Navaho religion can we possibly understand what it meant to the Navahos to be exiled from a homeland immemorially bounded by the sacred four peaks which figure in their myths and ceremonials. Not until one tries to transplant Indian corn does one realize what it means to uproot the Indian from his earth.

Bosque Redondo, with Fort Sumner in its center, was part of a military reservation forty miles square, occupying the bottomlands of a bend in the Pecos River. The land had belonged to the Mescalero Apaches, and the four hundred imprisoned survivors still regarded it as their own. Confined on it with them the 8,500 Navahos felt like interlopers, even in imprisonment.

The White authorities, however, saw no reason why both tribes should not farm the land and become self-supporting, contented citizens. Accordingly, the bickering tribes were set to work plowing and planting two thousand acres to wheat and corn, and digging thirty miles of irrigation ditches. The Navahos, nomads for centuries and free roving shepherds since the arrival of the Spaniards, had never bent back nor pride to the hoe. Everything went wrong. Even nature conspired against them with droughts, floods, insects, frosts. Every crop planted in three years was a failure.

Late one night the entire group of four hundred Mescaleros fled the reservation. The Navahos were in too dire straits to care. Wandering Kiowas and Comanches had run off the sheep and goats they had not eaten. They could not accustom themselves to wheat flour, their staple ration. Wood was scarce; they shivered in flimsy shelters of canvas and brush. The alkaline water sickened them. They gave in at last to hopeless despair and planted nothing.

The supervising Whites were in a worse mess. General Carleton, military commander of the territory, had conquered the Navahos. That was his business. Let somebody else be their nursemaid. That was Matthew Steck's business. Steck, superintendent of Indian Affairs in New Mexico, had no appropriation for feeding the more than eight thousand Indians suddenly set in his lap. He did not favor the Bosque Redondo removal plan. Let Carleton clean up his own mess.

The argument threw into relief the long-standing controversy between the War Department and Department of the Interior. Until 1849 the War Department had charge of Indian affairs, in accordance with the national policy to destroy all

Indian tribes completely. The control of Indian affairs was then passed to the new Department of the Interior, which was to carry out the procedure by which their tribal lands were to be assimilated into the national estate. By 1868, the problem was acute. During the last five years, Indian wars with the Sioux, Cheyenne, and Navaho alone had cost the government $100,000,000. Yet, to institute a policy of clothing and feeding them on reservations would run much higher. Neither department wanted the responsibility of solving such a problem, yet each department was convinced it could handle Indians more effectively than the other.

Finally a special committee from Congress came out to inquire into the Navaho controversy. It found, at Bosque Redondo, 7,200 Navahos remaining out of the original 8,500. The first year it had cost the army $700,000 to maintain them. The cost for the second year had been reduced to $500,000. The expense now had been reduced to $300,000. At an average of about twelve cents per head a day, this seemed a bare minimum. The Indians were being issued each day only a pound of corn and a pound of beef with a pinch of salt.

Obviously they would have to be removed. Lieutenant General W. T. Sherman, who had made the famous march to the sea through Georgia, and Colonel S. F. Tappan, peace commissioner, were selected to supervise their removal and to negotiate new terms of a lasting peace.

Wrote Sherman on June 11, 1868, three weeks after arrival:

> . . . Now this was the state of facts, and we could see no time in the future when this could be amended. The scarcity of wood, the foul character of the water, which is salty and full of alkali, and their utter despair, made it certain that we would have to move them or they would scatter and be a perfect menace. So of course we concluded to move them. After debating all the country at our option, we have chosen a small part of their old country, which is as far out of the way of the whites and of our future possible wants as possible, and have agreed to move them there forthwith, and have made a treaty which will save the heavy cost of their maintenance and give as much probability of their resuming their habits of industry as the case admits of . . .

The bondage was over. A week later The People started home: "7,111 Navajo Indians, viz: 2,157 under 12 years of age, 2,693 women, 2,060 men, and 201 age and sex unknown."

The "small part of their old country which is as far out of the way of the whites and of our future possible wants as possible," to which they were returned, consisted of some 5,500 square miles of almost uninhabitable desert, located in the very center of the wilderness hinterland of the United States—the heart of the Four Corners.

What did it matter? Surrounding Cañon de Chelly, it in turn was surrounded by the four sacred mountains of their religious cosmography. It was the mystical center, the vibrating heartland of the world itself.

The terms of the treaty provided that they were to be given a small clothing allowance yearly for ten years. They were to be issued fourteen thousand sheep and one thousand goats, an average of two animals per person. To each head of a family desiring it, a tract of land not exceeding 160 acres, seed, and implements were to be given to encourage farming. And for every thirty children a school was to be provided.

As the land was a sandy wind-swept desert without rain for twenty-five months at a time, and where water holes were often fifty miles apart, there was little likelihood that the people would turn into farmers overnight, especially after their showing at Bosque Redondo. The promise of schools was impractical and it was never kept. The clothing allowance was equally farcical in intention. What could women do in petticoats? And with a sheep and goat apiece they were confidently expected to die out soon without embarrassment to the remote public.

What did it matter? They strode off into the trackless desert with their sheep and their goat. A bunch, a clan group, a family, a couple. Destitute, without horses and wagons, camping equipment, cooking utensils, tools, guns, adequate clothing, matches. Hunting for the spring, the canyon, the group of rocks, or water hole from whose place-name had derived their own clan-name.

And from the hidden canyons and secret caves crawled out to meet them the few relatives and friends who had preferred to live like beasts rather than to endure captivity.

They were home.

Impoverished as they were, they were better off than

the Utes who had helped to track them down. The Utes were paid in full by their employers by having taken from them their fifteen million acres of tribal land on the western slope of the Rockies and being placed on equally barren reservations in Utah and Colorado. To the south, in Arizona, the Apache tribes were still continuing a prolonged resistance. Conquered and placed on a reservation they were yet to break out and run rampant before final capture and imprisonment in Florida—the end of Indian warfare in the United States.

When it was over, only the tribes in the Four Corners remained rooted to their ancestral homelands. The Pueblos of the Rio Grande, on its eastern boundary; Acoma, Laguna, and Zuñi, along its southern border; and the Hopi pueblos, in its center, within the Navaho reservation. The titles to Pueblo lands, held in common under grants from the Spanish crown, were finally confirmed by the United States Court of Private Land Claims. Some of it—as high as 90 per cent of all irrigable land—already had been confiscated. But what remained was henceforth designated reservations.

Such was the status of the Pueblos and Navahos, under those people who, four score and twelve years before had created on this continent a new nation conceived in liberty and dedicated to the proposition that all men were created equal. . . . Under the jurisdiction of Commissioner of Indian Affairs Francis C. Walker, who, in 1871, stated that he would prefer to see the Indians exterminated rather than an amalgamation of the two races, and to further this end stated, "When dealing with savage men, as with savage beasts, no question of national honor can arise. Whether to fight, to run away, or to employ a ruse, is solely a question of expediency."

A tribe of savage nomads accustomed to ride far and free with arrogant disdain for any other power on earth, they had endured as complete a subjugation of a free people as any in all history. And they never forgot it. There are old people living today who suffered it all, and there are few Navahos who have not heard of Bosque Redondo from their fathers' lips. It was a psychological and sociological holocaust whose devastating effects are imprinted upon their character, which are embodied in the very blood and sinews of their daily lives. Their remarkable adaptation was but the mask of Anglo-American citizenry. Behind it was hidden the Indian, the integument of a faith clinging to the imperishable rock.

Fort Defiance

Of all the forts established in and around the Four Corners—Fort Marcy, on its hill above Santa Fe; Fort Canby, near the site of the prehistoric Pueblo Colorado; the fort successively named Fort Fauntleroy, Fort Lyon, and Fort Wingate; Fort Craig, Fort Stanton, Fort Sumner, and Fort Garland in Colorado—Fort Defiance was the most typical, most important, and longest lived.

It was established on August 17, 1851, by Colonel Edward V. Sumner, with four companies of dragoons, the most remote army post on the western frontier and the first military post in what is now Arizona. Strategically located in the heart of the Navaho country, it was of equal significance to the Navahos. From it they had successfully retreated into Cañon de Chelly. Past it they had marched in bondage to Bosque Redondo. And to it they were brought upon their return.

Thereafter, for thirty years, Fort Defiance remained the only federal agency in the reservation. From an army establishment it grew into administration headquarters for the Indian Bureau in all its dealings with the Hopis and Navahos—as it still is. In 1938, it and adjacent Window Rock became the site of the $1,500,000 Navaho Central Agency buildings constructed with PWA funds to take the place of the many different agencies scattered through the reservation. Throughout its history of nearly one hundred years, it has been the stage across which has walked every leading character of the Four Corners.

Here came Na-tah-lith, one of the greatest medicine-men; old Barboncito, the black-whiskered Hostoowie; Ute-scarred-chested Manuelito, Mr. Blackweed, who was one of the signers of the treaty at Bosque Redondo. With Ganado Mucho, he later became one of the two most prominent chiefs and was sent to Washington to meet General Grant. The trip was his undoing. He fell out of favor with his people for accepting presents from the Whites and allowing his son to be sent to the White man's school. Unfortunately the son died; Manuelito took to liquor and died soon afterward.

One of the most engrossing stories is that of Henry Chee Dodge, who was born in the fort. In 1859, trouble broke out at Fort Defiance when the cavalry troops killed some Indian horses pasturing in the meadow. Located, as it was, at the mouth of Cañon Bonito and called by the Navahos "Meadows Between the Rocks" for its good grass, the spot was regarded by the Navahos as their favorite range. They swiftly retaliated. During the ensuing cavalry raids, a Navaho girl was captured and imprisoned in the military guardhouse. Here she gave birth to a child. The boy was named Henry Chee Dodge after Captain Henry L. Dodge, who had been previously killed by Apaches while on a reconnoissance trip. Five weeks later, in April, 1860, some two thousand Navahos attacked the fort. During the fighting mother and child vanished. The mother to appear and disappear again in one of the Hopi pueblos; and Henry Chee Dodge, half a century later, to become the last chief spokesman for the Navaho tribe.

It was here, upon the Navahos' return from Bosque Redondo, that they were issued their two sheep and goats apiece; the animals being led for counting through a hole called Window Rock in the sandstone "haystacks" of Tse-Bonito, a short distance away. Clothing allotments were given out, additional sheep; orders were issued; supervision carried on. Here, in 1873, was started the first school; in 1880, the first hospital; in 1882, the first boarding school. It was disastrous that none of these functions was successful. For Fort Defiance, as the sole federal agency, was to all intents and purposes the concrete home of the Navahos' dominating authority. By it they judged their nation of conquerors.

The outstanding neglect was the lack of medical attention. At Bosque Redondo hundreds of Navahos had died from a disease producing "big sores," presumably smallpox. Further weakened by their starvation diet, the alkaline water, and long walk home, they were accompanied by a military doctor. He stayed about a year, vaccinating against smallpox the few Indians who came to the fort. When he left, there was no medical attention for the Navahos for the next ten years.

When doctors did start coming again, in 1880, it was to stay only a month or so. In his speech given at the dedication of the new hospital in 1938, Dr. Peter, its medical director, humorously reviewed their qualifications. The title of doctor did not imply a very arduous or prolonged training. Often three to six months sufficed for a candidate to get his degree. His salary was poor—from $1,000 to $1,500 per year; life in the fort was dreary; and very few medical supplies were furnished. The positions of clerk and physician were soon consolidated, and evidently the incumbents were not held in high esteem.

Commissioner Henry Price wrote the agent, Major Dennis Riordan, asking whether there was a doctor at Fort Defiance, and if so, whether his services were required. To this inquiry the agent replied, "I beg to say that there is a person carried on the payroll as physician, but I don't think we have one. Instead of his being a doctor he was formerly an editor, a lawyer, and a sewing machine salesman."

Against this medical incompetency there came the epidemic of smallpox in 1883, and, in 1888, the greatest known epidemic to assail the Navahos. More than one thousand died of "sore throat," possibly diphtheria, without help; the only known decrease in Navaho population since The People's return from Bosque Redondo.

It is not surprising that such men learned little and cared less about the Indians around them. One of them, Dr. Jonathon Letherman, after spending three years at Fort Defiance, disposed of the matter authoritatively in a "Sketch of the Navajo Tribe of Indians, Territory of New Mexico," printed in the Smithsonian report for 1855. He wrote: "Of their religion little or nothing is known, as, indeed, all inquiries tend to show that they have none . . . The lack of tradition is a source of surprise. They have no knowledge of their origin or of the history of the tribe . . . They have frequent gatherings for dancing . . . Their singing is but a succession of grunts and is anything but agreeable."

For twenty-six years this view was held valid by all the visiting doctors at the fort, as well as by the Army and the country behind them. There then loomed, as the one notable exception, the incongruous figure of a young Dublin-born Irishman who joined the Army Medical Service in 1866 and was sent to Fort Defiance in 1881. His name was Dr. Washington Matthews. Discovering that the great nine-day massings of these heathen savages, yowling and leaping around a fire, were sacred ceremonies, and moreover healing ceremonies, he set himself to their serious study.

The result was the first recording of Navaho ceremonialism. His "Night Chant," "Mountain Chant," "Navajo Legends," and other reports later issued by the Smithsonian Institution form the basis upon which all later Navaho ethnology has been built, and have never been superseded for accuracy, completeness, and enlightened understanding. And until his death at Cape May, New Jersey, in 1903, he retained his deep interest in Navaho life.

Meanwhile, in the early summer of 1873, there had come to the door of a wealthy, retired lawyer in Rochester, New York, an obscure history student from Highland, Illinois, who hoped to find a position "as assistant-librarian or something similar."

The retired attorney was Lewis H. Morgan, who was devoting his time and money to the study of Indians. He had made the first study of the government and social organization of the Iroquois—the first real study of any American Indian tribe. It was he who developed the theory that the Aztecs were Pueblo people who had migrated from New Mexico—a theory still later developed into the most comprehensive study of Indian migrations throughout the continent. Morgan, in fact, was the "Father of American Ethnology."

The short pale-faced student of 33 who came to see him was Adolf Bandelier. With their meeting, Bandelier began his own career as explorer, historian, and anthropologist. He made his first trip to New Mexico in 1880, being allowed $100 a month for all expenses by the new Archaeological Institute of America. On this pittance he discovered the ruins of El Rito de los Frijos, on the Pajarito Plateau, which have been now designated for him the Bandelier National Monument. The following year, while Matthews was beginning his study of the Navahos, Bandelier travelled south to Mexico, substantiating Morgan's views by reporting that "the key to aboriginal history of Mexico and Central America lies between the city of Mexico and the southern part of Colorado."

While Matthews and Bandelier were beginning to study the Navahos and Pueblos, a geology professor, who had lost one arm at Shiloh had first traversed the Colorado River. For this service Major John Wesley Powell was given the task of organizing, in 1879, the U.S. Geological Survey, and then the new Bureau of American Ethnology.

One of his first employees was young F. W. Hodge who was working in the Geological Survey in 1884; entered the Bureau of American Ethnology in 1889; and became an executive of the Smithsonian Institution in 1901. As early as 1884, he uncovered the ruins of Hawikuh, one of the "Seven Cities of Cibola," near Zuñi. As a scholar, he later was a founder of the Quivira Society; editor of the narratives of Coronado and Cabeza de Vaca; annotator of the records of Fray Alonso Benavides; and is now the eminent director of the Southwest Museum.

It was inevitable that all these should meet Frank H. Cushing, one of the greatest ethnologists of all time, who, in his early twenties, was beginning his great basic study of the Zuñi creation myth and Zuñi legends.

Fort Defiance then, as now, was the focal point of the Indian Four Corners, while a lawyer, doctor, one-armed geology professor, and a history student were beginning their great task of laying the foundation for our present scientific study of Southwestern Indians.

The Navahos gave them plenty to study, growing into the largest tribe on the largest reservation in the United States. And the women did learn to wear petticoats—a half dozen, all big and flounced and ruffled, surmounted by a velveteen blouse, and with their hair tied into a *chignon* at back. Just like the officers' ladies at Fort Sumner. The New Look of 1948!

It was certain that further support did not come from Fort Defiance. It came from another new group of men gradually infiltering the Four Corners.

6 The Trading Posts

A Book Review

D*esert Wife,* Hilda Faunce. Little, Brown and Company, New York, 1928.

Many years ago, in Colorado Springs, my Columbia grade school teacher was a tall, slim young woman named Ruth Jocelyn Wattles. Her penmanship was exquisite and she knew Navaho. Aside from these accomplishments she must have been a remarkable woman, for the debt I owe her seems to gain interest daily.

The school was on the edge of town, its windows opening to the empty prairies on one side and to the shining mountains on the other. Too, we were an unruly class. Miss Wattles cured our predilections for both misbehavior and day-dreaming by the most novel of expediencies. Instead of punishing us, she rewarded us at the end of the day for good behavior by telling us stories of the Navahos. Gradually we quieted down to earn this last half hour.

As far back as Miss Wattles could remember, there were Navahos sitting about the big fireplace of her home ranch waiting to be fed. But inevitably we learned that many of the stories she told us were taken from letters being written her by her cousin. At times she even read us excerpts directly. Who this cousin was we never learned nor cared. It was the stories themselves which held us, amplified by Miss Wattles' own experiences, her eye for significant detail, her feeling for life, and her unbounded enthusiasm.

When school let out I forgot her stories completely. Life replaced them. I found myself for a time on the Navaho Reservation too; then in Wyoming, California, Mexico.

Miss Wattles meanwhile had been busy. Enthusiastic over our reception of the letters from her cousin she had sent excerpts of them to Harper's Magazine. Published there, they roused the enthusiasm of Little, Brown, and Company, who persuaded her cousin to arrange them in book form. The book was released in 1928 under the title *Desert Wife,* by Hilda Faunce, Miss Wattles' cousin. Not until it was reprinted, in 1934, did I run into a copy; and then, over twenty years later, it all came back to me—the quiet schoolroom at the close of day, and the snow beating like moths against the window-panes; Miss Wattles' tall figure and resonant voice; the simple, homely stories themselves, oddly familiar and amply confirmed by my own experiences at Shallow Water.

It is a beautiful, terrible, compelling book, one of the best that has ever been written about trading posts.

Ken and Hilda Faunce are living in Oregon. The fog and perpetual rain are depressing. The bank fails. The wife can endure these reverses and discomforts. But not the man. He was desert-bred, had once been an Indian trader in New Mexico and Arizona. That is the trouble. Homesickness. The land had touched him, he had to go back, as we all do. Such a strange man! In seven years of marriage the woman had never understood him.

They abandon the place, pack supplies in a light road wagon, and start driving back the old Oregon Trail. Up to the top of the Coast Range, down the eastern slope. Oregon. Idaho. Utah. There are few automobiles, few fences. The ground where the ox teams had formed a square by the water holes is still trampled flat. The woman cooks over a campfire, sleeps beneath the wagon, disconsolately eyes each small village with its tidy homes and shady trees. The man drives steadily on. He is moody, taciturn, stranger than ever to her. It is 1913; it might have been 1848.

At last they reach the Four Corners. Hilda is terrified. The vast emptiness and barrenness threatens her, as it always threatens the White. "To keep from going mad in the stillness," she closes her eyes and mutters a silly jingle about the Eohippus:

> There was a little animal no bigger than a fox,
> And on three toes he scampered over these Tertiary rocks.

Ken is home. From a prosperous trader at Lugontale he

leases the abandoned trading post of Covered Water. It is twenty miles from the trading post at Chin Lee, their nearest neighbor; 105 miles from Gallup, the nearest town.

The post is a decrepit, two-room shack of rough planking held together by box boards, with battens covering the cracks. The back door opens into a storage tent for goat pelts, sacks of wool, supplies. In front, the seepage from a spring fills a hole covered with boards: "Covered Water."

There is not a tree, a blade of grass, a house in sight. All around, interminably, spreads the vast, naked plain. From it into the post seeps snow, sand, loneliness—the strange place-spirit of America so inimical to the alien newcomer.

With the Navahos comes stark fear. Those strange dark faces. Queer customs. A language Hilda does not understand. Threats; the place has a bad name . . . The sheathed animosity between the White and the Red races.

Ken ignores his wife's terror. He speaks Navaho, feels perfectly at home. He keeps busy trading, making friends. Hilda huddles in the other room, but there is no door for privacy. Through a hung blanket she can always hear Indians begging coffee, glimpse them spitting on the floor and picking fleas from their hair.

How wonderfully, terribly, Hilda's fear is built up to its climax. She becomes seriously ill. She cannot eat. Her hair falls out. She "seemed to be turning into an Indian," becoming "a deep, burnt orange color all over." If she died in the house, the post would be a total loss. No Navaho would ever step inside it. They might burn it; that is their way. The Indians have stolen the shovel; Ken would be unable to dig her grave outside. There is no escape, even in death. So she worries in moments of consciousness.

The doctor arrives from Gallup. He stays twenty minutes and charges $225. It is not too much for the 105-mile ride. He leaves some pink pills and advises an operation in Gallup if she lives.

Hilda lives and undergoes the operation. A month later she walks out of the hospital. Ken has not written nor come to see her. Yet she knows he loves her. She returns to Covered Water, and asks him if he would have come to her funeral if she had died. "No," he answers. "I would have ridden the other way." That, she realizes, is what makes him so strange. It is the Indian way. Not to fail when they can help; when they cannot, to ride hard to forget.

This is the psychological turning point in the book, as it

is the psychological turning point of every alien race on a new continent. To meet in mortal combat the inimical spirit-of-place. To succumb to it and die. Or to accept its terms and henceforth be molded by its invisible forces.

How wonderfully now, throughout the rest of the book, Hilda opens up to the land and its people. She sees its naked beauty, its subtle colors, feels its strength and rhythm. She learns Navaho, makes friends with Old Lady, Slender Girl, Hosteen Blue Goat. En-Tso's tonic restores her hair. She sees ceremonies, learns to estimate the amount of sand the Indians put in their sacks of wool.

Trouble comes too. The Navahos kill one of their young school-Indians for selling turquoise stolen out of a grave. They threaten to kill Ken for befriending some prospectors hunting for gold. Smallpox wipes out family after family. Hilda rides from hogan to hogan to persuade them to let her immunize them with vaccine. She allows Ken to sell her favorite Navaho blanket to a rich tourist in order to save money for a small place of their own someday. The First World War comes and Ken averts a massacre of all the Whites around before soldiers like Kit Carson and his troops come . . . Episode after episode, they all show a deepening awareness of The People and the land.

And finally, having saved their small stake for a ranch, the couple leaves. Parting with mutual respect and understanding and sorrow, but still heeding the call of their own irrevocable destiny and leaving the Navahos to theirs . . .

A wonderful book. It reveals not only the outer conflict of two races, and the inner conflict of the individual, but how both may be transcended by admitting and facing their realities. And it throws into relief not only the life and needs of the Navahos, but the traditional function of the trading posts as a bridge between them and the impinging Whites.

The Traders

The usual trading post was a utility building rather than a country home. It was built to trade in and to live in, miles from any town or human habitation. It was necessarily built crudely with Indian help and from native material, and it was built strongly to withstand driving sand and wind and rain, heavy snows, and possible trouble. There was no set pattern. But with all their variations, they conformed to a general type. The post at Shallow Water, remembered from boyhood, differed little from those found almost anywhere in the Four Corners. Smaller or larger, they were all solitary oases in the desert; sturdy little forts on the frontier.

The walls were of sun-baked adobe bricks, from two and a half to four feet thick. No bullet could pierce them; they retained the heat in winter and the coolness of night in summer. The roof beams or *vigas* were huge logs of pine or spruce, hauled down from the mountains. Stripped of their bark, well seasoned, and cured like hams from the fireplace smoke of many years, they gleamed dark and smooth as honey. The roof itself was a layer of cross boards heaped with earth. The floor was of hard, pressed adobe until flooring could be freighted in, covered with innumerable Navaho blankets grown into rugs with the coming of the traders, and so durable that they out-lasted the floors. There was a fireplace in every room.

The main room was at best a huge hall. The walls were flanked with shelves of trade goods—bridles and spurs, bolts of flowered ginghams and solid-color velveteen, canned goods, staples, Stetson hats, knick-knacks, articles of clothing. Down one side and across the back stretched the long counter and showcases. The floor was littered with bushel baskets of onions and pinto beans, bags of flour, salt, and sugar put away from mice each night. Strings of dried chiles and coils of rope hung from the rafters. In the center of the room sat a squat-bellied stove surrounded by boxes of sand to spit in.

Adjoining this was the rug room, often serving as a general storeroom. Its windows, if not every window in the post, were stripped with iron bars. Here were piled stack on stack of rugs, perhaps two hundred averaging $50 in value apiece and representing $10,000 in all. There was an iron safe full of silver currency and valuable pieces of pawn silver, a few loaded rifles.

Behind the big room and built at right angles to it were the living quarters of the trader, one room to a half dozen, depending on the size of his family and the help he required. In one of these might be a woman working on a loom or a man pounding silver if the trader was trying to improve the design and color of the wares in his district.

At sunrise the doors were opened. All day The People straggled in from the vast empty plain. Riding their shaggy ponies.

Bumping along in their springless wagons, the man slimly erect in front, the woman slumped in her blanket beside him, the box full of children. In the post they stood spitting around the stove and sitting on the floor picking lice from each other's hair. The children knelt at the candy case rubbing dirty noses against the glass, silently staring at the peppermint sticks inside. A woman would inspect ten bolts of velveteen, dicker for a piece of calico.

Outside, the horses and wagons multiplied. People stood or squatted against the sunny walls, rolling cigarettes. Talking. Saying nothing. Everything was relaxed and easy. But pervaded too with a lurking tenseness, a sharp awareness. The trading post was a country store, but it was also the verbal newspaper of the region, a common meeting ground, and the focal point of perhaps a thousand square miles.

The undeniable master of all this was the trader. He supplied all the staples necessary for a people's changing existence, and was the only outlet for their wool, blankets, and silverwork. Loaning money on goods or articles given him for pawn, he tided them through drought and famine. He was their only contact with an alien, encroaching civilization. He interpreted this to them and them to it, excusing the ignorant foibles of greedy government Indian agents and missionaries, and protecting The People from the hasty anger of local sheriffs. He acted as law-maker, a judge and jury, a schoolteacher. At any hour of the night he might be awakened to set a bone or break a fever. He was often called upon to bury the dead, as Navahos would not approach a dead body. He contributed to all "sings" or ceremonials held in his area . . . All this required courage, absolute self-reliance, a quick wit, and a diplomacy as subtle as ever existed.

This writer could never subscribe to the obsession held by Oliver La Farge and other extreme romanticists that the traders were invented by Satan expressly to plague and cheat the Navahos. Among them, as among other groups, there were some who did cheat and contrive trouble of all kinds. They were few and they did not last. If they were not killed outright, they suffered peculiar accidents, became bankrupt, or disappeared. The traders were the first group of Anglos not expressly bent on obliterating the Navahos. Individually each became, to all purposes, the Great White Father in his wide domain. For during the first thirty years after the Navahos moved back from Bosque Redondo to what was now a reservation, twenty successive men held the post as government agent—a comedy of Indian administration.

What would have happened had the traders suddenly been expelled from the country? An interesting parallel is the case of a group of rural Chinese storekeepers, who established themselves among the Yaquis in the remote slopes of the Sierra Madres of Mexico. Parsimonious and scrupulously honest, they built their humble stores into the only banking structure of Sonora. Then late in the 1920's, while I was down there, Mexico decreed that all Chinese should be expelled. Hill-traders with thousands of pesos in beans and corn and beef in their ledgers, the Chinese storekeepers were suddenly driven out. The result was predictable. With no one to supply goods or credit, the abandoned stores were pillaged, groups of bandits formed and ran riot through the tiny villages, and another Yaqui uprising followed.

But in the Four Corners the traders were unmolested by the government, and it was they who enabled the Navahos to come through the difficult period following Bosque Redondo.

Probably the first trading post devoted primarily to the Navaho trade was established at Lee's Ferry, the principal articles exchanged being Mormon horses and Navaho blankets. "Al" Lee, grandson of its famous Mormon founder, John D. Lee, started the post at beautiful Tselani which his son, "Art" Lee, now runs. His other son, Hugh Lee, operates the post at Ganado and is currently president of the United Indian Traders Association.

A man named Leonard, about 1875, opened the first post at Ganado. In 1876, J. Lorenzo Hubbell opened a post three miles upstream from Leonard, on the Pueblo Colorado wash—near the site of the former Fort Canby and the ancient Pueblo Colorado. Three years later he moved down to Ganado, bought out Leonard, and took C. N. Cotton as partner. Later he moved to Gallup, founding the oldest and largest Indian trading firm in the Southwest. Hubbell was, by all odds, the most famous trader in the area. For half a century his post was a mecca, his hospitality a legend.

In 1876, there was but one licensed trader on the reservation proper, Thomas V. Keam, a former government interpreter. In 1882, he took up a homestead and established a post in the canyon now named for him. It was in Hopi territory, just ten miles east of First Mesa, but drew Navahos as well. He later sold out and retired to his old home in Cornwall, England.

A man named Brown opened the first post at Manuelito, named for one of the two signers of the treaty at Bosque Redondo. In 1882, J. W. Bennett and S. E. Aldrich also located there, soon branching out with another in Washington Pass, in charge of Elias S. Clark and Charles Hubbell. Aldrich, in 1890, then established a post at Round Rock on Lukachukai Creek. For a new partner he took Henry Chee Dodge, destined to be the last great spokesman of the Navahos.

The first store at the important trading center of Chin Lee, at the mouth of Cañon de Chelly, was opened by Hubbell and Cotton. It was later replaced by one built by William Stag. The Lynch brothers, in 1881, started a post at Navaho, the farthest west; George W. Sampson, in 1883, located at Sanders; "Billy" Weidemeyer, in 1885, at La Cienega, later settled by the Franciscans and now called St. Michaels; "Joe" Wilkins, a freighter, the old post at Crystal, in 1890; and Charlie Fredericks opened a successful post at Navaho Church, the towering red cliff eight miles east of Gallup.

By 1890, there were nine traders on the reservation and some thirty traders surrounding it. The main article of trade was Navaho blankets—the best obtainable. Apaches, Utes, and Paiutes preferred them to the blankets issued by the government. Spanish-Americans still used them for *serapes* and *ponchos*. Anglo-American cowpokes and settlers used them for bed blankets and lap robes. For the first time an estimate was made of the yearly output—a total of $40,000, of which $25,000 worth were sold to the traders and $15,000 worth kept for tribal use.

Fifty years later the business had grown to enormous proportions. There were 146 trading posts, most of them licensed and bonded under government control, paying, in 1940, some $1,865,000 for Navaho products, selling $3,640,000 worth of goods, and advancing $190,670 on pawned articles.

The first quarter of the century was the "golden age" of the trading posts, when, for a brief span, the integrity of Indian work and Indian thought achieved its only recognition. It was the traders who made this possible, and it is these old-timers I remember with a boy's love and respect for their high traditions.

Sam Drolet and Bruce Barnard, at Shiprock. Walter Beck and Dick Simpson, at Fruitland and Farmington. The Kirks, of Manuelito and Gallup . . . So many more, too numerous to record. Primarily and paradoxically they were not just "business" men. Like the Wetherills, at Kayenta, they made among the most important archaeological discoveries in the Southwest. Like the Newcombs, they recorded some of the first sand paintings. Like Ralph Myers, of Taos, they were accepted by ethnologists as authorities on Indian life as well as Indian handicraft. Their remote posts were oases in the desert, landmarks in an unmarked wilderness. They were bankers, doctors, interpreters, school teachers, art agents, representatives of an encroaching White civilization to the Indians, and champions of Indian tribes against an inimical government. Scarcely 150 men in an area of over 25,000 square miles for a period of fifty years, the Indian traders were the media through which were exchanged the values of two ways of life.

The Trading Capital

Midway between Fort Wingate and Fort Defiance there was built, in 1880, a general store and saloon called the Blue Goose. The site was ideal for a trading center. The Navaho reservation lay to the north, the pueblo of Zuñi and its reservation to the south. Past it streamed the tide of westward expansion following the 35th parallel route to California. To provide safer accommodations for travellers and to speed the delivery of mail, the Overland Stage was established and the Blue Goose was made a way station.

Next year surveyors came laying out the line of the new transcontinental Atlantic and Pacific Railway, followed by grading and bridge crews camping in tents around it. The following year, a locomotive engineer, named John Gallup, galloped the first iron horse into the tent city, the smoke billowing from its funnel stack and the whistle shrieking. A new town had been born and named . . . That's the story, although by prosaic coincidence the comptroller of the Frisco Railroad which was associated with the Atlantic and Pacific was also named Gallup.

There was nothing prosaic about Gallup's growth.

Coal, to fuel the locomotives, was discovered in the hogback near the new town. It became a mining center of Slavs and Italians, a division point on what is now the Santa Fe Railroad.

East of town, near Grants and Bluewater, were wide open grasslands for grazing cattle and sheep. Settlers came in, American ranchers and Spanish-American shepherds. Gallup became a frontier town in the noisiest tradition, with cowpokes riding in every Saturday night to shoot up its row of saloons and gambling halls.

From up in San Luis Valley of Colorado, John Wood came driving an ox cart filled with potatoes and bringing his wife to be delivered of the first white child in the new town. From the Navaho reservation came the traders in wagons piled high with wool and pulled by ten spans of horses. Other traders moved in from remote trading posts to establish large trading companies. Gallup became the trading and shipping center of the whole area.

Always there came Indians—a continuous straggle of Zuñis on foot and Navahos on spooky, quick-stepping ponies, to gawk and trade.

This was Gallup. The trading capital. The Indian capital. The metropolis of the Four Corners.

And this is Gallup today. Saloons and trading posts, bars and stores catering to the Indian trade. The Blue Goose infinitely and repetitiously multiplied. A frontier town with a backdrop of majestic red sandstone cliffs. Elevation 6,500 feet, population seven thousand. Still the largest, busiest town in the wilderness of the Four Corners. Still running high, wide open, and handsome.

It seems impossible that it can be so little changed since I first rode into it in a squeaking wagon. There are the tracks, the same grimy smell of smoke always so redolent of the far off, romantic, and unreal. The squat black buildings of the trading companies, each with their wooden loading platforms. And there—by all that is holy and ironic!—stands in one of their high facades the same wooden Indian, an unbelievable Hiawatha with the paint peeling from his feathers. Isolate in its cinder patch bulks the Fred Harvey hotel, a traditional haven of clean white sheets, famous coffee, and stacks of golden brown pancakes fortified by eggs and strips of bacon. Alongside it runs Railroad Avenue, with its row of ghastly bars, greasy little lunch rooms, pool rooms, and tawdry stores. Upstairs are the four-bit flop-houses, the dollar throws, and the privately public bedrooms.

The stubby block-short side streets run uphill to another street which has succeeded only in being more dull. One sees boarding houses, rooming houses, and little hotels, whose dreary parlors are impregnated with the odor of cheap cigars and the talk of railroad men whiling away time between runs. And these dwindle away into the wooden shacks and squat adobe huts of the Spanish-

American half of the population, to the edges of town with its cheap dance halls.

No. It seems impossible that such an insubstantial bit of flotsam could have endured so persistently on this vast and naked earth with its heaving undulations of brown short-grass plains, the great bulks of the vivid red cliffs and the distant flat-topped buttes and mesas spreading out eternally under the strange, dark wings that hover about it—the spirit of endless time and illimitable space which is at once poignantly and forcefully evoked by no more than the haunting whistle of a train at night, the fresh smell of sage after rain, and the slight and almost imperceptible movement of the grass under the constant wind.

Yet Gallup endures. An ugly town. As tough as any that one might find. It seems to belong to no one and no one belongs to it. Neither the casual tourists, the alien Slavs and Italians, the week-end cowpokes, nor the passing railroaders. Groups of dark-faced Spanish-Americans, with black, sad eyes and thin, bitter mouths, stand idly on the corners waiting to take quick offense if they are called Mexicans. Everywhere wander Indians in cheap, faded, cotton blankets bought from Montgomery Ward. They slither aimlessly along the walks in fawn-pink moccasins with upturned toes and twinkling silver buttons. They squat along the walls, nursing babies, interminably picking lice. They reel drunkenly into the gutters with wild, red-rimmed eyes. The Whites step by them sprightly in white collars and shined shoes as if dreading to see fall upon them the inevitable hand of the law or the club of order. And in all their faces, the white, the brown, the red, there is evident the same quality of alien remoteness, the same fear and shame and horror that lies equally heavy on each.

Gallup, as the Capital of the Four Corners, expresses on every street corner the outer conflict of its two major races, the deep inner conflict inherent in its *mestizos*, and the psychological conflict first evident in the early Mountain Men and now in us all.

Upon it impartially, too, descends the weather. Gallup has more kinds of weather per hour and square foot than any place you can find. You can be stuck there by snow in May, by rain in October, by driving sand in March. The heat is scorching. The cold is freezing. And the wind keeps blowing through the cracks of all seasons.

Yet we all—all we Wops and Dagoes, Greasers, Gringos

and Indians—seem bound together here as nowhere else by some strange enchantment that dismisses all this misery, poverty, and shabby sinfulness as a transient chronicle of human error; a phantasmal spell that seems to substitute a hidden reality for an obvious illusion, and which again and again and again sets it down at the end of all trails and all roads as a gleaming image of all our unspent hopes.

7 Warp and Woof

THE FOUR CORNERS, following the consolidation of the rest of the country from coast to coast by the predominately Anglo United States, still remained chiefly Indian—the last Red island in a White sea.

Along the eastern boundary were the pueblos of the Rio Grande: Taos, Picurís, San Juan, Nambé, Santa Clara, San Ildefonso, Tesuque, Santo Domingo, San Felipe, Cochití, Santa Ana, Zia, Jemez and Isleta. Along the southern boundary were the pueblos of Laguna, Ácoma and Zuñi. In the center were the Hopi pueblos of Walpi, Sichomovi, Mishongnovi, Shipaulovi, Shumapovi, Oraibi, and Hotevilla. Southeast of the curving San Juan was the Jicarilla Apache reservation; north of it was the Ute reservation; and just south of it, near its junction with the Colorado, was the Paiute reservation. The rest was preponderantly Navaho land.

Titles to the communally owned Pueblo lands had been confirmed by the government. The limits to the Ute, Paiute, and Apache reservations seemed as frigidly fixed. But the Navaho reservation kept growing by constant additions. From the original 3,500,000 acres around Cañon de Chelly, granted in 1868, it finally embraced 15,000,000 acres extending almost from Chaco Canyon to the Grand Canyon, and from San Juan to the Rio Puerco—practically the entire 25,000 square-mile area that had been the traditional domain of the tribe.

The People were increasing rapidly from the 7,000 who had returned from Bosque Redondo to an eventual 60,000. From two sheep apiece they were increasing their flocks to the enormous maximum of 1,370,000 in 1931. There were traders on the reservation to buy their wool clip, hides, pelts, blankets, and silverwork; a trading and shipping center on the transcontinental railroad and highway running along the southern boundary. Over this route came a steady stream of Whites bringing new knowledge and customs, a new religion and economic ideology, the pattern of a whole new life.

It was a time of transition, a time of conflict between the

old and the new. What were the economic factors that were to be the warp and woof of their future? The psychological influences that were to weave Indians and Anglos together into one living people, enriched by each others' culture and heritage; or to separate them completely and irrevocably—one with an incurable neurosis of fear, secrecy, and deception, and the other with an ever-growing psychosis of fear and resentment against all races with colored skins?

The Navaho Blanket

I can never recall a time when there was not a Navaho blanket on the floor for us to sit on while popping corn in the fireplace. Another held down our bed covers at night, and served as a lap robe in the buggy by day. Firm, heavy, and durable, the Navaho blanket was a household necessity throughout the West; as inevitable as the hooked rag rug of old New England families. Beautifully colored, incomparably woven, it was a work of art as distinctive of its place and time as a Gobelin tapestry or a Persian rug. With a design so bold, spontaneous and infinitely varied that it was never repeated, and yet so simple, strong, and conventional that its origin could be identified at first glance, it is still a symbol of that wind-swept plateau, the solitary mesas glowing red on the horizon, the sound of a distant drum—of all that is essentially Indian.

In the Navaho blanket was woven the whole history of The People. On it met the two races.

To the Navahos, shepherds since the arrival of the first White men, the sheep was the primary physical means of their existence. Every bit of the animal was used. The choice ribs were roasted over the coals. The stomach was stuffed with a dressing of the blood and fat and a little flour, and boiled. Heart, lungs, and windpipe were cut up and fried. The intestines were washed and roasted on green sticks. Head and feet were singed, then cooked in hot ashes. And finally the bones were boiled for soup.

To the Anglos, whose whole social structure was based on the supreme sanctity of property rights, sheep was the principal property with which the Navahos proved their right to exist. It was the economic factor that determined the increasing size of the reservation and limited it through the opposition of private White grazing interests with political power; measured The People's wealth and poverty; fixed the limit of population and finally marked their degradation.

The Spanish Merino sheep brought by the first Spaniards into the Four Corners were of the finest strain in Europe. This was the stock later imported by the King of Saxony, in 1765, to make Saxony yarn the best in the world.

Little wonder that the Pueblo weavers adopted them immediately, substituting their fine silky fleece for the cotton they had grown for centuries. They did not adopt the Spanish horizontal loom, preferring to retain the vertical loom originated by their prehistoric ancestors. On this the traditional cotton *manta* or cape became a woolen *serape,* a shoulder blanket. The Hopis were the outstanding weavers, and it was the men who wove.

After the Spaniards were temporarily driven out by the Pueblo Revolt of 1680 the Navahos took up weaving. They adopted the Hopi loom; the modern Navaho loom is still thc prehistoric Pueblo loom. Replacing their buckskin clothing with wool serapes and leggings, they wove saddle blankets, saddle throws, and girths or cinches for their horses. The Pueblo woman's shoulder blanket developed into the Navaho man's shoulder blanket—the so-called Chief blanket which folded in from the four corners still repeated the original pattern of the open whole.

But among the Navahos, unlike the Hopis, it was the women who wove, who owned the sheep. Sitting out on the range with her flock, her loom lashed upright to a gnarled piñon or cedar post, the design emerging as spontaneously and effortlessly as the shapes of the clouds overhead—this is the immemorial Navaho weaver still seen from the highway today.

The Hopi men, in weaving as in everything else, stuck fast to their indomitable selfhood. They refused to capitulate; the embroidered dance kirtles and sashes still used in all the pueblos reflect this. To the writer, nothing is more beautiful than the old, soft, loose-woven Hopi blankets of pure white simply striped with blue and black. But they lack the hardy utility of Navaho weaving.

The Navaho women were bound by no such tradition; by the time the Spaniards returned they were doing better weaving than the Hopi. They were imaginative, versatile, and supremely adaptable. "Slave blankets" woven by Navaho captives of the *hacendados* were in great demand. As far south as Chihuahua, Mexican shepherds and herdsmen slept on the *serape Navaho.*

"Chief blankets" were found among all the distant tribes of the Great Plains, the mountain Utes and Paiutes, the Apaches, and the Havasupais, of the Grand Canyon. All were passionately fond of red, a native vegetable color difficult to obtain, and the Navahos soon found the means of accommodating them.

A bolt of brilliant red cloth that could be cut into squares and ribbons, suitable for tying into the shaggy manes of horses and the hair of their riders, to wrap the quills of their feathers and head-dresses, to flutter from spear shafts! Traders to savages the world over have found this their most appealing commodity. And here to the wild highlands of America as to the dark jungles of Africa they began to bring it.

Stout, close-woven flannel of deep rich red. Manufactured in England, exported to Spain, carried to Mexico, and brought north to the Four Corners about 1800. Bayeta, Castilian Spanish for English baize. This was the cloth obtained so eagerly by the Navahos from the first traders at the annual fairs of the Mountain Men at Taos, or stolen on their raids on the Spanish settlements. Never had they seen such texture, such a brilliant red. It was expensive and it was rare, and the weavers used it with utmost skill. Patiently they raveled the cloth and respun the threads to weave into their blankets.

With bayeta, the Navaho blanket changed from the simple pattern of horizontal stripes, old as the pattern of prehistoric basket weaving. The plain stripes began to zigzag, to form right angles, to build up into terraces like the serrated sandstone cliffs. From the background of neutral white, female blue, and male black, brilliant red stood forth like the jutting mesas. Solid blocks were broken. With rhythmic freedom the pattern emerged with the classical severity of old pottery designs.

The terraced style, the deft blending of coarse native wool and bayeta, the four rich colors—with these the Navaho blanket reached its zenith in what both Charles F. Lummis and Charles Avery Amsden called the bayeta *poncho serape*. It was made almost wholly of bayeta, this rich red background crossed with a pattern of blue and white. It was six feet long, four and a half feet wide, of so fine a texture that it would hold water. Such a blanket was obtained from a Navaho war chief about 1859 by the governor of the pueblo of Ácoma, who sold it thirty years later to Lummis to hang in the Southwest Museum, which he founded, and which, in 1934, was reproduced in color on cloth for Amsden's exhaustive book * as one of the finest specimens of Navaho weaving.

With Bosque Redondo the bayeta blanket vanished—all blankets, even the sheep which supplied the wool. The few sheep supplied The People upon their return were an American breed. They increased slowly; the wool was coarse; and the freedom and uplift of aesthetic expression had been broken to the will of the Anglo.

It was a strange coincidence that the impetus toward new growth came from the same source as had the first sheep of the Navahos three centuries before. From the same Spanish Merino wool the textile industry of Saxony was producing the finest yarn in Europe. It was soft, silky, and colored with pure vegetable dyes —a yarn ready for the loom without the tedious process of raveling and retwisting. And German traders were bringing it into the Four Corners over the Santa Fe Trail, selling it to the Hopis for their beautiful embroidery.

Saxony yarn restored the art of weaving to the Navahos and bridged the gap of Bosque Redondo. It was in a Saxony yarn *serape* that the famous Cheyenne, Chief White Antelope, was shot down with all his tribal encampment on Sand Creek, Colorado, in 1864, by Reverend J. M. Chivington and a party of Whites, including the most prosperous banker of my home town—"the foulest and most unjustifiable crime in the annals of America" as reported by General Miles and General Sherman. The blanket was six and a half feet long and four and a half feet wide; a light yellow background on which was an intricate design in red, dark red, pink, blue, green, orange, and black.† But it was only a gesture of farewell to the passing vegetal colors and the classical terrace pattern.

That same year the first American dye factory was built, and a protective tariff stopped the importation of Saxony yarn. By the time the Navahos were resettled at the Four Corners, aniline dyed Germantown yarn appeared, named for Germantown, Pennsylvania, where it was manufactured. With it came the first cheap aniline package dyes later known as Diamond Dyes. The post trader at Fort Defiance taught the Navaho women how to use them.

A pot of boiling water. A little envelope of powder. A stick to stir it with . . . How quick, cheap, and efficient, this Ameri-

* *Navaho Weaving*, Amsden. University of New Mexico Press, 1949.
† This blanket also is reproduced in full color in *ibid.*

can way! What did it matter if the colors were muddy or garish? Here, take along this ball of cotton twine too. It'll do for warp . . .

Thus, about 1880, began the period of Germantown yarn, cotton warp, and cheap aniline dyes. And with it a new pattern. The immemorial background stripes, straight or zigzag, reared erect and ran vertically instead of horizontally in this topsy-turvy world of change. On them were diamonds, half-diamonds, everywhere. With little American flags and square-wheeled railroad cars. Why not? Spanish sheep, Hopi loom, English baize, Saxony vegetal dyed yarn, American aniline dyes—what is an artist but the reflector of the changing life around him? Even so, Navaho blankets were still the best obtainable.

There was but one more step for the enterprising traders to take: to create a market for them back east. Cotton, of the Cotton and Hubbell trading post at Ganado, took it. With a mimeograph he "circularized the whole country" with such success that he soon moved to Gallup as a wholesaler. By a stroke of undeniable genius and shrewd salesmanship he had suggested that the best grade of blankets, because of their durability, be used as rugs. The lower grades, the "dougies," could still be sold to Apaches, Utes, and cowpokes as shoulder blankets and *serapes.*

Hence, about 1890, the Navaho shoulder blanket began to grow thicker and heavier. It became a rug.

The demand increased rapidly. With it came a revolt against gaudy dyes, synthetic designs, and poor workmanship. All the best traders banned purple, the use of cotton string for warp. Lorenzo Hubbell employed the artist, E. A. Burbank, to make color paintings of old Navaho blankets with which to encourage his weavers. Dick Simpson, up near Farmington, insisted on his weavers copying the old classical "Moqui" pattern of Navaho designs on the Hopi blue and black striped background. J. B. Moore, at Crystal, sent wool to eastern mills for carding and dyeing, and helped his best weavers to evolve the intricate Crystal rug.

Due largely to his influence, there developed the Two Grey Hills rug in whose excellence this writer was brought up to believe, and which still has the reputation of being the best modern Navaho weaving. Two Grey Hills was about fifty miles south of Shiprock and just across the Chusca mountains from Crystal. It was a comparatively well-watered range protected by forested mountains, a neighborhood conducive to the development of excellent sheep and a pride in weaving. Here Moore insisted on the elimination of all dyes, using only the natural black and white wool. Combining these, a background of soft grey resulted, giving the blanket its distinctive tone. All the nearby traders co-operated, including Sam Drolet and Bruce Barnard, of Shiprock.

Cosy McSparron, of the Chin Lee trading post at the mouth of Cañon de Chelly, revived native dyes. From his experiments with green and yellow from rabbit brush or chamisa, a brownish red from cedar bark, red-browns from juniper and yucca root bark, and bright scarlet from raw hackberries, he evolved the Chin Lee rug with its clear green-yellow; and he still guarantees a native dye above aniline.

In 1931 the traders established the United Indian Traders Association to set standards of material and workmanship on all Indian goods. It defined the blanket or rug: "Material used shall be virgin wool or virgin angora wool, the same shall be hand-washed, hand-carded and hand-dyed, the warp shall be all wool and hand-spun and the blanket shall be hand-woven by an Indian."

Out of all these efforts and discouragements the Navaho blanket emerged not only as a rug, but in a new style. Life no longer swept freely through the Four Corners. Nor did the patterns sweep freely in unbroken horizontal bands across the blanket. They did rear in bold terraced shapes like the mountain ranges, break up into jutting blocks and diamonds standing alone in empty space like isolate buttes and mesas. The reservation was enclosed. The People's lives were confined within strict limits. And so was the blanket. Everything within it was enclosed, top, bottom and both sides, by a border. The pattern was no longer rhythmic, dynamic and unconfined. It was a static, a framed picture. Even that monstrosity of late years, the pseudo-ceremonial blanket supposedly copied from Navaho sand-paintings, in which the figured Yei were portrayed. Imagine gods confined within a frame!

The Navahos knew better. The bordered blanket was as foreign to their nature and their belief as the White restrictions confining them on the reservations. But they had learned at last to wear the kachina mask of the American business man, the successful commercial weaver.

Yet always, if you search carefully, you will find a telltale colored thread leading out through the border—a hidden path of escape for the soul of the weaver, the life of the blanket . . .

Charles Avery Amsden, who has made the most exhaustive study of the technic and history of Navaho weaving sums it up thus:

> With the establishment of the Navaho reservation in 1868 the isolation of the tribe was broken and the American government undertook a deliberate (although not openly declared) campaign of economic dominance as an adjunct to the mailed fist so recently shown its new wards. Clothing was distributed yearly over a period of ten years, it will be remembered. Thus the loom was deprived of its prime function, thrown almost into disuse, as the Navaho learned to depend on the Yankee machine for their clothing. That was one of the shrewd points of Government policy. Another was the encouragement of established traders. They seized upon the outmoded loom quickly enough, taught it to weave rugs for the white man's taste and purse; and again the loom figured in the growing economic vassalage of the prostate tribe. It happened that cheap dyestuffs had just come into use: aniline dyes. These the trader assiduously planted in the heart of the new industry along with commercial yarns and cotton twine. Obviously, the traders' advantage lay in selling the materials of weaving rather than encourage the Navaho to provide their own.
>
> The demand for rugs grew steadily, fostered as it was by many shrewd and zealous minds. Grew too the Navaho demand for American goods, temptingly displayed on every trader's shelves. So the tribe was molded, quickly and easily enough, into that hybrid, pathetic object, the reservation Indian. Even so, the Navaho was lucky: the white man coveted his weavings, not his land. His sheep and his loom enabled him to play the new game of living the white man's way . . .

Thus the Navaho blanket. Its story in all essentials is the story of Navaho turquoise and silver work, of Zuñi mosaic work with silver and petrified wood, Hopi embroidery, Paiute and Apache basketwork, the pottery that gained the band of Apaches their local name of Olleros Apaches, of the beautiful yellow Hopi ware, the two-toned black and the lustrous red of Santa Clara, of the vividly colored Ácoma ware, of San Ildefonso, Santo Domingo . . . They were all native handicrafts that rose to the level of high arts—the only native American art, and gradually deteriorated under the press of the Yankee machine to little more than tourist gee-gaws. Each is a subject for serious study, each has its own tradition, its experts and connosieurs. They were all utilitarian. But their chief importance is that as art, which speaks a universal language, they gained friends for their makers among the inrushing Anglo Whites.

The Harvey House

One of the staunchest of these friends was that novel institution known as the Fred Harvey system, which had been granted the concession for lunch and dining rooms, news stands, curio shops, and hotels along the Santa Fe Railroad.

These Harvey Houses were an integral part of the railroad stations, and they were spaced meal times apart so that passengers could break their journey by meals or by overnight stops.

In contrast to the dreary Grand Rapids style of the period, each Harvey House was a proudly functional part of its regional background. The *Castañeda,* at Las Vegas; *El Ortiz,* at Lamy; the *Alvarado,* at Albuquerque; *El Navajo,* of Gallup; *La Posada,* of Winslow; *Fray Marcos,* at Williams; *El Tovar,* at Grand Canyon; the *Escalante,* the *Havasu*—these were the only true inns of the West and in the Western tradition.

With their long *portales* and intimate *patios,* their floors covered with Navaho blankets, their walls hung with Spanish *santos* and *retablos* or painted with mural reproductions of Navaho sandpaintings, their great fireplaces smoking with piñon . . . their newsstands full of the finest books, photographs, and monographs on the region, their curio cases of Navaho and Zuñi silver, Pueblo pottery, and Apache baskets . . . their tidy horseshoe-counter lunch rooms, fragrant with the best coffee in the West . . . their hotel rooms with their cool, clean beds—the Harvey House was not only a haven in the wilderness, but an institution that had no parallel in America. Perhaps more than any single organization, the Fred Harvey system introduced America to Americans.

Of the three persons largely responsible for the Harvey House, John Frederick Huckel, director of the company, supplied the initiative and authority. Beginning with an instinctive appreciation of Indian crafts, he established, in 1900, the Indian Building at Albuquerque. Here were put on display the finest pieces of Indian handicraft that could be obtained, pieces that eventually stocked museums. The Santa Fe Railroad was so impressed with the interest it evoked that it arranged for all its transcontinental trains to stop here thirty minutes. This created a tremendous stimulus in the use of Indian products. To meet it, Huckel upheld the highest standards.

As one of the largest buyers of Navaho blankets, he fought the use by others of cheap materials, bad dyes, and spurious designs. When an eastern company brought out an imitation Navaho rug, the Fred Harvey Company bought a large consignment. Samples were hung in every Harvey House with big placards telling what they were. "This yarn is not Indian spun!" The Harvey Company contracted for the entire output of Lorenzo Hubbell's best blankets, and fixed prices which soon became standard.

Meanwhile Huckel made the study of pottery, baskets, silverwork, and ethnology his personal hobby. With his wife, Minnie Harvey Huckel, daughter of the founder of the system, he spared no efforts in his study. The most competent geologists, archeologists, and ethnologists were employed to write, in simple terms, the history of the country.

At a time when Congress refused to authorize the marking and official supervision of all authentic Indian goods for their protection against imitation and unfair competition; when the Beacon Manufacturing Company was advertising its machine-made bed blankets as "Indian"; and the Federal Trade Commission was trying ineffectually to stop the Maisel Trading Post, Inc., of Albuquerque from selling silver jewelry made in a mechanized shop by Indians employed to sit in the street windows—only when we remember these do his courageous efforts loom in true perspective.

As a Fred Harvey boy myself, a station newsboy, I knew Huckel only from a respectable distance. Hours before his arrival I was duly put to polishing the company brass buttons which, slipped on over the buttons of my old coat after school, made me an official employee. I was then allowed the great pleasure of meeting Mr. and Mrs. Huckel, helping their chauffeur to unload their baggage, and running errands for them afterward.

As a future reward for this distinguished service and the favorable attention I was sure to attract some day, there was the post of manager of the Indian Department. Mr. Herman Schweizer filled it meanwhile. A former train "butcher," he had attracted the notice of Mr. Huckel. With a discerning eye, a resourceful nature, and a background of several trips to Europe, he was soon put to work carrying out Huckel's ideas.

The appearance and tone of the Harvey Houses themselves were chiefly due to an artist of rare talents, our friend Miss M. E. J. Colter, their decorator and designer. It was she who suggested the use of Navaho sand-painting reproductions as murals for the lobby of the new *El Navajo,* built in Gallup in 1922. She persuaded Sam Day to sell a series he had been collecting for twenty-five years; a singer, Miguelito, to paint them; and Sam Day to act as interpreter. Because of the Navaho reluctance to record sand-paintings in a permanent medium, even though they were unnoticeably altered because they were not for ceremonial use, Miss Colter was "brought to trial" by several Navaho singers. Nevertheless the hotel was dedicated on May 25, 1923, with a Navaho house-blessing ritual conducted by Little Singer, Little Stern Man and Miguelito. The sand-paintings began the Huckel Collection, complimenting those of the Bush Collection of Columbia University, and the accompanying legends were obtained from Miguelito.

Six years later Miss Mary Jane Colter instigated and built the Hopi tower at Grand Canyon. It was built by Hopi workmen using the same structural design found in prehistoric pueblos, and decorated by Hopi artists. Two days before it was opened the Hopis held a dedication ceremony. She was the only White invited.

Nothing in her work, large or small, has escaped her careful study. To create the present *La Posada*, of Winslow, authentically Spanish in structure and mood, she travelled throughout Mexico studying architecture of the Spanish Colonial period and selecting furnishings. For a simple design for the demitasse saucers used throughout the Harvey Houses she selected from an old piece of Mimbres Apache pottery the symbol of a rabbit standing on a new moon, and traced its origin through the Codex Borgia back to the fifth sign of the Aztec calendar. For years an incomprehensible woman in pants, she rode horseback through the Four Corners making sketches of prehistoric pueblo ruins, studying details of construction, the composition of adobes and washes. She could teach masons how to lay adobe bricks, plasterers how to mix washes, carpenters how to fit viga joints.

Her collections of old baskets, and Navaho and Zuñi silver, are the best I have ever seen. But it has always been life itself which has interested her most. And to it she has brought both an Irish mysticism and Irish wit, a tender heart and a caustic tongue. Indian medicine-men know her by one, her Anglo business associates by the other. If ever she can be induced to write her memoirs it will be as valuable Americana and as penetrative a study of Indian life as any we have obtained.

Such was the Harvey House, which has left its mark on the Four Corners. . . .

8 

There were the traders buying Indian merchandise, teaching The People to wear the masks of American business men.

There were Fred Harvey and other friends trying to keep on them their masks of artists, and trying ineffectually to convince the public that there did exist such a thing as a native American art and culture—culture being officially defined as "any given people's way of life."

But there were also the Church and the State, conversely trying to impress upon the Indians another religion and culture. The spear-point of this "American Way" was the government school.

The Government Schools

According to the terms of the Navaho treaty of 1868, whereby a school for every thirty children was to be provided, the first government boarding school was established in 1873 at Fort Defiance, described ten years later in an official report:

> It was managed as an industrial boarding school, though no system of teaching industrial occupations was in operation or could be under the conditions existing. This was owing to the usual failure of the United States to perform its agreements in connection with Indian work. The Government, by its failure, compelled the opening of the school in an unfinished building, without suitable appliances; even without a woodshed or a water-closet; with a roof in its kitchen and dining room that was about as good as a sieve as a protection; sans everything almost that was needed for success in a school of this kind.

In 1871, the Supreme Court had ruled that the Pueblos were not "wards of the United States" and hence not under government guardianship. Nevertheless Congress appropriated funds for other schools at Tuba City and Tohatchi, at Keam's Canyon, just east of the Hopi First Mesa and at the bottom of the mesa. They were no better.

Thus among the Pueblos, where schools were not legally permissible, children were forcibly taken from their parents by government troops to fill the schools. But among the Navahos, where ample provision of schools was required by treaty, few were thereafter provided.

With the failure of reservation boarding and day schools, non-reservation or "away" schools were established. The precedent was set by the Carlisle Indian School in 1879. Colonel R. H. Pratt, who had served in the Indian Wars of 1874–75, had taken a liking to the young prisoners placed in his charge. Lamenting that the few Plains Indians being schooled by the government were sent to Hampton Institute, Virginia, an institute for the education of Negroes, he suggested that a school be provided for Indians alone. Accordingly, he was allowed to use the abandoned army barracks at Carlisle, Pennsylvania, which had served previously as a cavalry depot. His success with 139 Kiowa, Sioux, Comanche, Cheyenne, and Arapahoe children proved his point. There were built Haskell Institute, at Lawrence, Kansas; Sherman Institute, at Riverside, California; and similar schools at Phoenix, Arizona, and Albuquerque and Santa Fe, New Mexico—all drawing Indian conscripts from all Indian reservations in the United States. The theory was to remove the children from their home reservations and educate them out of their Indian background by a militaristic routine. They were then expected to find work in White communities and forget they were Indians.

One of the outstanding pupils of this government schooling is the present Sun Chief of Oraibi, Don Talayesva. Persuaded by Leo W. Simmons, of the Department of Sociology, Yale University, to write a full account of his life for the Institute of Human Relations, he has given in *Sun Chief* not only the most intimate glimpse of a government school, but the frankest and fullest autobiography of a Hopi ever recorded.

He was born in 1890 of the Sand Clan and named Chuka, meaning a mixture of sand and clay. Fear of Whites and the

United States government was the compelling worry of all Hopi. Negro troops were always coming to take children by force to the government boarding school at Keam's Canyon or to the school at the foot of the mesa. Among these was Chuka's sister. Her hair was cut, her clothes burned, and she was named Nellie. Within a few weeks she escaped. A year later she was recaptured and taken back to school. The teachers had forgotten her old name, Nellie, and gave her a new one, Gladys.

Chuka's brother was kept hidden for several years. Then he too was captured, his hair cut, his clothes burned, and he was named Ira.

At the age of nine, Chuka entered school. To save his clothes, he wrapped himself in a Navaho blanket and went down the mesa barefoot. The blanket was confiscated, his hair was cut; he was dressed in shirt and overalls, and named Max. The first year he learned six terms in English: "bright boy," "smart boy," "yes," "no," "nail," and "candy."

The second year his parents took him back to school because they were too poor to feed and clothe him. The mother was rewarded with fifteen yards of dress cloth and the father with a hoe. Little Max was given a new name: Don. During the winter, several boys were caught visiting the girls' dormitory. Each was given from fifteen to thirty lashes with a rawhide, depending on his age. On Decoration Day all pupils were given American flags and flowers, and marched to the graves of two soldiers who had been killed fighting the Hopis. That year Don learned that a White person "thinks with his head instead of his heart."

During his seven years there he worked in the kitchen and cleaned out the stables of manure; in the summer he was taken with groups of boys to the sugar-beet "plantations" at Rocky Ford, Colorado. They worked twelve hours a day for fifteen cents an hour, of which ten dollars was paid them and the rest sent back to the Agency.

In 1907, he was sent with fifty picked children to the Indian School at Riverside, California. Here Don remained three years. In the winter he learned to eat tomatoes, name the states of the Union, sing Christian hymns and shout football yells. The Hopi language had no curse words in it. Don learned to swear habitually in English. When he refused to debate in the auditorium before six hundred students, the disciplinarian offered him the alternative of being thrashed. Don chose the thrashing and was given fifteen blows on his bare skin with a rawhide. In spring and summer the youths were sent to harvest canteloups in Imperial Valley. Don acquired a good knife, a suitcase, and a five-dollar watch. He was "half-Christian and half-heathen and wished that there was some magic that could change his skin into that of a White man."

Then something happened—what Don ever afterward considered the most significant event in his life. He caught pneumonia and lay for a month in the death ward of the hospital. Late one night he began to feel the cold, numbing rigor of death creeping up his legs . . . when suddenly he saw standing by his bed a tall kachina dressed in dancing kirtle and sash, and carrying a blue feather in his left hand.

"Now, my boy, you are to learn a lesson," said the kachina. "I am your Guardian Spirit, *dumalaitaka*. I have been guarding you all your life, but you have been careless. I will wait here and watch over your body; but I shall also protect you on your journey."

Don felt himself lifted like a feather and swept over the mountains by a gust of wind; "like flying." Well, here was a flat mesa! Here were the old water holes on the ledge at Oraibi! He walked into his home. His mother was combing his father's hair. They didn't see him . . . Don walked out—into what? The Department of Sociology of Yale University, the Institute of Human Relations do not know. It was beyond sociology, beyond rationalization, beyond the limits of human relationship. It was a realm of myth and legend, a time-space dimension in which everything that had existed and was to exist had being in a perpetual, unified, living now . . . There were the Two-Hearts, the Kwanitakas, Mount Beautiful, the House of the Dead, Grand Canyon, all the kachinas, all the places of legend. There were trials to endure, decisions to make . . . It was done.

"Now, my nephew, you have learned your lesson," the kachinas said. "You have a long time to live yet. Go back to the hospital and to your bed. You will see an ugly person lying there; but don't be afraid. Put your arms around his neck and warm yourself, and you'll soon come to life. But hurry, before the people put your body in a coffin and nail down the lid."

Don obeyed and soon he became warm. Nurses were about the bed, one of them holding his hand. "The pulse beats."

The head nurse said, "Sonny, you passed away last night, but did not cool off quite like a dead person, so we did not bury you. Now we will get the credit for saving your life."

Next day his Guardian Spirit appeared again.

"Some day, my boy, you will be an important man in the ceremonies. But if you don't obey me I shall punish you again, but for only four trials—then let you die. I shall hold you lightly, as between two fingers, and if you disobey me I will drop you. Good-bye and good luck."

He made one step and disappeared. Don saw a soft eagle feather rise up from the floor, float through the door and vanish.

All his life Don remembered his admonition. He returned to Oraibi and took up the frugal life of his people. He was initiated into the secret societies, learned the rituals and in time was made Sun Chief.

Today, as an old man, he says: "We might be better off if the Whites had never come to Oraibi, but that was impossible, for the world is full of them while in numbers we Hopi are as nothing. Now we have learned to get along with them, in a manner, and we would probably live much worse if they left us to ourselves . . . I do not care for fancy clothes and fine living . . . I want to be buried in the Hopi way . . . If (my boy) wishes to put me in a coffin, he may do even that, but he must leave the lid unlocked, place food nearby, and set up a grave ladder so that I can climb out. I shall hasten to my dear ones, but I will return with good rains and dance as a kachina in the plaza with my ancestors—even if Oraibi is in ruins."

Except for his one unusual experience his life was typical. It is that of a friend of mine long considered by the Whites in town as one of the most promising young men in the pueblo. Today, ten years later, he is difficult to recognize. He will have nothing to do with Whites. He is a council officer and in time will likely be named ceremonial head of the pueblo.

That he went back as Don Talayesva, as they all went "back to the blanket," is ample proof that nothing the White school gave them was more than a thin patina. Once captured and sent to "away school," the Pueblo children suffered everything possible that could be done to erase all vestiges of their race and culture. Their hair was cut—and to the Pueblos this was a cultural castration. They were forbidden to speak their own language, to wear their own clothes, to keep their traditional customs, even their own names. Dismissed from school, they were untrained for anything but manual or menial labor. Developing a sense of inferiority under the racial discrimination of White employers, they hung around the edges of town, unkempt, drunk, and unwanted in company with that other racial minority, the *mestizo* Spanish-Americans. When finally they did straggle back to the pueblos they did not know how to adapt themselves. Little wonder then that the Pueblos fought conscription as something that would utterly destroy the core of their faith—another wave trying to submerge the Rock.

The Mission Schools

Meanwhile it was as incumbent upon the government to break the still resistant will of the roving Navahos, as it was to break up the traditional self-enclosure of the Pueblos within their independent city-states. Both government reservation schools and "away schools" being failures, various denominational Christian churches and missionary societies were encouraged to establish schools on the reservation. The Indian Bureau agreed to the proselytizing of Navaho children and later subsidized the schools with Indian funds held in government trust. And the churches, grasping at the opportunity to bring salvation to the souls of heathen savages, agreed to give them primary schooling.

For a generation then, the result was the same. Cruelty and stupidity in government schools, kindness and incompetency in civil and ecclesiastical schools, combining to widen still more the gulf between the Red and the White.

The first of the mission schools, the one with which I was most familiar and whose background is an integral part of my own childhood, was the Navaho Methodist Mission School along the bend of the San Juan.

When our family's two old maid aunts, previously fictionized as the Vrain girls, went there in the early 1890's the region had all the elements of a movie frontier epic. Farmington, at the convergence of the San Juan, La Plata, and Las Animas rivers, was its center. Ten miles west was the little Mormon village of Fruitland. Twelve miles east was Bloomfield, home of the cattle rustling Stockton Gang. To the north was the Ute reservation, to the east the Jicarilla Apache reservation, and to the south and west the Navaho reservation. There was nothing at Shiprock but Hubbard's Trading Post. Gallup was four days travel by wagon away. Durango, sixty-five miles north in the Colorado Rockies, was the closest railroad junction.

Farmington's main street was two blocks long. It was filled with swaggering cattle rustlers, unruly cowboys, Indian traders, Utes, Apaches, and Navahos. Here from Hon-Not-Klee, the trading post at Shallow Water on the Gallegos which the Vrain girls made their headquarters, they came on rare occasions to catch the stage and to bring to a boy those vivid reels of their incredible life and that of the women with whom they were associated.

The first of these was Mrs. Mary E. Eldridge, the first missionary in the region. A member of the Woman's Home Missionary Society of the Methodist Episcopal Church, she founded the first mission near Hogback, about twenty miles west of Farmington. Her work consisted mainly of administering to the sick out of meager funds contributed by the church and the government. The second was Miss Mary Tripp, who started the first school about 1893, assisted later by Miss Edith Dabb. In September, 1899, Miss Frances E. Rykert came from upper New York to help them as a teacher. I remember her vivid description of her frightening journey by train from Albany, by stage from Durango, and by wagon to Hogback.

A half-dozen women limited in funds, knowledge, and experience, with little support and supervision, trying to convert, teach, and heal the Navaho nation! In the movie they would have succeeded. In life their attempts were at once ludicrous and heroic.

Mrs. Eldridge homesteaded the land and offered to deed it to the Home Missionary Society of her church. When it was refused, she deeded it to the Presbyterian Church, which took over the site. She then located three miles west of Farmington, across the San Juan River, establishing a new post from which one of the Vrain girls worked as a field matron.

The Methodists moved up the river and re-established the Navaho Methodist Mission School on bottom land about four miles west of Farmington, on the west side of the San Juan, near the La Plata suspension bridge. Here Miss Mary Tripp established a small place under the auspices of the Indian Rights Association, of Boston, which she had interested. Here too Miss Rykert worked as a teacher; assisting her was the other Vrain girl.

The work was progressing, but as in a movie plot it was

also developing complications. If it were not rivalry between the Methodists, Presbyterians, and the Indian Rights Association, it was the admonitions of the government Indian agent conflicting with the advice of experienced Indian traders, the demands of cattlemen and townspeople. Medical supplies were short as was money to buy them. Only the women held together, riding to remote hogans by horseback, teaching the "Jesus Way" and how to sew and read.

How wonderful the children were! There was Enogah, the spunky little girl named Kigpah, "on the warpath," and Yabatya meaning "brave" because he always "dared to do right." One of the most inspiring children Miss Rykert ever taught was a boy of five. He could read and embroider as well as a woman. Of him she wrote, "He left us when he was only nine. I think of him now in the place that our dear Savior went to prepare." Unfortunately there was no medicine to cure him when he became fatally ill. His father carried him away and held for him a last sing. One of the Vrain girls followed on horseback and looked after his burial.

It was discouraging work. Miss Tripp died in 1909; and after serving five years as a teacher and three years as superintendent, Miss Rykert returned east seriously ill.

The new superintendent of the Navaho Methodist Mission was Mr. Simmons, with his wife, new to the country. With him were Miss Brown, a teacher; Frankie Damon, a blind half-breed interpreter; an old Mr. Western, who boarded there; and a Mr. Tice, from Illinois. The buildings consisted of a six-room adobe used as their living quarters, a two-story adobe, whose downstairs was used as a schoolroom and whose upstairs served as a dormitory for the twenty-seven Navaho schoolchildren, a laundry building, and corrals and sheds for stock and chickens.

Here it was then, as I remember it . . . No! It is too hopelessly tragic to be recalled in actuality. It had best be characters and setting of a movie after all. The plot reaches its climax in September, 1911. It is raining.

A thin drizzle obscuring the sage with a wet, grey mist. Recurrent showers. A steady downpour. Then cloudburst after cloudburst in the mountains. The San Juan, Las Animas, and La Plata rise ominously. By Thursday, October 5th, the rivers are overflowing their banks.

Townspeople, ranchers, and traders are in an uproar. Messages from Colorado warn of an oncoming flood; the Rockwood

Dam, above Durango, is weakening. All people in the lowlands are notified to move to safety. Particular anxiety is felt for the Mission School, as it is located on the bottom lands of the San Juan, roaring with the flood waters of both the La Plata and Las Animas. Mr. Simmons is notified.

It is noon. He is praying at the head of the dinner table. Around it patiently standing are Hortense, Alice, Geraldine, Percy, Abigail, John, Ira—twenty-seven Navaho children neatly named, learning the Jesus Way.

"We will not move," he answers. "God will protect us."

Mr. Western is seventy-five years old. "The river has never risen this high in all the years I've lived in this part of the country. Take my word for it!"

Mr. Tice grins. "I am an expert swimmer."

Lessons resume. But late that afternoon Frankie, the blind interpreter, steals out to measure the water. It is waist deep before he reaches the approach to the bridge. He comes back to propose they all move to a vacant homesteader's house on higher ground nearby.

"No!" shouts Mr. Simmons. "God will protect His children from the flood!"

This raises an ecclesiastical argument in the blind half-breed's mind. According to the Whites there is God and there is the rain, the flood, the mud, and all inanimate nature. But, according to the Navahos, there is God in the heavens, God in the rain, the flood, the mud, God in his children, The People, and all these Gods together are one God, the God of all the living universe. What does it matter which manifestation of God is pre-eminent for the moment? It is most confusing. Still he is inclined to believe that for the present it would be expedient for God-in-the-children to remove to higher ground from God-in-the-flood lest they coincide, with some inconvenience to all concerned.

So while the children are ordered off to bed and the White staff obdurately retire, he remains at the telephone. More calls come. Angry calls from the Indian Agent, Mr. Shelton, demanding that something be done by somebody for the wards of the government. Imploring calls from neighbors. Mr. Simmons refuses to answer. Abruptly the line goes out.

It is still raining. Blind Frankie cannot hear it for the roar of the flood.

He gropes toward the dormitory, rouses Hortense, Percy, Abigail, Geraldine—all the twenty-seven Navaho children. They lead him out to the corral and help him harness the horses. Inside the house the two frightened women, Mrs. Simmons and Miss Brown, hear them. They beg to go too. It is still raining.

The blind man loads them all into the wagon and takes the reins. The water has risen. It covers the hubs, is belly deep on the horses. They cannot get to the abandoned homestead. But they do make it upriver two miles to Mrs. Eldridge's place.

At 2 A.M. the first rise takes out the suspension bridge. At 4 A.M. the second rise strikes the Mission.

The sight at daybreak is appalling. The river looks like a monstrous brown snake writhing back and forth, uprooting huge cottonwood trees, gouging holes in the ground. The Mission buildings are all gone except the floor of the laundry, held down by heavy machinery. On it stands Mr. Tice and the Mission dog. Nothing can be done to save him. They watch him desperately all morning.

Indians come. They are carrying a bedraggled and unconscious old man. It is Mr. Western. He had jumped from the window, crawled through the water to a mud bank. Mrs. Eldridge manages to restore him to life, but he has lost his mind.

Suddenly Mrs. Simmons screams. Through a neighbor's field glasses she sees her husband perched in a tree top emerging from the river. When the walls had collapsed he had been washed away, clinging to the stairway. Luckily he had grabbed on to the tree. Here he clings several days until rescued, more dead than alive.

Near noon the laundry floor rises and tips Mr. Tice and the dog into the river. The dog is washed toward shore and rescued by some cowboys with lariats. Mr. Tice disappears instantly. Two days later his body is found twelve miles downriver encircled by buzzards flying overhead.

And now the finale. Hundreds of Navahos lashing their horses up the muddy road toward Mrs. Eldridge's place. Is it an Indian raid? No! They are the parents and relatives of the twenty-seven children who had seen the Mission destroyed and had believed their children drowned. Close-up of the hero: Frankie Damon, the blind interpreter, who had saved their lives . . .

Next year the Mission was rebuilt on a new site upriver, just a mile west of Farmington, and Miss Rykert was induced to return and help it get started. But the Vrain girls had gone. Something mysterious had happened to one of them. She had been converted by the Navahos. Becoming "queer," adopting their beliefs and customs, she vanished into the far reaches of the San Juan and has never been heard of since . . . Strangely enough, one of the children she had taught loved her and took her name. Today he is a singer or medicine man; and with his wife, Tah Dez Bah, he is living in a hogan near Fort Defiance.

Ganado Mission

A few years later the Presbyterians, like the Methodists, abandoned the site at Hogback and sent the equipment to another small mission established at Ganado, Arizona, in 1901. The site was fifty-six miles northwest of Gallup, near the location of the prehistoric Pueblo Colorado, and just one mile from Lorenzo Hubbell's Trading Post, the first post established on the reservation. For a quarter of a century it persisted as no more than another insignificant and ramshackle outpost in the wilderness.

Today, owned and operated by the Board of National Missions of the Presbyterian Church, Ganado Mission is the largest Indian mission in the United States. Nothing describes it so aptly as an exclamation made by a recent tourist-lady to its director, "Why Doctor, it's an A-osis in the Desert!"

An oasis it is. Two hundred acres of green lawn threaded by flagstone walks and gravelled driveways, shaded by rows of elms and cottonwoods, and supporting seventy buildings. It is as tidy as a college campus, modern as 1950, self-contained as a small city.

The million-and-a-half-dollar plant includes a power plant, ice plant, deep freeze unit, steam laundry, carpenter shop, swimming pool, commissary, and a farm with pigs, chickens, and a registered Holstein dairy herd to supply food for the four hundred people who are fed three meals a day. Several miles away the Mission owns and operates its own coal mine. The Salsbury Memorial High School is the only Indian high school to be state accredited. In the "Cathedral of the Purple Sage" sermons are delivered in English, then translated into Navaho and transmitted by loudspeaker into the wards of the Sage Memorial Hospital. With its 150 beds, its iron lung, X-ray, Wassermann baths, operating room, and laboratory, the hospital is the backbone of the Mission. In connection with it is conducted the only nurses' training school for Indians in the United States; over one hundred girls, representing fifty tribes, have been graduated.

The whole place is a memorial to its superintendent and medical director, Dr. Clarence G. Salsbury.* A missionary doctor in China for thirteen years, he came home in 1927 to accept a temporary assignment among the Navahos. When he arrived at Ganado he found a ramshackle infirmary of twelve beds trying to serve a people much worse off than the Chinese. Putting up tents to hold typhoid, diphtheria, and tuberculosis patients, he talked the Presbyterian Board into building him a two-story, stone hospital. Then he struck out into the reservation to find patients.

Today his fame as the Sagebrush Surgeon has spread throughout the world. He has been elected to fellowship in the American College of Surgeons, the American College of Hospital Administrators, the International College of Surgeons of Geneva, Switzerland, and named President of the Arizona Hospital Association. To watch the Big White Doctor—235 pounds big—do a Caesarian in twenty minutes was a pleasure this writer declined with thanks; but watching him clean a mess of catfish for two Navaho nurses was just as revealing of character—both his and theirs, for traditionally Navahos do not eat fish. There is nothing slow or awkward about his driving either. He hits the rutted dirt roads at an eighty-mile-an-hour clip that leaves no doubt he knows every stone, wash, and curve. He is a kindly man, a real character, and his mission is the most famous in the United States.

Today it is expanding its activities beyond its sphere of influence around the mission proper. One Saturday we went with the Doctor, two nurses and interpreter to a field clinic held thirty-five miles north, at Tselani. Here, to a little stone building near Art Lee's trading post, rode Navahos, from their remote hogans on the distant Black Mesa. Of the fifty patiently squatting on the floor only two spoke English. But one by one they got up, baring their arms for the needle. At Cornfields, Nazlini, and Greasewood similar scenes took place weekly—field clinics with inoculations and emergency treatments carrying the Big White Doctor's powerful medicine to The People.

On Sunday we went with Reverend Douthitt, the mission minister, and his interpreter on still another field trip. His field

* Retired July 1, 1950.

is every hogan within the two thousand square miles around the mission. His job is to convert The People to Christianity. In one hogan after another he stood before the family, the friends or neighbors who had been induced to attend. The Belicana Short Coat so incongruous in his black suit, white shirt, and black bow tie. Praying, telling a Biblical story, singing *Jesus Loves Me* or another gospel hymn translated into Navaho:

Jesus a-yo-a-so 'nih,
Bi nal-tsos yeh sil hal-ne,
Al-cin-i-gi a-nis-t'eh
Do si-dzil dah, Ei bidzil.

After months of hearing about the "Jesus Way" a Navaho "makes his decision for Christ and the Church." Then he is brought into the Mission compound for baptism in the church. The children are enrolled in the Mission school, are taught to forget the old ways and to make a complete transition to the new.

Yet it seems a pity that there is nothing to relate Ganado Mission to the immemorial traditions of the land and the people around it.

The buildings all seem stone transplantings from New England, and are named with neat placards like "Shangri La." The tidy green lawns are covered by signs carrying Gospel quotations. The "Cathedral of the Purple Sage" is a frigid, dressed-stone church. Few of the staff speak Navaho, and most are dependent upon interpreters. Native dress, customs, decorations, and language are discouraged. Navaho ceremonialism is held an abomination. Nobody is permitted to attend the neighboring sings. They are regarded as "pagan rites," and the people who attend them as "shaman ridden." The title page of the *Gospel Hymns* handbook definitely states that the hymns are to be sung "in competition with the heathen chants of the medicine-men." And on the classroom wall of the nurses' training school hangs a large pictorial chart divided into two vertical columns of opposing symbols: a squalid hogan versus a tidy hospital room, a native Singer versus a Doctor in starched white. For all of this the guiding motto is emblazoned on a huge sign erected in front of the Mission: "Tradition is the enemy of progress."

It is a fight to the finish to eradicate completely the Navaho culture.

St. Michaels Mission

The Catholic St. Michaels Mission, manned by the Franciscan Fathers and located at Cienega, between Ganado and Gallup, operates just as efficiently, without a hospital, but with reluctance to directly oppose tribal ceremonial life, and with the tremendous knowledge of Navaho psychology made possible by Father Berard Haile.

It maintains a large boarding school for over three hundred Navaho children, and supports ten buildings, including a chapel, dormitories, gymnasium, a light and water plant, a barn and shops in which farming and practical trades are taught. Father Berard Haile opened the school in 1901. His admitted purpose was to teach Christianity to the Navahos. But seeing the barrier of language which alienated them, and the more difficult task of teaching a religion to a people who have no word for religion in their own language, he set about learning their language and the meaning of their ceremonials.

Ednishodi Yazzie, "Father Shorty," first learned Navaho fluently. Then he set about transcribing it on paper with characters to fit the sounds. The result was a standard written Navaho language utilizing English and Greek characters, glottal stops, barred l's and other symbols. To reproduce these he set up a monotype of his own with a special keyboard, and began printing his own books. Meanwhile he began compiling a complete encyclopedia of information on Navaho thought and customs, and this led to an exhaustive study of the great Navaho sings or "Ways."

His text books now include: *Learning Navaho,* a *Navaho-English and English-Navaho Vocabulary* and *An Ethnologic Dictionary*—in which he devotes thirty-four pages of description to the name "Navaho" and why this is the spelling preferable to "Navajo." His religious translations are *A Catechism Of Christian Doctrine in Navaho, The Holy Gospel For Sundays, Holy Days,* and *The Catechism and Guide.* And for posterity he has recorded *The Origin of the Navaho Enemy Way,* for the Yale University Press; *The Flint Way,* for the University of Chicago Press; the *Navaho Fire Dance,* and the *Navaho War Dance.*

Little wonder that The People have nicknamed him "The Little Priest Who Knows." Father Shorty, grey-haired, felt-slippered under his long brown robe, has done more than any man to codify their language, and probably knows as much about them as any White man living.

Thus religious instruction was given to the children in their native tongue. Father Anselm Weber, a great missionary and linguist, rode horseback to Klagetoh, Cornfields, Tohatchi, and Lukachukai gathering pupils. With this close personal contact he also fought for Navaho rights against White aggression, and through his influence at Washington was able to obtain more grazing land for Navaho sheep, The People's chief source of livelihood.

At St. Michaels, no tuition is required. Classes are held up to the ninth grade, half the day being spent in the classroom, and the other half in learning practical arts. All students are encouraged to become Girl Scouts or Boy Scouts. Upon graduation, they are given opportunity to attend St. Catherine's Indian High School, at Santa Fe.

There are several other small missions on the reservation: the Rehoboth Mission, of the Holland Christian Reformed Church, east of Gallup; the Seventh Day Adventist Navaho Mission, near Holbrook; the Good Shepherd Mission, at Fort Defiance, and St. Christopher's Mission, at Bluff, Utah, both sponsored by the Protestant Episcopal Church; and the Catholic Tegakwitha Mission, at Houck, dedicated to Catherine Tegakwitha, the Lily of the Mohawks, first North American Indian to become a Catholic, in 1655.

There is also that strange, familiar, and beloved travelling mission known as Shine Smith.

Shine Smith

Years ago, they say, during the long hunger when The People were dying from an evil sickness, a tall, broad-shouldered Belicana fought his solitary way through wind and snow to their remote hogans. To one he brought good medicine. To another a bit of food. And to all he brought "hope and life like the sun shining upon the earth." So they called him Sunshine Smith.

That was in the winter of 1921, during the influenza epidemic. During the long hunger in the terrible winter of 1948, when The People were dying of malnutrition and cold, Shine Smith appeared again. He was giving a Christmas Party at Shanto to his old friends way up in the remote confines of their desolate wilderness. Nearly a thousand came. Each received a filling mutton stew, an outfit of warm clothes and another generous helping of the sunshine he had been dispensing continuously for thirty years.

One could call him an unfrocked, free-lance missionary. Or a jovial foot-loose Robin Hood continually on the prowl through 25,000 square miles of sand and sagebrush to help The People wherever he found them. But Shine Smith fits into no neat category. He is a character for an unbelievable novel, the hero of a thousand tall tales, a constant reproach to the organized, and a whispered scandal among the orthodox religious. He is a myth, a legend. You don't believe him. But there he is. Six feet tall, sixty-six years old, wide shouldered, white headed.

He was born in Rome, Georgia, and christened Hugh Dickson Smith. His father was Edward Reed Smith, an aide to General Nathan B. Forrest, of the Confederate Army. His mother was the former Susan Claudia Cothran, daughter of Wade Cothran, judge of the Supreme Court of South Carolina. His uncle was Charles Henry Smith, the famous humorist "Bill Arp" of the Atlanta *Constitution.*

After attending the Presbyterian University, at Clarksville, Tennessee, and then the Theological Seminary at Austin, Texas, young Smith was ordained a minister in the Presbyterian Church of Coleman, Texas, in 1911. For six years he preached to the cowhands of West Texas, receiving his first nickname of the "Cowboy Preacher."

Receiving a call to go to the Four Corners as a missionary to the Navaho in 1917, he was first stationed at Ganado, then successively assigned to Chin Lee, Kayenta, and Tuba City. During these four years Zane Grey gave him another knickname, "Parson Smith."

Apparently he did not behave himself in a manner becoming an orthodox parson. Brothers of the cloth accused him of misconduct. He was charged with departing from his station and making a trip to Navaho Mountain without proper authorization; of dancing with the Hopi at Moencopi; of assisting at pagan Navaho wedding ceremonies. Rumor sums up the scandal: he was unfrocked by the church.

Actually he resigned out of a growing necessity. He had observed that the Protestant missionaries seldom got out into the field. When they did, they were dependent upon interpreters and thus lost face as well as personal contact. Lorenzo Hubbell was right.

He must live with The People to learn their needs and language.

Shine did. And out among them he has remained ever since. Travelling in an old truck, always running out of gas. Jolting along with the Navahos in their creaking wagons. Thumbing a ride with a tourist. Unsupported by any church, he obtains contributions wherever and however he can get them—an article in a newspaper, a speech before a chamber of commerce, a gift from a generous friend. He preaches no specified creed. His message is simply help. Food and medicine, a bed in some hospital. Simple sanitation and child welfare. He can set a bone, deliver a child, will dig a grave. Fluently speaking Navaho, Hopi, and Paiute, he participates in their ceremonials. During 1941, a delegation of Navahos asked him to be their spokesman against the sheep reduction plan. As they were in bad standing with the authorities at Window Rock, Shine manouvered them off the reservation and took them to Washington. Refused official hearing, he got them to Mrs. Roosevelt and through her they were successful in obtaining $200,000 for farm lands.

Today he still remains an enigma. To him cling mistrust, suspicion, and scandal, and respect, awe, and legend. To both, Shine is impervious. He is like a man who knows that the factual brotherhood of man is at once the simplest tenet of mankind and the most complex problem of modern civilization.

9 Tide from the West

THE WHITE TIDE from the East had swept across the land and reached the blue Pacific. It could go no farther. But there still remained islands of Red occupancy remaining to be possessed.

One of these was the seven-million-acre Sioux reservation in the Black Hills of Dakota. To this land the Sioux Nation had been granted "absolute and undisturbed" possession by a solemn United States treaty, ratified by the Senate in 1868. But when, in 1874, gold was found in the region, General Custer was sent with United States troops to protect the prospectors. After the massacre of the troops the full force of the Army was summoned to eject the tribe and throw the reservation open to Whites. The United States Court of Claims subsequently upheld the legality of the procedure.

Another island was the so-called Indian Territory, set aside as an "everlasting home" for several other tribes. The Choctaws, one of these "five civilized tribes," had named the land "Oklahoma," meaning "Red People" or simply "The People." The Cherokees, to whom it was the end of their "Trail of Tears," had made such progress in their new home that when Senator Henry L. Dawes, of Massachusetts, paid them a visit, he reported as follows:

> The head chief told us that there was not a family in that whole nation that had not a home of its own. There was not a pauper in that nation, and the nation did not owe a dollar . . . Yet the defect of the system was apparent. They have got as far as they can go, because they own their land in common . . . *There is no selfishness, which is at the bottom of civilization.* Till this people will consent to give up their lands, and divide them among their citizens so that each can own the land he cultivates, they will not make much more progress.

Hence, in 1887, the "Dawes Act" or "General Allotment Act" was passed. Briefly, it provided that instead of communal, tribal ownership, every Indian was to be allotted a piece of reservation under a fee simple title. The unallotted residium or "surplus" was to be bought by the government for $1.25 an acre and thrown open for White settlement.

The rush began. White settlers, land sharks, lawyers, and politicians began grabbing up Indian lands for a quart of whiskey and a black cigar. From 138,000,000 acres, Indian-owned land dwindled to 52,000,000 acres by 1933.

The advantage of this was soon apparent. Oil had been discovered in Oklahoma. To two thousand Osages, to whom the richest deposits belonged, the government paid out in cash $265,-000,000 in oil royalties. Of this it was estimated that 90 per cent was lost to corrupting Whites—a mess of pottage for which the Osages had been forced to trade their birthright.

Such was the pattern for further despoliation when evidences of oil were struck on the Navaho reservation during President Warren G. Harding's administration. His Secretary of the Interior, Albert B. Fall, immediately introduced two bills. The Indian Omnibus Bill, passed by the House, proposed to appraise and pay each Indian the value of his share of all tribal assets in order that the land could be sold to individual Whites for development. The Fall-Bursum Bill, passed by the Senate, sought to transfer the title of Pueblo land to the Anglo- and Spanish-American squatters encroaching on the land.

Fortunately the movement struck a snag when the ever-indomitable Pueblos heard of the bills. A Council of all the New Mexico Pueblos was held at Santo Domingo pueblo on November 22, 1922. All night long the Fall-Bursum Bill was read and interpreted in the Tanoan, Tewan, Keresian, and Zuñian languages. Aided by a host of sympathetic Whites, the Federation of Women's

Clubs, and the American Indian Defense Association, a delegation was sent East to appeal the case. As a result of the publicity the Senate recalled the Fall-Bursum Bill, and in 1923, the Indian Omnibus Bill was killed. Fall, previously involved in the Doheny, Sinclair, and Teapot Dome oil scandals was later indicted and imprisoned.

The Pueblos and Navahos of the Four Corners were the primary survivors of the pitiful remnant of 204,000 Indians still remaining in the United States. They still retained their land and their religion—the immemorial Rock to which they had clung for four centuries.

America's Century of Dishonor was over. The savage flood tide of Anglo conquest and extermination had run its course. Now came the inevitable reaction, an ebb tide of sentimentalism and impractical idealism which undermined the Rock itself.

Another Proclamation of Emancipation

In 1933, Franklin D. Roosevelt took office to become one of the great presidents of the United States. Under him the whole country was awakened to a new sense of social responsibility. In all governmental departments efforts were made to restrain the ruthless flaunting of property rights above human rights that had grown out of the political philosophy of the country's Puritan founders. To carry this New Deal to the Indians, John Collier was appointed the new U. S. Commissioner of Indian Affairs. He—

But it all goes back to Mabel Dodge Luhan. Poor Mabel! To her hospitable doorstep has been laid every crime, conspiracy, and peccadillo occurring in the Four Corners for the last thirty years. Poor Mabel, nothing! She has loved it.

To begin with, she married an Indian, an Indian in the pueblo of Taos, an Indian who wore a blanket and his long black hair in pigtails. And to add insult to injury, she persistently proclaimed that there was something spiritually sound and wonderful about Indian life not to be found in the materialistic mental life of the White. For this unprecedented audacity the public never forgave her. It was too much! She became fair game to be shot at by all gossips, feature newspaper copy at all times, a permanent butt of ridicule for all occasions—and for twenty years the most controversial and influential personality in the Four Corners.

Poor Tony! He came in for a devil of a time too. For

marrying a White woman his people forbade him taking part in ceremonial work, stripped him of his Indian clothes, and practically pushed him out of the pueblo. But Tony pushed right back—with shoulders broad as a house, and a loyalty that could not be denied.

On the edge of Tony's pueblo land they built, about 1920, the Big House that immediately became a mecca for famous visitors. To it came painters like John Marin, sculptors like Maurice Sterne, poets like Robinson Jeffers, writers like D. H. Lawrence and Willa Cather, and musicians like Leopold Stokowski, to make the little town of Taos the art center of the West. With the artists came the Freudian psychologist, Dr. A. A. Brill, the ethnologist, Elsie Clews Parsons, government agents, state politicians, Harold L. Ickes, soon to become Secretary of the Interior—a continuous parade of notables and hopefuls.

One of these hundreds of visiting guests was a discouraged young man of thirty-five, in search of a permanent career, named John Collier. He had done social and public recreation work in New York, had been Director of Community Organization in California, and was now on his way to camp out for a year somewhere in Mexico, far from the press of human relations. Receiving Mabel's urge to detour, he came to Taos.

Here he stayed for a year or more, visiting Indian pueblos with Tony and meeting influential friends of Mabel. It was 1922 and the infamous Bursum Bill was being discussed. Tony took him with some other Whites to the All-Pueblo Council called at Santo Domingo. That meeting and his year at Taos convinced Collier of the ethnic value of Indian life to the world at large, and it offered to him the career he had been seeking.

He immediately set out to become the executive secretary of the Indian Defense Association, and then, returning to California, began an involved political struggle to secure White support and Indian signatures to a petition asking for his appointment as United States Indian Commissioner.

Eleven years after reaching Taos he was sworn into office under a new Secretary of the Interior, Harold L. Ickes.

Such was the background and contradictory character of the new Indian Commissioner: a little bent man with large deep-sunk eyes and a small thin-lipped mouth; an inherent sympathy for the underdog in general and a developed appreciation of the Indian in particular; a sincere and lofty idealism and an unrestrained personal ambition; a messiah complex and a trained knack for politics.

His first move was to draw up the Indian Reorganization Act. As its name implied, the bill sought to reorganize completely the administration of Indian affairs. All the lofty idealism conceivable was embodied in its principles. The Indian societies were to be regenerated. Their ancient ways were to be recognized and protected. They were conversely to be given every opportunity to "acculturate" to the "higher rather than the lower levels of white life." The land allotment system was to be abolished. The tribes were to be organized like federal corporations, and their tribal funds administered by the Indian Bureau for their benefit. Adequate schooling was to be provided, not only for children, but technological and business education for adults. Cultural, religious, and economic liberty was to be guaranteed—all the four freedoms. The Indian Reorganization Act, in short, was another proclamation of emancipation for Indians.

But it also contained a requirement, before it could be enacted into law, that every tribe should accept it by a secret-ballot vote.

Hence, to the Navahos and all the Pueblos, the bill was offered for discussion and referendum. The Pueblos voted for it. The Navahos rejected it. And, in 1934, it was duly enacted by Congress as law.

There began now the political administration of an idealistic concept by government bureaucracy.

The Lotus Eaters

When the Spaniards conquered Mexico they found some of the Indians eating the root of a cactus, which produced strange visions.

Gradually, through the centuries, the use of this root spread slowly northward through the Huicholes, Tarahumares, and Coras. Sometime about 1880 the Kiowas adopted it, and gave it to the Cheyennes and Arapahoes.

In 1909, a group of twelve Taos Indians visiting them in Oklahoma, then eighteen days by horseback away, were invited to a ritual in which this "pā-ō-té" was eaten. They returned with some of the "peyote" buttons, the songs and the ritual proceedings, and established the cult in Taos.

Outside the pueblo walls, a Plains tepee was erected by the Peyote or Road Chief. It was built with twenty-one poles, and with the doorway facing east. At dark a small fire of seven cedar sticks touching at the points was started with flint by the Fire Chief. In front of the fire was laid a small crescent-shaped mound of clean sand. Behind it sat the Peyote Chief, with tobacco and corn husks for cigarettes. Beside him sat the Drum Chief, with a small water drum; the Fire Chief, with a turkey wing for sweeping the ashes into a crescent; and Cedar Man, with sage and cedar. Around them in a circle sat those ready to take the Peyote Road.

The ceremony was simple. The Peyote Chief placed a button of peyote the size of a small onion, Our Father Peyote, on the moon-shaped mound of sand. He rolled tobacco in a corn husk, passing the makings to his left. The Fire Chief rose with a brand from Grandfather Fire, lighting the cigarette for him and then everybody else, passing around the circle to the left.

When all had taken four puffs, the Peyote Chief prayed. Each in turn prayed after him. The sack of peyote buttons was now passed around to the left. Each man took four, placing them on the ground before him. One at a time he cleaned with his knife, chewed into a fine paste, spat into his hands, rolled into a ball, and then swallowed.

The Drum Chief began beating the little water drum. The Peyote Chief sang four songs. Then the drum was passed along to the left, and the next man sang four songs. So it continued all night.

Sage was passed around clockwise to rub over hands and face so that its sharp clean smell would prevent dizziness. If a man became ill the Fire Chief removed the vomit with a shovel, and Cedar Man smoked him by lighting a branch of pungent cedar and fanning the smoke with a fan of feathers set in buckskin and embroidered with colored beadwork. At midnight, water was passed to drink. All went outside. Returning to the tepee they were smoked by Cedar Man. More peyote was passed around. The singing resumed.

At sunrise when the male sun looked in the doorway upon the female moon of sand, more water was brought. Then the wife or daughter of the Peyote Chief came with stewed fruit, and corn and raw beef or jerked venison ground together and sweetened. The members slept till noon, and then feasted.

They had travelled the Peyote Road. It was good. Our Father Peyote, Our Father God, had given them strange, beautiful visions. He would give them a good life.

The old men of the Council resented the intrusion of this alien cult. It had nothing to do with the ancestral ceremonies and kiva rituals of the religion they had fought for so long and indomitably against Anglo and Spanish encroachments. "It is not the work given us." The peyote tepee was raided, the fleeing members' blankets confiscated and identified. Three kiva members who participated were ousted and fined in communal land holdings. Two boys were publicly whipped in the plaza.

The peyote eaters, particularly the young men returned from government boarding schools, to whom it appealed most, retaliated by wearing American clothes, shirking their ceremonial duties and openly defying the Council. Every Saturday night, until dawn, the little peyote water drum could be heard beating softly and steadily across the pasture.

It was natural that the cult persisted in Taos. Since time immemorial this northernmost and easternmost pueblo had been the meeting ground of the Pueblos and the Plains tribes. The Kiowas still came to visit, being honored with gift dances up the canyon; and the Cheyennes and Arapahoes came in wagon and truck for the long straight tepee poles cut in the mountains above. Here, as nowhere else in the Four Corners, the Taos men wore their hair in long braids interwoven with bits of fur or colored cloth—an adopted Plains custom. There were so many words in their language bearing a resemblance to those in the Kiowa tongue that linguists linked them in a common Kiowa-Tanoan linguistic stock. Too, dreams had more significance in Taos than in other pueblos.

Yet, though it persisted, the cult had few members. Most of them resumed their duties in the kivas, participated in ceremonial work, and each year looked forward to the sacred pilgrimage to Blue Lake. The Peyote Road was but a detour for a small minority.

To the Plains tribes also it was not an integral part of their religion. It had gained no foothold until the buffalo were gone and the free-roving tribes were penned in reservations and the sacred Sun Dance was abolished. With it went the old power. What new power could restore their faith, their old life? For the Nez Perces there rose the apocalyptic cult of "The Dreamers"; for the Sioux the cult of the "Ghost Dance," founded by a Paiute in Nevada;

and for the southern Plains tribes the "Peyote Road." All were based on dreams and visions of a better time to come when the White man's power would be broken and the Indian restored to his own.

Of all these various cults only Peyote had survived. The ritual was simple and took the place of the gorgeous ceremonials, which were prohibited by the expense and lack of costumes, buckskin, great feasts. At the same time it was Indian in its origin and vastly more appealing than the predominant frigidity of the Christian Church. Peyote was a drug easily obtainable. It had two primary effects. It produced visions in miraculous colors blended in ineffable harmony. Also it enhanced the sense of hearing so acutely that a discordant sound was excruciatingly painful; hence the use of singing and the rhythmic beat of the water drum as an accompaniment while it was being taken.

Whether it was an injurious habit-forming narcotic was controversial. But as a substitute for the valid, deeply integrated religion of the Pueblos to be discussed later, or as a bridge to Christianity, the Peyote cult was valueless. It merely offered a colored lotus land to dreamers.

One of Collier's sons, however, drew up a paper concluding that "extensive research finds peyote to be not habit-forming or deleterious." The new Indian Bureau then officially recognized the Peyote Cult as the Native American Church.

> In Peyotism there is fused much of the ancient religious experiences of the Indians and some phases of Christianity. In a sense, then, the Indian has become modern or universal in spirit. . . . For Peyotism is not only a religion, but a way of life, a life that accommodates itself to the present and hopes for the future . . .
>
> One might compare this Peyote Road to the Taoist Way, but unfortunately we do not have the mataphysical (sic) material on which to base the comparison. The investigator is shut off from it because he does not know the language in which the prayers and speeches are made and because, so far, he has refused to become a disciple. But Peyote, the Compassionate, is there to guide and help the traveller. The journey is painful, but the rewards are great. It returns man to his pristine goodness . . .
>
> Peyotism has been organized as the "Native American Church" and it may be liberalized to admit non-Indians and its leaders may teach its doctrines to members of all races . . . It is claimed that no white man can fully grasp the meaning and significance of Peyotism, and there is a large element of truth in that. Peyotism having sprung from the historical

experiences of the Indians and being based on his own cultural drives, how can an outsider fully understand Peyotism? This will largely depend on the leaders who may develop and on the degree of their ability to be articulate not only before their own people, but before the whole world . . . The Peyotists are realists. They recognize change . . . But a great responsibility rests on various governments to keep open the gates for the genius of the race to express itself in modern life . . . Keep Open the Gates!

Such were the contradictory, confused and perfervid reports of the cult in official declarations of the new Indian Bureau. Under government sponsorship the Native American Church grew to a membership of some 25,000. The use of peyote spread westward. In the Four Corners one pueblo after another took it up, and its use began to seep into the Apaches, Utes, and Navahos until now it is a major menace.

By 1948, it had spread to tribes in North and South Dakota, Wyoming, Montana, and the Northwest. In a meeting of the American Medical Association that year it was urged that peyote be outlawed nationally as a habit-forming drug.

Unfortunately, reported the committee, the Indian Bureau permitted its use several years ago on the grounds that it was part of an Indian religious ceremony.

We are informed by the Narcotics Bureau that peyote is not covered by the Harrison Narcotic Act, but that its use is prohibited by law in some of the Southwestern States.

It is high time that the sale and possession of this drug be restricted by a national law.

But to get back to 1940, at the First Inter-American Indian Conference, held in Mexico, a lengthy paper was presented by a United States representative of the Indian Bureau. Embodying the above quotations on the spiritual value of peyote, and later reprinted in the official organ of the United States Department of the Interior, Office of Indian Affairs, it pointed out the "great responsibility"of the "various governments" of the twenty Latin Amerian countries to "keep the gates open" for the Native American Church.

There seems little doubt that the misguided attempt of the Indian Bureau to foist such a cult into prominence as a national church and to sponsor its adoption throughout all North, Central, and South America stemmed directly from a messianic complex too blind to question the propriety of governmental intervention in the domain of the spirit, and to the reality that no faith founded on an outside stimulus has ever endured.

The political advantages of the Indian Bureau policy, however, were soon apparent in the Four Corners. The traditional immuration of the pueblos was broken. In every pueblo, like Taos, there was a schism between the older conservatives trying to maintain their ceremonial life and the young liberals taking up peyote. For the Indian Bureau, with reforms and innovations of all kinds, this was a decided advantage. It had only to select members of the peyote minority as representatives of the pueblo and a vote for the project was forthcoming "by will of the people."

Thus the granting of religious freedom to the pueblos under the idealistic reforms of the Indian Reorganization Act. The Bureau had accomplished in twelve years what the Spanish Catholic Church and the Anglo Protestant Church had failed to do in four centuries. It had driven a spear-head directly into the heart of the ancient Pueblo religion—into the very depth of the Rock which was still the core of their faith.

There remained the Navahos.

Bedrock

Under the new Indian Reorganization Act the various surviving pueblos and tribes were no longer simply social groups. They were "federal corporations chartered for economic enterprise" —a new kachina mask.

There was one notable exception, the greatest nation of Indians yet remaining. The Navahos, who still considered themselves The People. They had rejected by secret ballot the Indian Reorganization Act.

Wherefore, logically enough, they were denied "access to the credit fund, the land purchase fund and the system of orderly devolution of powers to the tribe which were provided in the act." Being a people rather than a federal corporation they were now to have taken from them the one economic enterprise on which their lives depended—the sheep, whose mutton was their staple food, whose wool they wove into blankets to trade for flour, sugar, coffee, and silver with which to make bracelets for resale.

It was all very proper on paper, and it threw into perspective the inevitable result of the flood tide of Anglo conquest.

Recently Louis Cottam, Supervisor of the Carson National Forest, and Pat Murray, the forest ranger at Tres Piedras, included me in one of their flights over the country. We took off one clear Sunday morning above the deep gorge of the Rio Grande and followed the slashing, muddy river north into Colorado. Northwest over its goosenecks as it curved in a great bend down through San Luis Valley. West over Alamosa, Monte Vista, Del Norte, over Wagon Wheel Gap to the lofty Rockies, from which it now fell in a narrow sparkling stream.

By the instruments we were twelve thousand feet high and travelling 120 miles an hour. But the wall of mountains was rising higher and faster than the little 150 horsepower Stinson could climb in the thin rarefied air. Many a plane has been crashed headlong against its rocky peaks by pilots who still underestimate these ancient barriers to man's encroaches. Pat turned, circling for more altitude. 14,000 feet. 15,000 feet. Then he cleared the peaks so closely we could see the trembling leaves of the highest aspens, the moss on the bare ledges, the patches of snow.

Below us lay Creede, the old boom mining town, and on the high ridges the crumbling foundations of long forgotten gold camps. A patch of cleared meadow: the highest landing field in the United States. There was Wolf Creek Pass, nearly 11,000 feet high. And here were the headwaters of the Rio Grande and the San Juan. Two tiny trickles of melting snow. One flowing east and south to mark the eastern boundary of the Four Corners. The other flowing south and west across the focal point of the Four Corners, crossing three states, to join the Colorado River, as its greatest tributary, and to help carve in the Grand Canyon its western boundary. This was the Continental Divide, the massive Rockies, the high wall of its northern boundary.

It was still difficult to clear as we headed south. Out of stupendous gorges rose sudden up-drafts which lifted the plane six hundred feet before we could catch our breaths, or dangerous down-drafts which sucked us down so close we could barely skim the frost-shattered granite. Summit Peak, Cumbres Pass, Gobernador. Abruptly the earth fell away beneath us. We were floating safely over that vast mountain-rimmed bowl at last.

The plane lowered and the land spread out. Long as time, wide as the imagination. A vast grassy plateau seamed with arroyos, topped by buttes and mesas, darkened with low slops of cedar and pinon. A solitary trading post. A tuft of dust resolving into a toy wagon drawn by two mousy horses. A handful of sheep, trickling like water among the rocks. A lone Navaho horseman . . .

But the joy-ride was over; school was called. And Louis and Pat began teaching me that frightening, saddening lesson that all America must unavoidably learn: a lesson in soil erosion and soil conservation.

There was the mountain stripped clean of giant pine and spruce by a private sawmill operator. "I begged him to let me mark the trees to cut," said Louis, "begged him to leave the saplings for a future crop. We offered to build him a road at government expanse to take out his lumber so the undergrowth would not have to be cut. But he was in a hurry and he had only a lease on the area. So he stripped it bare."

"It isn't the wood," said Pat. "Look at that gulley. Ten feet wide and ten feet deep, and growing every year. With the trees gone there's nothing to hold back the run-off."

There was the arroyo staggering drunkenly across the plateau from left to right, tearing chunks from the land, its sides caving in—a raw and jagged wound.

"Let's take a look at the range," said Louis. "Be careful, I don't want to walk home."

"What range?" asked Pat. Mile upon mile there stretched out a desolate plain barely covered with sage and bunch grass. "Hell! It would take fifty acres of that to support one sheep."

"I remember crossing this area on horseback years ago," said Louis. "The grass brushed the stirrups. It's the same old story. Overgrazing. Nothing to hold the water."

The day before, we had ridden and walked to a similar overgrazed area that had been fenced off twenty years ago as an experiment to see how long it would take the grass to come back. Except for the fence there was nothing to distinguish the plot from the area around it.

And now we saw the *ritos* and the rivers into which these arroyos poured. Huge sandy courses a quarter of a mile wide, fifty feet deep. All choked with silt and topsoil washed from the unprotected, barren land.

We turned back, heading for the Brazos and the Rio Grande. This ancient valley, that had been the homeland of three successive races, was widening with flood upon flood. Down it, unless something could be done, would wash croplands and grasslands, towns and cities, the very Rockies, into a desert of silt fit only for the explorations of a future race's archaeologists.

No sermon was necessary. The savage tide of Anglo conquest across the continent had not only exterminated the Indians. It had gutted the peaks of ore. It had stripped the mountains of forests. It had stripped the plateaus of grass. Now the topsoil was going down the drain. The nation had literally reached bedrock.

This was the condition of the Navaho reservation. Since 1868, The People had been forced to graze sheep as their principal means of subsistence. Time and again as their population increased, the size of the reservation had been expanded. Always against pressure. In 1908, 3,500,000 acres were added, but White cattlemen brought political pressure to bear so that the land was returned, in 1911, to the "public domain," enabling them to obtain it. In 1934, the Arizona Navaho Boundary Extension Act provided for the exchange of White land for land from the public domain in order to ameliorate the condition, but similar action in New Mexico was blocked by political interests.

The reservation now consisted of fifteen million acres of upland desert of which only 32,000 acres could be used for planting. It was so badly eroded that the topsoil on 45 per cent of it had been washed away—delivering only 2.5 per cent of the water received by the Colorado River above Boulder Dam but 37.5 per cent of the silt. The rest of it was so badly overgrazed that, on nearly one-third of it, fifty acres were required to support one sheep, and on one-fifth of it, sixteen acres were required.

On this vast wilderness of 25,000 square miles, as harsh and empty and heartbreakingly beautiful as any area in the world, scarcely five thousand Whites could have existed. But over it ranged sixty thousand Navahos (even so, only two per square mile) increasing in population twice as fast as all Whites and all other Indians in the country. And on it they were grazing 1,594,000 scrawny sheep, their sole means of existence.

In 1934, the Indian Bureau confronted the alternative of saving the Navaho land from further erosion or saving the Navaho people from starvation.

Under the Indian Reorganization Act, conservation of natural resources was mandatory. But as the Navahos had rejected it by popular vote, it was necessary to secure their permission to drastically reduce their flocks to prevent further overgrazing and erosion. The Navahos were within their rights in refusing.

"It takes three hundred sheep to support my family of five. If you allow me to have only fifty sheep, four of us will starve." This was the gist of every Navaho's argument against reduction.

"Give us more land." This was the natural counter-proposal. They had the money to buy it. For by one of those tragicomic paradoxes this half-starved tribe was potentially one of the richest peoples on earth. Their 25,000 square miles of eroded desert contained thousands of acres of valuable timber; underneath were vast pools of oil with proven wells, sixty billion tons of coal, and some of the most valuable helium deposits in the world. In addition to all these natural resources they owned water-rights to the San Juan River, which, if made available by construction of a diversion dam, would open up from 100,000 to 160,000 acres of their land to irrigation.

But the Navahos had rejected the Indian Reorganization Act which would have allowed them to organize as a "federal corporation chartered for economic enterprise." Hence they had lost "access to the credit fund, the land purchase fund and the system of orderly devolution of powers to the tribe which were provided in the act." Congress withheld their money which might be used to buy new land, or to open up their land to irrigation, pending authorization from the Indian Bureau.

It was the familiar American problem of "play ball with me or else," and the new administration had been rebuffed.

The alternative still remained: to work for the Navaho people, ignoring the rebuff in light of the past injustices done them and their present and future needs; or to enforce soil conservation in order to bring them into line with the pueblos, like Ácoma, which had allowed its sheep to be reduced from 33,000 to 8,500 as a consequence of the provision mandatory upon acceptance of the Indian Reorganization Act.

The choice was made easy by the seriousness of soil erosion and the lack of cohesive tribal government among the widely-spread, semi-nomadic Navahos. Sheep reduction was recommended by the Soil Conservation Service, legalized by the Taylor Grazing Act, and enforced by the Indian Bureau. The program to reduce Navaho sheep from the 1932 peak of 1,600,000 to some 400,000 in 1944 began.

The reservation was divided into some eighteen districts, each patrolled by White agents, range riders, soil conservation experts, and law enforcement officers. A Navaho capital was established at Window Rock, nearly as large as the state capitals at Santa Fe and Phoenix, with administration and office buildings, cottages, and dormitories. Here were centered the activities of thirteen hundred federal employees (one for every forty-three Navahos) of the Navaho Service.

By 1940, the expenses were running about $3,850,000 annually. This amounted to about $71 being spent yearly by the government on each Navaho, compared to his total average income of $81.

Out of this mountain of activity and its pyramiding cost, the individual Navaho squatting in his hogan received no benefit whatever. He still remained illiterate, could speak no English. His wife's flock had been reduced from 250 to fifty sheep: not enough to feed mutton to the family, to provide her with wool for blankets which could be traded for flour and coffee, or silver for him to work. Day schools were built, but as there were only one hundred miles of all-year roads in the 25,000-square-mile wilderness, there was no way to get his children to them. There was still only one doctor for every six hundred Navahos. More than one-half of all Navahos died before the age of five. And still the tribe was increasing twice as fast as all Whites and all other Indians. More mouths to feed, more children needing schools, more people needing medical attention—and every year fewer sheep.

From an administrative viewpoint this was a decidedly successful program. But the monument to its memory was yet to come—in the disastrous winter of 1947, two years after Collier resigned as Indian Commissioner and steps were taken to abolish the Indian Bureau.

Meanwhile preparations were under way to extend these Indian reforms on an international scale.

Pátzcuaro Postál

In the fall of 1930, with an Indian boy named Chotuqua for a guide, I had ridden horseback from the east end of Lake Chapala, below Guadalajara, southeastward to Lake Pátzcuaro in Michoacan, Mexico.

Pues. There it was. Blue pine mountains surrounding a blue lake. Tiny white villages with red-brown roofs. Tarascan Indians swarming the great ancient plazas, the men in brown *serapes* bordered with red, the women in full, pleated, red skirts, and blue aprons. All set in red Indian earth under a turquoise sky, with white clouds unraveling overhead. As beautiful and poignant as any remote spot on earth. A *tarjeta postál* in red, white, and blue—a perfect postcard of undiscovered Tarasco.

But now, in April, 1940, it had been rediscovered. And we were going there. Mabel and Tony Luhan and I. The governor of Santa Clara pueblo. Some Navahos, Hopis, and Papagos, with Emma Reh, of Albuquerque. All to attend the First Inter-American Conference on Indian Life, sponsored by the Anglo United States and the twenty Latin-American republics. Tony and the Indians as Indian delegates. Emma Reh to present an ethnological paper. Myself with an assignment to cover it in a syndicated article for King Features Syndicate. Mere excuses! We were going on a vacation! Riding on the cushions, bowling over a new paved highway cut through jungle and sierra alike.

Pues. There it was again after ten years. But how changed! The little Toonerville Trolley drawn by six mules was gone. The cathedral, with its ancient olive trees and the old bells hung between them, still stood at Tzintzuntzan, ancient capital of Tarasco. But one no longer had to be paddled there in a canoe; a new paved road swung over the hill. A huge new statue rose from steep-walled Janitzio, out in the lake. No one seemed to remember Ciedro Echo, the Buenas Dias tree. Indians no longer gambled at baccarat, listening to the continuous cry, "*Que tiene bola?*" They were all hawking *tarjetas postáles* of the president's new home and the great tourist hotel swarming with people. We fled back to the old hotel, with its charm and grace, open toilets, and bad cooking . . .

Mexico itself had been rediscovered by Mexicans a quarter of a century before.

In Mexico "the revolution" is not the revolt against Spain led by Hidalgo in 1810. It is the revolt against the domination of White values begun in 1910. Villa in the north, Zapata in the south, Felipe Carrillo Puerto in Yucatan—under these revolutionists, Porfirio Diaz was driven out, Huerta fled, Carranza was killed, and the country swept by one of the bloodiest revolutions in history. "Land

and liberty!" cried the Indian peasantry, clad in white *calzon* and *camisa,* and shod in *huaraches.* Back from Europe came Diego Rivera, Orozco, Goitia, and Sigueiros to paint them and begin a renaissance of art. Back from the United States came D. Manuel Gamio to study them and evolve a new ideology. Up popped Indian presidents, Calles and Cardenas, to carry it out with the agrarian reform.

All this comprised the revolution. Liberty from absentee landlordship, the domination of European culture, the tyranny of American "dollar diplomacy." Restoration, to the 80 per cent population of Indians and *mestizos,* of the land held by feudal *hacendados,* the Church and United States industrialists. A return to native values, spiritual, artistic, ideological.

Dr. Manuel Gamio, the anthropologist, worked it out in detail in the Valley of San Juan Teotihuacan. Here, for seven years, he made an exhaustive study, embracing every aspect of life, to "weld a *patria.*" By welding a *patria* he meant not a government attempt to "civilize" the Indian, to "incorporate" him to modern progress. But a unification of land, race, and tradition in order to extend, in a living continuity, the style and spirit of the native culture. Otherwise governments were "doomed to failure, for they cannot logically rule people whose nature and way of living they ignore; and the people, unable to live under systems arbitrarily forced upon them, will degenerate and become weak, or will explode their justified protest in revolutions."

This voluminous report and Mexico's initiative in recognizing the validity of her Indian heritage gained attention throughout all the countries of Latin America. At the International Eugenics Congress, their concern was readily apparent. In all the twenty countries south of the Rio Grande there were sixteen million Whites. But there were eighty million Indians and *mestizos.* And they were increasing twice as fast as the population of the United States, at a rate that would double the population in thirty-five years.

Hence the First Inter-American Conference on Indian Life, originally scheduled to be held in Bolivia, and now called to order at Pátzcuaro, Mexico.

The conference lasted ten days. Prepared papers totaling eleven hundred pages were read in the four sections: economic, legislative, educational, biological. Occasionally there were plenary meetings. Proper resolutions were passed. A permanent Inter-

American Indian Institute was established. A great stride forward had been taken.

The conference, however, was not without its lighter moments; and for the Indian delegates from the United States these added up to a full ten days. It was immediately apparent that they had been brought down by the Indian Bureau as mere window-dressing. Through the crowded hotel, into one section after another, they wandered like ghosts. What they saw and heard seemed unbelievable. Most of the Indian Bureau's White delegates conformed to type. Few had ever seen Indians or been west of the Mississippi. None seemed aware of the profound difference between Anglo United States, with its less than 1 per cent Indian population and the Spanish republics with the 80 per cent Indian population. Nor that, of all the countries, the United States, which alone had almost completely exterminated the Indians, had the least right to recommend ways of saving them. Yet with Yankee aplomb and aggressiveness they stood reading their papers with the implied attitude of "This is the way we think it ought to be done, and therefore, the way for you to do it!" The Peyote Way! "Keep open the Gates!"

Tony and the poor Indians were badly confused. They inevitably wandered into the cocktail room. Here, outside their own country, they could buy a beer. And in the neighboring villages they could buy *serapes* to take home. These were the only tangible benefits they derived from the conference.

At the conclusion of the conference it was announced that a permanent Inter-American Indian Institute had been established, pending ratification of the governments represented, and that Mr. John Collier, United States Indian Commissioner, was president of the governing board.

On June 7, 1941, by formal treaty, the United States became a member of the Inter-American Indian Institute. And on November 1, 1941, by executive order, it created its own National Indian Institute as a member country.

What did this mean in actuality?

Quoting the Commissioner in 1947:

> The Senate repeatedly has voted the funds for its operations but the subcommittee on Interior Department appropriations of the House Appropriations Committee has repeatedly refused them. Thus, in spite of the treaty-making Senate, the United States has breached the Inter-American Indian treaty.

Why?

Among the resolutions passed at the Conference one reads as follows:

> Where there exists an over-concentration of the ownership or control of land, the respective governments shall take appropriate measures, in accordance with equity and justice . . . and we recommend that they adopt measures appropriate to their own situations to help the Indian populations in building up their economic life, providing them with needed land, water, credit and technical facilities.

Another states:

> . . . Indian agencies or offices should not monopolize the administration of Indian services, but should operate to focus upon the problems of the Indian all the resources of the governments as well as all the local resources.

It will clearly be seen that neither the practically-minded, obdurate government nor the impractically-minded, idealistic Indian Bureau could now comply either with the spirit or the law of these ratified resolutions. The era of sentimentalization had drawn to a close.

10 Tide from the North

AGAINST THE Spanish invasion from the south, the Anglo tide of conquest from the east and its ebb tide of sentimentality, the Rock still stood. But now there was gathering a storm that was to accumulate all these forces and break upon it.

It was postponed by Pearl Harbor. America's entrance into the war benefited the surviving tribes of the Four Corners like the citizenry at large.

Unlike World War I, in which Indians were not subject to Selective Service, World War II required their full support. They gave it gladly. Most of the thirteen hundred New Mexico boys in the Philippine campaign and the four hundred lost on Bataan were Spanish-Americans and Pueblos. Despite the fact that 88 per cent of the four thousand registered Navaho males between 18 and 35 were found to be illiterate, 3,600 Navahos entered the armed forces. Bearing such official names as "Algernon," "Popsicle," and "Angel Whiskers," they served with distinction. The Navaho Marines in the South Pacific were particularly acclaimed for their use of a secret communication system using the complex and undecipherable Navaho language as a code.

At home some fifteen thousand Navahos left the reservation to engage in war work on railroads and in factories, in the lettuce and cotton fields of Arizona, the beet fields of Colorado, and the sheep ranges of Nevada and Idaho. A war production personnel authority in California rated the ability of Navaho workers above Negroes, Mexicans, and lastly Whites.

During the war, prices for sheep and wool rose. Boys sent home their military dependency allotment checks. Absent family members brought back cash earnings. Altogether $15,000,000 trickled into the reservation. For the first time in years The People ate enough.

Then suddenly the boom was followed by the bust. The war workers and servicemen returned to the reservation; their dependency allotments ceased; their readjustment allowances expired within a year; their sheep were gone.

Sergeant Abner Jackson, a Navaho veteran of Tes Nes Pes, in a published letter now on file in the United States court at Phoenix, spoke for all the returned servicemen:

> After Pearl Harbor, as a United States soldier, when I landed in Scotland I could talk very little English, especially the Scottish variety. I had a smattering of Spanish picked up at Gallup (N.M.) railroad yards and a splendid Navajo vocabulary. I had just turned 18.
>
> They sent me to North Africa under Gen Patton and there I became a sergeant. I was with Patton until they took him from us in Sicily. We were given over to Gen Clark and I marched through Rome with him.
>
> I learned French in Africa, Italian in Sicily and finally, when we took the Siegfried Line, was soon able to talk German as well as I speak the language of the United States.
>
> I am back in Arizona, but the medals I received at Salerno and in Germany are of little use to me as my people are still in utter darkness of the Navajo reservation and even I can't vote because I am a Navajo. I can't go back to the blanket for we have none left and no sheep with which to make new ones.
>
> While I was in Sicily I received a letter from our Indian agent at Window Rock saying that I need not worry about my sheep being taken away from me on account of the soil erosion program and that they would be waiting for me on my return to the reservation.
>
> Yet on my return I did not have a single head of sheep left, but only a credit at the agency permit general store of $2.80 each for my sheep they had taken, when sheep were selling on the open market at from $8 to $14 a head.
>
> I want to vote and 6000 other G.I. Indians in Arizona want to vote. We want to be Americans, not former reservation Indians. We want to listen to radio programs both in Navajo and English.
>
> We want adult and child education in State schools—not bureau schools. Also better housing and irrigation for our land on the San Juan River, on our reservation.

Our people are not lazy, but are so very tired and poorly nourished that we are unable to work well.

Give us the same free opportunity that is given to the Negro and Mexican and aliens and we will be happy.

When we are free, then $65,000,000 will be saved for taxpayers and the Indian Bureau will be a thing of history.

Who was to help them now that Commissioner John Collier had resigned to extend his reforms not only throughout all the Indian populations of Latin America but throughout all the dark races of the Far East as head of his new Institute of Ethnic Affairs, Inc.? What was to happen to The People now?

The Long Hunger

It had been long coming, but now it came with all the cumulative evils of nearly a century. It was the eighty-fourth winter since they had been defeated by Kit Carson and marched away on the Long Walk. It was the winter following the summer drought of 1947. The winter of the fashionable "New Look," when inflation was climbing to a new peak, when butter and bacon and ground round sold for a dollar a pound, and the United States voted seven billion dollars relief and reconstruction aid for Europe and Asia.

But for The People there was little bread and coffee, no reconstruction aid. For them, the most destitute of all minorities, it looked like the "Long Hunger," the "Winter of Death," the "End of the Navaho Trail." As snow began to whiten the sage, the news blackened the front pages of the country's press. Facts old to the Navahos but fresh to the public as printer's ink.

On a reservation of 25,000 square miles, three times the size of Massachusetts, sixty thousand Navahos, the largest surviving tribe of Indians in the United States, faced starvation. The land could not support twenty thousand people. Of the total 3,500,000 acres only 32,000 acres could be planted.

For over a century, sheep had been The People's primary means of support. Now only 161 of the 11,117 families owned as many as two hundred sheep, the number needed to maintain a subsistence level of living. Due to the loss of sheep, there was no wool with which to weave blankets. The sale of blankets now supplied only 9 per cent of the Navahos' total yearly income, estimated by the government at less than $400.

Living in a state between malnutrition and starvation, the Navahos existed on an average diet of 1,200 calories, compared to the post-war Japanese diet of 1,300, the Germans of 1,500, and the United States average of 3,450.

Their death rate was 386 per 100,000 compared to forty-three for the United States as a whole. The infant mortality rate was so high that more than one-half of all Navaho children died before reaching the age of five.

Disease ran unchecked: trachoma, diphtheria, pneumonia. Their tuberculosis rate of 45 per cent was fourteen times that of the United States. Yet there were but 135 government hospital beds for tuberculosis patients, and 316 beds for general patients. There were only two field nurses and two dentists.

To whom were they to cry their misery?

Over 80 per cent of all Navahos were illiterate and spoke no English. Though the United States government, by solemn treaty, had agreed, in 1868, to supply one school for every thirty children, and the Indian Bureau had spent $1,000,000 a year for sixteen years for day schools, now abandoned as impractical, there were school facilities for only 5,000 of the 24,000 Navaho children of school age.

Since 1924, The People had been declared citizens by act of Congress, and, by virtue of the Fourteenth Amendment, they were automatically citizens of the state in which they resided. Yet they could not vote because of legal technicalities: in Arizona because they were classed as "persons under guardianship" or wards of the government, and in New Mexico because they were not taxed. Disfranchised citizens, they were denied benefits of the G. I. Bill of Rights, old age pensions, social security benefits.

From out of their snow-swept wilderness, from out of government files, the facts kept coming. Into the Four Corners poured photographers and reporters to discover still another: that in the whole 25,000 square miles there were but one hundred miles of all-year roads. And now came leading articles in *Time* and *Collier's*, photographic spreads in *Life* and *Look*, feature articles in *The Denver Post, Phoenix Gazette, Christian Science Monitor, New York Times,* Los Angeles *Times, Examiner*, and *Daily News,* Albuquerque's *Tribune* and *Journal*, to lead the parade of the country's press in exposing the Navahos' plight.

The public—already groggy over the expenditure of $400,000,000 aid to Greece and Turkey, $332,000,000 to Europe and

$570,000,000 to China—dug still deeper into its pockets. Led by Navaho Assistance, Inc., a non-profit corporation organized by Editor A. W. Barnes, of the *Gallup Independent,* to distribute relief supplies, organizations began sending in money and supplies. The Red Cross, the Navajo Trails Relief Caravan of Hollywood, Amvets' Indian Assistance, sponsored by American Veterans of World War II, the Quakers, labor unions; planes from Washington and Oregon, convoys from Denver and Salt Lake City, and a truck of relief supplies from Drew Pearson, the columnist who had started the Friendship Train with aid for Europe rolling from Hollywood past the starving Navahos.

Early in December, Congress completed action on a bill authorizing appropriations up to $2,000,000 in emergency relief for the Navahos and Hopis. The Bureau of Indian Affairs, however, asked for only $450,000. And two weeks later the House Appropriations Committee recommended granting only $200,000 unless the bureau was "staffed with people who have a desire as well as the capacity to carry it forward to administrative fruition," pointing out that the conditions were "directly the result of the short-sighted policies of the Bureau of Indian Affairs."

The winter tragedy was not without its comedy relief.

Many people declared that the plight of the Indians "was not nearly as bad as emotional extremists would have us believe." Mrs. Agnes Morley Cleveland, for one, displayed fancy frocks, from fashionable New York and Hollywood shops, sent to Indian women. "Someone decided the Indians should have better horses so they sent a carload of Percherons. Percherons on the desert! Well, they were so nice and big and fat that the Indians ate them!"

At the same time, Dr. Salsbury, of Ganado Mission, asserted in a public statement, "No one should get the idea that there are sixty thousand Navahos starving . . . It is possible there are more hungry bureaucrats in Washington than there are hungry Navahos on the reservation." He urged the abolition of the Indian Bureau, saying, "Exactly the same policies, personnel and schemes are in the Indian Bureau today. The present pseudo-starvation scare is being blown up out of all proportion in order to secure $80,000,000 more to play with."

What he meant was soon obvious. J. A. Krug, Secretary of the Interior, had just released his report, "A Long-Range Program for Navajo Rehabilitation." Drawn up by Charles A. Collier, son of the former commissioner, and Max M. Drefkoff, government industrial consultant, it presented a 10-year program to cost $90,000,000 in capital improvements.

With its release the tragi-comedy got into full swing.

In bold front-page headlines the *Los Angeles Times* announced the discovery of the first attempt to create the first "Russian-type 'Soviet' on the American Continent" among the Navahos. In a series of leading articles it proclaimed:

> First hand study also shows that the sensational "starvation" stories circulated about the Navajos by some newspapers and magazines last winter were untrue almost in their entirety, and in fact were used as a build-up for the present attempt to establish a "cooperative state" within the United States.
>
> Many generous and sincere persons were drawn into the Navajo "relief" program, which finally bogged down when the facts of the Navajos' relatively great prosperity began to come to light.

Ironically, this villain who had attempted to "Sovietize the Navajo Tribes" was cut from the same cloth as the ultra-conservative, staunchly reactionary and Republican *Los Angeles Times*. He was a wealthy, retired Indiana furniture manufacturer, a died-in-the-wool Republican named Max M. Drefkoff, an industrial consultant in the Department of the Interior, who had helped prepare Secretary Krug's $90,000,000 Navaho program.

In his study he accused the 105 traders on the reservation of maintaining an economic stranglehold by charging exhorbitant prices for goods, and interest on pawn silver. To correct this he had persuaded the Navaho Tribal Council to demand that the traders' mark-up prices be regulated to 25 per cent instead of the alleged 200 per cent, and a levy of 1 per cent up to the first $40,000 gross income against each post per year. He also had recommended the establishment of forty-nine small industrial plants on the reservation, whereby the Navahos could process their own wool, leather, and lumber. These recommendations were approved by Secretary Krug and embodied in his report—which report received the public endorsement of Oliver La Farge, novelist and former president of the Association of American Indian Affairs, who always had voiced great antipathy to the traders.

Repercussions of the Krug report were immediate. Indignation meetings were held throughout the reservation by Indians and traders alike. Navahos protested the action of their own Tribal

Council. The members themselves accused Drefkoff of having given them an ultimatum to vote for his scheme under the threat of withholding all relief funds. Votes of confidence were given the traders, whose posts were, indeed, the cornerstones of Navaho life. A delegation of traders hurried to Washington to attend the hearings. With Hugh Lee, president of the United Indian Traders, went the wealthy William Lippincott, of Wide Ruins, who straightway offered to bet Drefkoff $100,000 that the traders could not operate one year under the new regulations. Under all this pressure Drefkoff resigned.

On top of it all, Norman Littell, counsel for the Navahos, asserted that the reservation could support 100,000 more sheep. E. R. Fryer, superintendent of the reservation, who blamed the sheep reduction program on John Collier, was promptly replaced. Collier's successor, William A. Brophy, formerly of the Albuquerque office, became ill, resigned, and was replaced by Acting Commissioner William Zimmerman, Jr.

And on May 2 the *Los Angeles Times* reported:

Spring has come to the vast tableland which is the Navajo Reservation . . . . The joyous spirit of spring is animating the tribesmen. Naturally full of humor and pranks, the Navajos this year are bubbling over with laughter.

Some persons look askance at hogans. But they are part of functional living here, a link with the soil which the Navajo loves. To stand on a mesa studded with trees like an illimitable park and to look out over the grand vista of canons and sharp buttes etched against the brilliant sky to a far horizon where snowy peaks shimmer, is the rare privilege of these Navajo homebuilders. No city noises assail their ears, only the sigh of the breeze in the cedars and the tinkle of sheep bells and the calls of the lambs.

The Navajos seem quite content in their isolated hogans, with blue haze on the mountains and warm buzzings in the air. They have lived this way a long time. They feel free.

Indian Epilogue

Yes, the anticlimax is exactly that. After nearly a century of serfdom and the almost complete obliteration of their race, the surviving Pueblos and Navahos are still as they were.

That same summer, however, they were given the right to vote as American citizens. In Arizona, they had been disqualified on the grounds that they were "wards of the government" and hence incompetent to vote. But on July 15, 1948, the Arizona Supreme

Court declared this disqualification void, and granted all Indians the franchise. In New Mexico, they had been denied the vote on the technicality that their reservation land was not taxable. Yet on August 3, a federal court held that this disqualification, according to the State Constitution, was in conflict with the Fifteenth Amendment to the United States Constitution, and that the right to vote could no longer be withheld from any Indian in New Mexico.

It was election year; and the rulings roused fear that the voting privilege, if used by the Indians, would upset the balance of power in these sparsely populated states. Hence the new spectacle of power politics creeping into pueblo and hogan. But in the national election in November, practically no Pueblos voted. Roughly three thousand Navahos, out of the sixty thousand population, registered; and of these scarcely a third voted. They were all possessed of the same ever-present fear—that by exercising their voting privilege and paying taxes, they would lose their land.

We shall see that these fears were valid.

Secretary Krug, of the Interior Department, had proposed in his report that some $88,500,000 be authorized by Congress to rehabilitate the Navahos and Hopis over a ten-year period. The reservation would be supplied with paved roads and trails, graded air-strips, telephone and radio systems, boarding schools and hospitals. Studies would be made as to how industrial development could open up vast resources of timber, oil, gas, copper, helium, and fourteen billion tons of coal. Irrigation projects would be initiated. The Shiprock-San Juan irrigation project would reclaim 117,000 acres; the Animas-La Plata project 110,000 acres; and the South San Juan project, on the Rio Blanco and Navaho rivers, 75,000 acres more. Even so, the area would not be able to support more than 35,000 people. At least thirty thousand Hopis and Navahos must seek a living elsewhere.

Hence, attempts would be made to move some of them to the Colorado River Indian Reservation, south of Parker Dam. The current irrigation project there would reclaim 100,000 acres, of which the present Mojaves and Chemehuevi tribes would require only 25,000 acres.

In 1949, most of these provisions were embodied in what became known as the $89,000,000-ten-year Navaho Hopi Rehabilitation Bill. That October it was passed by both the House and the Senate and sent to the President for approval.

It was then discovered that a rider had been added by Representative A. M. Fernandez, of New Mexico, which provided for bringing the Navahos and Hopis under state control, instead of continuing their jurisdiction under tribal and federal laws.

This amendment was unprecedented in Indian affairs. It would have placed the Indians at the mercy of state and local politics, disrupted their social organization, destroyed their culture, and permitted their land to be appropriated for debt. The bill concerned only the Navahos and Hopis. But by implication and precedent, it might later have concerned equally all the Pueblos.

Not since 1923, when Albert D. Fall's Indian omnibus bill nearly succeeded in getting enacted, had any Indian measure roused such a storm of controversy. The whole West split sharply on the issue—churches, leagues, organizations, newspapers.

On the last day of the ten-day period allowed him to sign or veto, President Truman vetoed the measure. He stated that the Fernandez amendment, to which he objected, was "heavily weighted with possibilities of grave injury to the very people who are intended to be the beneficiaries of the bill." He also admitted that he had been "greatly influenced by the attitude of the Navaho Indians" whose Tribal Council had opposed the bill.

In the spring of 1950, the bill was again brought up—minus the Fernandez rider—and passed. Immediately afterward Fernandez declared his intention to demand a congressional investigation of the Tribal Council of Taos Pueblo, and to introduce in Congress a Bill of Rights for the Indians of Taos Pueblo. By the same implication and precedent, this bill, if passed, will affect all the pueblos by restricting their ancient rights of self-government and bringing them under state control.

There is still another factor of primary importance that points toward the Indians' eventual loss of control of their reservations—the presence of rare deposits of uranium and helium within the area, so necessary in this dawning Atomic Age.

Without indulging in either political controversy or idle speculation, it is obvious that the Pueblos and Navahos, as a people living their own communal life in their traditional homeland, are doomed. And with this ends our history here of the Pueblos and Navahos.

There is no defined long-range Indian policy. There never has been. Either of preserving the people ethnologically intact with a continuity of their ceremonial life, customs, handicraft; of preserving their reservations as we do national parks, national monuments, and wilderness areas; and their prehistoric pueblos as examples of the only native architecture in the United States. Or of feeding, clothing, schooling, and properly preparing the people for eventual assimilation into the impinging white culture. The Indians have gradually disappeared under the banner on which has been emblazoned our only consistent national Indian policy during two centuries—public antipathy and professional neglect, ruthless exploitation by private interests, and ineffectual government diddling.

Today, all Indians in the United States comprise less than 2 per cent of the population. Politically, economically, and socially, they seem inessential and unimportant. Yet psychologically they are today a tremendous fact. Our Indians lie heavy on our national conscience. They have given us a hangover, a racial psychosis, which we can't cure.

The result has been the crystallization of our peculiar Anglo antipathy against all dark races. It began with the Red, which we killed off; extended to the Black, which we enslaved; carried through to the Yellow, against which we erected rigid racial barriers; and now holds for all the Jews, whom we seem to be finding difficult to tolerate. Only to the White did Liberty hold up her torch. America as a melting pot held true only for white European races, not dark.

What does this psychosis mean to the richest and most powerful nation on the face of the earth? This impenetrable stronghold termited from within by its racial hatreds, its deathly inhibited fears, its complete lack of understanding of what it has destroyed? How long can Miss Liberty nurse these mental and spiritual ills, these impediments to growth? What does she see looking southward past her torch?

Prologue to the Future

Of the twenty-two nations in the Western Hemisphere, only the United States has almost completely decimated its indigenous race.

From the Rio Grande south to Tierra del Fuego, the land is predominantly Indo-American. Of Mexico's nineteen million people, fifteen million belong to Indian Mexico—"a nation within a nation."

Peru, Bolivia, and Ecuador are over 80 per cent Indian. Guatemala, 70 per cent. Venezuela and Colombia 75 per cent *mestizo* and full-blood Indian. Paraguay is still Guarani. In Chile, says Herring, "The mark of the Araucanian is upon every Chilean face of high or low estate . . . on the features and skins of the people, in the vengeful suspicion and bitterness of the rebellious masses." . . . One-fourth the entire population of Latin America, over thirty million, is pure Indian.

From deep underground, this socially and economically submerged bottom layer is steadily rising with a record birth rate. Of all the countries in the world which have reported birth statistics to the United Nations, the first nine positions are held by Indo-American countries. Their populations are increasing nearly twice as fast as is that of the United States, and at a rate that will result in a doubling of their populations in about thirty-five years. The increase is all Indian.

The top layer—the pure white—comprises scarcely 12 per cent of the population, and it is steadily decreasing. The great mass in-between, almost two-thirds of the entire population, is *mestizo*, and it is steadily growing darker.

The net result is the growing dominance of Indian influence, even in government. A current phrase in Mexican argot states it succinctly: "The government is growing darker"—a significant allusion to the many Indians elected to the presidency and official posts.

What is happening, as Toynbee asserts, is that after a long withdrawal under Euro-American domination, Indo-America is returning into the world arena as a dominant force again.

What is the trend of its influence?

Mexico, in 1810, was the first American nation to issue a decree abolishing slavery. Chile, in 1925, set up the first social-security system in the Western Hemisphere. Brazil's social insurance laws not only pre-date those of the United States, but contain provisions which ours still ignore. Uruguay, as far back as 1915, instituted the first eight-hour working day. In 1945, the first Indian Congress to assemble since the fall of the Inca empire, in 1533, assembled in Bolivia. Of the fifteen hundred delegates, all heads of ancient Indian communes, only three hundred spoke Spanish. One of their great accomplishments was the establishment of an agrarian code. It was patterned after the agrarian reforms of Mexico. Here, where 1 per cent of the people had held 85 per cent of the land, sixty million acres were taken from the huge haciendas and distributed in small plots or *ejidos* to village ownership. Each *ejido* group was a co-operative, collective society. Their success, in turn, parallels that of Peru's one hundred co-operative Indian societies and co-operative fisheries. The modern United States co-operative stems from these modern Indo-American derivatives of ancient Indian co-operative forms, the co-operative principle having been the base of the economic system of the Inca empire.

For this trend of collectivism and social progress, the President of Brazil, in 1944, had a ready answer: "Economic progress should not be considered as the primary aim of governments unless the ultimate goal of such progress is of a social nature."

All this, then, gives outline to the shape of things to come: the fusing of a new world-culture within the vast frame of Indo-America, by an ever-darkening, ever-increasing Indian and *mestizo* people. And this may mark at long last the end of a saga that has no parallel among the peoples of the world . . .

In such broad terms and within such a large "frame of reference" must be written any adequate history of the Indians of the Four Corners. From the start, their story has been one of continental ramifications, and it reflects the life-course of two peoples and their effect upon one another.

This brief outline, striving for this perspective, is neither a biased indictment of Anglo-America nor a romantic epitaph of Indo-America.

The Indians were communal, obdurate to change, non-individualistic, and hence not competitive enough to meet the challenge of the Whites. Although they have originated five-sevenths of the agricultural wealth of the entire world today, they were not adaptative enough to keep abreast of industrial developments as did their white neighbors.

Nor could anything have held back the progress of the Anglos, with their lusty individualism, Yankee wit, and mechanical genius. With these they have given the world the technological miracles of the age—the power to fly in the air, travel under the sea, talk across the world, preserve food indefinitely, undergo operations without pain, lengthen the life span.

But what we are concerned with here is not the mere objective record of one of several successive peoples rising to secular dominance over their neighbors, weakening under their own inherent faults, and being submerged in turn.

We are concerned with the subjective record of the evolutionary development of man through successive, well-defined stages. Through these stages each individual, each race and civilization, evolves alike. At each stage, tremendous conflicts take place. In the individual it is the inner conflict between instinct and ego. Between the Indians and the Anglos, as races and cultures, it has been the same basic psychological conflict objectified and extroverted on the field of war, economics, and politics.

In each case, the outcome must be the same. If the instincts win, the individual disintegrates morally and psychologically. If the conscious ego wins, his life is impoverished to sterility.

In the evolutionary development of mankind through this phase, we will see more clearly that it was inevitable for the conscious ego of the Anglo to assert dominance over the instinct of the Indian. But now a new phase has been reached. Man must transcend his own dominating conscious ego lest he impoverish his life to sterility.

For we, too, have reached an impasse. Our own human rights menace the very concept of property rights on which our civilization is founded. Our racial psychosis self-isolates us as a minority from the predominate dark population of the world as a whole. Neurotically ill, obsessed by a nameless fear of a kingdom of the spirit forever beyond our technological and economic mystery, we feel, for the first time, a lack of momentum, a loss of a sense of direction, the absence of a guiding faith.

How can we find it? Where do we go now? What, in reality, was the essential, unreconcilable difference between the Anglo and the Indian, whom we have never understood?

To answer this question is the purpose of this inquiry. For only by understanding the Indian as representing one phase of our development, and the Anglo as another, can we reconcile the tenets of both in a still higher stage as true citizens of our common universe. For we know now, like Eli Faure, that to refuse to perceive the unique face of man under the masks that cover it, is no longer a sign of force but rather of senility.

Behind his masks of archeological specimen, ethnological type, heathen savage, noble redskin, and underprivileged social minority, stands a man whom the Puritan Father, Pilgrim, brave pioneer, Indian fighter, rugged individualist, go-getter, and imperialistic Yankee has never seen. A man who by his own space-time concept of reality refutes as illusory and irrelevant all that we have here so far learned about him.

But first we must discern the invisible Rock to which he has so obstinately clung through so many centuries of defeat.

Part Two: The Gods

The modeler of gods, at bottom, is the spiritual universe hastening unceasingly in pursuit of its center of gravity . . . .

ELIE FAURE

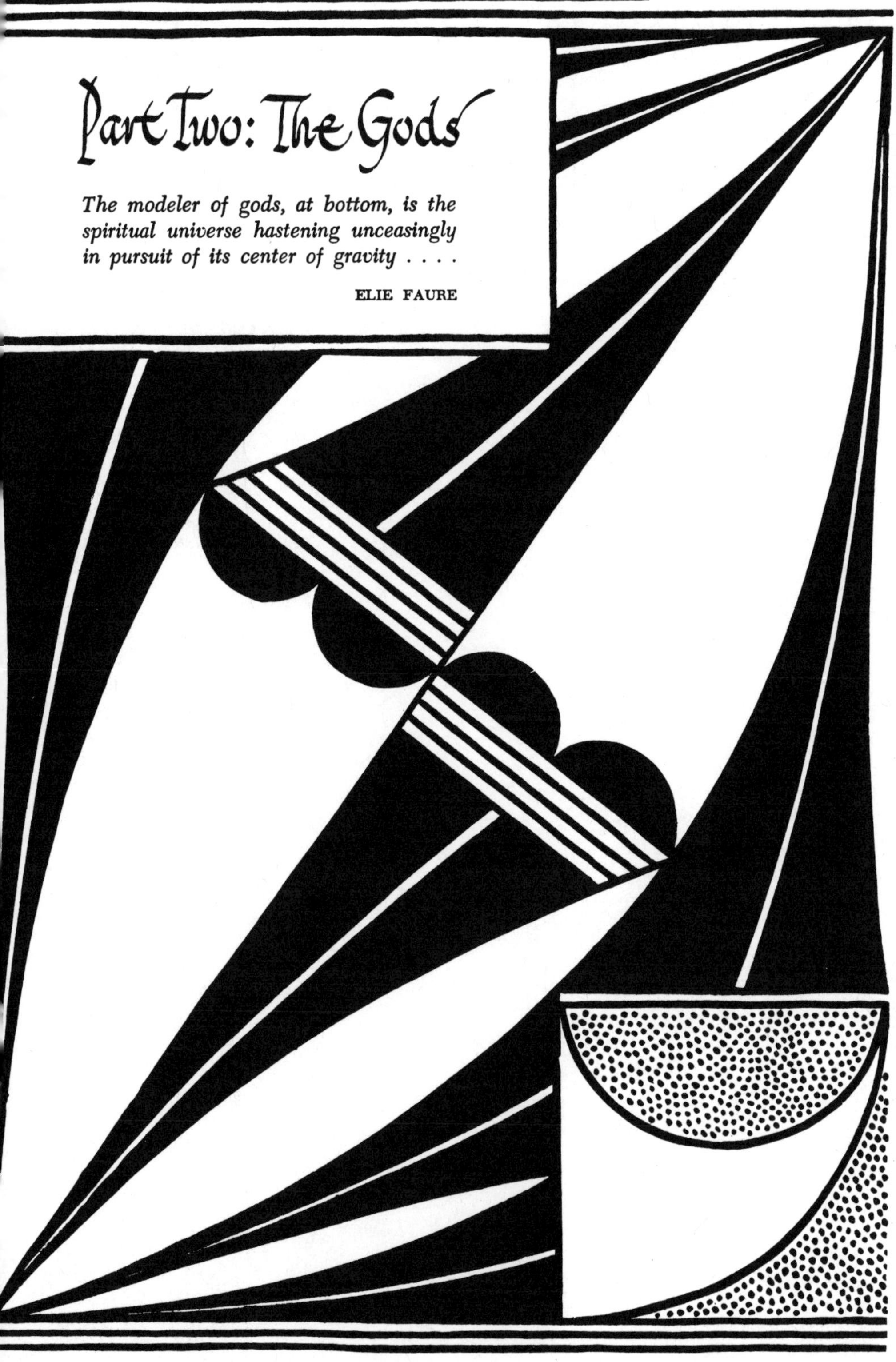

CONTENTS OF PART TWO

1 The Beginning

So what? The bow is broken. The thing is all over, done, finished—one thinks. When suddenly they come. Out of the kiva, out of myth and legend, out of the depths of America itself.

They come filing into the open plaza, shuffling unhurriedly, in dusty moccasins, with their loose-kneed walk. A line of figures, part man, part beast, part bird. Bare bodies splotched with paint, sinuously bending at the waist. Wearing ceremonial kirtles, a ruff of spruce around the neck. Carrying gourd rattles and twigs of spruce. But staring with tiny or bulging eyes from great wooden heads—bird heads with long beaks, animal heads with large-toothed snouts, square heads, round heads, cloud-terraced heads hung with tufts of feathers and bearing the symbols of lightning and rain.

They stop. There rises a yell. A single, piercing, off-pitch cry that lifts your scalp. There comes the authoritative stamp of a moccasined foot. A stamp that jams down your heaving insides and jars the mountains squatting on the plain.

They are dancing. Barbarically beautiful, brilliantly colored. Gently waving their twigs of spruce, shaking their gourd rattles. Singing like the soughing of wind through the pines. Stamping rhythmically as the beat of the drum, insistently as the pulse of the earth. No longer part man, part beast, part bird. But forces which sway the squatting mountains, which shape the cloud terraces building overhead. Dancing as gods have always danced, embodied forces of earth and sky, commanding the comprehension of the heart alone.

It is all one: the dancing gods; the pulsing cries and the

singing drum; the whirling horizon; the mountains in the sky; the white clouds squatting on the plain. And no one longer thinks it is all over, done, finished, for in this evocation of spaceless space and timeless time which obliterates the illusion of straight-lined progression from a distinguishable beginning to an ordered end, nothing ever is all over, done, finished. Seed and fruit, form and substance, deed and intention—everything fuses in a whirling circle that encloses an undivided, undifferentiated, ever-living wholeness.

One does not think: this is how it was when I first saw it as a boy! This is America before the white men knew it, the America that they have never known! For he is carried back beyond his childhood, beyond the time when the Druids thronged Stonehenge and the pagan Greeks danced to the pipes of Pan. Back into the archaic wonder and mystery and pristine purity of man's apperception of his cosmic role.

One does not think at all. He soughs with the deep-chested wind through the forest of spruce twigs. He writhes with the mountains in travail. He licks at the cloud terraces with serpent tongues of lightning. Part bird, part beast, part man, he wings into the sky, holes deep in the rock, and stands naked and defenseless and exalted before the gods of the storm. For he too is a god, and all their potencies are his potencies in selfless and fleshless communion with creation . . .

Suddenly it ceases. Man's temporal illusions rush back to fill this gaping vacuum; his insides start to heave again. Joe steps up to hand him something out of his blanket. "Chew this piece dry bread. That the way it is when drum stops beating."

The dust-covered, sweat-splotched figures shuffle back to the kiva. The mountains squat heavily back down on the plain. The cloud terraces crumble to ruins in the sky. But now one knows that it is not all over, done, finished. Here on this desolate rock-ribbed island in the emptiness of man's disbelief, it can be re-evoked again from the well-springs of his deepest instincts—a complete world as old, as new, as different as any man has known . . .

The analogy comes readily enough, but nothing more. The Indian world is co-existent with the one we know, but it has no connection with it whatever. Against its changelessness the long, negative, downbeat of history makes no mark at all; archaeology, ethnology, politics, and sociology are all off-limits. It is not a rational world of facts, of extroverted action, of cause and effect.

It is a world in-turned, with its own symbols, its own rhythm, its own values, and none of these can be rendered comprehensible by our own. A vast realm of instinct, intuition, faith, it is invisible and indescribable. And yet as real, within its own space-time continuum, as ours, and more enduring.

For this continuum, by the same miracle and mystery of life, yet embraces us—that secret and eternal part of us which responds to the movement of the stars and the phases of the moon, which finds tranquillity in sorrow, which leaps awake to something in the beat of an Indian drum. To this hidden capacity for wonder, for truth, for growth, nothing is wholly unintelligible. Not even the faintly visible horizon of a world hidden by the mists of our professed disbelief.

The Rock

In the Beginning the people lived in several worlds below. Successively they emerged from them to a new world above. In the middle of this new world stood a great rock. Extending through all the previous underworlds and protruding above this one, it was the core of the universe, rooted in time and space. It was oriented to the four directions, and its sides glowed with their corresponding colors —white on the east, blue on the south, yellow-red on the west, black on the north.

Emerging from the world below, the people gathered at its foot. And when they planted seeds to make the earth spread out, and when they called to the Holy People to help them plant the Holy Mountains, it was around this great natal rock. Hence they called it simply the Mountain Around Which Moving Was Done, the Mountain Surrounded by Mountains, or the Encircled Mountain.

To the east of it they planted the Holy Mountain of the East, made of sand and white shell. To the south they planted the Mountain of the South, made of sand and blue-green turquoise. To the west, the Mountain of the West, of yellow-red sand and abalone. And to the north, the Mountain of the North, of black sand and jet. In each they placed a Holy Person, a Talking God to guard the mountain and to listen to the prayers and songs offered it. Extra mountains they transplanted, and seeds of the four sacred plants. They made a fire with four kinds of wood and a hogan with four logs. Everything—the stars, the winds, the seasons—they put in order and named, and they became. For "when you put a thing in order, give it a name, and you are all in accord: it becomes."

Thus the pattern of the Navaho world at the Emergence. The great central Encircled Mountain. The four directional Holy Mountains. The lesser transplanted mountains, the plants, the trees, with the winds, the seasons, and the sun and moon and stars above. A world spread out like a four-petalled flower as seen from above. This today in a Navaho sand-painting is the symbol of the great axial rock, the Encircled Mountain: a four-petalled flower, like a four-leafed clover, like a lotus.

The four sacred mountains still bounding the ancient Navaho homeland are physical mountains: the Mountain of the East variously identified as Mount Blanca, in Colorado; Wheeler Peak, above Taos in the Sangre de Cristo range; or Pelado Peak, near the pueblo of Jemez; Mount Taylor, of the San Mateo range, as the Mountain of the South; the San Francisco peaks, in Arizona, as the Mountain of the West; and a peak in the La Plata or San Juan range as the Mountain of the North.

The Encircled Mountain is something else. It has been identified as Huerfano Peak, above Chaco Cañon, which bears its name. But by its very nature it cannot be so constricted. Being the core of the whole cosmos, it existed when the First People were still in the lower worlds; and spanning a time and space beyond our earth-dimensional comprehension, it is too great and too powerful to be visible. This is its metaphysical reality. El Huerfano is merely its material image, its physical counterpart.

The meaning of this is amplified by reference to the cosmography of Tibetan Buddhism, in which is found the most striking parallel to the Encircled Mountain.

The core of the cosmos is Mt. Meru. It is shaped like a truncated pyramid, three of its four sides glowing with the same directional colors of the Navaho world-axis: white on the east, blue on the south, red on the west, and yellow on the north. It is eighty thousand miles high and eighty thousand miles deep. Within it are several underworlds and several heavens. Around this mighty cosmic core are seven concentric circles of mountains separated by seven encircling oceans. Each of these fresh-water oceans and its corresponding wall of mountains is a separate universe with its own sun and moon and planets.

Outside these seven universes, and floating in the outer

salt-water ocean of space, are four main continents or land masses spreading out in the four main directions. The eastern continent is crescent in shape, white in color, as are the faces of its inhabitants. It is nine thousand miles in diameter. The western continent is round in shape, red in color, as are the faces of its inhabitants; its diameter is eight thousand miles. The northern continent is the largest of all, being ten thousand miles in diameter. It is of square shape and yellow color, and its inhabitants have corresponding faces. The southern continent is our planet Earth. It is the smallest of the four, being seven thousand miles in diameter as now verified by our modern scientific measurements. It is pear-shaped—and we agree that rather than being round it is flattened at both ends and bulges in the middle. Blue is the color assigned to it; and the faces of its inhabitants are oval shaped and greyish blue.

Below this mighty Mt. Meru the cosmos thus spreads out like a great four-petalled flower, a lotus. Each of the world-petals is protected by a Lokapala, or World Guardian, as each of the four Holy Mountains of the Navahos is guarded by its Talking God. And just as the Navaho world and the Encircled Mountain is symbolized by a four-petalled flower, so is the Buddhistic cosmos represented as a lotus.

These are striking pictorial and mythological parallels. But their full significance would be lost without their metaphysical meaning. The whole cosmos is represented as a lotus; but this cosmos is also identical with the goddess-mother called "The Lotus"; and our earthly universe is located within her "at about the level of her waist." In its duality, then, it is both that which was created and that which created it. And each living being, himself created in the image of the Goddess Mother of creation, also duplicates within his own psyche the complete cosmos.

Only by this can we understand the cryptic opening sentence of the legend of the Navaho ceremonial *Where The Two Came to Their Father:* "When they put the extra mountains around, they took Mountain Around Which Moving Was Done out of First Woman's belt."

This too explains the Zuñi references to the Sacred Middle which their ancestors found at Zuñi after their emergence from the underworld, and the location of their corresponding Mountain of Generation as being just below the navel of the Earth Mother. Above all is their striking conception of the Earth Mother as the goddess-mother of creation, through whose successive womb-worlds they emerged to this one.

The conception of this four-cornered world structure is not confined to them alone in America. In the sacred *Popol Vuh*, recording the creation myth of the Quiché Maya, the world is described as "four-pointed, four-sided, four-bordered." In the *Chilan Balam of Mani* this cubical world-block is further alluded to as the altar of the gods. The truncated pyramid temples of the Toltecs, Zapotecs, and Aztecs themselves suggest such world axes.

Hence we understand now, at the outset, that in Pueblo and Navaho mythology we are dealing not with easily comprehended, childish legends, but with a cosmographic concept as abstract, imaginatively vast and old as that of any people on earth. It is strangely consistent that the area today still contains this mythological meaning in its name of the Four Corners. Its original prototype, its greatest physical image, may well have been, not El Huerfano, but the Colorado Pyramid, the high hinterland heart of America. Its central section, the Colorado plateau region, is still the sacred middle, their traditional homeland. The Pueblos and Navahos have always regarded life as dual: the physical and the psychical. And it is both of these realities of the Rock to which they have clung against the assault of erosion and materialism alike.

The Canyon

Here is the visible world, four-pointed, four cornered, bounded by the four directions. One terrace, one plane as it were, of the pyramidal universe extending below and above.

One of its two great polarities is the Encircled Mountain, which extends invisibly upward towards the Sun Father.

The other is an equally tremendous hole, a navel, the *sipapu**: the place of emergence whence came man from the dark underworld, the place of beginning. It leads back down into the depths of the earth; into her who is known as the Goddess Mother of creation, Our Mother Earth.

It too is a mighty rock, as long as a mountain range, as high as its highest peak. But upside down. A deep cleft in the earth, a monstrous chasm. Like the Encircled Mountain, the Grand Canyon is impervious to time and change; and paradoxically, the more

* Also *shipapu, chipafunta, shipapuliva, shipapuni, shipapuna,* etc.

it has been assaulted the larger it has grown. Its spires and pinnacles have lengthened, its clefts and chasms have deepened, its buttes and mesas have broadened, until it seems as immeasurable and indestructible as the Rock itself.

This Upside Down Rock is visible. But unbelievable. In its abysmal depths whole mountains contract and expand. Clouds ebb in and out of the gorges like frothy tides. Everything changes shape constantly in the shifting light. And all these mutations of form, these permutations of substance, are suffused with infinite variations of color. Never static, never still, it is inconstant as the passing moment, and yet durable as time. It too is a realm of the fantastic unreal, Maya, "a world of illusion."

For us, as for the Hopi, Grand Canyon is the largest and deepest *sipapu* into the nebulous past.

Its walls are twisted, folded and compressed layers of rock three miles thick, one mile deep and 217 miles long. On the plateau out of which it has been cut there stand around it tall rock pillars like Vermilion Cliffs, Cedar Mountain, and Red Butte. On top of one of these lies a small pebble. And on this rests a speck of dust.

This speck of dust represents the age of the earth according to Archbishop Ussher, who, in the authorized version of the Bible of his time, sanctioned the statement that God created the world at 9 A.M., October 26, 4004 B.C.—scarcely six thousand years ago. . . . But there! It has blown away into the shifting, dissolving illusions of the canyon.

The small pebble represents the one million years since man first appeared on earth; the Age of Man, according to present scientists. In this little time-span man has walked through all history —lumbering out of a dark cave to discover fire, through the resplendent castles and kingdoms of vanished civilizations, to stand on the threshold of our Atomic Age. . . . But there! It has rolled off into the soundless depths of the canyon.

The pillar on which it rests is all that remains here of the sixty million years of the Cenozoic or Modern Era. In this short Age of Mammals appeared all the forms of life now known on earth—the continents, mountains, seas, and rivers; the hardwood forests, cereals, fruits, and grasses; the birds; the mammals and man-apes. But the pillar is crumbling into the canyon. There! It is carried away by that river of time which in only twelve million years has carried away, sand by sand, all the great mountain peaks around it.

Another butte still totters on the edge. It is all that remains of the one hundred and forty million years of the Mesozoic or Medieval Era. This was the Age of Reptiles—of great, slimy monsters, huge, toothed birds, and mammoth dinosaurs; of insects; of tropical plants and flowers; of the almost immortal evergreens. Soon it too will crumble and wash away with all the footprints, skeletons, and fossils imbedded in its rock.

Here now are the upper rock layers of the canyon walls. Kaibab limestone, named for the plateau on the north rim, Kaibab being a Piute name meaning "Mountain Lying Down." Coconino sandstone, named for the plateau on the south rim. Then the Supai shale formations which form the walls of Cataract Canyon, in which the Supais still live. Redwall limestone. Finally the Tonto group. . . . Over 3,500 feet of rock remaining to attest the three hundred and forty million years of the Paleozoic or Ancient Era. The Age of Fishes and the Age of Amphibians, of shell-bearing mollusca and corals, and the first appearance of land plants.

Below all this lie the Grand Canyon series of formations, twelve thousand feet thick. The Unkar and Chuar groups containing Hotauta basal conglomerate, bright red Hakatai shale, and Shinumo quartzite, appropriately named for the old Hopi confederacy. These thick, complex formations leave a record of the Proterozoic or Primitive Era, fifteen hundred million years long. The Age of Marine Invertebrates, primitive marine forms of life, trilobites and brachiopods, little groveling crustaceans.

Thus in a three-mile thickness of rock, in a vertical drop of one mile, there lie the remnants of an earth at least two thousand million years old. A whole world rising and sinking beneath the sea and rising again with the almost imperceptible, rhythmic pulse of eternity. Really different worlds successively emerging, each with its own physical pattern, its own forms of life. All lost now and forgotten in the illusory depths of time. Mere kachina worlds, of which are left but fragments of their masks.

But here now at the bottom of the canyon protrudes the oldest rock system known, part of the original earth's crust. Great vertical layers of gneiss that formed before the planet had cooled. Huge blocks of granite forced into them in a molten state by heat and pressure. Pegmatite. Vishnu schist. In it are found traces of the earliest known larval life—bits of carbon remaining from microscopic plants and single-celled animals.

Now we know what it is. The Rock, a protruding fragment of the Mountain Around Which Moving Was Done, the cosmic core of the universe.

Vestiges of visible time go back no further than this Archeozoic Era. The lengthening pulse beat—one million years, sixty million, one hundred and forty million, three hundred and forty million, fifteen hundred million—grows into a steady hum. In a whirling nebula Archeozoic Time merges into Azoic Time and it into Cosmic Time; and in the fantastic unreality of this palpable fourth dimension, this beginning links with the Psychozoic Time yet to come.

All these names, these physical remnants of vanished worlds and vanished life forms are but discarded kachina masks. Through this *sipapu* we come to the deep underworld, the heart of the rock, the womb of Our Mother Earth. It is the revered Place of Beginning whence came man.

The Kiva

Roughly corresponding to Buddhist cosmography, both the Navaho and Pueblo universes embrace four successive underworlds below the earth. A system of waterways exists underneath, connecting ultimately with four encircling oceans. Various springs and lakes, like the Lake of Whispering Waters of Zuñi, Sand Lake and Blue Lake of Taos, are openings to this system.

In each of the lower worlds a color predominated, the same colors which now designate the four quadrants. Not until the people emerged to this world was there light.

The Navahos generally designate the First World as the Dark or Red World, with its sky-opening to the east; the Second World, the Blue World, with its sky-opening to the south; the Third World, the Yellow World, with its opening to the west; and the Fourth World, the White World, with its Place of Emergence toward the north. Often called Center of the Earth, it is variously identified as being Silver Lake, in the mountains of southern Colorado near Silverton; Spirit Lake, at the head of the South Fork of the San Miguel; or Island Lake, near Ophir.

The Hopi, in their sand paintings, symbolize these lower worlds as four concentric, colored squares: yellow, blue, red, and white, with a small square in the center representing the *sipapu*, the canyon, the Place of Emergence.

All this is abstractly symbolized in the Pueblo kiva—the secret, underground ceremonial chamber. For the kiva itself, with all its many variations, recapitulates in structural form this four-world universe common to all.

The kiva may be four-cornered, rectangular in shape as those of the Hopi. It may be circular like those at Ácoma, just as the earth and the sky look circular when glimpsed from a midpoint. It may be sunk into the earth like a well, as those of Taos; or its upper portion may protrude above ground with a beautiful inset adobe staircase to the descending ladder on top, like those seen in Santo Domingo and San Ildefonso. Or as the hogan of the Navahos who, having no kivas, use their homes or build ceremonial duplicates for use during sings—it may be octagonal in shape, oriented to the four primary directions and the points between, with the doorway always facing east. It may be made of stones as in the Hopi kiva, of beautifully modeled adobe, like those of the Rio Grande pueblos, or of rough-hewn cedar logs chinked with bark and earth, as are the Navaho hogans. But for all these minor variations, it is still a carefully constructed model of the universe.

In the floor is a small hole, the *sipapu,* leading down into the first underworld. The floor level is the second world into which man emerged. The raised seating ledge represents the third world. And the ladder rises up to the roof opening, the fourth world to which man has climbed. As in Ácoma, the ladder may duplicate in meaning the Navaho rainbow bridge over which the gods travel; and the great hand-hewn *vigas* or roof-beams the Galaxy seen in the sky above, Beam-Above-the-Earth, a visible vestige of the invisible Rock.

In the kiva, man is ever reminded that he lives in the whole of the immense and naked universe. And he is constantly made aware of the psychic, universal harmony which he must help to perpetuate by his ceremonial life.

For the kiva is not only an architectural symbol of the physical universe. The universe, with its great axis rock and its great *sipapu* canyon, is itself but a structural symbol of the mystical soul-form of all creation. And both are duplicated in man himself.

The first world was of fire. The primordial fiery mass that broke off from the sun to become our planet. That derivative first element of life given by the supreme creator of all life, Our Father Sun. Fire, the Zuñi's Grandmother of Men, our Parent Fire. Hence in the kiva the fire is kept burning all year. At the beginning of each new cycle of fifty-two years, the Aztecs obliterated all fires throughout the empire and lit new ones from a sacred flame. Similarly in Zuñi today at the end of each year are all fires extinguished and new ones lit from a fresh flame struck on sacred Corn Mountain. With fire, life begins. And from the first world of fire man begins his journey upward.

From the fire pit a line of sprinkled cornmeal runs to the altar. On the altar are prayer plumes of eagle down. They are a symbol of the second world of air. For as the fiery, molten earth cooled, an atmosphere of vaporous air surrounded it, and man emerged into his second state of existence.

The fire element of the first world gave man his life heat. This air element of the second world gave him the breath of life. Hence to all the Pueblos breathing is an act of prayer. In their ceremonials the Zuñis breathe in and out upon their hands. To the Apaches breath is the manifestation of life. Wind gave the Navahos the breath of life; their *kethawns* or prayer sticks are made of feathers, its symbol. Similarly in the south, Quetzalcoatl, the Feathered Serpent of the Toltecs, who preceded the Aztecs, is the personification of the breath of life.

On the altar beside the prayer plumes sits a bowl of water taken from a sacred spring or lake. It is the symbol of the third world of water, which was formed when the second world of vaporous air condensed into water, when rain and floods came, forming the primeval, warm and spumy seas. From it man derives his life stream, his blood and all the watery constituents of his body, his urine, sweat, and sputum. It courses throughout the universe of his body just as the great system of waterways is an integral part of the Pueblo universe and the Buddhist cosmos.

The waters subsided and the earth arose; and now upon it emerged man as we know him today. It was a wonderful moment, perhaps the most wonderful within the living memory of man, when he emerged to live upon the loved earth we know today as our ordered own. In the Navaho sand-painting we see the first people emerging from the third world of water on the Raft of Whirling Logs.

The Turtle Dance at Taos depicts them emerging to our fourth world of earth. It is in the freezing wintry dawn of early January when the first light illumines the frosty peaks, just as in the cold dawn of life on earth, that the people emerge from the kiva. Spectrally they trudge between the snow banks to the open plaza, naked save for breechcloths, in the freezing cold. One side of each dancer is painted white, as water; one side is painted brown, as earth. And from ear to ear in a broad band running across their lips, they are painted with huge mouths. Just like the mouths of great turtles crawling out of the water upon dry land. And then in the growing grey light they begin the dance of life.

This earth element of the fourth world gave man the solid constituents of his earth-body, his flesh. Hence man as we know him today is truly born from Our Mother Earth. She gives him everything he needs to sustain life; she gives him his immemorial bread of life. Thus, as in Taos, the perfect ears of corn, those without blemish and with the tips ending in four kernels, are saved for kiva ceremonials and are called Corn Mothers. With fire, feathers, and water, corn takes its place in the kiva as one of the major symbols of the four worlds, often synonymous with the earth itself.

The Aztecs believed in the periodic destruction of the world by the agencies of fire, air, flood, and earthquake. Certainly in the 2,000 million-year geologic history of the earth as we know it, it has undergone the major cataclysmic changes of which the Archeozoic, Proterozoic, Paleozoic, Mesozoic, and Cenozoic eras, with their distinctive life forms, bear witness.

But still in the diastrophic changes, the eternal palingenesis in which whole continents sank under seas and rose again smoking on the horizon, the world continued to exist in isostatic equilibrium. Snow-covered peaks bore sea shells on their summits. Tropical jungles changed into deposits of coal imbedded in frozen tundras. One seeming world gave way to another. And yet the structural harmony remained unchanged.

To this the Navahos bear witness. For, upon emerging to the present world, they brought up with them the soil-seed of other mountain forms which had been present in the previous underworlds. These mountains were transplanted in the same sacred, relative positions they had occupied below, and they still remain chronologically named: the Sangre de Cristos, the "Third Mountain in the Third World"; Jemez Range, "Fourth Mountain in the Third World"; and the Chuskai, Black, and other ranges westward, "Mountains Made in the Fourth World." With the sand that was left they made eight more new mountains in addition to the sacred four mountains of the directions. Their general name was "When the Mountains Get Finished They Get New Again."

The kiva is beyond the confines of these four transitory, successive worlds. It is the heart of the immortal Rock, the universe itself. In its architectural structure and its symbolism it attests all changes. In it man is made conscious that each successive world was a new world, a different world, but that each was composed, in part, of the elements of the preceding ones. And so is man whose road of life has led through all. Like the Navaho ceremonial name for themselves, he is "Made From Everything." He too is a living kiva, a living universe, an architectural and psychical symbol of the soul-form of creation.

The Road of Life

Here then is the Pueblo and Navaho cosmography of four successive underworlds. But all these underworlds are embodied within the Goddess Mother of creation, from which man has been successively reborn.

Rooted in the first Zuñi underworld was the Mountain of Generation, corresponding to the Navahos' Encircled Mountain.

The second cave-world to which mankind emerged was "dark as is the night of a stormy season." It was located near the navel of the Earth Mother and hence called the "Umbilical-Womb or Place of Gestation." Here beings separated to become fathers of the six kinds of men: the yellow, grey, red, white, black, and mingled.*

The third cave-world was lighter, "like a valley in starlight." This world was named the "Vaginal-Womb or Place of Sex-Generation." For here peoples and things began to multiply apart in kind.

In the fourth world-cave—"the Womb of Parturition"—it was "light like the dawning," and men began to perceive according to their natures.

Finally into this great upper "World of Disseminated Light and Knowledge or Seeing," which is called *Tek'ohaian ulahname,* mankind emerged, first blinded by the light and glory of the Sun Father, then looking for the first time at one another.

The creation myth is thus not only the story of man's

* Terminology according to the translation of Frank Hamilton Cushing.

journey up through these four underworlds, but of his evolutionary development on the way.

The Hopi kiva sand-paintings symbolize the lower worlds as four concentric colored squares: yellow, blue, red, and white, with a small square in the center representing the *sipapu*. From this place of emergence, and running to the east, toward the rising sun, is laid a line of cornmeal, the Road of Life. On it are marked the four crooks of longevity; and between these are placed footprints, as in Aztec codices. In the Zuñi kivas, the thin line of cornmeal leading from the fire pit to the altar is also called the Road of Life. The ceremonialism of all pueblos refer to it constantly. It is a motif in the ritual songs of Zuñi, some of the most beautiful poetry known.

> . . . That clasping one another tight,
> Holding one another fast,
> We may finish our roads together;
> That this may be, I add to your breath now . . .
> May our roads be fulfilled.
> May we grow old,
> May our people's roads all be fulfilled . . .

Even to the fast riding horsemen of the Great Plains, the Cheyennes, Arapahoes, and Sioux, it was known as the long trail Where the Pony Tracks Go Only One Way, because they knew man would never retrace his steps.

The ancient Chinese Taoists called it Tao, The Way; to the Navaho it is still The Way—the Moving Up Way, Mountain Way, Life Way, as variously designated by the great ceremonials which teach it. The Buddhists call it The Path, the Buddha Path, because Gautama the Buddha taught them how to travel it.

Its symbolism to us of the Western World since Darwin's time is at once apparent. The Road of Life is not merely the duress of individual man's four score and ten years. It is the complete process of mankind's evolution. For according to modern scientific theories, our planet broke off from the sun in a fiery mass; an atmosphere of vaporous air surrounded it; this condensed into torrential rains that formed the seas; and from these rose the continental land masses—the whole process duplicating the divisional four-world periods recognized by Pueblo and Navaho ceremonialism.

Despite scientific gaps, the radio-biogenesis theory asserts that life evolved from a living organism created by the agency action of the sun's ultraviolet rays on water charged with mineral salts and carbonic acid, and that man gradually evolved from the simplest organic form.

How far back man's evolutionary beginning may eventually be proved to rational science is still in question; it is not yet granted an extension through plant and mineral life. Nor has all religion yet caught up with science; the dispute between church and laboratory over the priority of Adam and the monkey is still echoed from some orthodox pulpits. But again in Buddhism we find another striking parallel to Pueblo and Navaho belief.

Affirming that man began his evolutionary journey as a spark of life in the fire of creation, Buddhism traces the evolution of man through the mineral, vegetable, and animal kingdoms with the derivative elements of each. From the fire element of the first world, man derived his life heat. From the air element of the second, his breath of life. From the water element of the third, his life stream, his blood. And from the earth element of the fourth, the solid substance of his earth-body, his flesh. Hence man is a derivative summation of the four states of existence through which he has passed. As the Navahos say, he is "Made From Everything."

But man is more than a highly developed, physical organism. He is both physical and psychical, flesh and feeling. Hence Buddhism asserts that from each of these four worlds he also derived corresponding psychical qualities or aggregates.

With fire, man received an aggregate of feelings. With air, an aggregate of volition. With water, an aggregate of consciousness. With earth, an aggregate of touch.

Also with these psychical qualities which lift man from the level of a physical organism to that of a sentient, conscious being, he received corresponding passions.

Fire and feelings gave rise to his passion of attachment and lust. Air and volition, the passion of envy or jealousy. Water and consciousness, the passion of anger. Earth and touch, the passion of egoism.

But evolution is more than a mechanical process. It takes place on both physical and psychical levels; and it can, at this stage, be hastened or retarded by man's perception of his responsibility in the cosmic plan. Thus the Buddha Path is often called the Noble Eightfold Path from the eight things one must do to keep on traveling it: "Right Belief, Right Intentions, Right Speech, Right Actions,

Right Livelihood, Right Endeavoring, Right Mindfulness, Right Concentration." Hence with the Compassionate Pity of Buddha, one does not eat flesh nor even kill a gnat lest he retard its evolutionary development.

In his *Human Destiny* * the late eminent biologist, Dr. Lecomte du Nouy, substantiates this faith by giving it a scientific basis.

> . . . The evolution of living beings, as a whole, is in absolute contradiction to the science of inert matter. It is in disagreement with the second principle of thermodynamics, the keystone of our science, based on the laws of chance. The reason and the fact of evolution are, therefore, not of the realm of our present science . . . Everything has taken place as if, ever since the birth of the original cell, Man had been *willed* . . . This Will manifests itself, therefore, through evolution, and its goal is the realization of a morally perfect being, completely liberated from human passions—egotism, greed, lust for power—hereditary chains, and physiological bondage . . . Henceforth, evolution develops on a different plane, a plane no longer physical but psychological . . . And psychological evolution is expressed mainly by the improvement of abstract, moral and spiritual ideas.

The Road of Life, then, is not only a mechanical process of geological and biological change. Nor is it solely a religious doctrine. It is an ethic, a way of life participated in by every physical organ and psychic faculty of individual man, by all mankind, and by all forms of life. For life is a continuous, unbroken progression from the parent fire, the breathing mountains, the living stones, the cornfields and pine forests, through the fish of the waters, the birds of the air, and the animals of Our Mother Earth.

Hence Indians regard man as chief over all the lower forms of life. But he must recognize his kinship with them, and his responsibility and debt to them, by not destroying them lightly or without good reason. To the pine tree he is about to cut he says ceremonially, "We know your life is as precious as ours. But we also know that one life must sometime give way to another, so that the one great life of all may continue unbroken. So we ask your permission, we obtain your consent first."

Also to the deer he is starting out to kill he says the same thing ceremonially. And when he kills the deer he lays its head to the east, towards the Sun Father, sprinkles it with pinches of corn meal, and lets fall drops of its blood on the ground for Our Mother

* Longmans, Green & Co., New York, 1947.

Earth. And afterward when he builds its flesh into his flesh, when he dances in its robe and antlers, he knows that the life of the deer is continued in his own life.

From this superlative regard for life stem all the wonderful animal stories of wise Old Man Coyote, Grandfather Crow, the Gopher People, and the Crane People; the deer, turkey, bear, mountain lions, and antelopes that fill the old legends and delight children on winter nights. They tell of the time when man was incarnate in the animal world and understood their nature. And many of them recapitulate man's Road, like the old Ute legend of The Grizzly Bear Who Married the Aspen and created the mountain Ute; the aspen representing the vegetable kingdom, the grizzly the animal kingdom, and the Ute, man who stemmed from them.

The Road of Life then is the process of evolution. Yet for all its biological truth, it is still symbolic. For it still lies ahead of us. And as Du Nouy affirms, we must travel it on a psychological plane into still another world.

2 The Cosmic Dualities

In the same terms as Navaho and Pueblo ceremonialism, Buddhism affirms that man has travelled his Road of Life through four main stages of development.

The same concept has been held by many systems of teaching. Gurdjieff, the Armenian mystic with whom the Russian writer Ouspensky studied, held that man consists of four bodies. Man number one is the man of the physical body, whose center of gravity lies in the moving center. Man number two is the man in whom the emotional functions outweigh all others. Man number three is the man controlled by the intellectual center, the man of reason. And man number four is an intermediate stage.

In early esoteric Christianity these correspond to the "carnal," "natural," "spiritual," and "divine" bodies. In theosophical terminology they are successively called the "physical," "astral," "mental," and "causal" bodies. And in certain Eastern religious-philosophies they are referred to as the "Carriage" (body), the "Horse" (feelings, desires), the "Driver" (mind), and the "Master" (consciousness, will).

We today are beginning to understand these stages of development. Some psychologists hold that man first develops into a naive consciousness from mere bodily perceptions and auto-erotic desires. Controlled by feelings and instinctive impulses, he then develops an ego, a personal or self-consciousness dominated by rational thought.

But he is yet incomplete. For just as Buddhism postulates a fifth world into which man is already beginning to evolve, Gurdjieff maintained present man as being in an intermediate stage, and du Nouy affirmed that he must henceforth develop only on a psychological plane, so do some psychologists hold that we now must evolve into a consciousness of the self that transcends both instinct and reason, the non-personal and the personal, the unconscious and the conscious. This tendency to evolution is apparently inherent in every living organism, and its result is the enlargement and unification of personality necessary to further growth.

But this enlargement is accomplished at great cost. And always when the conflict between instinct and reason, the personal and non-personal, the unconscious and conscious, is too great to be borne. Then only does man transcend both these dualities by another Emergence to the new stage of consciousness above.

It is a portrayal of this conflict between the opposing dualities of man's nature that we approach on a bright, snowy, Christmas afternoon at Taos pueblo.

The Cosmic Dualities

The Christian Mass has been disposed of; the Spanish-American and Anglo-American holidays are over. Now, according to tradition, the Deer Dance is to be given.

There is nothing Christian about the Taos Deer Dance. Nothing Spanish. Nothing English. An ethnologist is authoritatively muttering something about its originating in commemoration of the great snow of 1880, when four thousand deer were killed to prevent the people dying of starvation. But there's nothing so ethnological or easy about the Deer Dance as that, either. Nor does it provide such a *participation mystique* as we might expect from John Collier's description:* . . . "The Red Deer Dance began, and the Sacred Mountain which haunts the sky northwestward from Taos shuddered, and poured out a cold, flaming cloud to the sun and all the stars. It seemed that way. And veritably, within its own affirmation, through a multitudinous, stern, impassioned collective outgiving, the tribe's soul appeared to wing into the mountain, even to the Source of Things." It's not even a dance, as are the Buffalo, Turtle, and Eagle Dances at Santa Clara and San Ildefonso.

* *The Indians of the Americas,* W. W. Norton & Co., Inc., New York.

It is a mystery play as old, as subtle and profound as were the ancient Greek Mysteries of Eleusis and the Egyptian mysteries at Sais. Its players are cosmic forces, and it dramatizes the dualism of all life.

Perhaps we can take it after our Pueblo dinner of beef smothered in amole sauce, beans, dried squash, chiles, tortillas, coffee, store cake, and canned peaches. Even Ralph, the old trader with me. He has been so long among Indians he wears his old brown coat wrapped round his shoulders like a blanket. Picking at his loose teeth, he lounges across the snowy plaza. Looking out from his huge battered Stetson at the brilliantly blanketed figures gathering on the terraces of the two "mud piles," at townspeople bucking the drifts with horse, wagon, and Ford, at the clouds lifting over the white mountain behind.

We call it Taos Pueblo as if it were one thing: one compact town, one united people. And when, on good days, we bridle a horse and ride around the high slope of the mountain above it, the pueblo does reveal a singular compact unity. We see below us the two five-storied mud pyramids like the halves of a kernel when a nut is split open; and all around, like a shell, traces of the old circular wall that once enclosed them.

But to a visitor in the plaza today this scene of unity is broken. The crumbled adobes of the old wall are hidden by snowdrifts. The white central plaza itself is divided by the icy stream. And the two halves of the pueblo on its opposite sides loom up separate and alone. The north pyramid is called "Hlau-oma" (cold-elevated); the south pyramid "Hlau-gima" (cold-diminish). The people too are divided into moieties or halves, the Summer People and Winter People.

There seems a constant rivalry between them. Twice a year—in May, on Holy Cross Day when the wild plum thickets are white with blossoms, and in September, on San Geronimo Day when the first aspens are turning yellow—the ceremonial races are held. The two groups, naked and painted different colors, run in relays as if against each other. Why? To see from which pueblo-half will come next year's governor you will be told.

It isn't true of course. But it seems like it. One house divided against itself; one people opposed to another.

All Indian life is permeated with an exaggerated sense of duality. One of its two great polarities is the Encircled Mountain which extends invisibly upward towards the Sun Father. The other is the canyon, the *sipapu* which leads back down into the depths of our Mother Earth. Day and night, winter and summer, sun and moon, male and female, mountains, rivers and rains, the colors and the directions, the kachinas, the sand-painting figures with their stylized round or square heads, the dual Hero Brothers—everywhere in nature, ritual, and legend is manifested this duality.

The ancient Chinese named these two opposite principles or dualities *yin* and *yang*. *Yin*, meaning shadow, stood for the north side of a mountain and the south side of a river. *Yang*, its polar opposite, stood for the south side of a mountain and the sunny north side of a river. From this meaning of "light" and "dark" the principles expanded to all polar opposites: male and female, active and passive, emotion and reason; and in the individual psyche of man to the bi-polar tensions of the cerebral and sympathetic nervous systems.

Upon recognition of this was developed in the eighth century the esoteric religion of the Golden Flower, whose teachings have been absorbed into Taoism, Confucianism, Buddhism, and all modern religions of the East. It was built on the premise that man's psyche and the cosmos are related to each other as inner and outer worlds, and from the one a way leads into the other. That way is Tao, the "Meaning," the "Way" of Lao-Tzu, the Road of Life. And its secret is *The Secret of the Golden Flower, T'ai I Chin Hua Tsung Chih*, the Chinese Book of Life.

For the best translation and explanation of this remarkable book we are indebted to the eminent Chinese scholar, the late Richard Wilhelm, who prepared the original German edition, and to the late great psychologist, C. G. Jung, for its interpretation in terms of modern European psychology.

According to the Chinese, man develops into a multiplicity of individuals in each of whom the central monad or life-principle is enclosed. But even before birth, at the moment of conception, it separates into bipolar phenomena.

There is the dark feminine *yin*-soul, the earthly principle; and the light masculine *yang*-soul, the spiritual principle. Each is separated into the dual phenomena expressive of its impersonal and personal elements.

The impersonal element of the *yin*-soul the Chinese call *ming*. Signifying a destiny beyond man's conscious will, his fate, the duration of life, and the measure of vitality, it corresponds to the *eros* of modern Western psychology. The impersonal element of the *yang*-soul is *hsing,* the essence or creative consciousness by which a spiritual being is made human, and corresponding to the Western *logos.*

To these impersonal elements there correspond in corporeal-personal man bi-polar tensions activated by the interplay of these two psychic structures. The personal element *p'o* of the *yin* principle Jung recognizes as the *anima,* the personification of the unconscious; and the *hun* belonging to the *yang* principle, the *animus.* They correspond in living men to the cerebral and sympathetic nervous systems.

The dark and the earth-bound *anima* is linked with the bodily processes. At death, as a ghost-being, the *kuei,* it decays and returns to the earth. The bright and active *animus,* on the other hand, is the higher soul. After death, as the spirit or *shen,* it rises in the air in a superconscious condition and flows back into the reservoir of life.

Looked at from the standpoint of progressive evolution this eternal, superconscious, transcendental, spiritual "soul" is "good" as compared with the unconscious, earthly "soul" limited with human faults. Thus do the Navahos view it with a striking parallel.

According to Navaho eschatology also, man is born with bi-polar opposites, good and evil. The guiding principle of this evil is "a little thing, small as a grain of dust, which Changing Woman (the Earth Mother) places in the back of a person's head (where you see the depression) immediately after birth when the infant makes its first sound. It remains there throughout life, causing the person to have evil thoughts, bad dreams, and to make mistakes. Everybody releases a ghost at death no matter how good he is, for some evil must have become attached to him through thoughts or unintentional deeds. At death this thing goes to the north—the dark afterworld—turning into a ghost four days afterward."

A Navaho ghost, then, is the embodiment, after death, of the evil in man's life. The Navaho *chindi* is thus the equivalent of the Chinese *kuei,* "the one who returns" to earth; the earth-bound soul, the *p'o;* the European *anima.*

The Navaho spirit, symbolized by the breath of life, is the "good" which also rises into the air and ascends to the sun; the

Chinese *hun* made up of the characters for "daemon" and "cloud"; the European *animus.*

Thus, from birth, man is possessed of two primordial life forces, related as the instinctual and intellectual factors of his psychology. United in embryo, they separate; and man's evolutionary life is the struggle for predominance between these two forces.

If the dark unconscious, goaded by earthly passions, forces the intellect into its service, then both powers leak away and life consumes itself. At death the *anima,* because it is linked with the bodily processes, sinks to the earth and decays. The *animus* rises and flows back into the reservoir of life whence it returns to earth, beginning a new experience.

On the other hand, if the light *yang*-soul is able to master the forces of the dark unconscious, then a release from earthly passions takes place. The ego withdraws from entanglements in the outer world which waste its life forces, and creates within the inner monad a life independent of bodily existence. Such an ego is a god on earth, a saint or sage who, in his earthly existence, has learned to merge the cosmos of his psyche with the great cosmos. These beings, however, retain their corporeal-personal character. Not until one has completely transposed his ego and is no longer limited to the monad does he become immortal. He has achieved the immortality of the Golden Flower, the immortal spirit-body. And the means for achieving this constitute the Buddhist teachings of meditative yoga, the ancient Chinese precepts which are the Secret of the Golden Flower.

Such technical practices are not for us of the West; we must continue to develop our own scientific techniques, like modern psychiatry, to abet the natural life process. For as Jung warns, this "overcoming the *anima*" is fraught with danger to a civilization adhering so closely to the Western Christian, and especially to the Protestant, cult of consciousness. We have a devilish impulse toward violent repression of the instincts, which makes our spirituality hysterically exaggerated and poisonous. "In order to keep to this height in some fashion or other, it was unavoidable that the sphere of the instincts should be thoroughly repressed. Therefore, religious practice and morality took on an outspokenly brutal, almost malicious, character. The repressed elements are naturally not developed, but vegetate further in the unconscious and in their original barbarism." The result is evident in our overcrowded insane asylums; we are a people ill with a mass neurosis.

Not knowing that we must depend on an equal interplay of both forces, we have become the modern machine-made Euro-American whose spirituality has been dominated by a cold mentality.

We see spectres of him walking about the plaza now on this bright snowy Christmas afternoon, staring almost incredulously at a remnant of American "savages" still clothed in blankets and moccasins, waiting for a pagan "show" to come off. This civilized man, states Jung, "regards himself naturally as immeasurably above these things."

Yes . . . Individual man achieves his dominating rationality at great peril. For the more powerful and independent his consciousness becomes, the more the unconscious is forced into the background. Till finally it breaks free from the dark, feminine principle with its emotions and instincts reaching back into the depths of time and rooting him to his past. Man breaks free—into a neurosis of anxiety and discontent, into a paralysis of frustration. And once more he must be led back to health and sanity, to his roots, to a harmonic relationship with all the living universe.

"Here," interrupts Ralph. "The buggars are comin'."

It is time at last to listen with our eyes and hearts. For it is in the Taos Deer Dance that Pueblo ceremonialism best dramatizes this one of the two truths of the cosmic dualities.

Taos Deer Dance

They are coming indeed. A long line of strange figures emerging from the kiva at the far side of the plaza. Emerging as out of the white shrouded forests with all the wonder and the mystery and power of unseen forces now made visible to all eyes.

The clouds have lifted over the mountain. The sun has broken through. The pueblo sparkles with a light fresh fall of snow. On its terraces and house tops the people are still: the bright-blanketed Indians; the Mexicans in black *rebozos* and black mufflers; the Anglos shivering in their overcoats. All watching in frosty silence the figures crossing the hand-hewn logs over the icy stream, passing between the banks of drifted snow, filing across the still, dazzling plaza.

At the far end of the line one of the tiny Cosmic Dualities slips on the ice and falls on its cosmic rump. Another helps him to his feet, tenderly chafes his bare leg. Ralph chuckles; having broken through the magic circle, he always recognizes the god in man and admits the profane in the divine.

One sees them closer now.

Two Deer Chiefs, beautifully garbed in snowy white buckskin from head to foot, with branching antlers mounted on their heads. Two Deer Watchmen, dressed in white buckskin shirts, long fringed leggings and moccasins, and carrying arrow quivers of white buckskin decorated with colored beads.

Escorted by these, two women, both tall and heavy, dignified and middle aged. Attired in loose, white, ceremonial buckskin gowns with the left shoulder and both arms free, and walking sedately through the snow in high white buckskin boots. From the back of their freshly combed hair rise two high eagle feathers; on top of their heads is fastened a small bright tuft of parrot feathers. Around their neck in back hangs the skin of a wild mallard duck with its iridescent feathers. On their cheeks are painted black spots; around their jaws runs a black streak. In her right hand each carries a gourd rattle; in the left, two eagle-tail feathers and a sprig of spruce. They are the sacred personages, the Deer Mothers. Arrayed and painted in the kiva, they are escorted across the plaza carefully so no one can touch them. So they pass in quiet dignity, with lowered eyes—not quite close enough to touch, inviolable.

Behind them, in single file, all the animal forms of plain and forest: men wearing the heads and skins of deer, antelope, buffalo, wildcat, coyote, and mountain lion. They stalk slowly forward, bent over, a short pointed stick in each hand to serve as forelegs; heads and horns raised proudly; their lower bodies bare and unpainted under the drooping skins and pelts.

And following them, small boys similarly masked as fawn and cub, accompanied by the grotesquely painted clowns, the Black Eyes or *Chiffoneta,* carrying tiny bows and arrows.

So they all pass in the dazzling white silence, neither gods nor men nor beasts, but forces made visible to portray this great blood drama of their common heritage.

The people draw back respectfully; in their reverent stares shine too the wonder and the mystery. The mountain walls close in, the gray skies lower upon the snowy clearing between two cliffs. In it now form two lines of waiting figures. Then, slowly at first, the drum begins.

One by one, from the two opposite lines, the animals begin dancing. The deer, the antelope, the buffalo, the coyotes, wildcats, and mountain lions. Bent forward, horns tossing, the short, pointed forelegs stabbing down the snow.

Then down the aisle between them, down and back from each end, come the two Deer Mothers. Sedate, middle aged women with long experience, they are the best dancers in the pueblo. Confidently and slowly, as women dance, they come dancing . . . Tall, impervious, silent, they come dancing. Their white boots never lifting above the clinging snow, their heavy bodies moving rhythmically within the loose, supple buckskin gowns. At the turn they pause, shaking their gourd rattles, raising aloft their sprigs of spruce and eagle-tail feathers. Each showing behind, the glimmering sheet of iridescent color on her back. And in front an impassive face made stern by her spotted cheeks and the black streak around her jaw.

They all give way before her, down and back. The wild deer and graceful antelope, the massive buffalo, the wild coyotes, the snarling wildcats, the little mountain lions, and all the shrinking fawns and cubs. They all draw back and crouch down shudderingly, with strange low cries, from the sacred, inviolable Deer Mother.

Then each Deer Mother turns back, eyes down as if unconscious of their presence. And led by the Deer Chiefs each file of dancers follows her in great circles, spirals, and diagonals. Follow her, dancing in the soft powdery snow, uttering their strange low cries of resentment, their snarls of defiance; but unable to resist and being led back again into a long oval.

Within it the drum keeps beating. It is the pulse beat of eternity keeping time to the alternate flow of life's bi-polar tensions.

The dancing oval constricts now as the cub lions and wildcats draw back on the outside from the prancing deer and antelope. With wild, frightened eyes one of them timidly touches a deer. A loud whoop, a chorus of shrill yells. The Black Eyes come scrambling and leaping through the snow. One draws his tiny bow and shoots the deer with a yellow straw. Then flinging him over his shoulder, he runs off through the snow.

But the Deer Watchmen are watching. One of them

leaps forward out of the circle and pursues the escaping Black Eye. Across the plaza he is caught. His burden is let down, its deerskin straightened; and he is led back to bondage, panting.

Great fun, this! The swooping Black Eyes. The kicking, captive deer. The pursuing Deer Watchers. Yells. There is a mad scramble and fall in the snow. Often concealment behind one of the large ant-hill ovens, much dodging and twisting. Sometimes a show of violence.

But the fun does not obscure the deadly seriousness. The people do not laugh. For they divine in it the inexorable power of the female *anima* which holds in bondage the masculine *animus* forever striving to break free. And when a Black Eye does escape with his burden, trotting across the hewn-log bridge, they see it as a violation that must be ceremonially atoned for in the kiva; an "overcoming of the *anima*" that, unless it is validated as a spiritual release, becomes only an aberration from the norm leading to the neurotic destruction of the psyche.

So it continues in the snowy down-trodden clearing between the adobe cliffs, high on the backbone of a continent—this ancient blood drama of the primordial forces unleashed in all its children. The leaping, clutching Black Eyes. The swift escapes foiled by the wary Deer Watchmen. And all the while the Deer Chiefs tossing up their branching antlers beside the drummer as, up and down, the sacred Deer Mothers dance softly before the animals held in bondage.

They give way before her as the male ever gives way to the female imperative. They try to break free of the magic circle only to be pulled back as the consciousness in its wild lunges for freedom of the intellect is ever drawn back by the eternal unconscious. And all the time they utter their strange low cries, the deep, universal male horror at their submission. Out of them it wells in shuddering sobs of loathing and despair, as still they answer the call. On all fours, as the untamed, archaic, wild forces they represent, impelled to follow her in obedience to that cosmic duality which must exist to preserve and perpetuate even their spiritual resentment.

The two Deer Mothers keep on dancing: impersonal, impassive, with lowered eyes, as if as oblivious of the power fatefully bestowed upon them as of the obedience they command.

Yes. One senses now something both of the force that

holds us back and the force that pulls us forward on the road of self-fulfillment. Which by their bi-polar tensions keep us in equilibrium, enclosed within the warm flow of human life. For man in all his powerful lunges toward freedom is still bound to the opposite pole of his earth bound existence till on a higher level of consciousness these opposites are united again as at the beginning.

And when they leave, the Deer Mothers leading the animal shapes silently away across the blue shadowed plaza, it is as if they all withdraw into the white-robed mountains. Embodied forces discarding their assumed shapes, but leaving in us the truths of their existence, the magic and the wonder and the mystery of their portrayal.

3 The Source

Our Mother Earth

CORPOREAL-PERSONAL man, with his allegiance to the dark pole of his dual nature, is truly born from the earth. Hence the personification of the Earth Mother is one of the two primary images in the Navaho and Pueblo pantheons.

In Navaho mythology she is commonly known as Changing Woman. Yet there is a profound and subtle difference between them. The earth-world was formed by the primal union of the Earth Mother and Sky Father—of the cosmic forces of light and dark, positive and negative, out of the fourfold womb of creation. But it was still in a nebulous fluidity. Its form had not yet hardened; it was still in semi-darkness; mountains, stones, trees, animals, and people were all anthropomorphic; and man had not yet been created in his present form . . . When at the foot of the Mountain Around Which Moving Was Done, Changing Woman was born.

Changing Woman was found lying on the east side of a mountain in a bed of flowers marked by a rainbow. She had been born of the darkness and the dawn. Under the direction of the Holy People, First Man and First Woman brought her up on sun-ray pollen, pollen from clouds and the dew of flowers—the sacred elements of the three preceding worlds of fire, air, and water. When she came of age a Blessing Way, Walking into Beauty, was given her.

Today the same Blessing Way is embodied in every other Navaho Way; and the puberty ceremony is given every Navaho girl when she reaches womanhood. A great feast is prepared to which relatives and friends, especially those with marriageable young men, come for miles around. A large cake, perhaps three feet in diameter, is made of blue cornmeal, salt, and water, and put to bake all night in a hole in the ground. At sundown the girl is washed, dressed in her best velveteen and silver, and her face painted red. A couch of cedar boughs and fine Navaho blankets is prepared for her. Around it are stacked gifts for the attending guests: saddles, blankets, silver and turquoise, foodstuffs, store dishes, cooking utensils. On it the girl lies facing east while her closest women relatives lecture her on the conduct, duties, and responsibilities of a mature woman. Meanwhile around the fire the men singers begin a series of songs lasting all night.

At the first flush of dawn the encampment stirs. Singers and guests shout and howl the debutante out of camp. She runs a mile or so and stops. Dawn is just breaking like her life as a mature woman. She faces the four directions in turn with a prayer to aid her with their invisible forces on the road of life. Then she turns and runs back on her life road with all the strength she can muster. All the young men who have concealed themselves behind clumps of cedar jump out, yell encouragement, and pursue her. But the girl is young and strong and agile. None will catch her! She is simple too. How her silver-buttoned moccasins skim over the breast of Changing Woman. The first ray of the Sun Father strikes her painted red cheeks. The winds of the Four Directions lend her their strength. Her full young breasts heave. Her eyes sparkle.

"Ai!" The People shout. "Her Road of Life will be long and happy! See how stoutly she travels it!"

Her race over, the runner flings herself down on her couch. Her women relatives pummel her belly, smooth her hair, massage her body, stretch her arms and legs to make her strong for the ordeals of life. Now the cake is taken out, broken, and passed around, the presents are distributed. Everybody laughs happily. She is a woman now. She will be married within a year, no doubt!

So it was at the Emergence. With the maturity of her prototype, Changing Woman, the earth-world solidified into form and substance; earth and sky, the mountains and the stars, plants and animals assumed their proper roles. Impregnated by sun fire and water, she immaculately conceived the dual Hero Twins, and then gave birth to a new race—the Navahos. Changing Woman is thus practically identical with Our Mother Earth. Because she changes aspect with the seasons the Navahos call her Changing Woman: literally A Woman She Becomes Time and Again. Initiates in the spring when she is young are called "Changing Woman's Son"; in the fall when she is old, "Changing Woman's Grandson."

Iatiku, "Bringing to Life," is her name at Ácoma, Zia, and other Keres pueblos because at the Emergence she created the four directional mountains and brought to life plants, animals, birds, and fish. The Eternal Woman, young in the springtime, fructified by the sun and copious spring rains, bearing abundantly in summer, and aging in the fall to die and be born anew—this to all the Pueblos also is Our Mother Earth.

In Taos the interregnum between her death and rebirth is observed as the Time For Staying Still. On December first, a kiva chief sonorously announces its beginning from the highest house top. Until January tenth, when everyone takes a sunrise bath in the icy creek to conclude the period, all townspeople must move back into the pueblo from their summer homes in the fields and mountains. For these forty days there must be no digging, no plastering, no wood chopping within the pueblo walls. No singing, no dancing either. The plaza is barred to iron-shod hoofs and wagon wheels. Wood may be packed in only on burros. Step softly brothers! Our Mother Earth is sleeping under her blanket of snow. It is her rest for renewal, a gathering of life for another period of gestation. It is the Time Of Staying Still.

Throughout their life she gives her children everything they need to sustain them; she gives them their immemorial bread of life, or as the Navahos call it, their "gift of life"—the indigenous New World maize.

Botanists formerly believed that corn was developed from a wild tropical grass called *teosinte* from the Aztec *teosintl.* Today they refute the belief. Corn has no ancestral forms. It has reached a genetic maturity so complete that it is the most domesticated of all cereals and probably the oldest. Excavations in Bat Cave, New Mexico, containing maize, reveal deposits that had their beginning not later than 2500 B.C. Corn has been proclaimed the supreme achievement in plant domestication of all time. And of the three great world cereals—Oriental rice, European wheat, and American corn—corn is the most nutritious, versatile, and valuable crop today.

Navahos and Pueblos still plant it as of old. Many kernels are poked into the ground with an ancient planting stick: "four for the cutworm, four for the crow, four for the beetle, and four to grow." Unlike modern methods, Indian corn is planted deep—nearly a foot, because of its elongated mesocotyl which brings it closer to moisture. It also develops a single large radical which descends to the sub-soil and finds water where ordinary corn with shallow roots would perish. The original dry farmers, the Pueblos do not disturb the weeds which hold the earth together and protect the growing corn. They use a shallow plow that merely loosens the topsoil for water absorption, without disturbing the deeper soil and exposing the desert earth to wind and soil erosion.

Despite their practicality, Indian life is impregnated with its growing mystery.

In most pueblos during early spring there are ceremonies when the *acequia madre* or mother ditch is cleaned out so that the fields may be irrigated. Among the many planting ceremonies the Hopi Planting Dance is one of the most dramatic pantomimes. Symbolizing the marriage, birth, and growth of the corn are nine dancers. Four maidens dressed in traditional wedding garb, each carrying two ears of corn. Four youths dressed in regulation Hopi dance kirtles, their bare torsos painted the dull yellow of the earth. And an old man painted black and white, wearing a headdress of corn husks, and carrying the age-old planting stick and a bag of seed corn, who leads the young men and girls through an intricate maze of dance steps.

From the time it sprouts, every bit of the corn plant is used. The young sprouts are boiled as greens, the young stalks roasted in the ashes. Undeveloped ears are made into soup, and the first milk ears into mush and bread. Throughout the year corn is the staple food.

At every pueblo feast corn is served. A favorite dish is a stew made of cracked white corn and mutton; and the fine ground, paper-thin *piki* bread is famous as the coarse ground humble *tortilla* is common. The corn is ground between two stones, the concave Aztec *metatl*, the "modern" Spanish *metate*, and the small *mano* or Hopi *tumuh* or *piki* stones. To lighten the work, Corn Grinding Songs are sung.

Out of corn, then, springs another image, the Corn Mother who is synonymous with the Earth Mother.

The perfect ears of corn, those without blemish and with the tips ending in four full kernels, are saved for kiva ceremonies. They are called the Corn Mothers. Hence at Zia, *Iatiku* is symbolized by such a Corn Mother. Its hollow cob contains her breath; "she blew her soul into it." Also a drop of honey for it to feed upon.

It was from two ears of corn that the prototypes of man were created, according to the Navahos. Hence of their sacred four plants—corn, bean, squash, tobacco—corn is given the ranking color, white, and the direction, east, in ceremonial symbolism. The turkey (which almost became America's national bird—and still is at Thanksgiving) supplied corn at the Emergence: four seeds of white, blue, yellow, and all-colors; and it was these seeds when planted which spread the earth out. In Navaho sand-paintings, corn plants are recurring symbols, the Male Corn with round heads, the Female Corn with square heads four cornered as is the earth itself. With corn pollen the Navaho buckskin masks of the *Yei* are sprinkled, as are the Hopi kachina masks.

"Corn is the Hopi's heart," says an old proverb. So the tray of sacred meal is never absent from a Hopi ritual. At Taos on the Day of the Dead when the harvest is over, a bit of corn meal is placed on each grave with the acknowledgment: "I am the seed of the husk that lies here, and I am the seed of the husks which will follow after me, and this meal I now place here is the bond between us all." It is in corn meal that the Road of Life is drawn in Zuñi kivas. With pinches of corn meal Pueblo householders greet the rising sun from their terraced house tops. In Santo Domingo painted cornstalks upheld the altar even in the Catholic church until a few years ago.

Little wonder that corn is so closely identified with the earth. In the beautifully colored Indian corn of the Four Corners with its ears of white, blue, red, and yellow, it bears the symbolism of all the four world-wombs of Our Mother Earth from which mankind was successively born.*

The sacred *Popol Vuh* of Guatemala reports that the ancestors of the Quichés were four perfect men made from yellow and white maize, corresponding to Navaho belief. Among the Aztecs this personification of the two identical aspects of the Earth Mother and Corn Mother was called Tinonantzin or Tonantzin which means "Our Mother." When the Spaniards came she was worshipped at a great feast held on the hill Tepeyac, on the twelfth of December, just before the rains. As we have already learned from Father Sahagún,† she was given a new Spanish name and recognized by the Catholic church. Hence today, clad in her sky-blue mantle

* See p. 173.
† See p. 51.

"dotted with stars like toasted maize grains," and under her new name of the Virgin of Guadalupe, the dark and ancient Earth-Mother is still the Christian patroness of all Indian America.

In the beautiful Basket Dance at San Juan the two long opposite lines of women dancers, dressed in their oldest embroidered *mantas* and carrying large baskets, kneel and go through the pantomime of grinding corn. And at almost every pueblo on its Saint's Day is given a Corn Dance.

These vary in quality and intensity more than any other single feature of Indian ceremonialism; perhaps simply because they are the most common and participated in by all members of the community, priesthood and laity alike, and are the one rite open to all visitors—with the resultant influences of deterioration.

At Santo Domingo the Corn Dance has reached its highest development as a ceremonial, and has maintained its greatest intensity. It is one of the truly great Indian dances of America. In its purity of conception and authority of execution, with its beauty of style, its intricate patterns and subtle rhythms, it is a highly developed art form sprung from the soil itself. Above all, it is in flowing fleshly prose a profound and moving invocation of the spirit to the Corn Mother of all men, Our Mother Earth.*

The Sun Father

With the primary image of the Earth Mother there stands that of the Sun Father. Opposed to the dark, feminine, earth-born, unconscious principle, he embodies the light, masculine, conscious, spiritual principle of man's dual nature.

Pueblos and Navahos alike recognize the sun as the most powerful creative force in the universe. Personified as the Sun Father, he is the great creator, the original impulse, the primal source of all life.

Of the four directions east is the most sacred; and the color of his radiant light, white (which is a composite of all colors), is assigned to it. Every morning when he "comes out standing to his sacred place" Pueblo householders greet him with pinches of corn meal. A new born child is held up to him that he may grant it a long life. When a deer is killed its head is laid toward the east while he is sprinkled with meal and pollen. Pueblo men rarely expose

* Described on pp. 263-268.

their completely naked bodies; then only quickly to swim and bathe, never needlessly. Not because of an overt modesty, but to avoid exposing the penis to the sun, who might think him boastful of his manhood and take his creative power from him. From birth to death, man acknowledges the Sun Father's supreme creative power.

The Sun Priest or *cacique* is the ceremonial head of the pueblo. He holds office for life, and his fields are tilled for him that he may devote his time to making solar observations for his people. Every day he watches from the highest house top the sun's journey overhead from the east to the west. He marks the solstices by the limits of its setting north and south on the western horizon, thus determining the planting and harvesting times for the people. In Taos, Tsikomo peak in the Jemez range is thus called "Sun-leaves-house-mountain."

Every spring the members of each kiva in turn "work for the sun." Confined to the kiva for forty days and nights, they wear no bright colors, no article of machine-made clothing, eat no canned nor prepared food, and are not allowed outside except on rare occasions. At these times an old friend may meet one of them in the home and in the presence of the governor or another officer. The visit is brief. One offers his head of lettuce or cabbage, the fresh greens which are received so gratefully during their fast, and the little bottle of mineral oil or laxative tablets needed so badly during their prolonged days and nights of sitting without exercise. There is not much to be said. The visitor is prevented by the attendant officer—if not by common sense and good taste—from asking pertinent questions. And his friend is not interested in the casual happenings of the outside world. He sits there wrapped in his somber blanket, completely withdrawn. His cheeks are pale; he gulps the fresh air avidly; his gaze is inturned. He is no longer an active member of society. He has withdrawn from the world as an emissary of mankind to give his strength and life back to the sun, that the creator of all life may return it again.

This also is the meaning and purpose of the ceremonial races common to so many pueblos. In former times long distance races of fifteen or twenty miles were run through the mountains, in early January just after the winter solstice when the sun begins its northward journey, and at night to give the moon power, the runners praying to the Morning Star for strength,—the "world around" race.

At Taos the great ceremonial races are held twice a year: in spring, on May third, *El Dia de Santa Cruz;* and in fall on September thirtieth, *El Dia de San Geronimo.* During the preceding nights the members of two kivas sing to give strength to the runners. The race track runs east and west as the sun travels. It extends across the plaza past the south pyramid, through a break in the old pueblo wall, and on out beyond town. Here it is worn deep below the level of the field by countless generations of runners.

Here early in the morning gathers a huge crowd. The terraced walls quiver with color in the bright sunshine. In the plaza, more spectators gather around ground displays of pottery, little clay figures of animals, Navaho blankets, Apache baskets, and silverwork brought upriver to sell and trade. Still the plaza fills with more visitors. While up and down the long, stone-pitted race course the old men parade, with their green branches, keeping back the crowd. Years ago the noted Colorado photographer, Horace S. Poley, showed me some old wet plate slides of the races he had made nearly fifty years before when photographs were allowed. Except for an Anglo in a bowler hat, there was nothing to suggest that they were not made yesterday. Nor would the scene have been changed in the least had a Spanish *conquistador* been snapped standing there instead.

But now the runners gather in two groups at each end of the track—practically all the men and boys in the pueblo. Those from one pyramid preponderantly painted grey; and those beside them from the other, brown. Really a grotesque and heterogeneous assortment in both groups: brown, grey, yellow, red, vertically striped and horizontally streaked. All with tufts of eagle down stuck to the paint. With hair gathered in a knot on top or at the back in a chignon. Wearing nothing but breechcloths and strings of fur around the ankles.

At a signal the first two runners leap forward. Hurtling down the track, heads up, straining like two hounds. To release at the far end, relay fashion, two others who come stumbling and panting back up the course.

So it keeps up under the climbing sun, between the shouting visitors and the silent blanketed throng. Two naked boys down and two back. Whipped along by the old men on the sidelines with their green branches, their anxious shouts. "Oom-a-pah! Oom-a-pah!"

The track is a long 440 and a rough one. But they keep hurtling forward on bare, bruised feet. One stumbles on a protruding stone. Another, sick with over-exertion, vomits in the brush. An old man kneads his belly with curative fingers, then pushes him back into the line for yet another effort. For they know that man cannot obtain the energies of life without returning some of it to the source.

And the racers know it too. So they run not to win from one another, but to extend all their strength to the sun for his daily and seasonal journey. Just as the Cheyennes and the Kiowas, in their Sun Dance, kept dancing around the tall pole, buckskin thongs tied to muscle and sinew, until they had ripped out their own ligaments without betraying pain. The race of the individual against the limits of his own flesh. And the unending race of all humanity, the valiant expenditure of man's puny efforts and unfaltering courage to run forward with the everlasting wonder of creation.

Such also was the meaning of the human sacrifices in Aztec Mexico. We cannot condemn these rites without realizing that human sacrifice always has been a custom of many peoples the world over. In the Old Testament of our Christian Bible, Abraham proffered his son Isaac in sacrifice. In our homeland of England, the Druids practiced it at Stonehenge. It was a common occurrence in our new homeland of New England when our Puritan forefathers put to death as "witches" so many innocent women and "unsaved" children as a sacrificial atonement for their own psychoneurotic sense of guilt and spiritual frustration. We can only attempt to understand the real, the deeper significance behind the framework of the deed. Just as a future civilization will understand our present monstrous and needless sacrifice of human life as an offering to the Machine God of speed, materialistic wealth, and temporal power which we worship. For no man can serve the image of any god without sacrifice in kind.

Like the Pueblos today, the Aztecs recognized the sun as God-the-Father, and their civilization was founded upon a faith as ritualistic and inclusive of every phase of life. Their *teocallis* or temples were built on pyramids rising terrace upon terrace to a citadel of altars built around a central platform. In the Place of the Gods at Teotihuacan, built by the preceding Toltecs, both the citadel itself and the Pyramid of the Sun were laid out astronomically rather than architecturally like the Greek structures. They were oriented to the cardinal points of the four directions, allowing true deviations. That is, the center line deviated from the west to the north at an angle of 17 degrees, the exact deviation from true west of the sun at that latitude on the day it passed through its zenith, showing that it was indeed dedicated to the sun. The proportions were in accord with relationships between the planets. The lines were inclined where straight would be supposed and the steps were placed asymmetrically on a deliberate tangent. So that what today may first look like faulty architecture is really planetary geometry. Standing in its immense, sacred city—itself four miles long, two miles wide, and almost one solid block of massive monuments—and still standing, the Pyramid of the Sun rises to height of 216 feet from a base 750 feet square, larger than the Great Pyramid of Egypt.

The great pyramid in Aztec Tenochtitlan (now Mexico City) stood in a court paved with stones polished so smooth that the horses of Cortéz could hardly walk thereon: three hundred feet square, it rose nearly three hundred feet high (by his measurements) to a summit crowned with two lofty towers fifty-six feet high. Down in Oaxaca, at Monte Alban, the Zapotecs leveled a great hill to support a similar citadel of religious structures. At Cholula today one climbs what he thinks is a brush covered hill to a Catholic church on top; it is a pyramid of hand-hewn stone.

On top of these *teocallis* burned sacred fires, nearly six hundred in Mexico City alone. From these new fires kindled by the sun at the beginning of each fifty-two year cycle, flames were carried first to other altars and then to the hills and homes throughout the empire. This New Fire Ceremony symbolized the birth of a new sun, a new cycle, and the reassurance of life. The same meaning is implicit in the corresponding yearly ceremony still observed in Zuñi.

Like the pyramids, Aztec life was laid out astronomically in accordance with the dominating place of the sun in their scientific world view. The twenty-four-ton Aztec calendar stone, with the year 1091 * established as its beginning, divided time into fifty-two-year cycles, each year divided into eighteen months of twenty days each, with an intercalation of five days to equalize the calendar at the end of each cycle. In full knowledge of solstices, equinoxes,

* Roughly approximating the date of 1022 established for the first arrival of the seventh tribe migrating south from Aztlan. P. 31.

eclipses, the year of Venus, and other phenomena, the solar synchronization of the Aztec Calendar Stone was more accurate than the European calendar even after the Gregorian reform which followed the conquest of the Spaniards.

From this vast astronomical and cosmological system rose the Pyramid of the Sun. And reaching from its apex to an emotional, intuitional, and cosmic level too high for any but symbolical representation, the institution of human sacrifice.

The victim was selected a year before from the bravest and most handsome captives. He was arrayed in splendid dress, given a royal suite. Wherever he went he was attended by a train of pages. People did him homage. Priests instructed him how to perform his part with grace and dignity. On the day of sacrifice he renounced this worldly acclaim. Ascending the pyramid he threw away his flowers, broke the musical instruments in his hands. On the summit six priests received him. Five bound him on the sacrificial stone. The sixth, with a knife of *itzli,* an obsidian hard as flint, dexterously opened his breast, and, tearing out his heart, still palpitating, held it up to the sun while the multitudes below prostrated themselves in humble adoration . . . Thus Prescott, who based his account on that of Father Sahagun.

There were other victims too. Tribal chieftains and children whose parents had gladly offered them for sacrifice. Captives from war: wars in which the warriors strove not to kill but only to capture for the ceremonial sacrifice which honored captor and captive alike. And when there was no war, strange Battles of Flowers whose only purpose was to allow contending tribes to capture victims for sacrifice. And towards the last Aztec cycle, beginning in 1507, when the practice had degenerated and the Spaniards were on their way, constant war and sacrifice of all enemy warriors—twenty thousand in one year it is said.

Yet even these degenerate extravagances were embodied in a faith and ritual whose significance was the constant renewal of the union between man and the source of all life, the Sun Father. A mass participation in which the victim regarded himself as an emissary of man giving his strength and life, like Pueblo runners, back to the sun.

Little wonder that when the Spaniards arrived, five years later, the first welcoming gift sent to Cortéz by Moctezuma was an image of the sun in beaten gold, big as a cart wheel. The

Spaniards had arrived from the primary direction, east; were white as its directive color; and their arrival coincided with the predicted return of the Toltec Quetzalcoatl.

Ever southward from the Pueblos of the Four Corners, ever backward into time, extend the prehistoric civilizations of the sun. Southward and backward from the Aztecs, Zapotecs, and Toltecs. Through the Mayas with their wonderful sacred cities; their great pyramids with four flights of ninety-one steps each, adding to 365 with the summit level to fit the calendar year; with a calendar itself so phenomenally accurate that it was possible to distinguish without duplication any given day in 370,000 years—a calendar so far in advance of European astronomy that Western science has barely now caught up with it. Still backward and southward to the Inca empire high in the Andes of South America.

The Incas too were "sun-worshippers," but not in the ignorant and pagan way that we suppose. What they really worshipped was the ideal of radiance in expansion as the supreme power of the universe. Just as *Ouranos,* the Greek word for "Heaven," actually means "infinitely expanding activity," so does the supreme power of God-the-Father, the Sun Father who lives in Heaven, manifest itself as the infinitely expanding radiance which imbues all things with life.

This conception embraced the whole religious, political, and economic life of an empire that spanned thirteen generations and 380,000 square miles throughout Peru, Bolivia, and Ecuador. Inca means sun. The Inca, the ruler, was regarded as the Son of the Sun: the living symbol on earth of the planetary ruler. "He was not the light, but came to bear witness to the light." Under him were priests who maintained the gold-sheathed walls of the Temple of the Sun with its huge ceremonial sun of solid gold and moon of gleaming silver; watched the "Sun Fixing Place" or great sun dial; conducted the rituals. There were Virgins of the Sun also, girls and women of all ages corresponding to all the stages in the growth of maize. Although it is asserted that there were no human sacrifices, it now seems certain that some of these were sacrificed at the Sun Temple at Pachacamac. Below the priests were the nobility and administrative officers who governed a communistic autocracy which we will learn was as novel, benevolent, and practical as any ever known.

Preceding the empire of the Incas and out of which it

grew was the Tiahuanacan civilization; and before this the pre-Tiahuanacan culture finally centering on the thirteen thousand-foot-high slopes around Lake Titicaca in Bolivia. Tiahuanaco means "City of the Dead," and it had been long a dead city when the Incas thus named it. But still there stands one of the finest specimens of stone cutting in the world—cut with mathematical precision before the discovery of metal. It is thirteen and a half feet long, seven feet wide and a foot and a half thick. It is the lintel of the Gateway of the Sun. On its eastern side is carved a visual representation of the Tiahuanacan god surrounded by twenty-four lesser gods; and on its western side are carved designs and niches for images. The god of Tiahuanaco was Viracocha or Pachacamac, the Uncreated Creator. Ages later the Ninth Inca presented this concept to his priests in an effort to restore the ancient postulate which placed Viracocha even above the sun. But the cult was too abstract even for the ruling caste.

With Viracocha, the Uncreated Creator, the abstract concept of that which unites even the concepts of the God Father and the Goddess Mother into one "Unbecome, Unborn, Unmade, Unformed"—which is also the most esoteric principle of Mahayanistic Buddhism originating on the other backbone of the world in the Tibetan Himalayas and held beyond conception by the finite mind—the mists of the past roll back beyond living stones, beyond memory. Beyond this present world of earth. Beyond the first world of primordial fire created by the sun.

Two thousand years. Twenty thousand. How can we measure the scope and depths of these great and ancient civilizations existent in a time sequence which we do not understand?

We only know that the Pueblo and Navaho concept of the Sun Father owes nothing to those of Tibet, China, Persia, Egypt. It is a belief common to all Indo-America. It was not new when the Navahos ground medicines for their Flint Way and Shooting Way ceremonials in that legendary Flint Home which was the Sun Temple of the Pueblo cliff dwellers at Mesa Verde. Nor was it new when the earliest Pueblos themselves carved their first kiva in the Rock. It is a faith rooted in and stemming from the soil of America, flowering in some of the most spiritually developed civilizations that have ever existed, and still bearing in the pueblo city-states of the Four Corners.

The Formulized Father

Let's not sell this short as sentimental nonsense. Inclined as we are to segregate mythology, science, and religion as irreconcilable domains, we must remind ourselves that we are as devout sun worshippers as the Pueblos, Navahos, Aztecs, and Incas.

Their Sun Father is to modern science also the center and supreme power of our solar system, the father of its family of planets and their satellites, the planetoids, the comets, and meteors.

From it was born our planet Earth as the first world of fire. According to the nebular hypothesis it was pulled out in an equatorial bulge from a spiral nebula whose core was the sun and shed as a ring of gas eventually cooling, liquefying, and solidifying. Or according to the planetesimal hypothesis, shot out from the sun in an explosive bolt of gas upon the near collision of the sun with a passing star, the bolt developing into a swarm of solid particles called planetesimals which finally congealed. Or as held by the gaseous-tidal hypothesis, drawn out from the sun in a long, streaming filament of gas by the tidal forces of a passing body, this breaking into sections and contracting into spheres which became our planets. In all cases first gaseous and self-luminous, full grown at birth, and cooling through a molten stage to solidify at the beginning of our geologic time.

Like the earth itself, life on it also derived from our Father Sun. According to the theory of radiobiogenesis the first living organisms were created by the heat and light energies of the sun—by the action of ultraviolet rays on water charged with carbonic acid and mineral salts. From this first unicellular protoplasm life evolved, as Darwin's theory of evolution first postulated, up through the animal world of form. Through Triassic theriodent reptile, bird, quadruped, simian, anthropoid ape. To man ape, primitive man, modern man. There now seems evidence that life evolved into the animal kingdom from the vegetable and mineral kingdoms as well—through the complete stages of existence suggested by the Pueblos' and Navahos' and Buddhists' four worlds of fire, air, water, and earth. Radioactive carbon 14 which lives at least five thousand years is no longer regarded as solely a product of nuclear bombardment in cyclotrons; it has been found in minerals and every living being, including man. As the Pueblos believe: there is no dead earth; inorganic matter has life. Places do not exist; they live.

They live by virtue of the infinitely expanding radiant energy of the sun, which provides the earth with life-giving warmth, lifts the vapors that return as rain and snow, sets the atmosphere in motion, and thus motivates all the life on the planet.

Nothing moves faster than light. Thus the speed of light from the sun, 186,000 miles per second, is the basic constant on which science builds all its knowledge, mathematical formulae, researches, theories, postulates, and probabilities. Without it there would be no Machine Age. No Machines. And no *Deus ex Machina* for us to worship as the soul of progress.

What is the composition of the sun? We only know that with a temperature reaching forty million degrees Centrigrade, it consists of no elements, no molecules, no atoms; just simply free neutrons.

What is its mysterious radiant energy, so sacred to us and the Indians alike? And how does it reach us? Science first thought that it travelled from the sun in a continuous wave motion like that of water waves. Then Max Planck discovered that it was shot out from the sun in bombardments of discontinuous particles of energy or quanta—true arrows of the sun.

High in the upper atmosphere such energy is formed when mysterious rays from outer space strike air atoms. According to the Fermi hypothesis these cosmic rays were born two million years ago, when tiny, positively charged protons collided with a magnetic field in a galactic cloud. Striking the atoms of the earth's atmosphere, they shatter the atoms into their component parts: the positively charged protons, the negatively charged electrons that circle the nucleus, the uncharged neutrons, and produce as new particles the mesons from the energy which binds the nucleus together. These mesons live only two millionths of a second, then disintegrate with a burst of energy. Hurtling down to earth. Piercing the bodies of men twenty times a second. Driving one thousand feet into the earth's crust. Compared to this energy the power derived from our fission of uranium, which releases only one-tenth of one per cent of the power stored within one atom of uranium, is manifestly negligible. This is the force that binds the universe into one living whole. The cosmic energy imbuing all matter with life.

But with the discovery that, since light is energy, sunlight has mass and is affected by a gravitational field, it remained only for Albert Einstein to come forth with the most significant statement made by modern man. All matter is merely condensed energy. In his now famous mass-energy equation he stated it mathematically in five symbols. $E = MC^2$. Energy is equivalent to mass multiplied by the square of the velocity of light.

This is modern Western man's mathematical definition of the infinitely expanding source energy which gives life. And the sun itself is that inconceivable mass which is defined by its boundless and infinite life-giving energy divided by the square of its superlative speed constant. $M = \frac{E}{C^2}$. The Formulized Father of Science; the Sun Father of Mythology; the Our Father Which Art in Heaven that Religion calls God. "In Him was life, and the life was the light of man." So spoke John the Baptist in the familiar terminology of Christianity.

It is not the purpose of this inquiry to offend the orthodox religious by drawing an obnoxious analogy. But it is neither an empty analogy nor a matter of propriety. For between the conceptual images of this one Divine Power as held by the church and the laboratory there is no correlation nor identity, as among those of the Pueblos, Navahos, Aztecs, and Incas. And it is due to this gap, this cultural lag, that we are faced with the tragic consequences which will be discussed in later chapters.

It may not be solely a coincidence, as we shall see, that the Los Alamos atomic research laboratory is located on "The Hill" above the old pueblos of Jemez, Santa Clara, and San Ildefonso, so close to that Navaho Mountain of the East, sacred to the sun.

Last year a significant thing happened. A ceremonial dance was scheduled to be held in San Ildefonso. When we went down to see it we learned that it had been called off for the first time in the memory of man. Most of the young Pueblos selected to participate were working up on "The Hill" above, and had been obliged to work an extra shift.

The incident marked the end of an era and beginning of another; the supersedure of one ritualism and symbolism by another. But without a break in the continuity; without a deviation from man's constant recognition of the Sun Father as the primal source of life.

4 The Return

THERE IS Our Mother Earth, then, from whose canyon-womb, the kiva *sipapu*, the Place of Emergence, man was born from the preceding four worlds into his present state of existence.

There is the Sun Father, the supreme power of the universe, the creator of all life, the primal source.

And there is the Road of Life. It is a long one and a difficult one. For man is at once born of the Earth Mother and the Sun Father and acknowledges allegiance to both of the cosmic dualities which they symbolize. Hence the supreme purpose of his life is to resolve within himself the conflict of these polarities so that he may finish his road in harmonic relationship with both and with all the universe.

But this introduces a paradox. In the Zuñi kiva universe the corn meal Road of Life runs from the fire pit to the altar. And in their ritual chants they sing: "From the Place of the first beginning we have come." . . . "From the Sun Father where our roads come forth." For the Sun Father created not only man, but the first world of fire. He is the original impulse, the primal source, the beginning of the road.

Yet in another aspect he is the final consummation, the end of the road. In the Hopi kiva sand-paintings, the Road of Life leads from the *sipapu*, the place of emergence, through the concentric colored squares symbolizing the previous worlds, out toward the east, the rising sun. In Navaho eschatology the spirit or breath of life in man returns to the sun at death. To return to "live in the sun" is the goal of all Pueblos. Hence to the Zuñis the Road of Life is synonymous with "The Road of Our Sun Father"; and in their ritual chants they pray:

> That our roads may reach to where the
>   life-giving road of Our Sun Father comes out;
> That this may be, I add to your breath now.

Thus the two paradoxical aspects of the Sun Father as the beginning and the end of man's evolutionary road, the source and the consummation of life.

How do we explain this? What is the meaning, the purpose of life? A life that ever turns back upon itself only to end where it started?

Since time began, the answer has been sought by all mankind, and the attempts to explain it have constituted all the great religions, all the divergent faiths and cults and creeds that have arisen throughout the world. None of them have answered it fully. Sometimes the devout seeker, in his despairing search, asks where is the final statement—the complete doctrine of life? Life alone is that statement, that doctrine. All others are partial. For it alone expresses the infinite thought, the infinite pattern, which in turn expresses the infinite creative will we call God. It is a road that must be travelled.

Hence in the cosmogenesis and eschatology of the Pueblos and Navahos we cannot expect to find more than barely visible traces of the pattern. But these traces are amply confirmed by the oldest, greatest, and most penetrating tenets of all religions. And the pattern they indicate in their own idiom, in their own symbolism, cannot be misunderstood. But to understand it we must recapitulate all that we have learned of Indian ceremonialism from its comparison with Western science and Eastern Buddhism and synthesize their physical and metaphysical meanings.

Withdrawal and Return

Conceived in his mother's womb, man recapitulates in nine months all his previous existences in the former worlds of fire, air, and water. Then born into the present earth-world he leads for some twelve years an earthly human-animal life of instinct, sense, and nerve. But this is not enough. For earthly human life is not sufficient to itself. It depends upon and is part of all life. So now he must be born again: into a consciousness of the greater life. And so another umbilical cord must be broken: the psychological tie which binds him to his earth-mother. From a child he must be reborn a man; from the lesser life of the flesh he must be reborn into the greater life of the spirit.

Hence, around the age of twelve, the Pueblo boy is entombed again in the womb. In that spiritual womb which is the complete symbolized universe and the heart of the Rock—the kiva.

The period of his gestation is long—twice as long as was his first, for the life it prepares him for is likewise longer. In these eighteen months the initiate is withdrawn completely from home, family, and pueblo life. Only at night is he allowed out of the kiva for fresh air and exercise. Under the tutelage of the older men he is taught by word of mouth the esoteric ceremonialism of the pueblo—the history, legends, and myths of the tribe; the long memorized chants; the symbolism of the kiva; the meaning of the masks, dances, and rituals; the names and attributes of the innumerable gods and the laws of world creation and world maintenance which all this articulates.

Aside from its primary purpose this long withdrawal has an immediate practical value. The mother's hold upon the boy is completely broken. There is no danger of his developing an oedipus complex through prolonged pampering at home. Nor does it allow the father an opportunity to assert a compulsive dominance, inculcating in the boy a resultant hatred of all authority. When the period is over and the boy walks out, it is in new moccasins, bearing a new name, and as a formally adopted member of the tribe. He is no longer a child living in his mother's house, but a man living in the wide universe. A sentient being awakened to his responsible cosmic role.

Such prolonged initiations are not the rule in all pueblos. Some are shorter. Others are intermittent. Still others more complex, involving a vast complicated rigmarole: presentations of the initiates by their ceremonial fathers, the bestowal of new names, their adoption into various priesthood, society, or kiva groups; fasts, vigils, pilgrimages, dances. In Zuñi and the Hopi pueblos, where kachinas are so prominent, it may reach a severe and frightening climax. At the beginning the kachinas flog each boy ceremonially four times each on legs, arms, and body with yucca whips. At the end the kachinas take off their masks and place them on the boy.

Then he in turn whips them, being warned never to reveal their secret lest the true kachinas which they represent cut off his head with a stone knife.

It is a moment of utter disillusionment to learn for the first time that the gods before whom the boy has cringed all his childhood are but his uncles and neighbors dressed in masks. Yet in that moment, as he himself wields the whip of authority within the sacred mask, is born the supreme truth that all men must sometime learn. There are no gods as we childishly know them. The gods are the invisible cosmic forces of the universe. And they reside in man who, if he wills, can evoke them for the common good. It is a prophecy and a promise of that time when man shall return to and be synonymous with the source power of all creation. Meanwhile from his long withdrawal, he returns to his daily life fortified by the powers that are his to evoke.

According to Bergson it is precisely through such individuals who withdraw from life for an inward development of personality and then return to perform creative acts in the field of action that society takes its great steps forward.

In a chapter of his long *The Study of History* under the same heading as this section, Arnold J. Toynbee adheres to the same thesis. "All creative personalities pass first out of action into ecstasy, and then out of ecstasy into action on a new and higher plane." This alternating movement he calls withdrawal and return. It is a characteristic found in all aspects of life. In individual men, great statesmen, soldiers, and philosophers who withdraw for a time from social toils and then return as leaders of the renowned movements in history. In nations and civilizations themselves.

He quotes Walter Bagehot: "All the great nations have been prepared in privacy and in secret. They have been composed far away from all distractions." Thus the withdrawals of Athens from political dynamics; of England from Continental entanglements during the Elizabethan era; of the "isolationist" United States;—all creative preludes to their return to mastery over their respective spheres of action.

In this sense we ourselves can interpret the present continental submergence of all Indo-America under Euro-American influence as but a long withdrawal—for building back its preponderance of Indian population, synthesizing its ancient culture with that of new technologies, restating its own values in modern terms

—preparatory to its return into the world arena as a dominant force again.

But pre-eminently the withdrawal and return motif as passive meditation and active application expresses itself in the religious field. It is fundamental to all mystics, saints, and religious leaders of mankind. Siddhartha Gautama, the Sakya aristocrat, renounces his life and family for seven years to become Gautama the Buddha, who re-establishes Buddhism as the religion which today holds the most adherents in the world. Muhammad after a withdrawal of fifteen years as a caravan-trader in the Arabian steppes, returns to Mecca as the master of Arabia and the Prophet of modern Muhammadism. Another world-religion, Christianity, is built entirely on the motif.

Jesus of Nazareth vanishes from Biblical-historical sight at the age of twelve, the age when a Pueblo initiate enters the kiva. Some scholars believe that He retired to Egypt and that He was there initiated into the mysteries by Buddhistic mystics from India and China, philosophers from Greece, and astronomer-priests from Egypt, who teach those esoteric truths underlying all faiths and creeds. He emerges again to view years later and, when He rides into Jerusalem, He is hailed by the multitude as the Son of God. Conscious of His mission and with His own idiom of parables, He withdraws again after His baptism by John into the wilderness for forty days—the time required of kiva members when they "work for the sun." And again, conscious of His impending betrayal, into the "high mountain apart" which is the scene of His Transfiguration. And now this great myth-drama, this passion and mystery play, this great sacred ceremonial, builds swiftly to its tremendous, spiritual climax. In the Crucifixion, Jesus duly suffers the death of mortal man. But only to withdraw into the tomb in order to rise immortal in the Resurrection. To withdraw from Earth to Heaven only to return again in the Second Coming—"a precedent in Christian mythology which has no parallel," adds Toynbee, this "future return to Earth of an historical figure who had already lived on Earth as a human being."

To us then the immuration of Pueblo boys in the kiva, and the traditional immuration of the very pueblos themselves from the materialistic life swirling about them, is easily understood. They both stem from man's basic need to go back to the source of all creation for a constant rejuvenation of his creative force.

Plato also was an initiate into the ancient mysteries. In his allegory of the cave he likens mankind to prisoners in a cave, standing with their backs to the light, imagining that the shadows cast on the back wall are the ultimate realities . . . until suddenly one of them is released to see the light and the realities which cast the shadows. That cave is the heart of the Rock, the Pueblo kiva, from which some chosen prisoners are indeed released to see the light stemming from the Sun Father.

They are all metaphors. The womb, the cave, the kiva, is the cavern of the human soul. Into it man ever retreats and emerges again on a higher plane. In this way only our gods are born. It is the Navaho Way.

Where the Two Came to Their Father

It happened just after the Emergence when Big Giant, Rock Monster Eagle, Big Horned Monster, Rock Monster That Kicks People Off, and all the other monsters were troubling the people. Changing Woman sat in the sun. Four days later she had a baby. Next day she sat in a pool underneath a canyon ledge and let the water drip on her. Four days later she had another baby. Both were boys. The elder brother was bold and active, the younger twin weak and shy.

They walked in four days, and they grew every four days, like corn. Changing Woman hid them from the monsters till they were twelve years old. Then one day when she was asleep they went to find their father, the sun, to ask if he would help them get rid of the monsters.

To start they stepped on two blue crosses, thence to a cloud, and from that to a rainbow. It was a wonderful and dangerous journey for the older boy, Changing Woman's Son, and his younger brother, Changing Woman's Grandson. The Cutting Reed People, Cat Tail People, Water Bug People, and the Rock That Claps Together all tried to kill them.

But Spider Woman, Rainbow Man, Little Wind, and Big Fly gave them charms, songs, and advice on what to do when they reached the House of the Sun. It was guarded by four big bears, four big snakes, four big winds, and four big thunders. Yet they were not frightened for they had the power to enter.

Once inside, a girl met them: she was daughter of the

sun, also Turquoise Girl, White Shell Girl, and Grandchild of Darkness. Wrapping one boy in a black cloud and the other in a blue cloud, she hid them from the sun.

Now (as in Jack and the Beanstalk!) the sun came home. Discovering the brothers, he and a man working for him, named Water Carrier, put them through a series of ordeals. The twins passed every test, answered every question. The sun then knew indeed that the brothers were his sons.

"My son," he said to the elder, "your name is Monster Slayer. My grandson," he said to the younger, "your name is Child Born of Water." To them he said, "I will give you my wisdom before you go down. You must always use it and hand it down, so that my wisdom will always be on the earth."

But they wanted to kill the Big Giant at the Mountain of the South. The Big Giant was also the sun's son. Yet the sun gave his permission, saying, "He has four lightning arrows, and he will shoot them at you first, and you must get all four arrows."

Now they were ready to return. All this happened at the time of the new May moon, which divides the year into half summer, half winter.

They went down to the Mountain of the South where the sun helped them to kill the Big Giant. Their lightning arrows cut the mountain in half, as is Mount Taylor today. They killed all the monsters, ridding the people of fear. Then they returned to Changing Woman at the Mountain Around Which Moving Was Done. But because they had killed too much the Heroes became weak and sick. So over them the Twelve Holy People gave *Where the Two Came to Their Father* for the first time, to cure them.

This ceremonial perpetuating the Hero Brothers' adventure and all the songs, rituals and wisdom they brought back is a Navaho war ceremonial formerly given over warriors before they left on a raiding party, and it was still given volunteers and draftees inducted in World War II. Like most ceremonials it is also used for protection against sicknesses of both body and mind. The ceremonial can last two nights and a day or five nights and four days. In the latter case dry paintings are necessary. Apparently there are only two remaining singers who know the ceremonial: Jeff King, seventy-five years old, and his teacher's son, Hosteen Belagan, eighty-three. It was due to this fact, Miss Maud Oakes told me, that she was able to persuade King to allow her to record and publish his sand-paintings and his version of the myth in one of the fine monographs of the Bollingen Series.*

Nevertheless we are not restricted to this one interpretation of a minor ceremonial. The hero of the major nine-night *Shooting Chant,* given Father Berard Haile by Grey Eyes, and given Gladys A. Reichard and Franc J. Newcomb by his pupil, Red Point, is the four-figured aspect of the Navaho twin war god, the Man Who Killed Fear. In his *Origin Legend,* Washington Matthews details his story, interpreting his name, Nayenezgani, as Slayer of Enemy Gods, and that of his brother, Tobadzistsini, as Born For Water. Haile identifies him as Monster Slayer with the spelling Na·ye· 'ne· zyané. Another complete ceremonial *Monster Way,* celebrates his slaying of the monsters. Parts of it are included in Haile's recorded *Enemy Way* and *Flint Way.* In fact almost every Navaho ceremonial mentions Monster Slayer or includes some of his songs.

In Cushing's transcriptions of the Zuñi creation myth we find a particularly striking parallel.† "Then did the Sun Father take counsel within himself, and casting his glance downward espied, on the great waters, a Foam Cap near to the Earth Mother. With his beam he impregnated, and with his heat he incubated the Foam Cap, whereupon she gave birth to Uanam Achi Piahkoa, the Beloved Twain . . ." who later descended to lead the people up through the four underworlds. "To them the Sun Father imparted, still retaining, control-thought and his own knowledge-wisdom, even as to the offspring of wise parents their knowledge is imparted and as to his right hand and his left hand a skillful man gives craft, freely surrendering not his knowledge . . ."

Uanam Achi Piahkoa, like the Navaho Hero Twins, is dual: Uanam Ehkona, the Beloved Preceder, and Uanam Yaluna, the Beloved Follower. They too are the Twin Brothers of Light, the Elder and the Younger, the Right and the Left.

Among the Hopi the War Twins are named Pookonghoya and Balongahoya; at Ácoma and other Keres pueblos, Masuwi and Ayoyewe.

But we are less concerned here with the ethnological background of the story than with the esoteric meaning of their

* *Where the Two Came to Their Father,* by Maud Oakes and Joseph Campbell. Pantheon Books, Inc., New York, 1943.

† "Outlines of the Zuñi Creation Myths," by Frank Hamilton Cushing. 13th Annual Report, Bureau of American Ethnology, 1891-2.

adventures. Monster Slayer is bold and active, with all the destructive potencies of the black north. He is addressed by Changing Woman as "my son." It is he who takes the initiative, who walks to the right, and accomplishes the death of most of the monsters.

Born of Water is weak and shy. His nature is akin to the benign blue south. By both Changing Woman and the sun he is called "my grandson." He walks to the left, on the heart side. Sometimes he walks behind. Later, in some versions, he merely stays behind to inspect the monsters which his brother has killed alone. Hence in these versions he is often called Who Gazes on the Enemy.

They are two, and they are one. For "except a man be born of water and of the spirit, he cannot enter into the kingdom of God."

These Hero Twins, the sun child and the moon child or water child, are the personalized representations of the two opposite reality principles, the cosmic dualities inherent in man: the *yin* and *yang* of Eastern philosophy, the *anima* and *animus* of Western psychology. But not yet are they polarized and split apart. Not yet do the brothers know their true natures and names. Both are still black in color; and together in the darkness of their unenlightened nature they start on the Way Where the Two Came to Their Father.

Their quest is for the secret of the Golden Flower, the Light which with life returns to itself; the Far Journey of Yu Ching and Lu Tzu. It is the Tao Way, penetrating the magic circle of the polar duality of all phenomena and returning to the Undivided One, Tao. It is the Buddha Path to Nirvana, as contrasted with Sangsara, the universe of matter and phenomena.

It is finally the universal psychical transmutation of limited human nature into the limitless divine nature, uniting the microcosmic consciousness of man with the macrocosmic all-consciousness. For not until man establishes this communion between normal human consciousness and the supernormal cosmic consciousness does he attain to true understanding of himself.

Joining the unenlightened human nature to the enlightened divine nature by the process of scientific meditation or yoga, which means simply "to join"—this is the symbolic rainbow path, spanning earth and heaven, which the Heroes travel.

Still children, still undeveloped, they are at first under the influence of the eternal mother, the feminine *anima*. She appears at the start as Changing Woman. Then as the crone, Old Age, who marks the bounds of human consciousness. Finally as Spider Woman, the fate mother or destiny who must help weave the cosmic pattern.

Spider Woman gives them the feather she has stolen from the sun. It enables them to proceed safely through the many dangers and obstacles which beset them. On the feather, as well as on the arched path of Rainbow Man, they travel. Little Wind also teaches them to "throw their breath" for protection. The feather we know. It is the breath of life which carries man beyond the precincts of mortal life; the divine essence which alone can raise to consummation in the great reservoir of life.

Thus by control of the breath, the in-breathings and outbreathings of the creative essence, do the Buddhist yogins in meditation make the same psychic pilgrimage. Rhythmically "sun breathing" through the right nostril, "moon breathing" through the left, just as the sun child rides to the right on his feather and the water child to the left. Rhythmically breathing: inhalation, retention, exhalation. With every change of breath a change of thought. Till all thought forms roll by, indifferent and detached as clouds . . . Till the yogic traveller reaches the realm of nonthought. This is called "The First Resting Place," the first stage of mental quiesence attained; and the yogin looks on, mentally unperturbed at the interminable flow of thoughts, as though he were tranquilly resting on the shore of a great river watching the water flow past.

This is the ocean Monster Slayer and Born for Water now reach, and in the corresponding sand paintings they are seen standing on its shore. It separates the world of reality from the shadow world reflected and inverted below. Hence the color symbolism from now on is reversed according to the color systems for above and below first pointed out by Washington Matthews.

Ahead stands the House of the Sun, on the water and yet in the sky where the two realms meet, prismatically gleaming in full glory with all the four colors of the directions. This realm of the true spiritual selfhood we vulgarly recognize as "Heaven" and the "Happy Hunting Ground." There is nothing mortal imagination can envisage that it does not contain; it is teeming with game, grain, flowers, all the bounty of creation. For this is the noumenal source, the fountain head of life.

But its treasures are not for the worldly; it is guarded by four powers of each of the four directions. Nor do the heroes desire them. They have been purged of all earth bound desires, and their true natures are perceived by their sister, the sun's daughter, who lets them in.

The sun discovers them. Water Carrier helps them prepare for their initiation. Another name for him is Moon Carrier. In his dual capacity of governing the waters and their tidal power, as opposed to sun power, he is the polar opposite of the sun but subservient to him. And now in the initiation comes the fiery furnace tests that every yoga adept must pass to achieve Nirvanic Enlightenment.

To understand them we must still keep in mind that the path travelled by the yoga pilgrim sitting in meditation in the Buddha posture is a psycho-physical process leading to the control of the triune aspects of man—physical, mental, and spiritual.

The first step of the yogin is to obtain complete control of the body so that he can direct or inhibit all its physiological processes at will. To demonstrate his proficiency he is often required to sit naked on a frozen lake and dry out by yogically generated heat a number of sheets dipped in the icy water and wrapped about him. And also to show his immunity to heat by sitting under the midday sun and surrounded by glowing fires placed at the four directions. Having attained bodily tranquillity he then attains tranquillity of mind by complete control of his mental processes. Thus the questioning, the sweat house, the mental and physical ordeals of the Hero Twins to prove that they have superseded the sangsaric tyranny of body and mind.

For the devout yogin this is only a blissful trance he has reached, a state of suspended animation. To achieve spiritual recognition he must now awaken the dormant or innate powers of divinity within himself. One by one the psychic centers of his body are brought into functioning activity. Situated in the perenium at the base of the spine, the vital force ascends through the median nerve in the center of the spinal column, and finally reaches the brain center. At this moment of mystic union is born that supreme result which Europeans call Illumination and Buddhists Enlightenment. It is the fruit of perfected meditation. The journey is over. The yogin has reached Nirvana, and is ecstatically overwhelmed with an all-pervading sense of at-one-ment with the divine . . . The Hero Twins have reached their Father's house and are acknowledged as his sons.

This is the moment of triumph, of self-fulfillment and self-knowledge. In full glory the True Son stands forth realizing his dual nature and is given his distinguishing names: Monster Slayer and Born of Water. Then the two separate into two more: Reared Underground and Changing Grandchild. All four aspects of the one, they stand in the four colors, facing the four directions, exhibiting the whole prismatic glory of their full development.

But this moment of supreme achievement is not permanent. It is merely the enlightened knowledge of the mind of its microcosmic and dual nature. The yogin is still a mortal man. And so as the vital force gradually descends again, he returns to his sangsaric or earthly life fortified by and aware of the nirvanic or divine reality of his true self. And so likewise do the Hero Twins prepare to return to earth to help their people.

They have one request: the lightning arrows and flint knives of their father, the sun, with which to kill the Big Giant and the other monsters. The Big Giant is also the sun's son, yet the Sun Father assents to his slaying and gives the boys lightning arrows, flint arrows, and armor. To understand this we must understand the nature and origin of the monsters.

It is already obvious that the vital life force residual in man is the sexual power. Used normally by ordinary man it perpetuates the race. Controlled supernormally by the yogin, this psychic fire-force corresponding to the purely physical sexual fluid is used to help transmute the limited human nature into the limitless divine nature during his experience of Enlightenment. But subnormally perverted the sex vitality leads to those crimes, insanities, diseases, and monstrosities of body, mind, and spirit so readily recognized the world over.

The Navahos and Pueblos, always frank and uninhibited about sex in ceremonial symbolism, develop this theme in outspoken detail. At the risk of offending the casual reader, we must record them clearly in order to understand how the monsters sprang from this subnormal sexual license.

According to the Navahos, First Man and First Woman, the prototypes of mankind, had been created before the Emergence, but they had no children. The emerging race was composed of anthropomorphous plants and animals and possibly of the earliest forms of primitive man. During the separation of the sexes, the women practiced masturbation. One used an elkhorn, one a feather quill, another a smooth stone stuck into the thick part of a leg sinew, and still another a whittled sour cactus. Hence the first conceived a horned monster, the second a monster eagle, the third a monster bear, and the fourth a monster that killed with his eyes. These monsters and their offspring were the ones destroying all the people.

It is clear then that rather than being the prehistoric saurians supposed by many ethnologists, the monsters but represent the evil thought forms resulting from the subnormal and misapplied use of the sexual force. This sexual power however still stemmed from the sacred psychic sun force. Thus the sun still must recognize the Big Giant as his child, the inverted or perverted aspect of his compassionate divinity. And for the same reason he must accede to the request of Monster Slayer and Born to Water to help them kill his monster son.

The return of the two heroes then, and their subsequent slaying of the Big Yei, Horned Monster, Rock Monster Eagle, Tracking Bear, and Slayers With Their Eyes by help of the sun's lightning arrows, is for the twofold purpose of ending the people's ignorant use of the sexual power, thus making way for the appearance of the new race, the present Navahos, and also to teach the Way of the sublimation of the seed for spiritual transfigurment.

Their mission accomplished, the sun takes back his arrows; the Twelve Holy People hold over the heroes the first ceremonial of Where the Two Came to Their Father to restore them from the illness of having killed; and Monster Slayer and Born to Water depart for "Where water flows together" * to live in the memories of mankind with all the great kachinas, yogins, saints, and sages.

Viewed universally, as it must to be comprehended at all, this ancient myth drama is the old, old parable of man's efforts to bring the human body and mind and heart into accord with the divine will. It is the Navaho restatement of Zuñi and Hopi kiva initiation, and of the Taos Deer Dance carried to its esoteric fruition when a deer has escaped. It is expressed in other idioms in the ancient Greek and Egyptian Mysteries, and the subtle *yin* and *yang*

* Said to be at the confluence of the San Juan, La Plata, and Las Animas rivers —just as Prayag, where the ashes of Mahatma Gandhi were consigned to the waters, is also known as "where the three sacred rivers flow together," the Ganges, Jumna, and Sarasvati.

doctrine of Chinese Taoism. But above all it finds its parallels in the Only Begotten Son returning to His Father through the ordeals of Gethsemane and Calvary, and in the supreme yogic dedication whereby Gautama the Buddha transcends the limits of normal consciousness and reaches at-one-ment with the divine.

In the purely scientific field, as in Jung's and Harding's expositions of Western psychology, its teachings are explained in modern terms. There are the two dual elements of man's psyche. The tremendous conflict in which the personal ego or finite mind is replaced by an infinite mind, a "non-personal psychic factor transcending the conscious ego in scope and power." And finally that "enlargement and unification of personality which comes from an acceptance of nonpersonal forces beyond our limited consciousness."

But it is the achievement of the Navahos to have expounded these abstruse truths with remarkable simplicity in a dramatic setting we know well. It speaks to us in the idiom of our own America—in the mountains standing on our own horizon, its swirling brown rivers, the cutting reeds and the cat-tail people, the bear and the eagle. Arching over the desert there we see the rainbow path the Heroes trod. Little Wind brings us their songs, the beat of the drum. On the cliffs we find the chips from their flint knives. Still the sons of Changing Woman hold the Way of beauty open to us, their brothers—that Way, once we perceive it, which is not only theirs and ours but that of all men under every sky.

The Magic Circle

For these men, the Navaho *yei,* the Pueblo kachinas, the Buddhist yogins, and the Christian saints, are but the vanguard of all mankind. We too are slowly travelling the evolutionary Road of Life back to its source.

In many versions of Pueblo and Navaho cosmography there have been four underworlds; in others three. Similarly, there may be either one or two upper worlds above this one. Buddhism holds to four and three, a total of seven states of existence. These minor variations are reconciled by the obvious fact that Emergences are psychic and not accomplished by mankind *en masse,* at once. As Gurdjieff states, there are living today many Number Two's and Three's. Likewise there are an increasing number of aberrant individuals, otherwise wholly normal, who manifest a high degree of extrasensory perception indicating their development to a higher stage of consciousness. Evolution or emergence thus is continuing to take place on both physical and psychic levels.

Following the corresponding Navaho and Pueblo and Buddhistic parallels of the preceding four worlds of fire, air, water, and earth, Buddhism teaches that the dominant element of the fifth state of existence will be ether, an aggregate of all physical matter. As the Navahos assert, there is no denying man's derivative, cumulative nature; he is "Made From Everything." The psychical attribute of the fifth state is the subconscious, a transcendental consciousness much higher than our normal consciousness first manifested in the third world.

The Buddhist doctrine further holds that there will be two more states of existence or "worlds." The subconscious mind is the storehouse of all latent memories; these go back to all existences in the previous worlds—to the "collective unconscious" of all mankind; and when it becomes dominant, man will be able to recall the complete past. Psychiatry would seem to confirm this in principle, holding that whatever man rejects falls back into the unconscious. Here it is held until man faces the conflict that arises. Then out of the unconscious in dream form will arise a "reconciling symbol which will bring the opposing dualities of the psyche together in a newly created form through which their energies can flow in a creative effort."

Both the conscious and subconscious having become manifest, the sixth element now emanates, which is mind—the Enlightened Mind emancipated from all elements and sangsaric illusions. Man is now perfected. He has attained the spiritual selfhood of the Buddha, of Jesus. And he is ready to emerge at last in the seventh state of existence, to cease to be a man and to be divine, returning to and merging with the timeless source. The evolutionary Road of Life is over. Like a circle it has turned ever in upon itself, returning whence it came.

All this is expressed in one abstract symbol, the encircled cross $\oplus$.

This is like the "reconciling symbol" of modern psychiatry. We recognize it in many variations as the Chinese Taoist Golden Flower, the Tibetan Buddhist lotus-cosmos, the Navaho four-petalled universe. It is the cosmic Mt. Meru surrounded by its four-universe continents, each of its world petals protected by a world guardian. It is the axial Encircled Mountain surrounded by the four directional Holy Mountains, each protected by a Talking God.

The four quadrants thus represent not only the Four Corners, the cosmic continents circumscribed by the outer ocean of space with its mountain ring, but the four directional colors assigned to them, the four stages of lower, material existence experienced by man until he surmounts them in the last three stages of spiritual development.

The encircled cross is the sign for the Holy Winds Basket in which the winds carried the corn pollen which was their only food before the creation of the deer. In the ceremonial basket sacrificial prayer sticks and cigarettes are laid in the shape of a cross oriented to the four directions. The prayer sticks, male and female, are made of feathers and different woods sacred to the directions. The cigarettes are made of the hollow joints of reeds filled with native tobacco. They are painted with the colors of the directions, sealed with moistened pollen, and lighted by a rock crystal held up to the sun. Such a multipointed cross as they form within the circular basket is the Zia sun-symbol which has appeared on the New Mexico state auto licenses, and which has now been adopted as the insignia of the Zia Construction Company doing all the construction work at Los Alamos!

The Navaho sand-painting of the Whirling Logs forms the pattern of the encircled cross. The cross is formed of two logs. At the end of each stand two male and female *yei*, the variation forming a swastika. This is surrounded by an anthropomorphic rainbow as the circle, and the whole is painted in the directional colors. It was a vision, says Matthews, of the originator of the Night Chant. But it also appears in connection with the myth of Natinesthani, He Who Teaches Himself, who lived near the Encircled Mountain and floated down the San Juan. His voyage of psychic self-discovery and his very name is again synonymous with the Buddhist doctrine that no man can depend upon church or creed, but must teach himself . . . Over and over in countless variations, in inexhaustible meaning, the symbol repeats itself. From it we are assured at last that the Road of Life through the successive worlds, or the evolution of man, is indeed accomplished within man himself, the microcosmic image of the macrocosmic universe.

Synthesis

It is only by such a synthesis of Eastern religious-philosophies and Western sciences with Navaho and Pueblo ceremonialism that we can see clearly the intent and meaning of the latter. In this respect our indigenous ceremonialism itself may be viewed as a symbolism reconciling those of the ancient East and modern West.

Hence it is not the purpose here to present the main principles of Mahayana Buddhism beyond an elucidation necessary for a fuller understanding of Pueblo and Navaho ceremonialism. The writer is aware of too many discrepancies between the various Pueblo and Navaho beliefs, and between the various schools of Buddhism, to assert a complete identity of both systems.

The same holds true for the many branches of Western science.

Yet in the basic outline of their common patterns their parallelism is too evident to be ignored longer, for to the writer's knowledge it has never been made the subject of a serious study.

There is an obvious reason for this. Pueblo and Navaho ceremonialism always has stood for an esoteric faith. Few have been the strangers allowed to enter a kiva or to learn the secret rites of the ceremonials. Even today paid Indian informants often impart misleading information to ethnologists; cameras are smashed at public dances; secrecy is the rule.

Buddhism always has been just as esoteric, an "ear-whispered doctrine" confined to believers in fear of persecution and perpetuated in secret lest its teachings be profaned. The distortions which have occurred have indeed been responsible for the Occident's strong aversion toward what it has always considered cheap Oriental mysticism induged only by fakirs and turbaned Swamis holding forth at ladies' afternoon teas. No less an authority than Mr. Winston Churchill regarded Mahatma Gandhi as a "naked fakir." Even Arnold J. Toynbee * adheres to the fallacious understanding that:

"According to the extreme Buddhist view, the soul itself is part and parcel of the phenomenal world, so that, in order to get rid of the phenomenal world, the soul has to extinguish itself. At any rate, it has to extinguish elements in itself which, to the Christian

* *Civilization on Trial*, p. 257.

mind, are essential to the soul's existence: for example, above all, the feelings of love and pity . . ."

Not until recent years have men of deep perception, like Richard Wilhelm, C. G. Jung, F. S. C. Northrop, and W. Y. Evans-Wentz, cleared the path for our fuller understanding of this philosophy which has endured since antiquity. We take this opportunity to refer to that clear exposition of Mahayana Buddhism given in *The Tibetan Book of the Dead* or *Bardo Thodol;* the biography of Tibet's great yogin, *Milarepa;* and *Tibetan Yoga and Secret Doctrines.* This superlative collection of seven treatises dating back as far as the first century, have been translated by the late Lama Kazi Dawa-Samdup, Lecturer in Tibetan to the University of Calcutta, noted Buddhist scholar and Buddhist initiate; edited and annotated by Dr. W. Y. Evans-Wentz, his yogic disciple, an Oxford graduate, a Celtic scholar and an Egyptologist; and published under the auspices of Oxford University.

It is both strange and naturally consistent that the traditional and deep rooted antipathy to Buddhism, of the Euro-American and especially the Anglo, does not hold in vast Indo-America below the Rio Grande. In his deeply penetrative *The Meeting of East and West,* F. S. C. Northrop makes a pertinent observation. Standing in the four corners of the court of the Encarnacion Convent, now housing the Secretariat of Public Education, in the heart of Mexico City, are four world figures cut in stone. These four men of primary importance are Quetzalcoatl, Las Casas, Plato, and the Buddha.

Quetzalcoatl of course is the feathered serpent of the Toltecs and Aztecs, whose conceptual image is so deeply imbedded in the subconscious mind of Indo-America that nothing has been able to erase it. Fray Bartolome de Las Casas accompanied Columbus and lived later in Nicaragua, Peru, Guatemala, and Mexico, where he was Bishop of Chiapas. Almost alone, he fought the ruthless exploitation of Indians by Spaniards, and proclaimed in lengthy Latin treatises that man is "a spark from the cosmic fire which burns toward God"—a Christian rewording of the concept held both by the Aztecs and the Buddhists. Plato, as we know, was an initiate into the ancient mysteries of Greece and Egypt; and Gautama the Buddha revived Buddhism.

As they reflect the attitude of modern Indo-America toward world culture the selection of these four cornerstone figures is of tremendous importance, as Northrop observes. Mexico is nominally a Spanish-speaking country. Why does not the figure of Cortéz appear instead of Quetzalcoatl? Her formal religion is overwhelmingly Roman Catholic. Why has not Christ been included in place of the Buddha? Why Plato instead of Aristotle? Why Las Casas instead of Hidalgo, who first rang the bell of independence for this modern democratic republic?

We can only conclude that the tenets of the ancient East have been more appealing to Indo-America than the principles of modern Western science. Yet today there is ample evidence that the East and West are approaching a new verge.

In this verge Pueblo and Navaho ceremonialism as a reconciling symbolism offers a significant means of synthesis. The whole field of the deeper meaning of our own indigenous ceremonialism lies practically untouched. The time has passed when we can view it superficially and academically as a dead mythology. We must see it as a profound living way of life, coinciding with the oldest and newest sciences of life yet stated.

Here then is its rudimentary outlines. Now we must understand better its expression in its own wholly American idioms —its sings, dances, and rituals.

5 Navaho Sings

THE FIRST frost has whitened the plains; now "the thunder sleeps," and it is time for the great Navaho ceremonials. Every boy grown up in the Four Corners knows them simply as "sings." For him they had the same fascination that the circus held for the country boy of the Midwest prairies and moving pictures for the city boy. But this "Greatest Show on Earth" is announced by no posters; a casual word by grapevine suffices. When is it? A shrug. Where is it? God only knows, it seems—or cares. As a trader in his remote post will answer, "Down the Chaco"—"Up from Tohatchi some'eres"—"Back on the bluffs, where the San Juan makes a turn." The sweep of his hand includes a hundred empty miles.

It is enough. Father loads the buckboard. Or the boy packs his saddlebags or flivver and rides off alone. But not for long. Out of the vast desert wilderness emerge The People, looming abruptly above the pelagic plain like barks upon waves, then lost for an hour in the trough of a sandy wash. A scraggly team, an old springless wagon filled with straw, pots, blankets, and children. On the seat the man, slimly erect, a crimson headband holding his straight uncut hair. Beside him the woman, shapeless as a collapsed accordion in her voluminous petticoats and brilliant velveteen blouse, and laden down with silver: bracelets, rings, a squash-blossom necklace, and pins of shiny dimes. Occasionally a lone horseman, perhaps two. Without greeting, they emerge from the silence into which they vanish again, like birds obeying a blind impulse to migration.

The place is where it is. Following them you come upon it. It is on top of the high bluffs standing above the big crescent of the muddy river, and on the wide, sandy desert which sweeps backward to the mountains.

In the deep dusk, in the silence, that lofty amphitheatre of mountain, river, and plain, where hundreds of The People have gathered, is like a scene swung forward from childhood, itself a memory of a farther childhood, shadowy and indistinct, now suddenly illuminated by hundreds of small fires.

They are cooking fires, red and thick as flowers blooming in the dark. They gleam on faces truculent and unsmiling, on youthful faces lit by simple wonder—on the collective face of a race on which is stamped, above all, its pride, dignity, and wild nobility. The People squat, hungrily stripping mutton ribs, rolling cigarettes. Mangy dogs, alert as wolves, prowl up and down the lanes between fires; one yelping from a blow cowers under a wagon tongue. A horse neighs. An axe bites into cedar. The cold thin air sharpens with frost, but is still tinctured with a pungent smell—the burning cedar, whose smoke wraps the calm waiting multitude and, rising upward, spreads like a blanket across the sky.

By the rising moon, the medicine hogan of logs looms up, and off to the east the flimsy shelter of evergreen branches where the dancers rest. Between, a great bonfire lights up a sea of high crowned Stetson hats. It is the end of the eighth day, "The Day" of the chant. Every evening, and growing longer each night, the sound has continued: the ceaseless eerie chant, the thud of moccasins on the hard packed earth, the clatter of gourd rattles. And each night the crowd has increased, swelling the vast encampment, gathering for the climax—the ninth and last night of the chant.

The Navahos have no collective center. Following their sheep, they gather for a sing anywhere in their 25,000 square-mile desert. It is more than a ceremonial; it is a great fair, an exchange of gossip, a renewal of their tribal solidarity. Without this deep sense of their remoteness, aloneness, and daily tribal life underneath, no sing can be fully experienced. Otherwise it is just a spectacle—a dreary desert stage, shabby costumes, a drab monotony. The show, the real show, includes The People themselves.

So one patiently spreads his own blanket at the edge of the encampment, and feet to fire listens to the faint, far off chant—hears it till one hears it no more, so gradually does it blend with night. Only the familiar sounds persistently intrude: the champ, the stamp of horses; the clatter of singletrees; the soft tread of figures passing in the sand; the crackle of dying flames. The moon arches high above the bare, black hills. The chant of the eighth night is over, and upon the face of the earth, the wild and bitter earth, The People sleep as they have always slept—vagrant and secure as their own sheep under the winter stars.

At the first streak of dawn there is a stir. The jagged mountain range stands out, black cardboard pasted on a grey blotter. The plain is a vast rumpled blanket coated with rime. And the dogs, the shivering, mangy, half-wild dogs—no one can sleep for the prowling dogs. Between their yaps one hears the soft scuff of buckskin in cold sand. The early risers shuffle past. There are no trees, no rocks, there is nothing but the immense plain grey with frost. The women squat in the sand, great brooding hens, with their six or eight voluminous petticoats outspread like wings.

The sun brings color: reds, greens, blues, and yellows, the vivid stains, to the shifting blankets; blood-red to the western hills; the sheen of silver to the frosty wagon rims; a lilac flush to the wavering lines of smoke. Freshly the axes ring out. There is more smell of burning cedar, the woolly stench of more mutton on the spits. In the bitter cold the women begin trailing down the bluffs to the river. Gingerly they wet their narrow-lidded eyes set in broad Mongolian faces, smooth the black straight hair tied with white string into a *chignon* at the back. Then dipping up pails of water they plod back up the trail. The sun gleams on their rose-red, purple, and green velveteen blouses, on their heavy silver necklaces and bracelets. Their full calico petticoats billow over their broad haunches; the concho buttons twinkle on the fawn-brown, ankle-high moccasins encasing their thin bare shanks.

And the watcher too, in the bitter cold, strains muddy water through a rag, and follows them up the trail to watch the day unfold—the ninth and last day of the chant.

Most of The People have arrived by now, perhaps a thousand are encamped on the plain. The sing which brings them together is a medicine ceremonial for an old sick woman. For years the family has saved for the expense, to pay the singer and his assistants, to provide firewood hauled from the mountains, and for the slaughtering of many sheep. While the sing is for her, all who come benefit also.

All the work and planning, preceding the nine-day chant itself, has been accomplished by the intricate ritualism whose legendary exactness has governed each step: the preparation of prayer sticks, the making of buckskin masks from the hides of deer killed without bloodshed, and the cutting of logs for the medicine hogan.

Octagon shaped with the one door facing east as always, the hogan is open to all. The day's painting on the floor is an intricate, stylized design in colored sand, handed down from antiquity in memorized detail. Its brief beauty attests, like the singer himself, the impermanency of its makers—and the enduring truth which remains. For as quickly as it is completed and used in the short ceremony, it is destroyed.

Now the painting is gone; the patient and guests file out. The old singer remains sitting cross-legged on the bare floor, in blue jeans and a blood-red velvet shirt, tail out, and held by a belt of heavy silver conchos. His long hair is as grey as the ashes into which he stares vacantly, like a man who sees beyond the remembered past and the ever living present which curves around and beyond us into the future, the completed rainbow ring of eternal truth. On the floor around him lie his helpers, sleeping through the day while awaiting night.

Outside, the multitude is awake enough. The night ceremony is good. But the communion, the stirring with others, the sparse words of greeting—that is good too, the change of rhythm after months of solitude. So they stir about, walking endlessly through the crowded lanes. A sharp, biting wind rises. Clouds of dust sweep over the desert. The patch of plain is a stinging blanket of sand. Young men race their ponies, hardly distinguishable in the gritty storm. Trading goes on endlessly: blankets, belts, jewelry, foodstuffs, a horse. And the women and children squat patiently on the ground, heads covered with blankets.

By midafternoon a stream of muddy clouds spreads over the sky like smoke erupting from the black Colorado mountains. There comes a pause, a dull apathetic deadness—the stupefying negation of Indian life. The crowd goes stale and heavy, at once and without warning. Humped over and cowering in blankets, they sit amid refuse, blowing ashes, and smoke, in the cold. They seem unresistant, dead. Even their bodies appear boneless. Their faces—the few uncovered—are impressive as stone yet betray a profound racial fortitude.

The Indian is capable of letting himself sink into this mindless torpor when he is hopelessly caught in a snow storm; when he must wait a day for a swollen arroyo to subside before crossing; when his gim crack Ford breaks down on a seldom travelled road—any time, and without provocation. He shows not only patience and the blind acceptance of conditions imposed upon him. He accepts it as a gestation period for a renewal of strength. For each, this inert torpor is not only an utter, instant relaxation but a complete surrender of mind and soul and body to the invisible forces, the great creative oneness in which the Indian acknowledges himself undivided from the breathing mountains, the house of the dark cloud, of dawn and evening twilight—a surrender to the great creative oneness which is recreative also, which renews in eternal flux the enduring strength of all. It is a mindless sinking down, for renewal, for refreshing, that once again he may rise from the spell and hear his heart sing:

Happily I recover.
Happily my interior becomes cool,
Happily my eyes regain their power,
Happily my head becomes cool,
Happily my legs regain their power,
Happily I hear again!
Happily for me the spell is taken off!
Happily may I walk
In Beauty, I walk! *

When evening comes The People are still grumpy, sullen, dead. They move about slowly on leaden legs, apathetically cutting wood and lugging water. The wind has died. A low canopy of clouds compresses upon the earth a bitter cold. The mountains seem to have dissolved in mist. There is only the great curving river immovable at the bottom of the bluffs, and the dreary expanse of treeless plain.

Then suddenly, unaccountably, one feels the quickening life. There is no outward change. It is simply that the human blood pulse seems to have quickened. The People come out of themselves,

* Washington Matthews' translation.

throw off the black negation, become positive. And the new rhythm, like a tremor, ripples through the crowd.

Already the first dry, pale snowflakes have dropped, like small breast feathers from a wild goose. Their warning is ignored. The people eat slowly, ravenously, but one feels an imperceptible haste. Greasy pots are wiped, horses fed, dunnage shoved under wagon beds. One by one the group breaks up, all moving casually and unhurried to the cleared space in the center of the plain.

It is the ninth and last night, "The Night" of the chant.

In two vast waves the crowd surges to the clearing leaving a lane between the green shelter and the medicine hogan. They squat down, packed solid on the plain, each family with a little blaze of sticks; not cooking fires though an occasional coffee pot sits in the coals, but small enough to crowd with moccasins, with brown hands and faces, to lean over without singeing blankets. It is the great log fire in the center that illumines the scene. The flames leap ten, twelve feet high. In their ruddy glow the squatting thousand or more are a mass of brilliant blankets. They all wear their best: the soft vivid Pendleton blankets, factory made; the good Navahos—Two Grey Hills, the yellow Chin Lees, the striped Chiefs; the tattered old ones; the bright new ones; and there are plenty of dirty quilts.

The men crowd near the shelter, crested waves of high-peaked grey Stetsons surmounting the sea of blankets. A trader in his truck has driven in. So now they stand, big-boned, dignified, inscrutable, drinking colored soda pop in the bitter cold. All chew gum of course—a full package. The Navaho, with all his other attainments, is the world's greatest gum-popper, vigorous, inexhaustible.

At last the blanket hanging in the doorway of the hogan lifts. The old singer comes out to sit head down under the sparse falling flakes of snow. For an hour nothing stirs but hundreds of jaws and the figures huddling closer to the burning sticks with the immemorial and repetitive gesture of wrapping blankets closer—left arm across breast, the right hand flitting to left shoulder.

There is a sudden stir in the crowd, as of a woman fainting. A group half carries an old woman forward. They set the patient on a stool in front of the hogan. The singer does not look up. Out of the darkness the snow pelts faster; the flakes float and shimmer briefly in the glow of the great center fire.

Then abruptly the grey haired medicine man rises and stands staring toward the invisible eastern horizon. Someone has placed a basket of corn meal in the lap of the woman sitting on her stool beside him. With handfuls of this he sprinkles a path along the lane. As he turns back there is a jangle of little bells. The crowd of men parts like waves. Through them, from the shelter, come the dancers.

In front is Talking God of the East, Hastseyalti or Xascelti; he is *Yei-bet-chai* (*Yei-bicai, Yebitsai, Yaybichy*), the maternal grandfather of the *Yei,* the gods. His head-mask is a hood of white buckskin surmounted by eagle feathers, and fringed with red horsehair. The black symbols surrounding the holes cut for his mouth and eyes are to represent the storm cloud hanging above and the mist rising from below. His nose is a painted cornstalk. Over his clothes he wears a buckskin robe, and on his shoulders hangs a circlet of spruce. His soft fawn-brown moccasins are secured with silver buttons above the ankles. He carries a little medicine basket.

Followed by four dancers, single file, he stops in front of the singer and the woman who has risen beside him. These two now separate, one to each side, and sprinkle the dancers with sacred meal. All turn, facing east. The singer chants a long invocation, repeated line by line by the woman. In the deep silence broken only by the sputtering logs, the voice rings out sonorous and guttural, with the faint female echo.

At the end there is a loud whoop. The *Yei-bet-chai* dashes down the lane, whirling his little basket. The line of dancers turns again, facing west and the hogan. Back comes Xascelti, followed by a whooping clown who has burst from the shelter. He shrieks, yells, kicks his bare legs, switches his foxskin tail at the flames. He is Xascelbai, Water Sprinkler, the god of rain and snow. Like rain, he brings joy and mirth.

Quiet during the long invocation, the people breathe their relief; in intense silence, they watch the four waiting dancers.

They too are masked grotesquely in painted buckskin hoods falling to their shoulders, with a broad band of evergreen around the bottom and two or three eagle feathers on top. Their bare bodies are smeared ashy grey to the waist. Each wears a short beautiful kirtle of hand woven wool, and down his naked back hangs a streamer of colored cloth.

They stand quietly. Then in unison they lift their hands

waist high; in the left a sprig of evergreen, the symbol of everlasting life; in the right a gourd rattle. Slowly the rattling begins. Like a snake, then a pelting hail. Their right feet lift and stamp. Then the left. The moccasin buttons shimmer in the red glare of the fire. The thin muscular legs move falteringly without shaking the spruce twigs stuck in the black cloth bands below the knees.

Then abruptly, as if a switch had been turned on, they break into the rhythm of the stamp, and as in one voice, they begin the *Yei-bet-chai* chant, the most eerie, the most piercing of all:

"Hu-hu-hu-*hu!*"

From the appearance of *Yei-bet-chai* and the sound of his distinctive call this ninth-night ceremony of the *Kledzi Hatal* or Night Chant is commonly termed the *Yei-bet-chai* Dance. Xascelbai, Water Sprinkler, also has a distinctive call; he is sometimes referred to as the dodi god because of his whip-poor-will dodi call. The third masked impersonator is Yaaskidi, the Humpback. The hump on his back is a sheep pelt drawn over a hoop, painted with white spots, and decorated with feathers. It is symbolically filled with black clouds and seeds of all kinds.

So it begins: the quick powerful tread in the soft falling snow; the accompanying rattle, the guttural verses of the chant each repeated the mystic four times—the chant that unvarying in endless, insistent repetition, keeps up hour after hour, through the long bitter winter night.

But there is more than one group of dancers. The first four men dance and chant for some twenty minutes. Then they file out to the shelter and are replaced by a team of six. It in turn is replaced by a team of eight. And then again the first four come out.

All are masked and painted similarly. But throughout the long, bitter night one gradually notices the variations. Some of the buckskin hoods are worn and wrinkled; in others the paint is clean and fresh. There may be one proud eagle feather or two or three. For one of the black cloth knee bands a faded Paris garter may be substituted to hold the spruce twig better. So too the short kirtles vary from the finely woven ceremonial Hopi kirtles used by all Indian tribes to a tattered silk piano scarf.

And at intervals the formation changes too, from single file to double line and back again.

But even the variations seem measured, repetitive. One after another the teams come through the crowd; quiet, bare bodies bent under the falling snow, like greyhounds slinking along the trail. There is the moment of suspense, the slow raising of arms and legs, faces uplifted to the midnight sky. Then, all of a sudden, the high-pitched cry. And again the full-throated chant filling the cold night.

Only the four chief figures never alternate: the whooping, leaping Water Sprinkler; the white buckskin Talking God; the Humpback; and the singer, the wrinkled grey-haired priest. For him, servant of unseen forces and mystic legend, nothing else exists. Sharp eyed, attentive, he stands through the night, a pillar of that doorway between present and past, a snow-stung prophet of the wilderness.

And the sick woman, who sits there head bowed and blanketed, the disregarded focus of an enduring rapt multitude.

This sing on the last night is by its very monotony, its forceful insistence, magnificent. Its unvarying drabness closes the mind. The rhythm of chant and stamp crawls into the blood. The stranger freezes, is blinded by the gusts of smoke; his limbs cramp painfully. There is no escape. He is caught in the rhythm; it is irresistible in its appeal.

The Indian loses himself quickly enough. He goes back to the root of his trouble, back to the root of all good. To him they are synonymous. The brassy sky which brings drought is the same that will fill with rain clouds; the bitter earth is also the fruitful earth. And with this assurance is the deep awareness of the living, animate gods about him: "with your moccasins of dark cloud"—"with your leggings of dark cloud"—"with your headdress of dark cloud."

The forces of nature are not to be hurried. They are not to be commanded imperiously with will and reason. Neither are they to be whined at, grovelled to, pleaded with. The Indian, conscious of his own strength, his oneness with them as a part of all, meets them on their own grounds with dogged persistence, with stubborn faith. So for hours, all night, night after night, he treads powerfully the hard frosty earth, he chants insistently with face lifted to the skies:

> With the zigzag lightning flung over your head, come
> to us, soaring!
> With the rainbow hanging high over your head, come
> to us, soaring!

With the zigzag lightning flung out on high on the ends
of your wings, come to us, soaring!
With the rainbow hanging high on the ends of your
wings, come to us soaring! *

And the gods gathering to themselves lightning and rainbow, allying themselves with the animate forces of the universe, themselves gods—perhaps they do come.

The People look little like converts waiting for a prophet. They seem to have sunk into night. Now past midnight the storm has ceased. The moon comes out. The low mud hills across the river stand forth. It is intensely, frightfully cold. The wide, sandy plain gleams silver with its light covering of snow.

The stranger huddles miserably, wrapped up in his bed and squatting beside his handful of burning sticks. He waits—and for nothing but a surcease from the awful cold. All around are the Navahos in a tangled mass. Children and dogs lie inertly entwined, whimpering in sleep. Women sit back to back, shoulder to shoulder, stoically. The standing men creep through the mass, sink down crosslegged in sheepskin or blanket, and stare patiently through the sluggish smoke. Even the old singer condescends to a blanket.

The dancers keep on. Their grey-ash bodies are besmirched with smoke. They seem to have shrunk into themselves from cold. Now towards dawn they come out showing greasy drawers or long underwear beneath their finery.

Those bitter hours just before dawn! Nothing can assuage the insatiable cold. It seems an element that lives unseen, gnawing at wrists and knees, at nose end and stiff fingers. The face feels drawn out and set like cement; the smoke-blinded eyes raw as holes burned in a blanket. There is no need to close them. The line of dancers, their soggy moccasins relentlessly stamping the ground, their rapt uplifted faces, the interminable chant—it is all a kind of mesmerism, really.

So comes daybreak. It is like a blanket slowly and pitilessly being pulled off night; the illusion of lost warmth in the vanishing darkness. And the naked earth spreads out wan and grey: the snowy plain, the lumpy mud hills beyond the river, the far mountains—the earth bleak and barren, the bitter naked earth, the earth that has been and will be always greater than its people.

A few traders arrive, a group of ranchers, and stand

* Washington Matthews' translation.

shuddering about a fire. There is a glow in the east, as if someone had set a lantern in the saddle of the hills. For a moment the clearing is empty of dancers. The singer throws off his blanket, stands erect, with his face lifted to the flushing east. To the right and a little behind him the woman stands with her basket filled with meal. The silence is taut, electric.

There comes a jangle of bells. Then suddenly, from night into morning, a new group of dancers trots in. They are big fellows, almost naked and freshly painted; their stamp is vigorous, powerful; their voices rise clear and loud. They are the special team reserved for this last, most beautiful dawn song.

It ends sharply. It is done.

In beauty it is finished.
In beauty it is finished.
In beauty it is finished.
In beauty it is finished.

And from the east, the revered east which first lights and which first shadows the steps of man, the sunlight floods the frosty plain and its silent throng. Refreshed, touched by the mystery surrounding their daily simple lives, made whole again, The People drift back to their camps, to their wagons—back into their wilderness with their scraggly teams, their blankets and silver, their strong and haughty faces.

And the old woman, the patient, her face is still touched by the mystery too. Exalted, she stands for the moment between the present and the long trail where the pony tracks go only one way—perhaps made well, made whole again, or perhaps with the disease really untouched. Neither matters in the awakened strength of her rebirth. For if hers is to be the trail that must soon lead from all, and which, in time, must be theirs after her, she will follow it in the beauty, in the deeper peace, and with the assurance of another, still brighter dawn.

The Dances

Such is the bare envelope of the Navaho ceremonials we commonly call "sings."

Seventy years ago the pioneer, Washington Matthews, discovered that the names of all the ceremonials contained the word *hatal* for sacred song or chant, and that the medicine man who conducted it was called the *hatali,* the chanter or singer. Hence he named them chants—as the Night Chant and Mountain Chant, which he recorded.

Of late years another authority, Father Berard Haile, claims greater accuracy in translating *Xatal,* his spelling for chant, as designating the manner or way in which ceremonials should be conducted. He thus calls them Ways—as the Flint Way and Enemy Way, which he in turn has recorded.

How many of these sings, chants, or ways there are nobody knows, although Dr. Kluckhohn has undertaken the task of classifying them. All are complete ceremonials of extraordinary complexity extending one, three, five, or nine nights. Each contains its own ceremonies—like that of the fire ceremony, the bath, and the emetic; its own rituals—the preparation of prayer sticks and of masks; its own dry paintings, myth, songs, and prayers. Their complexity extends to each separate function. In the major nine-night sings the first four days may be devoted to the cutting, decorating, and planting of the male and female prayer sticks; the last four to the construction, ceremony, and destruction of the sand-paintings, one for each day. In preparing new buckskin masks the deer must be killed ceremonially, without the shedding of blood, by suffocating it with pollen. Prayers are recited, songs chanted. Matthews records 576 songs for the Night Chant alone. These must be given in proper sequence, without deviation or omission of word or line lest the mistake nullify the whole ceremonial. And so it is with every phase of the whole: a vast and complex ceremonialism in which every countless detail is achieved within the confines of rigorous tradition.

For it the medicine man or singer is wholly responsible. Few singers conduct more than one particular sing. To master it he must apprentice himself as a child and make it his life work. Ceremonial myths, songs, and prayers are regarded as spiritual property just as inviolable as material property. Hence after ten to twenty years of work learning the ceremonial, the apprentice does not consider it his, or that he has the spiritual authority to transmit it to posterity until he buys it from his teacher. Over a period of years he may pay in soft goods (unwounded skins of deer, pelts, and blankets), hard goods (coral, turquoise, and silver), cattle, sheep, and money, to the equivalent of several hundred dollars.

The singer further tests his pupil's thoroughness and

astuteness by giving him only what he asks for—perhaps the literal songs and myths but not their meanings. In all cases he reserves to old age one of the songs or sand paintings for his own protection. In turn, the new singer never divulges his knowledge nor conducts the ceremonial gratis. But neither does he seek to enrich himself by material gains from his non-material property. He never boasts of his knowledge, and it is customary for him to disclaim any knowledge. The ceremonials thus constitute a body of esoteric knowledge which unfolds gradually as one learns what to ask for, and whose deeper meanings reside only within the hierarchy of singers.

Little wonder that their extent, their richness and profound meanings is yet beyond us. Not until recently were we even aware of their existence as structural ceremonials. The huge encampments were supposed to be purely social gatherings of a seminomadic people to trade, gossip, and witness one of their tribal "dances." Actually Navaho dancing, as differentiated from Pueblo dancing, is of minor importance. The dancers are called simply "the group that sings while it moves." And the dances are but phases of the complex ceremonials to which each belongs.

Primarily there are three of these Navaho dances. The most familiar is the *Yei-bet-chai* Dance; the most spectacular, the Corral or Fire Dance; and the most popular the Squaw Dance.

The *Yei-bet-chai* Dance, as we have observed, belongs to the Night Chant or Night Way. It derives its name from the appearance of Hastseyalti, the Talking God of the East, the maternal grandfather of the *Yei,* and his familiar call of "Hu—hu—hu—*hu!*" which punctuates the long chant of the dancing singers.

The spectacular Corral or Fire Dance concludes the ninth night of the Mountain Chant or Mountain-Top Way. A large corral of spruce branches, the "dark circle of boughs," is made with an opening some ten feet wide to the east so that spectators can enter. In the center is lit a great fire whose flames leap twenty, thirty feet high. Around it, in front of the hundreds of squatting spectators, are lit other small fires. All night long various singers of other ceremonials, groups of dancers, and sets of performers keep the crowd amused with tricks of magic. Red arrows representing the great plumed arrows of the Mountain-Top Way sand-painting are swallowed. A feather is made to dance on the ground. A yucca stalk grows blossom and fruit. A sun symbol climbs up and down a pole. Then, at last, the fire dancers come in, painted with white clay.

Circling ever closer to the unbearable heat of the great central fire. Lighting the brands in their hands. Then dancing, leaping, and cavorting around and through the fire, searing their own bodies and whipping each other with flames . . . a scene from Dante's *Inferno*.

The popular Squaw Dance is a part of the Enemy Way. It is held three successive nights at three different encampments, and owes its name to its public dances in which the women drag the men into the clearing where they dance in couples. A man must dance or pay the woman if he refuses. It is the only dance in which men and women dance together in the usual sense, and hence is most popular. The slow travelling by day to the next encampment, the songs and gossip exchanged, all this provides more fun and sociability for the chance visitor. That it is in reality a War Dance, and that he, the visitor, may be included as the enemy, seems incongruous at least.

But before perceiving the meanings of all these dances we must consider another aspect of the sings—that of myth-dramas.

The Myth-Dramas

One of the functions of the ceremonials is to perpetuate the myths and legends of the tribe. As The People have not had a written language, the long ritual songs with their connecting ceremonies constitute a series of myth-dramas handed down orally from one generation to the next. Each ceremonial myth is separate and unique. Their various characters are the legendary heroes of the Earth Surface People, the Holy People, the *Yei*, birds, beasts, plants, mountains. Over and over they reappear. And gradually we perceive a chronological sequence, and realize that all these separate myths combine into one vast interlocked myth: the complete evolutionary story, the only true history of The People.

Moving Up Way relates happenings in the pre-Emergence period when people were moving up from the underworlds. The race included plants and animals which were anthropomorphic in the sense that they were the spiritual counterparts of the present physical images, the inner forms of the inanimate forces. Also included were the primitive cliff dwelling Pueblos, substantiating their belief that they preceded the Navahos. This emerging race was created by First Man and First Woman, who had no children. The paradox is explained by the fact that First Man and First Woman merely represent the dual forces manifesting themselves as the prototypes of man. Mankind as such had not been created yet; but the separation of the sexes had taken place, and from the sexual license of this race—by masturbation—the monsters were created. These monsters—i.e. the perverted, undirected, but divine sex power of the sun—were gradually destroying the people, including the ancestral, primitive Pueblos.

Blessing Way, the Emergence myth, recounts the birth of Changing Woman, who is to correct this evil. Her puberty ceremony is still held today for every Navaho girl. She gives birth to the dualistic Hero, Monster Slayer and Born to Water who later destroy the monsters. Changing Woman then gives birth to a new race of men, the present Navahos, and to them thus becomes synonymous with Our Mother Earth. Blessing Way is the most important of all ceremonials; some of its songs are included as a necessary part of every other ceremonial.

In Night Way the people moving up to the present earth world found only darkness. Changing Woman (with her dual name of White Shell Woman) attempts to create light for them. On the floor of the world hogan she spread white for dawn; on the white she spread blue for morning; on the blue, yellow for sunset; and on it, black for night. Then she prayed. But there was no light.

Then she laid some turquoise and some white shell beads on the darkness, and prayed again. Faint light appeared.

Now the twelve Holy People answered with help. They brought more beads and turquoise, and made a magic circle embracing the whole. Over its face Changing Woman held a crystal. And suddenly a bright blaze resulted. It was so bright and hot that Changing Woman, the twelve Holy People, and the Earth Surface People had to keep raising it, and spreading out the world, to hold it up at a safe distance. After this ordering of light and darkness were created *Yei-bet-chai*, Water Sprinkler, Humpback, and other gods who later appear as mountain sheep to the Hero, giving him the songs and dances of the ceremonial.

With Monster Way begin the post-Emergence myths. It relates the journey to the Sun Father of the Hero Brothers and their destruction of the monsters. Where the Two Came to Their Father parallels this as a minor ceremonial, and the hero of Shooting Way is also Monster Slayer.

The physical death of the monsters, however, created a

resultant psychic evil. The vitality of the earth, the waters and the mountains was impaired by the jarring falls of the giant monsters, the flowing of their blood and the rotting of their corpses without compensation to the earth for these abuses. So also was weakened the vitality of the people themselves. A ceremonial was needed to destroy the ghosts of the monsters. Enemy Way served this purpose.

Today it is a war ceremonial to remove the ghosts of all alien enemies, every one not Navaho being regarded as foreign. But all these ghosts—scalped Utes, Anglos, and Spaniards, the ghosts of Germans and Japs killed by Navahos in World War II, the ghosts of syphilitic prostitutes met in town—are identified with the ghosts of the original monsters. The pot drum symbolizes the ghost. It is an earthen jar filled with water and covered by a taut buckskin in which is punched eye and mouth holes. The drum tap is a cedar or cherry twig bent into a loop. With it the ghost is thus beat into the ground to the accompaniment of the prayers and songs.

The Enemy Way myth is based on a war expedition to Taos soon after the death of the monsters and a scalp dance to celebrate its victory. The leader of the war party was Monster Slayer. During the march the party was overtaken by the Hard Flint Boys. They appear in the sky as the Pleiades, and on earth in the dual form of whirlwinds and waterfalls. In the ceremonial they are represented by the Black Dancers or Mud Dancers who smear a mixture of these two elements, earth and water, on their bodies. Father Berard Haile also points out that they emphasize the ritual requisite of corn from the pueblos of Taos and Oraibi, the extreme east and west limits of enemy country.

On the eve of the attack the party was joined by two old men, Bear Man and Big Snake Man. They were the ones who took the scalps of the two non-sunlight-struck Taos maidens, or virgins, one dressed in turquoise and the other in white beads. By this they earned the right to the two corn maidens held as prizes at home for the warriors who took the scalps of two Pueblo girls in compensation for two girls previously lost to Pueblo warriors. Yet the warriors refused their right and set the two girls free at the scalp pole dance.

The campaign took three days. Hence Enemy Way is a three-night ceremonial, being held the first night at the rattle stick receiver's camp, the third night at the patient's camp, and the second night at a place between them. A scalp is still used, one of old scalps dug out of a tin can saved for the purpose. And the War

Dance or Squaw Dance is the same procedure then followed when the two corn maidens encircled each warrior in turn.

During the dance they were enticed by the magic smoke of the two old men reclining some distance away. When the girls arrived they found Bear Man and Big Snake Man changed into two handsome young men. The elder girl took Bear Man as a mate, the younger Big Snake Man.

Next morning the warriors were furious. They made a fruitless search for the girls, ready to whip them with willow sticks. The girls escaped them by stepping on two clouds and floating away. The magic smoke of the two old men followed the girls, one east and the other west. The direction where the smoke of Bear Man followed the elder in her wanderings and adventures leads to Mountain-Top Way; that of Big Snake Man following the younger to Beauty Way. And at the ends of these two ceremonials the sisters are again united.

From this it is at once apparent why Beauty Way symbolically emphasizes snakes, and Mountain-Top Way bears. Washington Matthews translates the name for the latter literally as "a chant towards a place within the mountains," and the mountains undoubtedly refer to the sacred Mountain Around which Moving Was Done. The bear is also sacred, being the animal "truly reared within the mountains." The mythical hero of the ceremonial is synonymous in meaning with the bear. His name is Dsilyi 'Neyani, which means Reared Within the Mountains. Among the songs are the Songs of the Young Women Who Become Bears. The long myth recounts the adventures of Dsilyi 'Neyani, his meetings with the gods who gave him his name, taught him the dance of the great plumed arrows, and instructed him to give his people the ceremonial to cure diseases and to invoke rain and good crops.

In the long and involved myth of Flint Way, a young man out hunting seduces a woman. She turns out to be the wife of White Thunder who shatters the hero with a bolt of lightning. Big Fly advises the grief stricken family to seek help from the singer, Gila Monster. The singer proceeds to cut up his own body into tiny pieces. His flesh and blood is thrown to all directions. Thereupon the Wind People and Sunlight People reassemble the scattered particles. The Spider People respin his nerves. The sun restores his eyes and ears, the moon his body hair, the Dawn People his face. Talking God and Pollen Boy restore his mind, Corn Beetle Girl his "travelling means." The Medicine People sing. The living medicines themselves sing. All life breathes to restore life. And when Gila Monster's living pouch is made to step across him, the singer sits up perfectly restored. Having demonstrated his ability to restore life with life, the singer, Gila Monster, then proceeds to restore the hero. As White Thunder destroyed the hero's life, he too contributes to his restoration.

The hero then journeys to buffalo country. He commits adultery again with Buffalo Woman and her sister, the wives of the buffalo chief. The angered chief engages the adulterous hero in mortal combat. With the chief's death all the buffaloes are killed and the hero brings them back to life again. In return for this he is given their songs, prayers, and medicines like the prized buffalo blood, horns, generative organs, and buffalo track dust now used in the ceremonial.

Despite this, the sexually inclined and rather obtuse hero has not realized the import of all these adventures. Whereupon Gila Monster reviews his whole life for him, points out the motives involved in all actions, and explains the restoration ceremonies.

Flint Way was originally a nine-night sing. It is now restricted to five nights and four days, but in its duration no sleep is permitted as during other three-, five-, and nine-night ceremonials. As its purpose is the restoration of life or consciousness and vitality, it is synonymous with Life Way. It borrows from Blessing Way, and is intimately connected with Shooting Way. Like the latter it has male and female branches. As the Mountain-Top Way uses a spruce corral, and the Night Way uses a variation of it in the small spruce shelter which is the home of the *Yei*, Flint Way takes place in a flint corral called the Home of Flint.

Haile identifies the original Home of Flint as the prehistoric Pueblo cliff dwellers' Sun Temple in the Mesa Verde ruins. The whole ceremonial is too rich in symbolism and meaning to be exhausted. Its symbolic emphasis on the buffalo, sacred to the Plains tribes, confirms the fact that the Navahos travelled out on the Great Plains and that they must have obtained some rites from the Plains tribes as well as from the prehistoric Pueblos. There is also some evidence that the male branch originated with the Jicarilla Apaches.

The use and symbolism of flint offers too a ripe field for exploration. Flint has always been sacred in America. Among the

Pueblos it is a form of lightning. With a knife of flint or volcanic obsidian Aztec priests performed their human sacrifices. Derived from the power of the sun it was regarded as the source of life; from it sprang people, even gods like Itzpapalotl, the Obsidian Butterfly, and Itzlacolinhqui, Curved Obsidian Knife. In Mexico, peculiarly enough, its main quarry was a mountain near Timapan known as the Cerro de las Navajas, the Hill of the Knives.

In all the ceremonial myths recounting the journey of Monster Slayer and his twin brother, their father, the sun, garbs them in an armor of flint and gives them a huge flint knife. Gila Monster, the animal, is likewise still clothed in a scaly armor; and Gila Monster, the singer, used a flint knife to cut himself up, to slice the yucca plants for the ceremonial bath, and decorated his hoof rattle and pouch with flints.

So it is that all these countless myth-dramas lead into still more myths and ceremonials: the Navaho Wind Way and Chiricahua Wind Way, Hail Way, Water Way, Bead Way, Coyote Way, Ghost Way, and Down Way. All combining into one vast interlocked myth which is at once the complete story of The People and the whole story of man.

The Mystery Plays

That these myth-dramas are essentially mystery plays is beyond question. It is not enough that they perpetuate the mythological history of their people. Like the ancient mysteries of Greece and Egypt they teach in the medium of their own parables the universal truths of life.

There is a great difference between such mystery plays and the European morality plays as we know them. Navaho ceremonialism is not concerned with morality—"that negative and mindless imposture which pretends to be religious, while it only has to do with the body that is food for worms, and needs no religion." Whether the hero of Flint Way commits adultery is of little importance; he suffers no censure or penalty. But it is concerned with the fact that the deeds of individuals are not confined to their own spheres of social action; they vitally affect the earth, the waters, the mountains—the whole web of life. Nor is the influence of a character restricted to the term of his physical life. It continues through his ghost to be a psychical force. This interrelation of parts within the solidarity of the whole living universe, the psychic effects resulting from physical causes, the correspondence of inner and outer forms of life, and the continuance of causal action through the realms of life and death, all combine to give meaning and validity to the sings as profound mysteries.

We have already observed that the primary basis of all these mysteries lies in reconciling the two great primal forces, the cosmic dualities inherent in man. These polarities are not restricted to manifestation solely as male and female, but their expression in sex is as common and easily understood in the ceremonies as in our own life. When it is not understood and its use is perverted as in Moving Up Way, monsters are created. Rightly understood on the physical plane, it assures the creation and perpetuation of the race, as in Blessing Way and Monster Way. But this endless perpetuation of mankind on the same physical plane is not the destiny of man. He must surmount it; and by finally reconciling and uniting the opposite polarities on a higher spiritual plane, consummate all aspects of his nature in harmony with the divine Creator of all life. And this, as we have seen, is the meaning of Monster Way, Shooting Way, Where the Two Came to Their Father, and all ceremonials based on the Monster Slayer myth. Life assures this eventual destiny; all life contributes to this gradual understanding. It restores divine harmony, lost spiritual consciousness; it permits mistakes but it rectifies them; it is inexorable with all its mercy, for life itself is the Supreme Way. Hence Life Way or Flint Way. And life itself is sanctified by those supreme divinities which overlook and guide our slow but constant evolution. Hence Blessing Way which must be included in every other ceremonial, which alone sanctifies its use and validates its meaning.

Young Navahos are told that excessive sexual intercourse is injurious and in time *affects the spinal cord where it joins the brain,* reports Haile; Flint Way therefore employs a special ceremony for the removal of inordinate passions of men and women. This is a direct parallel with the practice of Tibetan Buddhist yogins in redirecting the course of sexual power up the median nerve in the center of the spinal column to the brain center and thus achieving the transcendental phenomenon of Illumination; and this yogic process, as we have learned, is the parallel meaning of the Hero Twins' journey to the sun in Monster Way and Where the Two Came to Their Father. The Navaho ceremonial preoccupation with sex we therefore glimpse as parables dealing with the understanding and transmutation of the physical life force into a spiritual power necessary for the evolution of man into his final states of existence.

With sex, death is of equal importance in the Navaho mysteries. At the time of death, according to Buddhism, the spiritual consciousness, or life principle, leaves the physical body at the crown of the head at the sagittal suture where the two parietal bones articulate, the exit of the median nerve: the Aperture of Brahma. In recognition of this spot many Buddhists shave the head save for a lock of hair on the crown; and at death a few of these hairs are symbolically plucked to insure the escape of the consciousness principle.

We recognize this spot on the crown of the head as the traditional Indian scalp lock. Among the Plains tribes the Osages shaved their heads except for this scalp lock; in Indian sign language Osages are thus identified by the gesture of brushing the sides of the head in an upward motion towards the scalp. The lifting of the scalp of a dead enemy is therefore not only a gesture of victory. It is necessary for the purpose of allowing his ghost to escape to the symbolic black north. Lest it return to trouble the warrior's slayer, a scalp dance is held.

The War Dance at Taos is similar to that of the Cheyennes. It lasts the traditional four days; is danced around the scalp-pole; and the warriors' bodies and faces are painted black, as are the faces of the women who dance in a circle outside them.

Hence the symbolism of Enemy Way and Monster Way: one appeasing the ghosts of the slain monsters, and the other ghosts of those slain by the war party at Taos. Monster Slayer's temples are blackened because they indicate the seat of ghosts. When he begins his journey to the sun his original color is black because his way leads through the black north, the dark underworld domain of ghosts. The patient of Enemy Way is always blackened as was he. And the Squaw Dance or War Dance is itself a dance around the scalp pole.

Appeasement of the ghosts of vanquished enemies is necessary as the psychical counterpart to their physical destruction. But the destruction of life is always wrong; for life, even destructive life, stems from the divine source; even the monsters are acknowledged sons of the sun. Thus Monster Slayer and Born to Water became ill from their slaying and must have Where the Two Came to Their Father held for them, just as modern participants in war still do. Moreover the killings affect all mankind, the earth, the waters, and the mountains by impairing their vitality, and Enemy Way must compensate for these abuses. It is easy to see why Navahos believed the influenza epidemic of 1918 was a result of the temporary disablement of the sun by the eclipse of June 8, and why they now believe the earth is turning sour and the streams are drying up as a result of the debacle of World War II.

Yet in Life Way or Flint Way we have a courageous affirmation of the power of life to restore life. And this mystery play in which Gila Monster cuts his body into bits and restores it to life, as he later does the shattered body of the adulterous hero, finds its exact parallels in the ancient Greek and Egyptian mysteries.

In the Orphic mysteries enacted only before neophytes and initiates, Dionysus-Zagreus is slain by his Titan brethren who cut his body into pieces. Apollo is then charged by Zeus to gather together the scattered parts. In the Omophagic Rites the myth was represented by the actual sacrifice of a man and the dismemberment of his body, the devotees eating the flesh. A similar rite dramatized in the Egyptian mysteries represented Osiris being slain by his brother Typhon and his companion. The body was cut up into twenty-six pieces, cast into the Nile River and afterward collected by Isis.

A rough parallel to Enemy Way also exists today in the Tibetan mystery play in which a human effigy called the Enemy is speared, stabbed, and torn into pieces after a War Dance. Another adaptation similar to Mountain-Top Way is the Snowy Range Dance, essentially a religious rite of purification celebrating the inner form of Kinchinjunga, the five-peaked sacred mountain of Sikkim, whose altitude is but slightly less than that of Mount Everest.

All these mysteries and their sacred rites—of death, restoration, and rebirth, the eating of the flesh or the corn cake in Blessing Way and the "no-cedar mush" of Enemy Way, the exorcising of evil spirits—are, in turn, paralleled by our own Christian mystery with its Holy Sacrament.

It is in this great tradition of antiquity, and teaching the universal truths of life, that the Navaho sings speak to us in their own allegorical art forms.

Our first appreciation of these profound myth-dramas and mystery plays as highly developed and rigidly stylized art forms is, of course, the classical appraisal of Dr. Jonathon Letterman in the first Smithsonian report.

The ceremonials he reports as, "They have frequent gatherings for dancing." Their rich symbolism and intricacy of ritual he does not notice. Of their lengthy myths and traditions he surmises, "The lack of tradition is a source of surprise. They have no knowledge of their origin or of the history of the tribe." Of their religious allegories he asserts, "Of their religion little or nothing is known, as, indeed, all inquiries tend to show that they have none." And the long chants themselves he describes as, "Their singing is but a succession of grunts and is anything but agreeable."

We can well forgive his lack of musical appreciation. Indian music sounds dissonant to the European ear. It is based on rhythm rather than on melody. This rhythm is marked by gourd, hide, or deer hoof rattles for the chants proper; no rattle accompaniment for the songs in Enemy Way and Blessing Way is prescribed, therefore they are not properly called chants; and in addition to this variation songs are sung while prayers are recited.

The rhythmic patterns are further complicated by the voice tones of the singers. There are half tones and minor tonalities outside our own chromatic scale, impossible to reproduce on a piano with its basic seven note octave. The falsetto is prominent, and contrary to the down beat of many Plains tribes the music is characterized by bold upward leaps which carry miles across the plain. The rhythmic pattern is thus so complex and subtle that it has been the despair of Euro-American musicians.

Some years ago Leopold Stokowski set out from Taos for an extensive tour of the Four Corners with all his paraphernalia for recording and transcribing Hopi and Navaho songs. The tour was a musical failure. He was unable to transcribe a phrase. Down in Mexico I remember meeting Miss Laura Bolton, who has made a successful career out of recording primitive songs. She later came to the Four Corners to obtain a collection. The present Victor Record album is the result, but not too successful. They seem difficult to record. While we were in New York, Lois Moseley, the head of Decca's Musical Comedy and Classical Music recordings, and an accomplished pianist, was often confused by the simple rhythm of Tony Luhan's singing in a taxicab or at home, while keeping time with his fingers on a small drum or on his knee, and was unable to transcribe a bar on the piano. The late Charles Wakefield Cadman made his reputation with so-called Indian songs. His *Land of the Sky Blue Water,* often designated as being taken from the Havasupais, in the Grand Canyon, does not even stem directly from the songs of the Chippewas and Omahas which Cadman always said inspired his own melodies although he could never transcribe them.

More fortunately as translations multiply, we are beginning to recognize the lyrics of the songs as pure poetry. Great poetry. Its rhythm sings even in the printed word. It abounds with metaphors and similies so subtle as to be almost incomprehensible to those who do not know the country and the intense feeling it evokes. Adjectives are unusual and inexhaustible as the shades of their symbolic meaning. Nouns and names, Changing Woman, Talking God, the Rainbow Trail, Pollen Boy, Where Water Flows Together, The Mountain Around Which Moving Was Done are striking images in themselves. The use of verbs defies imitation.

The buffalo is the "horned chief." Eagles are "those who glide next to the sky." A feather picked from a live eagle is always a "live one's plume." Plants and animals are named like the Cat Tail People and Red Ant People. A stretch of sand dunes is called Cutting Sands. The little rock wren "grinds" on the dark rock because her quick gliding movement back and forth is remindful of the movement of a woman's hands grinding corn on the metate. An arrow is "looking" when, shot into an animal, it begins to move or shake as if surveying its surroundings from the wound. Medicine beginning to show its effect "starts its flight" because the feathers of living birds are employed in the ritual. Beauty and happiness are synonymous; it is found in plants, water, trees, mountains. The Mountain Around Which Moving Was Done is also White Corn Mountain or Spruce Mountain; it is Mirage Mountain, Long Life Mountain, and Happiness Mountain.

These countless poetic images may also be qualified to denote direction, time, and relative importance by the names of the primary colors, and the trees, plants, or animals sacred to them. And by the use of repetition emphasizing the four-fold or six-fold aspect of the universal pattern, the song pattern itself groups itself into metrical four-line or six-line stanzas.

. . . With your moccasins of dark cloud, come to us!
With your leggings of dark cloud, come to us!
With your shirt of dark cloud, come to us!
With your head-dress of dark cloud, come to us!

With the zigzag lightning flung over your head, come
to us, soaring!
With the rainbow hanging high over your head, come
to us, soaring!
With the zigzag lightning flung out high on the ends of
your wings, come to us, soaring!
With the rainbow hanging high on the ends of your
wings, come to us, soaring!

I have made your sacrifice,
I have prepared a smoke for you.

My feet restore for me,
My legs restore for me,
My body restore for me,
My mind restore for me,
My voice restore for me,
Today take out your spell for me.

Far off from me it is taken!
Far off you have done it!
Happily I recover!

Happily my interior becomes cool,
Happily my eyes regain their power,
Happily my head becomes cool,
Happily my legs regain their power,
Happily I hear again!
Happily for me the spell is taken off!

Happily may I walk
In beauty, I walk!

With beauty before me, I walk
With beauty behind me, I walk
With beauty below me, I walk
With beauty above me, I walk
With beauty all around me, I walk.

In beauty it is finished.
In beauty it is finished.
In beauty it is finished.
In beauty it is finished.*

* Washington Matthews' translation.

All these components of the ceremonial as an art form—the rhythmic music of voice and rattle, the poetry of the song lyrics and recited prayers, the masks of the dancers, and, above all, the stage setting of mountain, plain, sky, and the embracing universe—are combined in the dry paintings. In visual, poetic images they sing the myth. They portray the characters and the setting. They give us, at a glance, the whole ceremonial.

Only for Navaho ceremonials of five nights duration or more are dry paintings commonly specified. In the major nine-night ceremonials the intervening last four days are given over to their preparation.

They may be made on an unwounded buckskin—the skin of a deer which has been ceremonially killed by choking with pollen. The head is laid to the east, and the paintings are executed in corn meal, corn pollen, ground flowers, and charcoal. White is made of corn meal; blues of dried larkspur blossoms; yellow of corn meal or pollen; red and brown of pollen mixtures; and black of charcoal.

Or they may be made of sand. The floor of the hogan is covered with a ground work of smooth sand perhaps three inches thick. The pigments are colored rock or sandstone ground to powder: red, white and yellow. Black is ground charcoal taken from a tree struck by lightning. And this mixed with white gives the grey which appears blue in contrast with the other colors.

The painting may be twelve feet or more in diameter and require the work of several men from sunrise till mid afternoon. Working swiftly from memory they squat or kneel, letting the powder slip from the hand between the thumb and forefinger onto the sand. The singer supervises the exact construction of each detail by his assistants. When two lines are crossed the lower is filled in completely and the upper is spread over it. If a mistake is made the faulty part is not erased; sand is poured on it and a new drawing is made with fresh powder.

Without doubt these dry paintings originated in the kiva ceremonialism of the Zuñis and Hopis who still use them. But appropriating them as they have the weaving, the Navahos developed dry painting to the supreme art that it is now. Today we commonly understand dry painting as Navaho sand-painting.

No other indigenous American art surpasses it in unique technique, in purity of style and emotional depth. Beside it primitive and pseudo-primitive art shows itself to be only crude and undeveloped. Modern abstractions seem childish. For these sand-paintings, so highly developed and rigidly stylized, are abstractions as pure as any ever known. Always symmetrical, equated to the four directions and perfectly balanced with the four primary colors, they are strikingly original designs of form and color whose origin can be felt as far as they can be seen. They are more sophisticated than the latest importations from the Beaux Arts of Paris and the newest innovations seen in the exclusive ateliers of Fifty-seventh Street. And yet they are realistic pictures so childlike, simple, and direct that they defy description.

Pictures of plants, of people, mountains, animals, the rainbow. No more than this.

But the plants—the corn, bean, squash, and tobacco—are always placed, whatever the design, in the same cardinal directions, and are colored with their corresponding colors. Human figures and corn stalks may be indistinguishable. They stand erect, always in twos or fours, the females with square heads, the males with round. Bodies are elongated into tenuous columns scarcely an inch wide. An arched rainbow bordering the whole turns, on close inspection, into a figure whose ends resolve into head and feet. A mountain may be a great four-petalled flower or a tiny spot of color on a flake of flint. Whatever they all are is determined by that aspect of their character which must be accentuated in relation to the structural whole. There is no background. For these stylized figures are the inner forms of life itself, whose homes, whose ambiente is the entire universe.

The Navahos are not interested in their artistic value, nor in their perpetuation by reproduction. As individual transcriptions the sand-paintings are perhaps the most transient the world has known. They do not last a full day. The day's painting is begun at sunrise and finished in the afternoon. The patient is seated upon it for a brief ceremony. Sand from it is applied to various parts of the body to the accompaniment of ritual, songs, and prayers. Then the mutilated painting is destroyed before nightfall, the sand being carried out on the desert again.

Like the songs, the prayers, the myth, the dances and the rituals, the whole ceremonial, it serves a practical purpose. In this lies its true meaning.

Healing Ceremonies

The primary function if not the sole purpose of Navaho sings is to cure illnesses of the body and mind. This aspect of healing ceremonies supersedes all such other aspects as social gatherings, myth-dramas, mystery plays, and art forms. To this practical purpose is bent all Navaho songs, prayers, myths, sand paintings, and rituals.

The ceremonial thus considered is a vast and complex thaumaturgical rite which has its parallels in modern Western psychotherapy, Christian Science, and Buddhist yoga.

The Tibetan Buddhist yoga system is divided into several parts or paths, all leading to the harmonization of body, mind and spirit with the divine, each practiced as required. *Mantra* yoga employs the use of words and sounds in *mantras* or chants, which aim to establish telepathic communication with the deities invoked for assistance. Each of the basic notes in the chants corresponds to a certain color of the same vibration. Certain times of the year or day are also specified for their use as in Navaho sings.

Yantra yoga depends upon the similar use of geometrical designs or *yantras*. As basic vibrations may be manifested audibly in sounds and chants, and visually in forms and colors, the designs like the Navaho sand-paintings express in visual form the audible pattern of the chants.

Often called *mandalas,* these geometrical designs have been extensively studied by Dr. C. G. Jung. He correctly points out the most beautiful are those of Tibetan Buddhism, and that those "found in the sand drawings of the Pueblo Indians" are notable examples. The oldest he discovered was that of a palaeolithic "sunwheel" found in Rhodesia. Others he finds in the Middle Ages of Europe, in Jacob Boehme's book on the soul, and in drawings of his mentally diseased patients who had no idea of their psychological meanings. *Mandala,* he asserts, means a circle, especially a magic circle; hence the "dark circle of boughs," the spruce corral of the Mountain Chant. Christian *mandalas* show Christ in the center, with the four evangelists at the cardinal points, as in Egypt Horus was represented with his four sons the same way. Other forms take that of a flower, of a cross, of a wheel, always with four as the basis of the structure. These compare, of course, with the previously described symbols of Navaho ceremonialism: the circle, the cross separating it into quadrants, and the Encircled Mountain as a four-petalled flower.

Whatever their origin, says Jung, these basic symbols come from two primary sources. One source is the unconscious which produces them spontaneously. The other source is life, which, if lived with complete devotion, brings an intuition of the self. When one becomes aware of the latter, it is expressed in drawings, while the unconscious enforces an acceptance of life.

We shall learn more about *mandalas* later. It is enough now to heed Jung's statement that the *mandala* does mark an effect upon its maker, and is an effective part of the technique of Eastern yoga.

The yoga system is divided into three main classes: *Hatha* yoga, which insures physical health and vitality; *Laya* yoga, which leads to control of mind; and *Raja* yoga, which leads to the perfection of spiritual man.

The Navaho sing may thus be compared to a complex yoga system employing all these methods or paths. Its immediate aim is to restore the patient physically and psychologically. His illness, whatever it may be, is never regarded as being solely organic; this is only its effect. Its cause is a basic disharmony which can be righted in him, the microcosmic image of the macrocosmic universe, by bringing him into harmony with his cosmic duplicate.

This aim coincides, to some extent, with the growing understanding of modern psychotherapy that the patient rather than the illness must be treated. The founder of our orthodox Christianity, Himself, believed that "evil spirits" could produce disease and madness in mankind. Mark and Luke record His healing of the maniac by driving out of him a legion of devils and allowing them to enter a herd of swine; and Matthew attests He gave His disciples "power against unclean spirits, to cast them out, and to heal all manner of sickness and all manner of disease."

Like modern psychiatrists, no Navaho singer is permitted to conduct a ceremonial unless he himself as a patient has had it held for him. The reason is obvious. A novice singer may be too weak to stand its great power and may suffer harm. Matthews asserted that mistakes made in the superlative Night Chant cause crippling and paralysis. Peculiarly enough, he himself suffered a paralytic stroke while learning it. And of late years Reichard, in her two-volume study of *Navaho Religion*, records that the singer,

Crawler, incurred paralysis of the legs (and his name) because he was too weak to stand the power of this same great chant. He then switched to learning and practicing the Mountain Chant successfully.

In accordance with the religious esotericism of the ceremonials, the singer must be sought out by the patient, and must give only what the patient asks for. The sing selected, and those parts of it to be given, are thus determined by the patient and his friends, depending on the nature of his illness and what he can afford to pay. A nine-night sing like the Mountain Chant, with its sand-paintings, rattle sticks, huge corral, innumerable specialty dances, the provision of sheep and firewood, etc., is an expensive ceremonial for which a man may save for years.

His illness may be caused superficially by a fall from a horse, a bad dream, or by standing near a tree when it was struck by lightning. For each physical or mental disorder there is an appropriate healing ceremonial.

Flint Way or Life Way is primarily concerned with restoring consciousness and lost vitality, and with the cure of internal injuries. Mountain-Top Way removes the bad effects caused by bears, and Beauty Way those caused by snakes. The province of Enemy Way is the cure of all sickness resulting from alien ghosts—that is, all non-Navaho causes, whether they be physical like contact with a "foreigner" in Gallup, or psychological like contact with a dead body or a grave. Evil Way takes care of all native ghosts. Big Star Way, for very bad dreams. The Shooting branch for recurrent dreams of falling and floods. Shooting Way proper for lightning and snakes. Moving Up Way when one has seen a spot of fire as an indication of ghosts. The superlative Night Way for mental disorders. Bead Way for skin irritations. Feather, Wind, and Bead Ways for head afflictions. Red Ant, Eagle, Hail . . . all are based upon the understanding that every physical ailment is equated with a psychical deformity, and their function is the treatment of the patient rather than the disease. Blessing Way alone is a preventive, not a cure; and for this reason, its rituals are included in most of the other ceremonials in the hope of rendering the patient immune from further attacks.

From this outline we understand that Navaho ceremonialism is preoccupied with specific healing, or restoring harmony between the individual and supernatural forces. Its function is the treatment of the patient, not the disease. In a later section we will understand better why it is no paradox that even a singer may submit to medical treatment, as at Ganado, with no distortion of his principles; any misconception lies in our own inadequate understanding that every physical injury is equated with a psychical deformity.

There is one branch of Navaho ceremonialism which can be briefly mentioned. Witchcraft is sometimes practiced by aberrant singers, as by some of our own professional practitioners, for their own personal ends. Needless to say the evil use of their power is censured and feared. Peyote Way, as it is now beginning to be called by the Navahos to whom use of the weed has spread, is no ceremonial at all, as we have learned. It is not a healing ceremony, a myth drama, or a mystery play. It is a new alien cult based on the use of a narcotic plant, permitted by government authority, and offering only a temporary escape from those realities of life as traditionally viewed by the Navahos.

6 Pueblo Dances

WHEN WE bravely start out here to a dance it's dollars to doughnuts that we are going to an Indian dance. And by this we usually mean one of the dances of the Rio Grande pueblos.

According to the old saying, "Councilors sing, they do not dance." It is a respectful way of saying that the old men on the council observe their ceremonial duties in the kiva and by singing during the public functions. The young men dance. Every young man and woman, every boy and girl, as their names are called out from the housetops, must participate in a ceremonial dance sometime during the year. They dance winter or summer. Night or day. Often between times for fun. Sometimes for profit. And always as if in answer to a powerful inner necessity for expression. It is no wonder then that the dances of the Rio Grande pueblos are by all odds the best in the Four Corners and doubtlessly in the country.

I once spent an evening in Los Angeles with Adolph Bolm, who, in 1910, danced with Nijinsky in the European premiere of *Petrouchka*. He stated that the Pueblo Indian dancers were the only indigenous dance art forms of any consequence in America, and that they were the best dances he had ever seen.

Nor have I ever seen an imitation of Indian dancing worth the trouble. The best attempts were made by the Denishawn dancers, famous when I was a boy. But Ted Shawn did not deceive himself. He said, "There is no place in the world where one can see men dance with such perfection as in the Hopi villages of the

Painted Desert, for here they put a lifetime into the perfection of their art."

Naked redskins dancing around a fire. That is our immemorial image of the American Indian. They live up to it fully. Every Indian dances. Any time, Anywhere. It seems to come to them as naturally as breathing.

Today is Monday. Clara comes from the pueblo to do the wash. With her comes little Red Bird to mind his manners meanwhile. He dances. All alone across the creek. Half naked, his little round navel stuck out. With a steady tattoo of small brown feet in the grey dust. Very simple. Almost too simple to be imitated. But the step, the rhythm is perfect.

Or maybe Ralph and Rowena are having a few folks in on a dull Saturday night. Why not ask Adam to bring some of his boys from the pueblo? Or Trinidad? So, of course, they dance while Ralph lazes back, belly out, thumping one of his drums.

Or perhaps it is a moonlit summer night at the pueblo, and all the people are out in the plaza, dancing slowly in a great circle which opens to let us in. A Round Dance. Just shuffling around and around in a great slow wheel. The women, pale figures in light shawls and snowy buckskin boots; the men wrapped in their white summer sheets like ghosts. The dance came from the Cheyennes and Arapahoes, who got it from the Sioux; the Ghost Dance round the pole. But now the Round Dance or Circle Dance. Held any time, anywhere, without meaning, merely for fun.

Why we go anywhere else to see Indian dances is a mystery. We have plenty of them here at home. And on the eve of January sixth, Twelfth Night, which is locally known as King's Day or *Los Reyes*, you can see most of the others in miniature. The newly elected governor invites us to his house to see them. The room is cleared, the adobe floor swept. The bright blaze of a piñon knot is the only light. It gleams on the brown, seamed face of the governor, on the men sitting against the walls on tiny benches, and on the women squatting on the floor. Everybody is cracking piñon nuts. Everything is relaxed, cheerful.

About eight o'clock the children begin making the rounds of the houses of the governor, the war chief, the fiscal and council members. One after another they knock and enter. A group of two, four, or five children accompanied by a father or a ceremonial uncle. Each has a specialty dance or an imitation of another pueblo or tribal dance. The Horse Tail Dance, a war dance derived from the Sioux. The ornamental Chief Dance from the Arapahoes. Two little couples do the Sun Dance of the White River Utes. Another boy does the Isleta Turtle Dance. Two little Devils imitate the Mescalero Apaches. And here is a tiny boy driven around the room with colored ribbon reins by a tiny girl: the rare Ute Sariche or Dog Dance. Now here's our boy! A lithe youth of twelve. Dancing rapidly. Passing willow hoops over head, arms, legs, down under the feet and up again without missing a step. The famous Hoop Dance which is a specialty of Taos and the delight of tourists at the Gallup Ceremonial. How wonderful he is, really. Maybe he will grow up to be as good as Trinidad! How wonderful they all are. Utterly charming, these small dark babies so completely costumed and painted, even to charcoal mustaches. Dancing in front of the leaping fire, the grave watchers, and the men around the drum holding out a flour sack for gifts of round bread, our cigarettes and "nickel-pennies."

It is from all these dancers, and the dances that were first held in front of prehistoric kivas when the world was young, that the great ceremonial dances derive.

The Corn Dances

"Dancing," says William Butler Yeats, "is the motion of desire in the lower, mortal world, as singing is its sound symbol. David, dancing before the ark, symbolizes the masculine before the feminine, the energetic before the secretive."

The rhythmic moving prayers for rain, for fertility and abundant crops we thus understand as man's ceremonial appearance before Our Mother Earth, the conceptual image of the feminine polarity. We call them Corn Dances because the Earth Mother and the Corn Mother are synonymous. They are also called *Tablita* Dances because the women so often wear *tablita* head-dresses. And because they invoke rain through a mimetic magic, Rain Dances.

They are the most common dances to be seen throughout spring and summer. They are held in all pueblos along the Rio Grande, and almost invariably they occur on the Saint's Day of the pueblo according to the Catholic calendar. They are thus often considered the pueblo's chief dance of the year.

They vary greatly in appearance and intensity. Our

home Corn Dances, here at Taos, are perhaps the worst. The lines of dancers are ragged, the costumes poor makeshifts. Women dance without *tablitas,* and wear gaudy piano scarfs and Spanish shawls. Girls giggle. Boys are sullen. The small groups, as a whole, lack dignity and rhythm. Many of the people are living away from the pueblo in their summer homes out in the fields. All their minds and energies are focused on the annual Blue Lake Ceremony. All this, as far as dances go, makes Taos a "winter" pueblo. The Corn Dances at San Juan and Santa Clara seem almost as bad. The plazas are baking hot, clouded with dust, and swarming with tourists; and the dancers lack homogeneity and intensity. Those at the small pueblos of Zia and Santa Ana are better, and those at Cochití and Jemez are good.

Here one glimpses the full pattern. The constant alteration of dance groups; one filing out from the Turquois kiva, dancing for a half hour or more, then filing back as that from the Squash kiva emerges to take its place. The Turquois group is identified with the Summer society, the masculine principle; the Squash group with the Winter society, the feminine. Thus winter follows summer, and summer again winter, with a constant compulsive reiteration, each group adhering to the same dance pattern.

In the small dances, where all participants are men, the dancers dance in one line. Here there are two lines, the men in one, the women in the other. Then four lines and circles in a slow changing pattern. The half or quarter turns are always made to the left; the right arm, the rattle hand, raised and swept over the head. There is the chorus of old men. The drummer. The *Koshares.* In their expressive pantomime one reads the symbolic gesture language. The lowering arms indicating the lowering clouds. The zigzag motion of the arm overhead symbolizing lightning. The jerky hands lowered palm downward bringing falling rain. And the gentle uplifting hands lifting up the corn shoots, lifting up the stalks of growing corn.

At the conclusion of each Corn Dance the spectators on the terraces above throw gifts to the dancers—cigarettes, sacks of Bull Durham, stick candy, chewing gum. This custom of throwing gifts to dancers, says Elsie Clews Parsons, stems from the old practice in Ácoma, where the kachinas threw away everything they had on except their masks to indicate how they wanted the people to act.

The epitome of all the Corn Dances are, of course, the

supreme spring and summer Corn Dances of Santo Domingo. In this dance are embodied all the constituents of the complete form—the full chorus; the participation of every one in the pueblo, men, women, and children; the *huitziton;* the *tablitas;* the splendid *Koshare,* with their gesture language; the stylized dance pattern. With perfect co-ordination and controlled intensity, it reaches its full expression in one of the truly great dances of America. Maskless, it is yet pure kachina. A whole people's rhythmic and moving appeal to that feminine polarity of all life which is symbolized as Our Mother Earth.

Santo Domingo Corn Dance

You could see it down there on the sandy plain between the lumpy mud hills and the chocolate-brown curve of the Rio Grande. It was just as I saw it for the first time nearly thirty years ago. A low mud town as if sliced out of a low mud hill. A few straggly corn fields outside. A patch of ancient cottonwoods across the river. And beyond, the pale cedar-splotched desert sloping up and away to a far blue rampart of mountains.

Santo Domingo. Lost and desolate in the universe of earth and sky. Stubborn and indomitable in the world of men.

Listen! You could hear it already. The faint, resonant beat of a drum. Like the almost imperceptible echo of a pulse within the lifeless, lumpy hills.

Leaving the car outside, we walked into the corona of filth and the acrid odor of urine and ordure that edged the pueblo; past the lanes opening between rows of squat, flat-topped houses. It was early spring. The snow and mud were gone. The air was sharp and dry, the wind strong. Dust eddied in the empty streets. A dog sprawled in the sunlight, biting at his fleas. Only the drum, full-toned now, betrayed the lifeless negation.

Abruptly we came to the long, wide street that served as a plaza. A stinging blast of sand swept up it and lifted. Revealing not only the pulsing heart, but the voice, the will, the blood stream and the ligaments—the hidden and working anatomy of the desolate town. Its function was the Spring Corn Dance.

At the near end of the plaza stood a high, cylindrical, adobe kiva, whose smooth wall was broken by a flight of terraced steps. On these stood resting a file of dusty, painted dancers. In front had been erected a little green shelter facing the plaza. And in this, on a rude altar, sat a wooden santo bedecked in bright cloths and silver.

Squatting on the ground against a wall, we stared down the dusty street. At the far end rose another kiva. Out of it, to the beat of a drum, was filing a long line of dancers.

In front, up one side of the street, came four rows of old men in their brightest colored shirts, tail out over gaudy flowered, full-legged pajama pants, and carrying in each hand a sprig of evergreen. In their midst one beat a small drum tied round his waist.

Beside them, up the middle of the plaza, walked a man beating powerfully a great belly drum. With him walked the flag carrier. The flag he carried was the ancient flag borne to battle by Aztec priests. A long smooth pole—the *coatl,* the serpent-staff of Quetzalcoatl, from which dangled a ceremonial fox skin and a narrow hand-woven kirtle. And bearing on top a bunch of parrot and hummingbird feathers—the *huitziton,* the crest of the war god Huitzilopochtli.

Behind them in two files slouched the dancers—perhaps a hundred and fifty men, women, and children.

Little by little as they straggled forward against the wind, colors screamed against the dun grey walls, a life emerged into the monotone of sand and sky. But it was not a show; there were no other spectators. It was a great ceremonial dance by which the corn must be lifted into life; corn for all. So everyone participated.

The men, naked to the waist, were painted a golden copper. Their freshly washed hair fell to their wide shoulders and held entwined a few blue and green parrot feathers. Each wore a white Hopi ceremonial kirtle embroidered in red and green, and tied with a red and black wool sash, the long fringe dangling from right knee to ankle. At the back, swaying between their legs, hung the everpresent fox skin. On their legs tinkled straps of little bells, sea shells, and hollow deer hoof rattles. Their ankle-high, fawn-colored moccasins were trimmed with a band of black and white skunk fur. They carried in the right hand a gourd rattle, in the left a sprig of evergreen.

The women, alternating with the men, shuffled along bare footed in the eddying dust. Their squat heavy figures were covered by loose, black wool *mantas* beautifully embroidered around the hem in red, leaving one bare shoulder free, and belted around the waist with a green and scarlet Hopi sash. Their waist long hair, like that of the men, rippled free in the wind. Each carried on her head a turquoise-blue *tablita* held by a string passing under her chin—a thin wooden tiara perhaps a foot high, shaped like a doorway, painted with cloud symbols and tipped with tufts of eagle down. They wore heavy silver bracelets and rings, silver squash-blossom necklaces, and strings of turquoise and coral, and carried in each hand a sprig of evergreen.

Everywhere evergreen, the symbol of everlasting life. It was as if they had chopped down a spruce forest and brought it down to the mud flats.

The two files stopped, facing each other, the children on one end. Between them the flag carrier dipped his long pole over their heads, the drummer began to beat the great drum.

The outside ends of the four rows of old men halted, curving round and inward to form a four-deep semicircle facing the two lines of waiting dancers, the small drum in the center.

Now in wind and dust the dance resumed.

The great belly drum throbbed hoarsely. The gaze of the fifty old men turned inward, became fixed. They began to chant —a powerful soughing like the wind among the pines. The *huitziton* dipped and rose. The sprigs of evergreen lifted and fell. Then came a tinkle of bells, the clatter of deer hoofs, a rattle of gourds. The lackadaisical dancers drew together like the segments of a chopped-up snake.

They were dancing.

In two long rows, the stable, stolid women alternating with the leaping men. Then in four shorter rows as the women stepped back to face the turning men. And now in a great, slow-moving circle breaking up into two circles, each woman a shadow at the heels of her man.

A powerful down-sinking stamp, insistent and heavy, from the men. Then faster as the drum quickens double time. Stamping to one beat and to the next marking time with bending knees. But from the old grey-headed crones, from all the submissive women, the barely lifted flat feet and the whole body subtly shaking with the rhythm.

Occasionally an instant's pause. Then a shrill yell, a quickening rattle of gourds. The thunder throb, the blood beat of the great belly drum. The chorus of the old men's rapt voices soughing through the spruce twigs. A spruce forest moved down to the mud flats to shake and toss in the acrid stinging dust, under the hard, alkaline sky.

The group danced for a half hour or more, then filed back to its kiva. But as the Summer People left, the Winter People came out from the opposite kiva. Thus alternating as winter follows summer, and summer yet again winter.

The insistent, down-pressing stamp that sinks down deep into the earth, as the throb of the drum sinks deep into the unconscious. And the insistent rising chant that lifts, lifts up into the shaking spruce twigs, up to the rain feathers on the pole, to the clouds in the sky. The two dual life-forces that flow downward and upward in man. But here now arrested, rigidly controlled and rhythmically freed as the psychic in-breathings and out-breathings of meditative prayer made visible in patterned motion. A prayer whose mesmeric beat closed the mind to sight and sound, to wind and dust. Beating through the flesh of the earth and the earth of the flesh, through the growing corn and the people who would envelop the ripened corn again for the strength and power to perpetuate both.

Late in the afternoon the wind increased. Swirls of dust blew down into the plaza from the bare mud hills. A choking grey mist through which little children, too, still kept dancing. The boys in little kirtles and doll moccasins, and the girls wearing on their heads diminutive *tablitas,* painted with tiny sunflowers. Two straggling rows of fresh-hatched chickens caught in a sand blizzard.

Easter had come to the mountains above with rushing spring torrents, the smell of fresh plowed fields. In the hot river lowlands below, the earth had been longer awake; the fruit trees were already in blossom, the bottomlands planted with chile and melons; the sun glared white and hot. But here on this dreary sandy plain no sign of resurrection had yet appeared. And so the people called it forth, group after group, with an enraptured and unrelenting persistence. The people who were themselves seeds of everlasting life planted between the mysterious depths and heights of the wide universe.

They shook the earth awake to give forth the tiny shoots of new green corn in the scrubby *milpas.* They stilled the serpentine clouds writhing overhead, they gathered the fat-bellied clouds hovering there over the far buttes and mesas, above the desert. They called down rain, they called the tall walking rain out of the doorways of cloud with the fluttering tufts of eagle down.

And all the while the *Koshares* pantomimed the insistent prayer as the old, grey-haired chorus sang it, and the people danced it. The eleven loose *Koshares,* the most vigorous and alive of all.

Two of them were divided vertically with paint: brown on one side, black on the other. The other nine were just alike. Naked save for dark blue loin cloths and kerchiefs, their ashy grey bodies were splotched with white and black spots, their faces weirdly streaked with zigzag lines. Their hair was drawn up into a knot on top of the head, plastered with white clay, and tied with a dirty blue rag. From the tuft stuck up a thick cluster of corn husks, dry, brittle corn leaves. Fantastic figures. Blackened ghosts of old cornstalks. But wearing sprigs of evergreen in their waist at back, and in their ankle-high white moccasins.

So beautiful of movement as they weaved continually through the lines of unheeding dancers like alert, spotted leopards. Head down, eyes lowered, they danced up and down, between and outside the lines. Their loose flexible arms with poetic gestures drew up the deep power from the blackness of the earth with which they were painted, drew up the hidden juices into the roots, drew up the corn shoots. Then at a change of rhythm their heads raised. They drew down the rain like threads, drew it down from the sky with all its sun power and moon glow, its pink-tipped arrows of fire, and its waters.

But also they were very watchful to correct a child's step, to hitch up a little boy's knee strap and tie on a girl's *tablita,* blown off by the wind. For the dancers must not hesitate to the end. And when a tot squatted down exhausted, one picked her up, piggy-back, to carry her off for rest.

So it kept on all day. The tossing forest of spruce twigs and the deep soughing among it. The leaping, golden-copper bodies of the men among the forest. And the women, powerful and subtle, holding the *tablitas,* the painted doorways, almost steady as they danced between the men. All in long lines, flexible as corn, straight as rain.

Till finally, towards sunset, the two groups merged. A hundred singing old men, three hundred dancers, two dipping poles, two great drums.

In the tremendous resurgence one knew now that this was prayer. But not prayer as we know it. It was not a collective supplication, not even communal in the sense that it was merely participated in by every unit of the whole. It was a unification and release of psychic forces through a rigorously constructed discipline into a communion with the forces of all creation. These were not men humbly beseeching the gifts of life. They were the forces of life made manifest in man as in earth, demanding by the laws that governed both an interchange of the energies potential in each.

Suddenly it was over. And in that first instant of cessation, in the terrifying absence of power rushing back to its different sources from a vacuum of sound and motion and feeling, one knew that the exchange of energy did, does take place. This is the secret of the tremendous impact of the Corn Dance, and the validity of its perpetuation from the prehistoric past.

The Animal Dances

In contrast to the spring and summer Corn Dances are the innumerable fall and winter dances which emphasize the symbolism of animals and birds through the use of masks. We call them Animal Dances.

Like the Navaho sings which also symbolize a beast or bird—the bear in Mountain-Top Way, the snake in Beauty Way, the buffalo in Flint Way—these Pueblo dances are more concerned with the meanings involved than with their pantomimic imagery. All the public functions conclude, like the Corn Dances, a four-day ceremonial whose rites are observed in the kivas.

The Turtle Dance is given at Isleta, San Juan, and Taos. We have previously described the one at Taos, held in the wintry dawn of January first. The twenty-five men emerging from the Water kiva just as the light shows over the mountains. Filing through the snowbanks to the plaza, naked save for breechcloths and moccasins, with a band of paint stretching from ear to ear like the mouths of great turtles. Standing in one line, Manuel, the leader, in front, swathed in a blanket, wearing an erect eagle feather in his hair. Then beginning, as did the people in their first dawn of life after their Emergence from the third world of water, the dance of life. This is the meaning of the Turtle Dance. And it is further expressed in the Turtle Dance song of San Juan:

Long ago in the north
Lies the road of emergence.
Yonder our ancestors live,
Yonder we take our being.
Yet now we come southward,
For cloud flowers blossom here,
Here the lightning flashes,
Rain water here is falling.

Unlike those in Taos, the San Juan Turtle dancers wear no face paint. But their bodies are painted the dark brown of turtle shells, and the step is the same. They stand in the same spot hardly lifting the feet, but turning at rhythmic intervals to dance in the opposite direction. In making this half-turn each swings his right, rattle arm high over the head of the next dancer—a pure kachina gesture, and practically the same gesture with which the Navaho *Yei-bet-chai* is begun.

Buffalo Dances are given at Taos on January 6; at Tesuque on San Diego Day, November 12; and others at San Felipe, Cochití, and San Ildefonso. Buffalo bring snow and carry away sickness. So at the conclusion of the dance a sick person may have the mask placed on his head and pressed to his palms and soles to help as a cure. In a small decadent pueblo like Tesuque—which may already have discontinued the dance—only a dozen dancers may follow the Hunt Chief out of the Winter People's kiva. But on King's Day at Taos it is a major ceremony. Mrs. Parsons records that, in 1926, seventy-two buffalo came out from the three north kivas, sixty-nine from the three south kivas, accompanied by four "hunters" and twenty-five singers. I have never seen more than fifty; but as they mill about, shaking their great shaggy heads in the gathering snow, their black massive bodies so ponderous against the adobe walls, they create an invisible force that seems almost tangible.

The masks are the heads of buffalo, or heads made of bear hair and cow horns to resemble them, slipped over the dancers' heads; the hoods rest on the shoulders; the black beards fall down over the breast. The tips of the swaying horns carry eagle down; and more down is stuck to the shaking heads, like snow. The bodies of the dancers are bare save for the usual dance kirtles and moccasins. From an armlet on the upper left arm dangle two eagle wing feathers. The legs, arms, and bare torsos are spotted with white paint. In the right hand is carried an arrow, tip down; the empty left hand is held at the waist.

Outside the four lines stand the four hunters or Hunt Chiefs, beautifully arrayed in snowy white buckskin leggings, shirt or robe, each carrying a white buckskin quiver of arrows slung across his back. With them stand the officers with their canes of office, from whom formal permission to hold the dance must be obtained. And behind stands the chorus of old men in bright blankets.

So they dance; in four lines, at four successive positions in the plaza, shaking their curving horns. Driving away sickness. Bringing the cleansing snow, the life-giving snow that covers the fields and swells the mountain streams above. And evoking surely, with their great power, the spirits of the vast herds that thundered across all America. You can see them there beyond the pueblo wall. Approaching across the empty fields, their great, shaggy heads fronting the thick storm, their beards frosted white.

They are real, of course. The tribally owned herd, kept in the great communal pasture behind the pueblo, along the base of the sacred mountain. Buffalo was the pre-eminent sacred animal of the Plains tribes. Its medicine, hoofs, hair, horns, hide, and dust have been carried through all the eastern pueblos to the Navahos, who embody their symbolism, as we know, in the Flint Way. To Taos particularly, which always maintained a close contact with the Plains tribes and often sent out buffalo parties, the buffalo is still a sacred animal. It is more than a legend, a symbol. It is a living reality. And here the Buffalo Dance is one of the three great winter dances.

The Deer Dance, already described,* is the greatest of the three; with the Santo Domingo Corn Dance it is one of the two most significant dances of all the Rio Grande pueblos. We know that it is more than a dance. It is a mystery play in the great tradition of the Navaho sings, of the ancient mystery plays of Greece, Egypt, and Tibet. And its meaning lies in an understanding of the two cosmic dualities emphasized constantly, not only in Indian ceremonialism, but in Eastern mysticism and Western psychology. That this meaning is expressed so explicitly in the medium of the dance rather than in song-myth and myth-drama, is the highest achievement of the Pueblo Dances; it creates a form world which holds the integrated substance of an art, a culture and a religion.

There are Deer Dances in many other pueblos. Some of

* P. 188.

these are combined with Buffalo Dances, as in San Felipe. The masks include elk and antelope as well. And this too carries out the same mystery play in pantomime. The animals break away from the feminine Game Mother; are caught and carried back by the Hunters; then the masks are sprinkled with corn meal and fed.

Almost twenty years ago I saw a Yaqui Deer Dance up the Yaqui River from Magdalena. As in the pueblos here, the dancers wore deer heads and skins; and bending over at the waist, used sticks as forelegs. The annual gathering of the Yaquis is at Magdalena on San Francisco Day, October 4, as I saw it in 1932. On this day too there used to be held an Elk Dance at Nambé. There was also a Goat Dance given at Santa Clara.

Eagle Dances are given by curing societies in San Ildefonso, San Juan, and Santa Ana, and occasionally as specialty dances by Taos. Symbolizing the second element, air, and the breath of life, the masks may be used afterward to brush those who come to the kiva for a cure. The dances are magnificent mimicry. The scrawny, thin-legged men stalk out stiffly as eagles. They bend forward, the great cruel heads over theirs, the feathered skins lying on their backs, the tails hanging outspread over their buttocks. They fling out their arms to spread the long swift wings. So they dance. Fluttering their wings, circling, turning, dipping; flinging up their curved beaks and staring fixedly at the sun; diving, gliding, whirling up again.

Bandy-legged, they look frail and unfed. One sees why. The dance is a terrific ordeal that a heavier man could not stand. But in it one reads the same old truth. Man is dual. Plant like, he is rooted to his tribe, his earth, the feminine polarity. Animal like, he is also free to will and move. So like the eagle he launches out into the blue, whirls and dips in space, the symbol of our freedom. The American Eagle. But all eagles wheel and dip, rise and glide over the cliffs the same way. Their freedom of movement is only comparative and transient. It expresses itself only in cycles, unchanged through the course of time. So are we all bound, in our freedom, within the limits of our transient earth bound existence until our ultimate release into spiritual freedom.

These dances, Eagle, Deer, Buffalo, and Turtle, all show, over and over, the masculine dancing before the feminine, one of the two great truths of our duality.

Years ago I saw a Parrot Dance at Santo Domingo.

I have never seen it since, but parts of it are still vivid in memory. The dancers were many, all attired in the usual manner. But the dance leader carried a cage in which were placed seeds of many kinds and a parrot carved of wood, painted the vivid colors of the directions. Over its tail spread an arched rainbow of feathers. The cage was presented to each of the directions, then handed to a woman who did likewise. The parrot is a sacred, mysterious bird; it is long lived, colored with all the directional colors, can look the sun in the eye without blinking, and coming from the fruitful south it brings warmth and fertility. In Taos there is a Parrot kiva.

I remember going to a little jungle town in Mexico with Tony Luhan to trade for parrot feathers. They had to be just so—quill and fletching, for him to take back home to the pueblo. This is where they all came from, these ceremonial feathers now tied to the tall flag pole, the Aztec *huitziton,* and bunched on the top of the dancers' heads during the Corn Dances. The jungles of Mexico. All carried north along the ancient trade routes connecting the Aztecs with their spiritual motherland, these northern pueblos.

To the Bear Dance of the mountain Utes, the Butterfly, Snake, Buffalo, and Antelope Dances of the Hopi, the Pueblos have corresponding ritual parallels. We must remember too that for each of the six directions, including zenith and nadir, there is a corresponding animal and bird. And the full meaning of these lie in the ceremonials, of which these public dances are but a part.

The Spanish-Indian Dances

It is to be expected that the dance-loving Pueblos have adopted many folk dances, customs, and beliefs of the early Spaniards, transforming them into their own dance forms.

Two of these are notable examples.

The *Matachina* or "*Matachines*" is a common Christmas dance in Santo Domingo, San Felipe, Cochití, San Juan, and Taos. Romantic belief holds that it was the dance of the Aztec ruler, Moctezuma, who taught it to the Pueblos on his long trip north by litter. It is really an adaptation of the old *Los Moros, Los Moros y Los Cristianos* or *Morismas,* introduced into Mexico by the Spaniards and first danced here in 1598 by Oñate, at San Juan.

The dance attracts many Spanish-American neighbors who still observe *Las Posadas,* the nine nights of traditional Christian hospitality from Guadalupe Day to Christmas. All the way to the pueblo the fire-walls and house tops of their simple adobes are lighted with little bonfires of crossed sticks or candles placed in paper sacks partly filled with sand. These *luminarios* give light to the Virgin on her journey. Formerly a fire was lighted on the mesa top north of San Juan, and tradition has it also that similar beacon lights on hills guided Moctezuma on his long trip north.

The characters are as mixed in conception. There is *Monarco,* the monarch; *Malinche,* the Indian mistress and interpreter of Cortéz during the conquest of Mexico; *El Abuelo,* the grandfather; *El Toro,* the bull; and the dancing *Matachinas,* each carrying a three-pronged stick. Each is appropriately masked and garbed. There is dancing, horseplay. The bull makes passes with his horns at the grandfather, who acts as if gored; after which the bull is shot by the musicians and falls dead. What it is all about no one seems to have the slightest idea. Possibly it is just a mock bull fight watered down from the old Spanish folk fight between the Moors and the Christians. To this writer it is a bastard offspring of three races through three centuries, but with a style predominantly Indian.

Mrs. Elsie Clews Parsons, with her special talent for detecting cultural affinities between Indian and Spanish ceremonies, once told me that the *Matachina* was danced among the Mayas, Yaquis, and Tarahumaras of Mexico, but without *Malinche*—probably because of the Mexican Indian's traditional sadness at her betrayal, and that the dance, like the *Pascolas,* was associated with death. A far cry from the pure fun-loving function is provides here.

The Pecos Bull of Jemez is held during the Fiesta of Porcingula on August 1 and 2. It carries out the same theme. The main character is the bull, a framework mask covered with colored cloth and painted with white rings, worn by the impersonator, who is otherwise dressed in the usual Hopi dance kirtle and moccasins. He chases around after several bull-baiters in front of the bower built for the image of Porcingula. Then from the Turquoise and Squash kivas emerge the large groups of dancers, each group appropriately colored and garbed, the women wearing *tablitas.* The name, Pecos Bull, derives from the fact that the last survivors of now extinct Pecos immigrated here to Jemez in 1840, bringing their patron saint and bull with them as well as their sacred Mothers.

Another survival of Spanish origin is found in Cochití, when on All Souls Night Kachina Society members go from house to house to dance for the spirits of the dead. This has its parallel throughout Mexico in *La Danza de Los Viejos,* the Dance of the Old Men, who follow the same custom. Aside from this, *Los Viejos,* with their fantastic masks is a favorite folk dance in Mexico.

Whatever the validity of these Spanish-Indian dances may be, they have lasted from the conquest to World War II, over four hundred years.

With all these primary dances of the Rio Grande pueblos, as well as the *Yei-bet-chai,* Fire, and Squaw Dances of the Navahos, there are the Devil Dance of the Apaches, the Bear Dance of the Utes, the Butterfly, Buffalo, and Snake Dances of the Hopis, the Katchina Dances of Zuñi, and many others. I am always learning of one I have never seen. Anytime, anywhere in the Four Corners, there seems to be a dance going on.

Aside from their meanings they offer a traditional art form that cannot be equalled in America. And it is vanishing swiftly with little trace. Nearly half a century ago, before cameras were forbidden, the famous photographer, Horace S. Poley, of Colorado Springs, made a series of slides of some of the best dances. In 1937, he invited me to see them. Among them were the Navaho *Yei-bet-chai,* the Hopi Snake Dance, and the Ute Bear Dance. Yes, the Bear Dance, one of the rare dances without a drum or rattle, in which two notched sticks are rapidly rubbed together to mark the rhythm —the first Indian dance I ever saw as a small boy. How wonderful they were, these old authentic slides. But Mr. Poley was getting old and wanted to find a place for them. Colorado College and the Colorado Springs Art Center had turned them down. He was still trying to find a museum, a society, that might be interested.

The dances have long been a favorite subject for painters, especially here in Taos. Everyone has taken a brush stab at one or another: Walter Ufer, Ernest Blumenschein, Gerald Cassidy, Andrew Dasburg, Howard Cook, John Sloan, a dozen others. Preliminary sketching of the dance itself is forbidden or difficult at best, the subject is too dynamic for static reproduction, and re-composition to meet European art standards distorts the original forms; the results, on the whole, have not been too successful.

Among the best I know is the colored sketch of a composite ceremonial painted by Nicolai Fechin, who has done the finest Indian portraits I have ever seen. It was reproduced in my book *The Colorado,* but so badly that it is a reproach to the subject.

For recording Indian dances in paint we must depend on Miss Dorothy Brett. No one is better fitted for this labor of love. With her ear trumpet and fishing pole stuck in her "dream of beauty"—a station wagon she can nap in—Brett has rumbled over every road, poked up every canyon, to become the best fisherman in the country. Now, thank Heaven, she has moved down from her little cabin high on Lobo and built a house of her own with Indian help. And she is painting a series of Indian dances. Painting Indians at last, after twenty years.

There is something strange, ineffable, and compelling about Brett's Indian paintings. They are not portraits like Fechin's, with their wonderful, realistic characterization, their vivid colors and bold, broad style. Brett is the only painter I have known who has blindly, intuitively caught the valid, mystical component of Pueblo character.

My favorite little color sketch hangs on the wall opposite. An old man is standing on a housetop, like the *cacique.* Below him a young boy is climbing up the ladder. Behind rears the snowy sacred mountain. But the white mountain gives the impression of great height, a stainless purity and serenity, as if it might be the tip of the remote Himalayas, far removed from the world of men. The old man's figure is so accentuated in length and leanness that it leaves him nothing of a corporeal personality. He is wrapped in a dark blue blanket which clings so close that it makes him look like a gaunt Buddhist priest, a Turkish sultan in jacket and pantaloons, a Persian ascetic, or a genie called out of Aladdin's lamp. Even his white buckskin moccasins suggest the Oriental slippers upturned at the toes. This major part of the picture is so remote and strange, so starkly blue and white, that it is like a mystical image of antiquity. And this is immediately counterbalanced by the boy climbing up the ladder. Wearing a short American hair cut, he is clad in blue Levi trousers to repeat the blue of the old man's blanket, and in a warm yellow sweat shirt to emphasize the sand yellow roof top. In composition and color and meaning this simple sketch is a profound statement of the two components of Pueblo life. It has height and depth, coolness and warmth, abstract mysticism and warm earthyness. It has style. After twenty years, Brett has developed a style which identifies her paintings as far as you can see them, and a style that suits her subject perfectly.

So far, in her new series, she has done the Deer Dance, the Buffalo Dance, the Turtle Dance, the *Matachina,* and the Feather Dance. There is no describing them. The dancers are alive with the spirits of their masks; they are a whirl of feathers, a maze of tossing horns, a moving phalanx of irresistible power, a fantasy of ancient Spain. And yet the background figures are so warm and earthy and realistic we can pick out the faces of our Pueblo friends. All are compactly composed, balanced of color. They are Indian to the core, and they are Brett.

Every day she gets Trinidad, the best dancer, to come to her house:

> We spend the morning going into the patterns of the dances, the details of the dress and so on. Damn it, all these years I have been held by that rule of no photographs, no drawings and so on. Then all of a sudden it seemed worthwhile to take the risk of offending the old men to record these dances before they disappear, and of course I should have started years ago, but I suppose one never starts anything until one is ready. These Indians are so funny!—came up to me at the Turtle Dance this time and said, "Now you put away that camera!" knowing it was my *ears,* his idea of being *funny* and how he laughed . . . I have most of the ingredients for the Races. I want to do the pueblo as we knew it in the old days . . . you remember how the colour piled itself up, and below the runners, and then a hint of the Aspen tree altar . . . After that with the help of Trinidad I may try to do some of the old dances they never do . . . We will pass off the scene, but we have seen the heyday.

That heyday of Pueblo dancing, as well as it can be framed, will be remembered in Brett's paintings.

7 Zuni Kachina

THE KEY SYMBOL of Pueblo ceremonialism is the kachina. It is an image with as many reflected images as there are spellings for the word: *katsina* or *katchina, k'atsena* and *k'ats'ana, thlatsina, koko, oxuwah, thliwan.* It is a spirit, a mask, a man, a cult, a way of life, and a visual language by which its meaning may be expressed. Subtle, profound, and simple, it is an ideology rooted in every pueblo.

Long ago, when the Zuñis were fording a river in their search for the sacred middle of the world, some of the children slipped off their mothers' backs and were transformed into water creatures. They went downriver to the junction of the Zuñi and Little Colorado rivers, some eighty miles west of present Zuñi. Here, under the Lake of Whispering Waters, they became kachinas, and established a kachina town. In answer to prayers they came back to dance for the people, bringing rain and fertility to the crops.

But after these dance visits many of the mothers followed them. Too many. So the kachinas informed the people that they would not come any more in person; only in spirit would they invest the masks and the personifications of them which the people were instructed to make. Their impersonators were to be given proper gifts of prayer sticks, and the masks were to be fed with sacred meal, lest drought and sickness result. At death the mask was to be buried, while the impersonator journeyed to the underlake kachina town, where he became a kachina. And so it is today.

The Hopi kachinas are the spirits not only of the Hopis' own clan ancestors, but of the stone, plant, and animal beings encountered during their early migrations and taken into the clan. They live on the San Francisco Mountains to the west. The kachinas of other pueblos—Ácoma, Cochití, Santo Domingo, Laguna, and Zia—live in Wenimats "under a lake with weeds growing in it." Also, like those of Zuñi, Taos kachinas live under Blue Lake, where their projecting ladder may sometimes be seen.

Kachinas thus are spirits. Spirits of the dead, spirits of all the mineral, plant, animal, and human forms that have traveled the Road, spirits of the mythical heroes, the stars, clouds, color-directions—all the spirits except the Earth spirits, as the Earth Mother and Corn Mother. This is an important distinction. For "the universe is endowed with the same breath, rocks, trees, grass, earth, all animals, men." This breath, as we know, is the breath of life. It is the immortal component which at death separates from the body, returns to the one cosmic lake of life, and then reactivates another material form to continue the evolutionary journey on the Road of Life. The kachinas, then, are the inner forms, the spiritual components of the outer physical forms, which may be invoked to manifest their benign powers so that man may be enabled to continue his journey. They are the invisible forces of life. Not really gods, but rather intermediators, messengers. Hence their chief function as rain makers, insuring the fertility and abundance of crops.

The masks are likewise kachinas because they are invested with their spiritual powers. Representing the invisible forces of the sky, the stars, clouds, lightning, and the directions, they may be abstract designs symbolically patterned and colored. Representing animals and birds and insects, they may be animistic and anthropomorphic creatures with horns, hoofs, claws, snouts, beaks. Representing mythical heroes, they may be human forms appropriately dressed to designate their identities. Or they may be a combination of all these; strange forms part man, part beast, part bird. Every boy who is initiated into a kachina group is given a mask. During his lifetime it is ceremonially fed and attended to properly. And when he dies it is buried with the distinct understanding that its supernatural power must be isolated or given back when it is not under rigorous control.

Also kachinas are the men, the impersonators, who wear the masks. During the ceremonial time they wear them they too are invested with supernatural powers. In all pueblos they belong to special kachina cult groups, societies, or kivas. In their ceremonial duties they must be above reproach. They must remain continent, refrain from contact with Whites, avoid quarrels, have good thoughts. If one stumbles or falls while dancing he is whipped; for this betrays an immoderation which might nullify the ceremonial, even bring drought. A kachina is always present at the initiation of young boys. The lifting of his mask, revealing his identity, is always accompanied by a full explanation of the rite he has undergone. This rite of initiation among Navahos takes place on the eighth day of the major nine-night Night Way ceremonial; the masked figures of all these Ways are of course kachinas also. All the masked figures that appear in Pueblo dances; the maskless figures that appear, like those in the Turtle Dance; fetishes on the kiva altars; figures in dry paintings—they are all kachinas. And, as in Nambé, if a boy or man dedicated to membership in a kachina group dies before he is initiated, he will be initiated after death under Sand Lake.

How many kachinas there are is unknown. In Zuñi and the Hopi pueblos, where the most important are constantly reappearing, those easily identified must run into two hundred or more. Children are taught early in life their names and masks. While dancing in the plaza the kachinas seek out the children who need to be punished. They surround a child, frighten him with their grotesque antics, ceremonially whip him with long yucca whips. Then they thrust into his hands a small wooden image of one of themselves.

This "doll" is also called a kachina. It has been made by a member of the child's maternal clan family and given to the kachina to present to him. It is carefully carved of soft cottonwood, painted correctly and decorated with the proper feathers. A collection of such dolls thus constitutes a whole pantheon, as it were, of the kachinas in miniature. And to the usual Westerner of a generation ago any Kachina Dance was usually gruffly referred to as a "Doll Dance."

These dolls are not properly kachinas. They are not invested with power; they serve only to help familiarize children with the names and masks of the real kachinas. Nevertheless they used to be regarded very highly in every pueblo household. Asked whether they might be bought, one host politely answered, "Would we sell our children? How then can we sell our kachinas? They too are a part of our family." Next day, however, the trader was courteously presented with three kachinas as a gift to this boy who had accompanied him—a gift, of course, which had to be recompensed with a gift of trade goods equal in value, amounting to a couple of dollars.

A few years ago when my wife, the Queen of the Bandits, returned from Europe she brought back some of her treasured costume dolls made by the famous Italian, Madame Lenci. She was equally fascinated by these pueblo dolls, which have so much more meaning. So we dug up some old ones, and we set out after some new ones. Only to find that the kachinas now "made for the trade" no longer sell for fifty cents. For a long time they had not been made at all, and those now being made will soon be museum pieces and collectors' items.

The invisible forces of life manifesting themselves through the spirits of the clouds, lightning, color-directions, the heroes, the dead; through the masks representing them; and through the men who impersonate them; the breath of life which equally permeates "rocks, trees, grass, all animals, men"—this is kachina.

We understand now that kachina ceremonials are forms of instrumentalism, mimetic rites for controlling the natural forces of rain, fertility, health, and soundness of mind through the supernatural powers invoked. Practically all the great masked or unmasked Pueblo dances are Kachina Dances or derivatives from them. Yet they are but the public functions which conclude, like the last nights of the Navaho sings, the long and intricate ceremonials of which they are a part.

In none of the eastern pueblos along the Rio Grande are they as important as in the Zuñi and Hopi pueblos to the west. For years we were always sure of running into a "Doll Dance" at Zuñi almost any time we happened there. This was no exaggeration. In Zuñi there are three primary series of kachina dances: one held for three months after the winter solstice, another for three months after the summer solstice, and the third during the *Shalako.*[*] In this latter, the climax of the ceremonial year, kachina imagery reaches full blossom. The *Shalako* is one of the greatest Pueblo ceremonials. And its masks are perhaps the largest known in the world.

The Shalako

Massed on a low hill above a little river, Zuñi has changed little in outline from the classic Cibola which Estevan, the "Black Kachina," saw four centuries ago. There were six of the reported seven walled cities, one for each of the six directions: Hálona, Háwikuh, Mátsaki, Kiákima, Kwákina, and Kianawa. They had up to two hundred houses, five to seven stories high, with a total population of about 3,500. Zuñi remains the seventh and newest. Still the largest pueblo in the Four Corners; and with Taos, also five stories, the highest. Hálona, Ant Place, it is still sometimes called. A human ant hill standing alone on the plain forty miles from railroad and highway. But at the sacred middle of the world. Hence its other name Itiwana, Middle Place.

"Native Zuñi history, 'from-the-beginning talk,'" says Parsons, "concludes with the arrival of the *conquistadores* and a flight to Corn Mountain, ever the mountain of refuge." To its impregnable top the whole population fled once for three years, and again for twelve. There it stands too, its sculptured terraces repeating like a shadow the outline of Zuñi itself. Both kachina, town and mesa. For both in the wintry twilight are obliterating the present, waiting to revive the past.

One shivers in the gathering dusk, damning the delay. All things Indian seem built on an interminable wait; it is as if they have outworn the centuries with patience. We wait at the edge of town, facing the open plain. A crowd of Zuñis, Pueblo neighbors, and visiting Navahos, a few Anglos. But no Spanish-Americans; they alone are forbidden since Estevan's time. Behind, over the little river and the new causeway, the pueblo recedes.

The dusk grows thicker, the cold thinner. Like a corrosive, it penetrates wool and leather. One sees nothing now but the

[*] Also Salako, Chalako, etc.

wintry stars and the effulgence upon the snow. Then suddenly—

The moment, like most things Indian, comes swiftly, unexpectedly at last. They rise abruptly from out of the dark plain, as from the dark aboriginal mind so impenetrable to the White. Six ghostly white shapes gliding effortlessly forward. It is a wonderful moment, one of the few that do exist.

The six spectral shapes look some ten feet high, without arms or legs. Swaying and dipping they keep gliding palely forward. Out of the cold silence comes too a woodeny clack-clack. One sees now the gargoyle heads with their up curving buffalo horns, their great bulging eyes, and their long black clack-clacking beaks. Man, bird, beast—they are not anything, really. But by their strangeness, the remoteness of the vision by which they were created, they embody in their moment of truth an aspect of all.

Long ago, before the wandering Zuñis found the Middle, they stopped to rest beside the little river. So now on this sacred resting place the six *Shalako* pause before the causeway. Priests greet them with a sprinkling of cornmeal. We see now that each of the *Shalako* masks is accompanied by an attendant and an alternate to relieve the man inside. It is an ordeal of endurance and skill. A stumble or fall would call for the whipper. But no one is permitted to see the changing impersonators.

Then darkness falls. In bitter cold the wait begins anew. The causeway, newly built each year, is reserved for the *Shalako*. Everyone else must cross by the bridge downstream. So all converge to the plaza. A thousand or more Zuñis. The slim arrogant Navahos. Stolid Hopis. Santo Domingos here to grudgingly compare the dancing with theirs. Silently they squat in thin-soled moccasins or lounge against the walls, cigarettes in mouth.

In the corrals down the dark slope a goat bleats. The little river washes over the icy stones. Across it, almost indistinguishable, loom the tall pale *Shalako*. Confounding, inexhaustible patience! It has rubbed off the edges of time.

The *Shalako* is a forty-nine day ceremonial, but preparations for it have required a full year. To receive each of the *Shalako* a new house has been built or an old one replastered and purified for use. The hosts pay dearly for the honor with succeeding years of debt and scanty living. For months they have been aided by the kachina impersonators, hauling *vigas* and stones from the mountains, garnering crops, gathering wood. They whitewash the walls, rub down the *vigas*. The long rooms are hung with skins and pelts, blankets, bright calico—anything to make a splash of color. When all is ready the host may need to butcher a dozen cattle and fifty sheep and goats to feed his guests. Women grind corn and bake paper thin bread day and night.

Meanwhile the chosen kachina impersonators have been working in the kivas, memorizing their songs and prayers, making prayer sticks. Every morning they must rise in time to offer prayer meal to the rising sun. Every nightfall they take a bit of their evening meal to the river and offer it with prayers. Each month during the full moon they plant prayer sticks at distant shrines. When they have helped build the new houses in which they will be received, they must build an altar and the new causeway across the river.

Early in October, on the morning of the tenth month of planting prayer sticks at the full of the moon, they receive two cotton strings tied in forty-nine knots, one to be untied each morning thereafter.

On the fortieth day the first kachinas appear in public, parading into the plaza, where they are greeted with sprinkles of meal and taken into seclusion for their eight-day retreat. We recognize them as the Mudheads, the *Koyemshi*, the clowns. Their masks are those of pitifully deformed human faces, colored like their bodies with the pinkish clay of the sacred lake. Like idiot children born of incestuous union they warn against sexual license. Theirs is the most dangerous of all masks. No one dares touch them for fear of going sexually crazy.

Another group of kachinas marches in on the forty-fourth day. They are led by *Sayatasha*, the Rain God of the North. He is called Long Horn from his turquoise-colored mask with a long horn on the right side of the face because "he brings long life." His right eye is small "for the witch people, so they won't live long." The left eye is long "for the people of one heart, so that they may have a long life." In the left hand he carries a bow and arrow. He wears white buckskin and much fine silver, showing that he is most important. He comes to make the days warm. Hence every day he has gone out to pray to the sun, to observe the moon and regulate the monthly planting of the prayer sticks. All this time he has lived under severe restrictions. He cannot leave the pueblo, engage in a quarrel. He is a man whose "heart is good."

Among his party is a little boy of ten, *Shulawitsi*, the

Fire God. His head mask and naked body are smeared black and splotched with the direction colors: red, yellow, blue, and white. A fawnskin pouch filled with seeds hangs over his shoulder. He carries a cedar brand. Attending him is his ceremonial godfather, unmasked, but robed in buckskin.

The group, like the *Koyemshi,* are greeted with meal and conducted to a kiva. Then, I am told, they go to a distant shrine where the little Fire God lights a fire with his cedar brand. It is sprinkled with meal. Prayers and songs are given over it. The curling smoke makes clouds. It also signals the *Shalako* to go into ceremonial retreat, and the governor to call from the house top reminding the people to burn food in their fireplaces for the dead.

Late this afternoon, the forty-eighth day, everything is ready. A ripple of excitement stirs the air. As the sun sinks they come. First *Sayatasha,* Long Horn, the Rain God of the North. With him is his war chief, the Rain God of the South, similarly masked save that he has no horn. *Hututu* he is named for his call. Being very important they walk with long slow strides, poising each foot in the air before bringing it down with a heavy thump. "Hu-tu-tu!" they cry, shaking their deer bone rattles.

Behind them come two *Yamuhakto,* warriors of the East and West. Their name, Carrying Wood, is said to mean "you are a tree and under your body the deer lie down to rest at your feet." So they carry deer antlers in both hands, and across the tops of their heads are sticks of cottonwood. They pray for the trees that there may be wood. Their face masks are blue, punctuated by small eye and mouth holes; their torsos are red; their limbs yellow; and they wear white buckskin kirtles belted with fox skins. Shuffling across the plaza with high lifted knees, twisting from the waist, they peer at the crowds standing reverently in line.

The last two are the *Salimobia,* the War Brothers of the Directions, zenith and nadir. They are the whippers, carrying yucca rods to punish stumbling dancers and whip spectators should one fall. Young men with beautiful bodies, they dart back and forth, always on the run, uttering high, clear calls. They are dangerous and carry the bad luck of crow's feathers. This year one is speckled, the other black. Their big eyes are connected like goggles, and they have long snouts. Like all kachinas they wear, somewhere, a downy eagle feather to symbolize the breath of life, a parrot feather to bring southerly rain, a turtle shell, and deer hoof rattle; and hidden in their belt is their "heart"—a pouch of squash, bean, and corn seeds of the four directions.

All kachinas make the round of the six ceremonial houses, planting prayer sticks inside the threshold. The little Fire God, shivering, clambers up the ladder to leave two more, male and female, in a box on the flat roof. All then enter the house on a meal trail laid to the altar. Here they place the seeds from their belts in a basket on the new altar and in a hole in the center of the floor. The walls, floor, and ceiling are marked with meal. Long Horn now blesses the house in a long poetic prayer.

All kachinas are now ritually seated by the host. They raise their masks, smoke reed cigarettes. The host casually questions them about their coming. The kachinas now begin to answer with a long recital that takes some six hours.

Meanwhile, in other houses, the *Koyemshi* are following a similar procedure. Thus the abiding places of the giant *Shalako* are made ready. The crowds outside now wait in darkness, cold, and silence. Dogs are shadows; people, poles. They wait as one must wait for the gods: in hope and patient humility, facing the dark slope, the freezing river and its new causeway of stones and sticks.

In a breathless moment they appear again at last.

The *Shalako* come! It is the incoming of the gods to Zuñi, an Indian Entrance of the Gods into Valhalla. Sound the drums. Let the gourds be shaken, the deer bones and the turtle shell rattles. We have waited long enough. Let's have a real show!

But the black curtain doesn't go up. There is no curtain, no spectators, no actors. There are no gods, really. There is only the timeless flow of the divine through all, a quickening perception of the spiritual essence in all things. Yet how wonderful it is. A moment like the first, not repeated again and gone instantly.

Palely the tall spectral shapes come gliding across the causeway. The immense crowd gives way, rolling back in silent waves, washing down the dark alleys.

As doors open and light streams forth you can see them clearly at last. Magnificent figures, their breasts top the heads of the retreating crowd, their eagle feather head-dresses reach above the roof beams. All six are alike. The head mask is turquoise in color, surmounted with a crest of eagle feathers raying like the sun. The huge up-curving horns are hung with red feathers. The bulging ball eyes roll. The long wooden beak clack-clacks. Each wears long black hair, and a ruff of raven feathers around the throat. The blue turquoise face is matched by a breast plate. The rest of the armless body is draped with double Hopi kirtles, pure white, with their beautiful border embroidery of red, black, and green. Below, barely visible and incredibly tiny, protrude the beaded moccasins of the impersonator inside. Now one sees his perfect co-ordination and sense of balance in the smooth swift glide, the tall figure swaying over the running feet, the eyes rolling, the beak clacking, and finally the swoop as each *Shalako* precariously dips its head to enter one of the ceremonial houses.

In each house the ritual is the same, and the same that was followed some hours ago by the previous, lesser kachinas. The *Shalako* is seated by the altar on the far side of the big room, "the valuable place." Reed cigarettes are passed around and the smoke is blown to the six directions so "that the rain makers may not withhold their misty breath."

Now while the host, surrounded by family, friends, and attendants, questions the *Shalako* about his coming, the impersonator takes off his mask and wipes off his sweating body. One sees now that he wears a small white buckskin cap, a black jacket; and that to his red-painted knees is tied a string of bells. But nothing interrupts his long, prescribed ritual. Monotonously it continues for two hours or more.

Among other things it is an invocation of fecundity, a blessing to all: "those with snow upon their heads, with moss on their faces, with skinny knees, no longer upright, and leaning on canes, even all of these":

> . . . I have passed you on your roads.
> My divine father's life-giving breath,
> His breath of old age,
> His breath of waters,
> His breath of seeds,
> His breath of riches,
> His breath of fecundity,
> His breath of power,
> His breath of strong spirit,
> His breath of all good fortune, whatsoever—
> Asking for his breath,
> And into my warm body,
> Drawing his breath,
> I add to your breath now.*

* Ruth L. Bunzel translation.

As we know, breath is the symbol of life, and inhaling an act of ritual blessing. Wherefore now at the end of the long ritual chant all inhale, holding their wrinkled brown hands up before their nostrils that they may partake of the sacred essence of prayer.

Meanwhile the house has been filling with spectators during the interminable ritual. No one is forbidden save Spanish-Americans; everyone is a welcome guest. So of course everyone comes. Zuñi's excellent dancing and generous feasts are proverbial. The forty-mile road across the desert and through the cedars, muddy, and slippery as a river of glue, has by now frozen hard. Cars stuck in adobe since afternoon lurch into the pueblo loaded with visiting Pueblos and Anglos. More Navahos on horseback ride in—as they will ride, a hundred miles, to buzzard at a feast. Trading posts close, and driven from their red-bellied stoves dozens more come to soak up the hot stench of the ceremonial chambers.

On the other side of the ceremonial chamber, the lofty center room, is the kitchen where the women are ladling out the feast. Patiently they work through the side rooms with pots of stew, platters of paper-thin bread, chunks of meat, sweetened corn, and chiles. The floors are a mass of squatting Indians. Wrapped in sheepskin coats, leather vests, and blankets—Navaho, the fine old Pendletons, the atrocious Montgomery Wards—the men sit gorging meat and washing it down with tin cans of coffee. The women nurse babies, cat nap.

In another side room, as in an opera box, favored guests sit on chairs—friends of the traders perhaps, or government agents. But uncomfortably, for there is no getting out. And soon these rooms are packed too.

The ceremonial room itself almost defies description. It has the visual impact of a mammoth, super-colossal, technicolor stage-setting for the court of Kublai Khan. There is the great, lofty room with its forty-foot *vigas* gleaming honey yellow; the crackling flames and curling smoke staining the fresh-hewn stones of the fireplace; the snow-white altar, with its clear turquoise and brilliant red, the prayer sticks "clothed in our grandfather, turkey's, robe of cloud," its altar painting "our house of massed clouds," its corn plants "stretching out their hands to all directions, calling for rain." There is the "Council of Gods," the masked kachinas, and all around them, save for a lane running the length of the room, the people. Packed with chairs and benches, it is a solid mass of people. One great vari-colored body with hundreds of heads. In back, along the walls, in the doorways, stand a hundred more. Everyone smokes, spits, pops his package of chewing gum. The stench is too thick to cut with an acetylene torch. To move ten feet is ten minutes' work. Caught in such a crowd the visiting Whites suffer their boredom with pale drawn faces running with sweat. Or nauseated by the stench, utterly fatigued, they fight to get out into the clear, freezing night. And ten minutes later, numb with cold and still paler, they fight to get back in. These interminable Indian ceremonials! Whatever else they are, they are ordeals requiring the guts of a statue.

About eleven o'clock the ritual chants of the kachinas end. Food from the feast is taken down to the river. All the dead have returned. Now the dancing begins.

From the "valuable place" rises the tall *Shalako.* He is no longer pale, remote. The flame light gives life to his snow-white kirtles. The woven stylized designs of clear turquoise and brilliant red leap out; the black condor-like ruff of ravens' feathers around his throat shines like polished ebony. In the silence the long beak clack-clacks with a terrific clatter. Below him faces turn upward. Twice the height of a man his buffalo horns hook the air. His headdress of eagle feathers almost brushes the beams.

He comes gliding up the lane. The tall body sways, then dips. The gargoyle head swings over the rim of the crowd. Its bulging eyes roll in their sockets. Then back again he goes dancing, really gliding with effortless precision and smooth stateliness. So till dawn the *Shalako* dances before his people.

They sit silently and calmly impressed. Only in the face of a child in his mother's lap does one see rapture in the presence of a god. His little black shoe-button eyes follow the great figure, the flower-like face quivers and is still again. What seed is implanted in that little center of emotion and subconscious thought? Will the government school and the mission church ever completely stifle its invisible growth? And one finds an answer in the face of an old man with "snow on his head" and "moss on his face." It is there, graven in the deep wrinkles and the half-closed eyes—the seed which has come to flower.

It is a silent, relaxed, easy-going crowd. There is only one disturbance on the steps, a dull angry murmur as a fool Zuñi makes a fool white man take off his hat. It is the only discord of the night, and it makes one sicker than the stench.

There is something honest and reassuring about a Zuñi scratching for lice or picking his nose, utterly at ease in the presence of his gods. But this holy and hypocritical "hats off, this is our religion, you've got to be respectful" attitude smacks too much of the White.

One stumbles out into the freezing December night. The dark lanes between the houses are chasms of frozen silence. One puts out numb hands, like tapers, to find the way. Then abruptly one stumbles around a corner to see a single petal of light on the rime covered earth. And then comes the faint clatter of the wooden beak inside.

In each of the six houses it is the same. In the *Sayatasha* house, Long Horn and *Hututu* are dancing together now. East and West, embodied in the *Yamuhakto,* join North and South. Then zenith and nadir, the *Salimobia,* flash in and out. The little Fire God, almost exhausted on the floor, is prodded to his feet again by his ceremonial godfather. In the *Koyemshi* house the Mudheads dance with the pink sweat running off their clay-smeared bodies. And everywhere, in all six houses, the *Shalako.*

Suddenly at dawn it stops. Long Horn clambers up to the roof. Facing east he unties the last knot, the forty-ninth in his string, and intones a prayer. The ceremonial houses are emptied and closed; the kachinas unmask and their heads are washed by the women of the household.

Outside, the darkness has faded. The mists rise. The sun touches the adobe walls with a yellow wand. It is the signal for a Navaho *Yei-bet-chai.* One sees it correct to step, timing, and every detail of costume. But thank God! the dancers, though naked to the waist, have clambered into woolen drawers.

The dance, reports Miss Ruth Bunzel, was first given long ago by visiting Navahos who, having nothing to eat, had come for food. At the same time the Zuñis were suffering from "a sickness of swellings." So led by *Yei-bet-chai* the Navahos danced by "two and two around the village." As they left, the Zuñis spat, saying, "Now you will take away with you this sickness"; and to the sickness they said, "Now you will go with these people." Since then the Navahos have wanted to dance in the pueblo again. But the Zuñis "just dance the Navaho dance with their own masks and it doesn't cost them anything."

A lone horseman, swathed to the eyes in his blanket,

creaks over the bridge. One follows him, shaking in the intense cold. The planks are white with hoar frost. The stones along the river are covered with ice. Tufts of buffalo grass seem dipped in silver polish. What a bitter December dawn. Anything for a cup of coffee!

At noon, on this forty-ninth day, the *Shalako* leave. Gliding past house tops thronged with people they gather at the river. In the bright, warm sunlight they loom bigger, brighter, stranger than at night. Escorted by flutists and singers, anointed with pinches of meal, they cross the causeway and glide swiftly away from reverent Zuñi. Glide back to their source, disappearing as suddenly as they came. But to come again and mingle with their people, to renew the faith, to quicken the old apperception that the spiritual essence is in man as in gods, and that the flow between them is unbroken.

That yonder to where the life-giving road
Of your sun-father comes out,
Your roads may reach;
That clasping hands,
Holding one another fast,
You may finish your roads,
To this end, I add to your breath now.*

The Zuñi Book of the Dead

For four days afterward there are dances in the plaza by each of the six kiva groups, ending on the last day with all groups dancing at once.

During this period there are other secret rituals at distant shrines. One of these is participated in by the *Shalako.* They take turns running across the plain to bury their prayer sticks in a hole. The alternates then run to sprinkle the hole with meal. Running is the last test of their strength. If one falls it is obvious that the impersonator has not been continent, has not kept a good heart. In this case he is whipped by Long Horn, and the waiting *Salimobia* are sent back into town to whip everybody they meet in exorcism. As the *Shalako* then depart running, men run after them and try to strike them. Counting coup, one cries, "I have killed a deer": The *Shalako* is then laid down as a ceremonially killed deer, his head to the east and sprinkled with meal. The act is suggestive of

* Ruth L. Bunzel translation.

sacrificing the *Shalako* who thus becomes a deer and imparts hunting luck to his "killer."

It is little wonder that the *Shalako,* with its vast unplumbed ceremonialism, has received from the time of Bernardino de Sahugún and the early Spanish priests more observation than perhaps any single Pueblo ceremonial. Of late years Mrs. Elsie Clews Parsons, Dr. Franz Boas, Ruth Benedict, and many other scholars have resided in Zuñi for anthropological study. The best of these studies, by far, is the paper prepared by Ruth L. Bunzel for the *Forty-Seventh Annual Report of the Bureau of American Ethnology,* containing translations of the long ritual chants. Pure poetry translated with deep feeling, they are embodied in a text that is among the finest apperceptive writings on Pueblo life and character yet achieved. But the ceremonial itself is too rich in meaning to be exhausted. We have transcribed and translated it, but we have not evaluated or interpreted it.

The interpretations so far attempted vary widely. As suggested by Mrs. Parsons, the *Shalako* may be a war ceremonial. Long Horn and *Hututu* are war chiefs. The *Salimobia* are the War Brothers of the Directions. The *Koyemshi* are scouts. The *Shalako* themselves carry war clubs hidden in their belts, and their crooks of office are associated with the scalp ritual. There is the signal fire, the ritual killing.

Or it may be a hunt ceremonial. The evidence for this are the *Yamuhakto,* representing the forest home of the deer. The *Koyemshi* do the dance of the mountain sheep. The *Shalako* are killed and laid out as deer. And there is a deer hunt held before the ceremonial.

Or it may be a ceremonial for longevity. Or like most kachina ceremonies, a ceremonial for fertility and reproduction.

It seems to this writer that we greatly underestimate the esoteric significance of all Pueblo ceremonialism by restricting ourselves to these purely surface and ethnological explanations. For above all, the *Shalako* is a ceremonial for the dead. The process of death, the return of the dead, the ritual feeding of the dead, the long recitals of the spirits of the dead, the psychological preparation for death—these combine into the one underlying motif of the complete ceremonial. This is what makes it one of the greatest Pueblo ceremonials and one of the unique rituals in the world.

To understand its meaning we must bear in mind all that

we have learned of Pueblo and Navaho eschatology and its parallels found in the *Bardo Thodol, The Tibetan Book of the Dead,* in *The Secret of the Golden Flower,* the Chinese *Book of Life,* and in the Egyptian *Book of the Dead.*

They hold that man is composed of seven principles. Each corresponds, with its physical and psychical attributes, to the seven worlds or states of existence he must pass through on his Road of Life: the four successive worlds he has already emerged from, and the three more successive states whose attributes are in him in embryo. They manifest themselves, as we recall,[1] in bi-polar structures and tensions which both complement and conflict with each other during his life.

What happens when man dies?

At the instant of death the "soul" escapes the body at the crown of the head, the scalp-lock over the sagittal suture where the two parietal bones articulate.[2]

But this "soul" is a dual bi-polar phenomena. Its dark, earth-bound principle, the freed *anima,* hovers around the body for four days. Then it disintegrates and returns to earth—or as the Navahos believe, goes to the symbolic black north. Hence to appease and dismiss it, the various scalp dance ceremonies common to the Pueblos and Navahos.[3] This is the Navaho *chindi,* the Chinese *kuei* and the Buddhists' so-called "astral body," a nebulous pattern of the whole which is also held to disintegrate after four days.

Differentiated from this "ghost" is the enduring life principle, the higher spiritual soul, the bright and active *animus.* It rises into the air in a superconscious condition and flows back into the reservoir of life. It is this "spirit" which eventually at the end of the Road of Life will return to "live in the sun."

Hence at Ácoma, when a person dies, his hair is parted over the forehead to represent the Milky Way, and the bangs cut with four corners in observance of the ceremonial four-day period immediately following death. At the side of the head are placed feathers of the sun hawk and corn husks to show that he has been initiated as a kachina. The body is "planted" (buried) with the head to the east so he will be reborn. For his spiritual consciousness still has three more worlds or states of existence to pass through. And it is with its experiences that we are now concerned.

The "dead" person after he dies, then, undergoes first a

[1] P. 186. [2] P. 248. [3] P. 248.

four-day period of unconsciousness. It is an embryonic state preceding birth into the after-death world which parallels the embryonic state preceding birth into the human world. He then wakes into the *Bardo,* after-death, dream or subconscious plane to which he has transferred his existence from the mortal, conscious plane. But all his experiences seem as real, as vivid to him as had those in his equally illusory "living" state.

They begin at once. According to the *Bardo Thodol,* he hears a series of four "awe-inspiring" sounds. A sound "as of a jungle afire"; a sound "like a thousand thunders reverberating simultaneously"; a sound "like the breaking of ocean waves"; a sound "like the crumbling down of a mountain." It is as if the world is disintegrating around him. His mortal body is. It is beginning to disintegrate and separate into the original elements of the four worlds of which it was composed: fire, air, water, earth. There are indeed only four ways of burial for his physical body: cremation by fire, leaving it exposed on a high cliff for birds of the air to devour, burying it at sea, and letting it return to earth.

But each of these physical elements has its mental and emotional attributes. So now begins a series of psychic experiences. There appear masses of light corresponding to the colors of the four worlds, which blind and dazzle him. Fearful figures which beset him. Wrathful deities which menace him. Peaceful deities which help him. Scenes of violent action which take place before him. These phenomena of course are but psychic reflections of his deeds, thoughts and emotions in previous states. A reading, as it were, of his Book of Memory.

From some figures and colors he flees; towards some he is inclined. The inclination of his own passions, desires, emotions and thoughts, according to his degree of development—his own conscience—is the determining factor in the direction he takes. This, as we understand it, is the Judgment. He thus follows a colored light path, white, yellow, red, or blue-green, to a corresponding realm or lake. These colored lakes are synonymous with the Eastern, Southern, Western, or Northern continents, previously described, into which he will be reborn to continue his road. They symbolize the state of development to which he is fitted.

In these lake realms he leads for a necessary time in his after-death state the life of what we variously term fairies or spirits; the Pueblos, kachinas; the Buddhists, *devas*. In this fourth dimensional existence all these beings of like inclination, development, and destination live consciously together, see each other with *deva* vision, just as they did in their incarnate world existence. But they cannot be seen by those of dissimilar orders, nor by man. They may pay visits to help mankind, but they are not gods.

Mrs. Rhys Davids, in *Buddhist Psychology* rightly "objects to the ordinary translation of the word 'devas' as 'gods.'" She explains that the *devas* who now and then pay visits on earth, at home, are nothing more than "so many ladies and gentlemen, pleasant, courteous, and respectful to great earth-teachers or earnest disciples . . . They will again be denizens of earth. No, Buddhist *devas* are not gods. And one way to understand Buddhist doctrine is to cease calling them so."

And so after a necessary time spent on this *Bardo* plane, he is released from the great pool of life into reincarnate existence on earth as man, again to continue his Road of Life on the conscious plane; alternating as night and day, with its wakeful and dream, conscious and subconscious states, his twofold existence. Until, as we have already learned, the cosmic dualities of his nature are finally reconciled and he is united at last with the divine source which has no beginning and no end.

All these phenomena of his mysterious transition to the *Bardo* plane take place, according to the *Bardo Thodol,* in a symbolical period of forty-nine days—seven days each for the seven states comprising his total existence. This is the precise time required for the Zuñi *Shalako* ceremonial, as designated by the cotton strings tied into forty-nine knots.

All life, in one respect, is a preparation for death. And since the preceding winter solstice, when the impersonators are chosen, they have been preparing for the ceremonial. But it actually begins on the tenth month of planting prayer sticks at the full of the moon when the sun chief or *Pekwin* gives them the knotted strings. October too is the beginning of the periodic death of nature; all the crops have come to fruition and have been harvested; the earth begins to withdraw into itself.

Each day one knot is untied as the ceremonial progresses. It is significant that the first group of kachinas to appear in public, on the fortieth day, are the *Koyemshi,* who warn against sexual license. They signify in man, as in nature, the necessary cessation of sexual activity, the beginning of the period of continence.

Four days later Long Horn, the most important of the kachinas, appears. With his long horn and long left eye (on the heart side), he "brings long life." This assurance seems paradoxical in a death ceremonial. But it can be better understood when it is remembered that, among Buddhists, longevity is also aimed at and aided by supplication to the Buddha of Ever-Enduring Life as an antidote or counteracting influence to the practice of some kinds of yoga which tends to shorten life, for it rapidly ripens the physical body for death.

With the appearance of all the other kachinas we see represented all the colors, all the directions, of the Eastern, Southern, Western, and Northern continents of the *Bardo* cosmography—those realms chosen by the spirits of the dead for future reincarnation according to their degree of development. *Sayatasha,* of the North; *Hututu,* of the South; the *Yamuhakto,* of the East and West. Over all of them the *Salimobia,* the whippers, have power. They represent nadir, the dark underworld domain of unhappy kachinas, and zenith, the above, lying in the direction of the sun father. *Shulawitsi* is a little boy for he represents fire, the original spark of life; and he is splotched with all the directional colors because all the previous worlds and all the future worlds of existence are equally imbued with life.

Indeed, the whole Zuñi cosmography is almost identical with that of the Buddhist. The underlake town of the Zuñi kachinas is similar to the lake realms of the *Bardo Thodol.* And this Lake of Whispering Waters as well as other lakes and sacred springs are openings to the system of waterways connecting with the four oceans encircling the four worlds, as also held by the Buddhist doctrine.

So it is from here that the kachinas come—these "many ladies and gentlemen, pleasant, courteous, and respectful"—to be received as honored guests and given cigarettes, food, and drink. They are not gods; no more than are the Buddhist *devas.* They are the spirits of the dead; of all the plant, animal, and human forms; of the clouds, the color-directions; the inner forms, the invisible forces of life. Wherefore their masks of horn, claw, snout, beak, or abstract design represent all aspects of life, as the great composite *Shalako.*

And why have they come? Why simply to recount their story to fellow travelers whom they have "passed on their roads," and to assure them of an equally pleasant journey. Especially "those with snow upon their heads, with moss on their faces, with skinny knees, no longer upright, and leaning on canes, even all of these." To bring a blessing of fecundity and fertility to all, man, beast, bird, and corn. For each there is a separate kind of rebirth according to the degree of his fourfold development. Birth by heat and moisture for the seeds of the vegetable kingdom; by egg; by womb; and supernormal birth by transferring consciousness from one state to another, as accomplished by all mythical heroes. Above all, to reassure their people of the naturalness of the death process and death state as paralleling their existence on earth. It is an assurance which avoids the fallacious terror that a soul exists only on earth in a human body for the short space of only one lifetime, and that it is irretrievably committed to the horrors of Hell or the celestial raptures of Heaven for all eternity on the basis of this short span. On the contrary, it reaffirms a belief in the ultimate evolution of every living thing, subhuman, human, and superhuman.

The "killing" of the *Shalako* and the belief that the *Shalako* then turns into a deer imparting hunting luck to the "killer," as postulated by Mrs. Parsons, seems at variance with this. It assumes that a human can be reborn into a lower plane, as into an animal form. This is contrary to both Buddhist doctrine and the tenor of all Pueblo ceremonialism; for man is Made From Everything, a derivative summation of all his previous states of existence; and life is a one way road.

So the *Shalako* dance and mingle with their people, who have no terrors of obliteration. And when they leave, the same motif of the whole orchestral ceremonial is repeated in the four days of kachina dancing afterward, until they have made their transition back into the *Bardo* plane. The winter solstice is at hand. All the fires are extinguished. The whole earth dies. But from the Zuñi *Shalako* we know that it is all simply a withdrawal that life may be renewed with freshness, increased vigor, and a deep sense of its continuous flow.

This is the simple and profound meaning of the ancient rites of the Chinese, of the Celts in Brittany and Ireland, of those described in the *Tibetan Book of the Dead* and the *Egyptian Book of the Dead.* It is in their tradition, written with Pueblo imagery and symbolism, that the *Shalako* is the *Zuñi Book of the Dead.*

8 Hopi Ceremonialism

NAVAHO CEREMONIALISM is preoccupied with restoring harmony between the individual and the supernatural forces of the universe. Its specific function is healing illnesses of the mind and body.

Pueblo ceremonialism is more abstract. It is ritually preoccupied with maintaining harmony in the universe. Its chief function is bringing rain.

To the Pueblos everything alive is significant; everything significant is alive. Nothing is differentiated except in degree. All combine into a rhythmic, interlocked web. No people emphasize this more than the Hopi.

The Hopi pueblos cling to three mesas in the heart of the Four Corners. Walpi and Sichomovi, on the high narrow peninsula of First Mesa; Mishongnovi, Shipaulovi, and Shumapovi, on the curving crescent of Second Mesa; Oraibi and Hotevilla on Third Mesa, and farther west, new Moencopi. No part of the vast arid wilderness is more inhospitable than their five hundred square miles of sandy desert. Looking no larger than Navaho blankets, small fields of stunted squaw corn lie far out on the plain, necessitating a daily ten-mile walk for their care. Patches of squash and beans are terraced into the rocky hillsides to catch underground flows of water. Orchards of a dozen trees bearing peaches the size of walnuts are watered from jars carried uphill on women's heads. Nowhere is life such a desperate struggle. And nowhere is it more serene, more beautifully framed by the slow-moving clouds in the turquoise sky, the vivid sunrises and sunsets, the oceans of color forever undulating over the immeasurable plain. The Hopi acknowledges the harshness and the beauty with equal acceptance. Armed with no more than an ancient planting stick he has nurtured his tribal life through a dozen centuries. And clad in the armor of an invincible faith, he has developed a ceremonialism that is as complex, abstract, and powerful as any ever known. It is a cabalistic maze. It is simple as prayer. It brings rain.

Doubtless it would be an exaggeration to say that Hopi ceremonialism is the root mother of all Pueblo and Navaho ceremonialism. There are too many profound differences. But to emphasize the differences is to miss the value of them all. Their significance lies in their common meanings. The Navahos recognize this. They have a profound respect, almost an awe, of Hopi "power." The other pueblos view Hopi ceremonialism with almost equal veneration. To Hopi dances couriers are often sent from other pueblos to pluck a twig of spruce from the kachinas to plant in their own fields. There is not a Pueblo dance that is not garbed in the traditional Hopi embroidered dance kirtle and sash. Among the Whites, from the earliest Spaniards to the present Anglos, the Hopis have been regarded always as the most aloof from alien contact, the most secretive, the most obdurate to change. The Hopis themselves are aware of their power. Their term for anything "bad" or irrelevant is simply *kahopi*—not Hopi. But this pride is far from being the arrogant pride of the Navaho. Unlike their warring, restless, adaptative neighbors, their traditions are rooted in peace. Hopi means literally "People of Peace." And this indomitable strength of character, this persistence which has outworn the centuries, is rooted in the prayer sticks buried in the pueblo plaza—the "roots of the town." Their ceremonialism is the rock to which they have clung.

A friend in a distant Rio Grande pueblo once was giving me some rare information. He described the rite followed, but he did not know its meaning. Yet he was sure of its efficacy. Why? "The Hopis know. Them people they know!"

The Hopi creation myth coincides in outline with those of other Pueblos and the Navahos, with which we are already familiar. Man emerged from four successive worlds corresponding to the Zuñi's Umbilical Womb, Vaginal Womb, Womb of Parturition, and World of Disseminated Light and Knowledge; and to the Navaho's similar four worlds as symbolized by fire, air, water, and earth. During part of the time they were in the underworld they were ants; just as the Red Ant People were among the first people of the Navahos, and Zuñi's ceremonial name is Ant Place.

In the preceding underworld the same separation of the sexes took place. Sexual license was practiced by masturbation with a "gourd of deer, hare blood, or eagle feather," corresponding to that of the Navahos' Moving Up Way. As a result, monsters were born as in Monster Way. Pookonghoya and Balongahoya, War Twins similar to Monster Slayer and Born for Water, were born through solar impregnation and rain drops. The mother deity—as Iyatiku, in the pueblos of Zia, Ácoma, Cochití, and others, and Changing Woman among the Navahos—lay on her back in the sun and rain. Like her, she has a dual counterpart in Nautsili. Among the Hopi she has many names to compare with "Bringing to Life": Dawn Woman, Thought Woman, whose every thought became a creation, and Hard Substance Woman, because she is the owner of turquoise, coral, and shells; and thus is identified with White Shell Woman.

The Hopi *sipapu*, the place of Emergence, is an actual spot in the walls of Grand Canyon. The first to emerge were the War Twins; Spider Woman, their ceremonial grandmother, who was also the fate mother of the Navaho Twins; and Mocking Bird, whose songs are still sung at the *Wuwuchim* ceremonial. The Twins grew in four days, as the Navahos hold. It was they who produced order after the Emergence, hardened the soft earth, led the people on their migrations, freed them from the monsters, and gave them their ceremonies.

The stars were thrown up into the sky by Coyote, as in Navaho legend. The moon was made of an unwounded buckskin and raised to position. The sun was made of a shield of white cotton. As in Night Way there was trouble raising it. First Turkey tried, burning his head feathers red. Next Buzzard tried, burning his head bald. Then Eagle, scorching his head yellow. Then the Hawk. Finally all together raised it.

Consistent with Hopi complexity in all ceremonialism, there are many myth figures which are not found among the other Pueblos and the Navahos. Behind Dawn Woman there looms Muy'-ingwa, a male maize spirit protecting all vegetation, chief of nadir, father of the Underworld. There is Masauwa, the first householder of Hopiland, a personage of death, war, fire, and night. To his underground house journey the spirits of the dead for initiation. The breath body is first met by Tokonaka, an Agave sentinel, who tests its fitness to pass on. Sand Altar Woman is the sister of Muy'-ingwa and wife of Masauwa. Conceptually she is like the Deer Mothers of Taos, the Game Mothers of various other pueblos, and is the patroness of all game animals.

As in other ceremonialism, a bird and an animal are associated with each of the directions, and the symbolism of all is important. Outstanding is the snake. Snake People were the first occupants of the Hopi pueblos. Water Serpent came from the south and is patron of the Water Corn clan. He is associated with nadir, and effects the floods and earthquakes caused by people's sexual misconduct. But feathered he becomes a personification of the breath of life; he is Quetzalcoatl, the Feathered Serpent of the Toltecs.

Closely associated with the snake is the antelope. The Horn People were the second to reach the Hopi pueblos, coming from the east. Antelope heads are placed on the altars of the Antelope Society at Oraibi, and the Agave Society, Walpi; and members of the Horn Society wear horns.

Eagles are captured and their heads washed "to take them into the tribe." They are killed for ceremonials, notably on the morning after the *Niman Katchina;* food and kachina dolls are given them; and they are buried. The eagle is associated with Zenith and the sun.

Locust is the Humpbacked Flute Player, who plays his flute on the Flute Society altar at Walpi. He keeps the kiva warm with his music, melts the snow and brings warm weather, and is as important a personage as Humpback of Night Way among Navahos. He went up through three worlds hunting for the *sipapu,* playing his flute and remaining indifferent to the lightning bolts hurled at him. Hence the ten-day Flute ceremonial, alternating with the Snake-Antelope ceremonial in different years, dramatizes the Emergence and the fertilization of maize by lightning. This is paralleled by the Aztec lightning god striking the corn, as shown in the Nuttall Codex. And it in turn is recapitulated in the Hopi sand painting which shows six ears of corn colored with the directional colors radiating from a bowl at the center, along with pebbles and bird-skins of the corresponding color directions.

As with animals and birds, plants are also symbolized with reference to the directions. There is the same major emphasis upon corn, "the Hopi's heart." Squash is the basis of high ritual and a stylized art famous throughout the Four Corners. Beans fill important ritual roles. Colored according to the directions, they determine sometimes the order of kachina initiation.

As with Zuñi, the Hopi kachinas play a pre-eminent role in all ceremonial life. Less spectacular perhaps, but possibly more numerous, they number over two hundred. At all times kachina ideology dominates Hopi thought. But like those of Zuñi their two major appearances occur near the winter and summer solstices, and they give rise to two significant kachina ceremonials.

The Powamu

The *Powamu* ceremonial is popularly called the Coming In of the Kachinas. Another common name for it is the Bean Planting Ceremony. *Powamu* means simply "put in order," and this is what it is. A ceremonial for exorcising the cold and wind of winter, for cleansing the fields for spring planting, obtaining crop omens from beans, initiating children (every four years), and curing the people of rheumatism. To put all these things in order the kachinas come back from their home in the San Francisco Mountains.

Preparations begin just after the winter solstice, when, at the full of the moon, beans are secretly planted in the kiva. On the morning after the February full moon appears, the Crier announces from the house top that *Powamu* has begun. Eight days later the kachina members gather in the kiva. They make the rounds of the pueblo ordering boys to hunt and girls to grind corn for them. For four days the children fast from salt and flesh, while the kachinas sing, pray, renovate their masks, and tend to the planted bean seeds. The earth-filled baskets are kept wet, a fire is maintained constantly and a blanket is stretched across the ladder opening. In this hothouse the seeds are forced to an unseasonable sprouting, and the tiny green shoots are further strengthened by song and prayer.

At the end of these four days, the children are initiated in the usual ceremony. The kachina masks are terrifying; the strikes of their yucca whips are light but meaningful. After the children are whipped and initiated, old people present themselves to be whipped to cure their rheumatism. All night kachinas dance in the kivas, masked, painted, and wearing beautiful four-petalled squash blossoms made of corn husks. The bean sprouts are carefully inspected and from their growth a prediction of the year's crops is read. On the last day a public dance is held, presents and kachina dolls are distributed, a feast given. The kachinas have come back. From now on they dance weekly in the plazas.

Niman Kachina

The *Niman Kachina* is the Home-Going of the kachinas back to the San Francisco Mountains.

It begins ten days after the summer solstice, when Intiwa, the *Powamu* society chief, sets up his standard at the entrance of the Horn kiva. It is a ten-day ceremonial. The first eight days are required for kiva rituals. Counterbalancing the *Powamu,* its emphasis, like that of the Zuñi *Shalako,* is upon the slowing pulse beat of life. Prayer sticks for Spider Woman are made, representing the prayers of old Hopi women, and hawk prayer feathers for the War Brothers, representing the prayers of old men. An altar of the directions is set up. On it four gourds of water are placed by four different clans. In a long, elaborate altar ceremony, songs and prayers are given. The plank over the *sipapu* is ritually knocked, calling for Muyingwa below. In sand in front of the altar are planted all the prayer sticks—hundreds, male and female, of all directions, color of all kinds. And on the eighth night an all night dance is held.

The public appearance of the kachinas begins at dawn and is almost continuous throughout the ninth day. It is a farewell of beautiful, barbaric pageantry. The pigments of the masks have been scratched off and buried; new paint put on. There are helmet masks topped with feathers and grass. High terraced *tablitas* are painted with cloud and rainbow, with corn and butterfly. Sometimes, on the back, a kachina doll standing on an ear of corn. The inevitable ruff of spruce around the throat, a sprig carried in one hand. There are six female kachinas with faces hidden by a long red fringe, their parted black hair done up in whorls, the squash blossoms of Hopi virginity. Just like those worn in the crowd by Hopi brides, who have been barred from seeing any dance during the year until this *Niman Kachina.*

How beautiful it is in the thick dust, the stifling heat.

The dancing kachinas. The men bringing them prayer sticks; flipping drops of water over them with an eagle feather; blowing smoke at them from a ceremonial pipe; sprinkling them with meal. Women bringing paper thin *piki* bread tied in bundles, sticky chocolate cake. Children shyly offering the first fruits of the fields: small ears of corn, little melons, tiny, pink-cheeked peaches. And the kachinas too have gifts for them: bows and arrows, kachina dolls in their image.

So they dance. Till sunset. Then, led by Intiwa, they leave. Going to the far mesa point, pursued by the people plucking spruce twigs from their costumes to plant in their fields. Silently moving alone now down the rocky trail toward the setting sun, a weirdly beautiful procession of figures struck by a strange enchantment beyond the touch of man. Vanishing at last, as all kachinas must vanish, into their immemorial home . . . But to reappear at sunrise on the point, only for a moment. An hallucination to the sleepy spectator. A promise of their return.

The ripe richness, grotesque imagery, and barbaric beauty of Hopi ceremonials are almost unbelievable and certainly indescribable. They fill the calendar year. The *Soyal* at the winter solstice turning back the sun to summer. The fire ritual of *Wuwuchim.* The *Powamu* and *Niman Kachina.* The women's ceremonials of *Marau, Lakon,* and *Oazol.* The Flute ceremonial observing the Emergence. The Snake-Antelope ceremonial. The Summer Solstice ceremonial turning back the sun to winter. The War and Stick Swallowing ceremonies. The spring races, the kachina races. The many dances—kachina dances, masked and unmasked, the women's beautiful Buffalo Dance and delicate Butterfly Dance. With all their perpetual prayer stick planting. Their dry paintings of sand, meal, and pollen, on the altar, in front of it, or around the *sipapu.* The kiva withdrawals, initiation of children, ritual songs, prayers, and myths, the directional color systems, the symbolism of stone, animal, plant . . . All these parallel those we have already observed in other Pueblo and Navaho ceremonials.

Like the Navaho sings, the major Hopi ceremonials are of nine nights' duration, but measured by the intervening and overlapping eight or ten days. They too are healing ceremonials. The *Powamu* for rheumatism, the *Flute* for lightning shock, the Snake-Antelope for swellings, the War for bronchial trouble, the *Lakon* for eczema, the *Maru* for venereal diseases. Like Pueblo ceremonials their last days end in great public dances. Like both Navaho and Pueblo ceremonials they are myth-dramas, mystery plays. They are, in a sense, a recapitulation of all Navaho and Pueblo ceremonialism. They stem back, as the symbolism of the Navaho Flint Way derives from the Mesa Verde Sun Temple, to the earliest cliff dwellers. They parallel the meanings and often the exact rituals of the ancient Aztecs, Toltecs, and Mayas. And their extraordinary richness and complexity is the despair of all ethnological and anthropological study.

Their specific functions are to heal, bring rain, fertilize crops, recount myths, preach sermons, afford fiestas, perpetuate tradition. But above all they are structured to maintain the harmony of the universe. Everything else is partial. Hence their ultimate meanings are rooted in the same old, familiar premise that the unplumbed universe within individual man is indivisibly linked with the immeasurable universe. Whatever distorts the whole warps the part; what can happen within the psyche can take place in the cosmos.

This truth is stated nowhere more clearly than in the ceremonial which is at once the chief goal of all tourists, the most fascinating and repulsive, and the least understood: the so-called Hopi Snake Dance.

The Snake-Antelope Ceremonial

This nine-night, ten-day ceremonial begins four days after the ten-day *Niman Kachina* which is given ten days after the summer solstice—which places it usually sometime in early August if you figure it out. Alternating with the Flute ceremonial, it is given on First Mesa on the odd years and on Second and Third Mesas in the even years.

So now, blinded by the sun and choked with dust, we are crawling westward from Keam's Canyon around the high rocky rampart of First Mesa. To sleep for the night at its foot. Below Tom Pavatea's trading post, where we can get water and groceries. In the ancient peach orchard on the soft sand. That is, if we don't spread our bed rolls in the dark right over the ant hills as Doc Harlin and I did late one night in 1932. The dance this year of course is not in Walpi, high above. It's in Hotevilla on the far end of Third Mesa. But there's no hurry to get there. The folks concerned are still busy in the kivas, tending to those rattlesnakes. Let's let Dr. Elsie Clews Parsons give us the horrible secret details. Being invited into a kiva is no fun. Sitting there hours on end is work; stuffy, smelly work. Let her do it while we loaf around the post.

"Howdy," says Tom. "How's tricks?"

"Hi," we say. "Good crop this summer?"

"Fair to middling," says Tom. "But they ask too many questions and don't buy enough souvenirs. Mebbe the bunch comin' in for the dance will be better. Don't know why I think so."

The dance is a Butterfly Dance late this afternoon up above. So off we go, leaving Pavatea to harvest his crop of tourists and Mrs. Parsons her crop of notes in the kiva, where she has been a week already.

On the first day of the ceremonial, she notes, the Antelope Chief sets up his standard on the kiva. Then he goes in for a smoke. The Snake Chief, in his kiva, smokes, sprinkles meal, prays, then begins to make snake whips—little wooden stems decorated with eagle feathers. They're in no hurry either.

Next day Antelope Chief spreads a mound of sand marked in corn meal with the lines of the six directions. On this he sets the *tiponi,* about two feet long, made of eagle wing feathers and decorated with feathers of the birds of the cardinal directions: oriole of the north, bluebird of the west, parrot of the south, magpie of the east; all bound in buckskin and tied with red thongs. Snake Chief receives more members of his kiva. He gives them some root of the beetle plant so if they are bit by snakes they can chew a little and spread it on the fang puncture. They go out and gather the first few snakes in a snake bag, returning at sunset.

In the morning the snakes are taken carefully out of the bag, being held in back of the head so that they cannot strike, and inserted in a large bottle. Then the Snake priests go out after more snakes. To the north, the west, the south, the east. Every day it is the same. Each man stripped to a loin cloth, his face painted red, his body marked with a red stripe, a red feather tied in his crown lock. Each carries a digging whip to dig snakes out of the ground if necessary, and a snake whip of eagle feathers to make them straighten so they can be grabbed.

In the Antelope kiva—But no. No more running back and forth between kivas, old Sikyapiki tells Mrs. Parsons gently but firmly. She must choose to observe the ceremonies in either kiva, and not enter the other. Only he can and must visit the Antelope kiva each day. So she stays in the Snake kiva.

But we know what is going on in the Antelope this fourth day. The altar is being made and set with bowls of water from the sacred springs, green cornstalks and vines of squash and beans. Then the dry painting is laid with colored sand. It is about five feet square. At the four corners are built the cloud-mountains—yellow, black, red, and white—each with a hawk feather thrust into its apex. On these the clouds perch, and in them the four chiefs of the directions live. The outer lines are similarly colored, and the whole makes the rainbow house.

Next day in the Snake kiva the snakes are fed with pollen, sprinkled with meal. Songs and prayers are given. It is an elaborate ceremony. Mrs. Parsons is busy making notes. She has to sharpen her pencil and is about to throw the shavings in the fire. No, no! Cedar charcoal is associated with Masawu. She must deposit the shavings on the floor under the ladder.

So the days crawl by, the sixth and seventh. The complexity, the intensity is mounting. Prayer sticks are being made. Set after set. For the cardinal directions, the Cloud Chiefs, who sit at those four corners of space, the sun, the moon. For that of the sun a journey food packet is made with meal, pollen, honey taken in the mouth and mixed with saliva. Systole and diastole, the songs rise and fall. Pale light steals down the ladder opening upon the naked backs of the painted priests, the jars of coiled serpents. Smoke blown to the directions drifts upward. The long myth chant continues.

In this cabalistic maze the snakes are taken out of their jars and loosed on the clean mound of sand. Bull snakes, rattlesnakes, whip snakes, snakes mottled, streaked, and patterned: a coiled, interlocked maze of sinewy serpents. The priests do not hesitate to pick them up while in coil. They stroke their heads with the feathers of the whip to make them uncoil, believing that only when a snake is coiled can it strike. The movements of their hands are "slow and gentle but sure and unhesitating." There is no snake drugging, extraction of fangs, nor inducing them to strike until they empty their sacs of poison. Even so a man is bit twice on arm and leg. He calmly rubs the wound with sand or the beetle-root. The dark stripe constrictors rear up five feet high, a monstrous sight.

Some rattlesnakes wriggle toward Mrs. Parson's flinching body. One lunges into her very lap——

"God, how they make me creep!"

Why, Dr. Elsie! Imagine that in the middle of a scientific ethnological report! There she is, the cold, objective, analytical scientist immersed in her research. Suddenly shaken smack-dab into the role of a mere woman.

Dear Dr. Elsie. I can't see you there at all. I remember you as I saw you during my first trip to New York, so generously and thoughtfully calling me to ask, "Have you ever been to Grand Opera at the Met? Wonderful! Friday night then."

How beautiful, strange and remote it all seems—the Metropolitan, that gaunt old stone kiva, the revered sanctum sanctorum of a culture ritual of a whole civilization. Like the Snake-Antelope ceremonial, it is a ceremonial of a vanished culture, observed by a civilization itself swiftly vanishing. Now indeed the Diamond Horseshoe is already gone. The deep canyons of New York with their crowded cliff dwellers are losing vitality as the tides of change beat upon the shores. The tall towers are shaking. But there, while the hour was still unspent, we sat as guests of our thoughtful and generous hostess. A gracious lady in brocaded scarlet, perfectly at home in her family box, held for years.

But now squatting in a dingy, stuffy hole full of crawling rattlesnakes while far overhead the clouds begin to form.

We can see them late this seventh afternoon, tenuous wisps of white gathering in the blue, as we jolt westward to camp tonight on Third Mesa. Thirty miles of grey sand, grey cliffs and a single old windmill and water tank, a dismal oasis.

We boil up the steep slope of the mesa. Past Oraibi, on the near edge, a clump of dreary stone and adobe huts that looks like a ruin. Across the wind swept tableland to Hotevilla, on the far edge. It doesn't look much better. None of them look like much, compared to Zuñi and Taos. Nothing seems alive. Everything seems to have retreated underground from the sun and wind. For us it is another dry camp outside the pueblo.

Before dawn we are awakened by a faint jingle. A file of shadows slips across the horizon. That other year when we slept at the foot of First Mesa it was the same. The Snake priests, palely outlined by white breech clouts, were moving by us to the spring. We could hear their low voices in prayer. And next morning when we went there we saw the planted prayer sticks and the ground white with sprinkled meal. Every morning of the last four they do so, a different spring each day. Sleepily we turn over. The clouds still hang threateningly above us, a little thicker and a little whiter in the black.

At dawn they are still there. Underneath them, on top of both kivas, are tiny figures laying bands of sand across the roof in all directions. On each band is sprinkled a line of prayer meal. These kivas are now the All Directions Altars, the cloud road markers, for over these roads the clouds will travel.

It is the eighth day. The intensity is spreading outside the kivas. A restrained air of excitement permeates the dusty, squalid village. Outside, everybody gathers for the Antelope Race. The prize is a bunch of prayer sticks and a bottle of water taken from a sacred spring. The winner will pour the water on his field and plant the prayer sticks. Along the course are deposited prayer sticks and prayer meal. The racers are urged along by kiva members whirling their whizzers or bull roarers, a stick whirled on a string to make the roaring sound of low thunder; and shooting their lightning frames, a jointed wooden frame which is shot out in a long zigzag like lightning.

Formerly racers ran naked, hair flowing loose like rain. Now the boys are short-haired, wear shorts, and their feet are daubed with mud. So they race across the plain at sunrise, forty brown bodies straining and panting. To be met by more men and boys carrying cornstalks and squash blossoms, with women and girls scrambling for these trophies when the race is over.

In the early afternoon a burro loaded with cottonwood branches is driven into the plaza. A leafy green bower is built; the *kisi,* the shrine, to hold the snakes. In front of it a shallow hole is dug, perhaps two feet deep. Over it is laid a board smoothed over with sand: the *sipapu.*

A few people are coming in by now. A band of Navaho horsemen, some visiting Pueblos in an old flivver, a sprinkle of Anglos with a case of soda pop which they generously pass around before the ice is melted. Everything is restrained and easy; everybody loafing quietly in the shadows. Till late in the afternoon, when the kivas suddenly begin to empty.

The Antelope Dance

The Antelope dancers appear first, led by the Antelope Chief carrying the feather *tiponi* on his left arm. All twelve are decorated alike. The chin is outlined by a white line from ear to ear. The lower leg from foot to knee, and the lower arm from hand to elbow are painted white. There are zigzag lines of lightning on the upper arm and leg, and white clouds painted on both shoulders. Each wears a white kirtle and embroidered sash, a fox skin hung in back, feathers in his hair, and beaded anklets. One carries gourd and prayer sticks; another a rattle; another wears a cottonwood wreath and carries a medicine bowl of water.

As they file silently across the plaza and around the bower, the Snake dancers come out. In contrast to the greyish-white Antelopes, the Snakes are reddish brown. Their faces are smeared dark red, with a splotch of white clay on the hair over the right eye. Their dark-brown bodies are spotted with white. Each man wears a fringed kirtle, a fringed deerskin garter on the left leg, a turtleshell rattle below the right knee. All wear necklaces of turquoise, shell, and coral, and carry a fringed bag of meal in the left hand and a snake whip in the right. The chief carries his bow standard.

They too encircle the green bower four times, each casting a pinch of meal. Each man too on reaching the *sipapu* stamps hard with one foot on the plank resonator, the foot drum. Then they line up facing the Antelopes.

Two opposite lines. The greyish white and the forbidding reddish brown. All held in a moment of suspense, a theatrical pause. Then suddenly it begins.

The Antelopes shaking their rattles, dancing their stamping dance, singing their deep voiced chant. The Snakes bending over, stamping their dance steps, shaking their leg rattles, waving their snake whips.

The lines dance forward and back. Up and down between the lines dances the Antelope Chief, followed by the Snake Chief stroking his back with his snake whip.

Then, in pairs, each Antelope and each Snake dance up between the lines, Snake's left arm resting on Antelope's shoulder.

Now the Antelope darts into the bower and grabs a bunch of cornstalks and bean vines. This he carries in his mouth while resuming dancing. The Snake helps to support it with one hand. When it is dropped he picks it up deftly as he would a snake and restores it to his partner's mouth.

Back in line again the Snakes wheel in unison, circling the *kisi* four times and stamping on the *sipapu* as before, every circle larger in radius, and then file back to the kiva. The Antelopes leave with the same ceremony. . .

It is over. It is sunset, and dark, and the eighth night of the ceremonial. Poor Mrs. Parsons! So busy still taking notes in her Hopi Diamond-back Horseshoe. Endless ritual, ceremony, costume, prayer, chant, song, and paraphernalia. Imagine trying to record a Grand Opera in similar detail without a convenient place to put your pencil shavings! Now she must fast for the busiest twenty-four hours of all.

The whirling whizzer will seem to whirl inside her empty stomach. The rattlesnakes will rattle inside her aching head. Near cockcrow the singing will commence. At daylight sixty or more prayer sticks will be planted outside at different shrines. Two of the Snakes will go to the roof of the Antelope kiva, whirling their whizzers and shooting their lightning frames to the four directions. Inside, perhaps, there begins the same ceremony as is held in other pueblos when a young boy and girl come in. The Antelope Youth painted and holding a rattlesnake in his hand. The Snake Maid ceremonially dressed in white, holding a jar of bean and melon vines, her hair whorled in squash blossoms. Both standing on the sand-painting during the ceremony. Mrs. Parsons must have her head washed. All Snake priests have their heads washed. The snakes must be washed too. Those snakes!

No. It is better to be a tourist. My earliest ambition in life was to be a tourist. To travel and see the sights, to travel on and see still more sights. A forever stepping out of Fred Harvey dining rooms, toothpick in mouth, with an air of smug satisfaction. A never-ending trail of indulgence requiring no work, no worry, no effort to understand such fuss and fol-de-rol on the part of such ignorant, heathenish savages as these.

So here for once we lie in our bedrolls while Mrs. Parsons does the work. Watching the clouds gather thicker and heavier around the morning star. Listening to the Crier on the kiva roof giving that resonant call which floats over the pueblo, across the mesa and out over the lightening plain. A call, like a muezzin's call to prayer; one of the most beautiful sounds on earth.

He is arousing the young men for the sunrise Snake Race which duplicates the Antelope Race of yesterday morning. Another fine sight to see.

There are more tourists to help us enjoy the day. We can see them beginning to come in already as we cook breakfast afterward. Like tiny black beetles far down on the immeasurable plain they look, crawling sixty, seventy miles along the rutted dirt road, puffing up the grade, disgorging. Fred Harvey tourist busses with uniformed drivers. Dudes in droves from guest ranches, all in elaborate, colored cowboy boots. Old jalopies. New Chevies. Long sleek limousines hunting vainly for a "Reserved" parking lot. Trucks and pickups jammed with laughing Spanish-American families. Ranchers. Casual visitors detouring off Highway 66. Station-wagons loaded with boys and girls from summer camps and schools. Government Indian Service agents, looking very important. Forest Service rangers in green whipcord. A group of bifocalled scientists. Mystified foreigners perpetually slapping the thick talcum dust off their shiny black suits. Wagon loads of Navahos of course, one after another. Pueblos springing up from nowhere. A movie star in dark glasses. Yes she is! Look!

All day long they keep coming. The whole American melting pot. Decorated with Tiffany diamonds, costume jewelry by Woolworth, turquoise and heavy silver from the Navahos. Under felts, stiff straws, scarlet head bands, Lily Daché creations, black umbrellas and colored parasols. Carrying fans, thermos bottles, sandwiches, and little black notebooks—no cameras please.

All broiling and perspiring under the blinding sun and the sultry clouds lowering over the kivas. Fighting for a place on the flat Hopi roofs. Swarming the terraces. Massing the plaza. Peering in the squalid doorways. Bargaining for Navaho jewelry and Hopi pottery at twice the price. Flocking everywhere like sheep.

But, on the whole, a tolerant and well-behaved mob. For all are drawn here to see only one thing. Native Indians dancing with live rattlesnakes in their mouths. If there is one thing that evokes the most shivering horror, the worst agony of tingling suspense, this must be it. The United States Indian Office has threatened to stop it as a "loathsome practice." La Junta, Colorado, Boy Scouts, calling themselves "*Koshares,*" imitate it yearly with $100,000 worth of costumes. Business men of Prescott, Arizona, annually calling themselves "Smokis," have tried to exploit it in the most derisive, cheap, and vulgar parody yet attempted. And still it goes on, year after year. So from the four corners of the world everybody comes here to the ancient wilderness heart, the nerve center of America. To see Indians dance with rattlesnakes in their mouths.

It is more than that. Though they may not know it, it is the oldest rite in all America, stemming unbroken from the earliest prehistoric cliff dwellers, deriving from the first era of human life on this continent. It is more than that. Although they do not realize it, it is an evocation of that dormant and stifled other component of all our lives, that intuition of the dark self which lies hidden deep within us. Towards this invisible, irrational, and unadmitted fourth-dimension they stand reaching out, hour after hour, with a confused sense of irritation and unbelievable patience, repugnance and longing, angry denial and intolerable suspense. And over them all, the thousands of tourists and the hundreds of Hopis, the squalid village and the majestic plain, the mystery lies heavy as upon the first naked prehistoric cliff dwellers who waited here watching the lowering, darkening clouds . . . Lies heavy upon the same mankind, the same earth, that are still dependent upon the same ancient verities of above and below for survival . . . Waiting till almost sunset for the concluding ceremony on this ninth day.

The Snake Dance

It always seems sudden and unlooked for when at last they come. And it is always new, though it is essentially a duplicate of the Antelope Dance of the day before.

First come the Antelopes. Twelve men, a pair like prayer sticks for each of the six directions. But today more somber grey with black hands and feet, black chins, and a white line across their upper lips, their bodies dirty ash grey.

Then the Snakes. Today their faces are blackened with charcoal, with smears of red-brown on the cheeks, their black and red-brown bodies covered only with black kirtles.

Grotesque and horrible they file somberly around the plaza, their loose black hair flowing in the breeze. Short, heavy, powerfully built, as if compressed to the ground.

Ash grey and reddish black, they each in turn encircle the bower and cast their pinches of meal. Bend forward, shaking their rattles. Then stoop and stamp powerfully upon the plank resonator or foot drum, the *sipapu.* All call softly with a deep, somber, wordless chant.

This is the one supreme moment of mystery. Here, now, at the mouth of the cavern world where the power gushes up on call. Everything later is an anticlimax, even the snakes.

So it begins. The dull resonant stamp like distant thunder, like a faint rumble underground, sounds in the silent sunlit square. It is echoed by that deep, somber, thunderous chant. The sound is one we never hear, so deep and powerful it is. And it reveals how deep these men are in the mystery of its making. Calling to the deep cavern world below. Summoning the serpent power. Calling up the creative life force to the underground streams, to the roots of the corn, to the feet, the loins, the mind of man.

And the power does gush up. It shakes the two opposite lines of Snakes and Antelopes into motion, into dance. And now it begins—what the crowd has been waiting for.

A Snake stoops down into the *kisi* and emerges with a snake in his mouth. He holds it gently but firmly between his teeth, just below the head. It is a rattlesnake. The flat birdlike head with its unmoving eyes flattened against his cheek, its spangled body dangling like a long thick cord. Immediately another Snake steps up beside him, a little behind, stroking the rattlesnake with his snake whip with intense concentration. Up and down they commence dancing, while another Snake emerges with a giant bull snake between his teeth. At the end of the circle the Snake dancer gently drops his snake upon the ground and goes after another. The snake raises its sensitive head, darts out its small tongue like antennae, then wriggles like lightning towards the massed spectators. Now the yells and screams and scramble! But a third man, the snake watcher, is waiting. He rushes up. Deftly he grabs the escaping snake, waves the long undulating body over his head, and carries it to the Antelopes. They smooth it with their feathers and lay it down on a circle of cornmeal.

Soon it is all confusion. The whole plaza is filled with Snake dancers dancing with snakes in their mouths. Rattlesnakes, huge bull snakes almost too heavy to carry, little whip, racer, and garter snakes curling in a frenzy about one's ears. A loosely held rattler strikes a man on the jowl and dangles there a moment before it is gently disengaged. The dance goes on. Snakes wriggling on the ground, darting toward the spectators. Brought back by the snake watchers, an armful at a time. Until all of the snakes have been danced with and deposited in a great wriggling mound by the ash-grey Antelopes.

Suddenly it is over. Two Hopi girls dressed in ceremonial mantles sprinkle the writhing mass with baskets of meal. Then Snake priests grab up the snakes in armfuls, like loose disjointed sticks of kindling, and run out of the plaza. Down the trails into the stark Arizona desert to four shrines where the snakes are freed. Released at last, after giving up their dark potency, to carry the meal prayers sprinkled upon them, the feather breaths of life, the ceremonial commands laid upon them, back to the deep spinal core of the dark source.

The setting sun spreads its effulgence over the mesa, the farther mesas, and distant buttes. The whole arid rock wilderness floods with twilight. The clouds hang heavy, dark and somber. A few drops of rain sprinkle the crowds. They hurry away swiftly. The motorcars start buzzing, filing in a funeral cortege down the slope. Quickly, to "cross the wash," to escape the coming flood.

The ash-grey Antelopes and the brown-black Snakes file ceremoniously back to their kivas. Each drinks a large bowl of emetic medicine concocted out of the root medicine and handsful of beetles and stinking tumblebugs. They go out to the edge of the cliff and vomit. If they didn't their bellies would swell up with the power like clouds and burst. Then they may eat and wash. But the dark power called up for nine nights and days is still within them. So tomorrow morning they must wash again: heads, bodies, necklaces, planting sticks. And again they must rub with the dry root medicine, must chew it and spit it in their hands and rub themselves. While the Snake Chief touches each with his snake whip, the last strike of the serpent, comes the vivid flame stroke of lightning which at last releases the sweet smelling rain, the torrential swishing floods.

The Rain-Makers

So it ends, as it always does, in pouring rain. It fills the underground reservoirs; insures forage for herd, flock, and beast; waters the parched fields and shrivelled little orchards; renews the stream of life in mankind; restores the whole balance of nature in this vast rock-ribbed desert.

The specific function of the Snake-Antelope ceremonial is to bring rain. But it is rooted in the primary purpose of all Hopi ceremonials—to maintain the harmony of the universe. Not only physically in the outer world, but psychically in the inner world. So, in man as in the desert, rain may be induced to fall by the same laws. Thus we can understand this external phenomena by a similar internalized procedure.

The snake, as we have learned, is one of the oldest symbols known for the primary sexual force residual in man. The Snake People were the first Hopis simply because they were the first of mankind, after the separation of the sexes and the Emergence to this earth world in human form, to be imbued with the sexual power of generation. Hence Water Serpent comes from the preceding water world and is patron of the Water Corn clan. Hence also he is associated with the fruitful South and with nadir. When his power is misused by people in sexual misconduct he causes floods and earthquakes; he upsets the whole physical world just as the blind misspent power of the sexual force upsets the whole psychic make-up of individual man. But the natural use of sexual power enables man to reproduce himself, to perpetuate mankind. So feathered with the symbolic breath of life, the snake appears in the benign aspect of Quetzalcoatl, the Feathered Serpent of the Toltecs. Double-headed to show both of these aspects, the malign and the benign, he is the Precious Twin. Thus he appears on the walls of ancient caves and cliff dwellings, on the kiva walls of Ácoma, and in Zia and Isleta. The compulsive power of sex, for good or bad, the most forceful of all instincts! So the serpent, among Pueblos, Aztecs, and Toltecs, draws all things to him with his breath; as in the snake swallowing of ancient Aztec ceremonialism.

The antelope is more abstract. For mankind cannot be left to travel the Road of Life blindly, driven only by the serpent power of sexual regeneration. It must be guided by that intuitive sense of the divine which permeates all life. And this is symbolized by the horned deer, mountain sheep, and antelope. Hence at Ácoma the head of the Antelope clan is the "father of the kachina" and the ceremonial head of the pueblo. It was in the shape of mountain sheep that the Holy People appeared to the hero of the supreme Navaho Night Way. In many Pueblo ritual chants it is the deer who stands "at the Place of Beginning, where our roads come forth, there where the deer stands." Thus the Horn People were the second clan to reach the Hopi, coming from the sacred East. Hence the antelope heads on the altars of the Antelope and Agave societies.

In the subtle *Yin-Yang* doctrine of Chinese Taoism, the *Yum-Yab* doctrine of Hindu Lamaism, and Tibetan Buddhism we find the same snake-antelope symbolism developed in the psycho-physical structure of man.

The human body is held to have a psychic counterpart of the physical nervous system. There are three primary nerve channels and numerous subsidiary nerves by which psycho-nervous energy is carried to all the nerve centers, therein stored, and thence distributed to every organ and part of the body. The whole system may be said to roughly correspond to the lake, reservoir, and tributary river system of the external body of the universe. The main median nerve extends through the center of the spinal column. Around it to the right and left, like serpents, coil the other two. The latent mystic fire force associated with the physical sexual force of the body is the Serpent Power, personified as the sleeping goddess, Kundalini, abiding "four fingers below the navel nerve-center." She represents the feminine or negative aspect of the universal force of the cosmic mind. The Hopi snake.

Roused from her slumber she slowly uncoils and ascends up her double-coiled path to the brain psychic center, represented by a personification of the masculine or positive aspect of the universal force. Here in union with her Lord, the Divine One, in the pericarp of the Thousand-Petalled Lotus, there results the phenomena of mystic rain. The navel center, the heart center, the throat center, the brain center—all the psychic nerve centers are filled. The median nerve channel is set in vibration. The whole body is recharged with psychic power. And man attains that sublime peacefulness, that yogic quiescence or True State of Mind in which alone the divine light of true perception can dawn.

This union of the moon fluid with the sun force, the transmutation of the two aspects of the vital force, the harmonization of the cosmic dualities, because it takes place in the crown of the head, is often pictured objectively, as in images of the Buddha, as a protruding outgrowth. It symbolizes an invisible psychic brain center, a psycho-physical outgrowth of the ordinary brain through which functions the divine or Buddhic consciousness—a phrenologically evolved bump of sublimity as it were: a symbolic horn. Hence a horn trumpet is often used in Buddhist ceremonies, and the horned antelope pictured on Buddhist temples is emblematic of the peacefulness of the True State of mind or yogic quiescence thus achieved. The process is called Kundalini Yoga; and like all yoga it means simply "to join" the two spiritual forces of the cosmic mind.

And so we can reread the ceremonial most clearly in terms of its Eastern parallel. But in the Hopi Snake-Antelope ceremonial we find a converse restatement of this doctrine based on the fundamental premise that whatever can be achieved within the psyche of individual man can be duplicated in the universe without.

The ceremonial begins with the Antelope Chief setting up his standard. For it is he, representing the masculine power of the divine, who takes precedence over the feminine and sanctions the awakening and loosing of its power. The Snake Chief then follows by setting up his eagle feather *tiponi,* symbolic of the snake completely feathered with the feathers of all directions and transmuted into the breath of life. Throughout the whole nine-night, ten-day ceremonial we see this alternation of the two groups in every ritual. But always it is the Antelope which takes precedence over the Snake. In the setting up of the altar, in the races, in the dances themselves. Always it is the Antelopes who appear first with the fruits of the finished transmutation—the green cornstalks, the squash blossoms, the bean and melon vines. And always later the Snakes follow with their lightning frames, bull roarers of thunder, the reptiles themselves—the sexual serpent power which is to be transmuted. And, day after day, it is the Snake Chief who dutifully presents himself at the kiva of the Antelope Chief—the means appearing before the end, the lower self before the higher.

But, little by little, as the sleeping goddess Kundalini is aroused and begins her ascent, we see the premonitory union of the two. The Antelope Youth painted and holding a rattlesnake in his hand. The Snake Maid dressed in white, her hair whorled in squash blossoms, holding a jar of bean and melon vines. Slowly everything is made ready for their eventual union in the objective world outside. The kivas—universes in miniature—become the All Directions Altars for the larger universe enclosing them. They mark the roads for the gathering clouds. All the sacred springs are blessed with prayer feathers. The four cardinal directions are appealed to with song and prayer.

Meanwhile from the deep nadir, the bowels of the earth, the manifestations of the serpent goddess Kundalini are called forth as from the base of the spine. They are received as honored guests; they are washed, fed with pollen, sprinkled with prayer meal. The dangerous fire power is there. It is recognized, but it is not dissipated nor destroyed. It is controlled by the symbolic breath of life, the eagle feathers on the snake whips; it is rigidly controlled, gently but without fear, as the powerful sexual force is controlled by the yogi.

The climax approaches. The first meeting of the two takes place. The Antelope Dance is the Snake Dance save that it is the Antelope priests who handle like snakes the stalks of corn and vines of squash and beans and melons. The dormant power is awake and spreading; Kundalini is ready to join her Lord. Now the final purification to sanctify their mystic union. The heads of the priests and of the snakes must be washed in the milky seminal fluid of the yucca root. And now as the dark storm clouds gather, and the gathered power lies heavy in the air, the thaumaturgical climax. The deep resonant stamp upon the *sipapu* unlocks the reservoir. The serpent power is unleashed. Kundalini is freed and mounts to union with her Lord. The lightning crackles. The thunder rolls. Masculine and feminine unite in storm and passionate embrace.

The whole body of the universe trembles and lies supine in a moment of utter quiescence. The mystic rain falls. It fills the underground lakes and reservoirs of the land as it recharges the psychic nerve centers of the body. The streams run full, the springs spout, the whole stream of life is renewed.

It is a great ceremonial; one of the greatest man has known. It is an hallucination, a hoax, and a fact as real as rain.

We need not accept its testimonial. But from it we realize how little we know of the components that achieved it. As little as the Hopi rain makers know of the physics and thermodynamics and stratospheric control we invoke to bring rain.

We both know so little of the deep, mysterious universe which lies unplumbed within us; of the immeasurable body of creation that encloses us in this tiny cell of earth and roof of sky. But someday when our rivers run too shallow to support the teeming populations of the future; and our countless great dams and vast reclamation projects give the lie to the omnipotence of science—when our need becomes as great as that of the Hopi—we too shall learn that the internal and external must coincide, without separation, without limit, in obeisance to the mysterious laws which control both.

9 Pole and Pilgrimage

BESIDES THE GREAT Navaho sings, Pueblo dances, Zuñi kachinas and the rich Hopi ceremonialism which outline the main body of Indian ritual in the Four Corners, there are innumerable other aspects giving substance to the form.

Symbolism, dry paintings, song, and dance build up the rituals; many rituals combine into ceremonies; a dozen ceremonies structure the complex ceremonials. A whole book could be written on prayer-sticks alone. Another on the simple rattle. And still another on the significance of the cane. Aside from the ceremonials or associated with them are great tribal gatherings like the annual encampment of the Jicarilla Apaches at Horse Lake. There are pilgrimages like those to the Zuñi Salt Lake for salt, to the Lake of Whispering Waters for turtle shells; of the Hopis to Grand Canyon; of Taos to Blue Lake. At both Taos on San Geronimo Day and at Picurís on San Lorenzo Day there are pole climbs. Merging into Catholicism there are Indian dances like that of San Felipe in the church on Christmas Eve. Throughout the year, running the gamut from pure native expression to forms watered with many faiths, ceremonialism holds sway throughout the Four Corners.

Where is it going? To what does it all add up?

Positive and negative, a dreary disintegration or a climactic sublimation, it seems best expressed in two ceremonials which stand at opposite poles.

The Pole at Picurís

On this and every tenth of August the old pueblo of Picurís still celebrates its patron San Lorenzo.

Picurís, to be honest, does not lie within the Four Corners. It rests in a small tuck of the Sangre de Cristos just outside the northeast corner. In the old days the pueblo was on a regular route of travel. Indians, Spaniards, and American trappers from Santa Fe followed up the Rio Grande past San Ildefonso, Santa Clara, and San Juan to that funnel in the cliffs called Embudo. There they turned east into the mountain valley past Picurís. Thence northward and westward to Taos over the lofty range that Colonel Price curtly named U.S. Hill.

Today the "old" road twists up the Rio Grande gorge and the new one skirts it above. But from west to east over the hill another road to the remote blue valley of L' Eau du Mort follows part of the ancient route. Tres Ritos, as the area is known: the heading of three little rivers, once among the great beaver streams of a century. Still out of the dark canyons deer, wild turkey, and occasionally a bear drift down into the clearings.

South to Santa Fe there is not another crossing between the river and the eastern plains. It is a wilderness area of high dark forests, aspens and scrub oaks, little mountain pastures dotted with tiny settlements of Spanish-Americans, descendants of the Spanish-Colonial settlers of three centuries ago. So that the people stop work in their little corn *milpas* and crowd to the doors of their isolated red-brown adobes to stare at our lurching car.

They are mountain people. And so they differ, like their high pitched roofs for winter snows, from those below. Their flinty black eyes have a repellent remoteness. Their dark muddy faces and hands, like their dark mud-brown adobes, are infused with a dull red as if the iron in the springs has stained both land and people. But more likely a mixture of the Pueblo.

For just south, if there has been no rain and the rutted road is miraculously passable, we cross a ridge and drop down into Picurís.

But first the village of Peñasco. A general store or two. Several cantinas. An old nunnery still a beautiful reminder of what it might have been. A church with a horrible white-washed sheet iron front. And a scatter of adobe houses along the dusty road.

The place is serene enough if you notice only the scenery. The bright yellow glitter of the summer sun on the wheat and squaw corn. The metallic glint of the steep pine slopes on either side. The point of Jicarilla Peak at the end of the narrow valley. Even the painted wagon wheels set in the adobe gables of the houses for decoration, lend it a picturesque individuality.

But it all has a harsh and repellent remoteness. A feeling of strained attention behind a careless front. At a hitching rail a row of horses switch away the big blue bottle flies. Some men squatting on the ground keep passing around a bottle. There is no laughter, no obscene jests, no talk. They drink, and drink again, and watch each other warily with black reptilian eyes. And the houses, the stores in two rows across the hot, sun struck road, face each other warily too.

Peñasco has a bad name. It is always quarreling, stabbing. Peñasco means "rock," and it is a folk belief that every quarrel begins with a thrown rock. So on every provocation they break out of the silence with a thrown rock, a knife thrust, and a clatter of a horse's hoofs into the night. And then again the heavy, sultry silence.

A woman cloaked to the eyes in a black cotton *rebozo* squeaks down the road in new high shoes with glass buttons. With her are two little girls. One wears pink muslin with many ruffles. The other faded green taffeta. Their braided hair is tied with yellow ribbon. Their eyes shine.

Goody, goody! Today is fiesta! We shall have greasy pink ice cream and *dulces*.

They may even get a ride on *Tio Vivo,* a decrepit merry-go-round with hand carved, unpainted wooden horses.

An old Studebaker wagon rolls in, its box filled with a family in wrinkled store clothes. A group of horsemen clatter up, look warily about before dismounting at the cantina. The town is beginning to fill.

Bravo! Today is San Lorenzo. There will be music, fiesta, and tonight a dance. But don't worry. Before the moon comes up there will be a stabbing, or shooting. There always is.

And all this latent violence, this lurking heaviness and tense silence bears down upon the old pueblo of Picurís scarcely two miles away.

It lies over a ridge, in a little *vega* sloping up into the dark pine forest. We come down upon it suddenly and unaware as the road lurches around the shoulder of a hill and drops as if drunk.

A desiccated mummy of a village. The creek is green and slimy in clotted pools. The sloping plaza is overgrown with weeds and full of cattle droppings. And the pueblo itself—with an immediate and unaccountable change in the texture and color of adobe—is a coarse, dull black. The walls of the houses flanking two sides of the square are cracked and crumbling. Roofs sag under earth sprouting still more weeds. Butts of protruding *vigas* are weathered grey. In back are the corrals, their heaped-up stone walls falling down again; and from them a single, lean, half-wild pig comes to root about in the hot sun.

But it is the dead oppressive silence one feels first. It eddies up as if from an opened grave. And one knows, instantly and instinctively, that the catastrophe has struck. And now Picurís and its people are dead, dead, dead.

But one stays. Possibly because of the pole. The tall, stripped, green pine pole planted securely in the middle of the plaza. And hanging from the top, feet bound and head down, with its throat cut, a dead sheep. Also a squash and a dirty flour sack full of groceries. The pole dominates the dusty, weed-grown square, the cracking, mud-black adobes, the dead, oppressive silence. It reminds us, faintly, that it is San Lorenzo Day in Picurís.

The pueblo is old, oh very old. One of the ninety reported by Coronado when first he came this way in 1540. It is still one of the twenty-five left intact and populated. And it is still one of the ten which has openly preserved its scalps instead of secreting them in the hills away from town. On top of the bald rise overlooking the valley and the pine-ribbed mountains behind, stands the scalp house. It has almost washed away, adobe to adobe, to complete the eternal cycle. But the walls still stand, slyly hung with the necessary turkey feathers, and the crumbling tower.

You don't get very close. For nearby is the newer kiva with its protruding spruce pole ladder decorated with feathers. Take a step toward it and on top will rise a guardian silent, dignified, and inscrutable in warning. The dead present, like the alive past, is still inviolable.

So we wander around in the blazing August sun. A little girl wades across the creek. Her eyes are black and bottomless.

"Pots. See my pots." Such a listless appeal.

Picurís pottery used to be famous. A dull lusterless black

or a bright gold, prismatically glittering with specks of mica. Everywhere in these *cerritos de talco* glitter the micaceous clay banks of which they are made. The substance still abounds, and the people still make pots. But the strength for form and the feeling for design is gone. No one knows how to fire them correctly. The bowls are untruly shaped, without a ring, often burnt and cracked. And so they sit in their doorways: old straggly-haired crones with a litter of worthless pottery at their feet.

Yet inside, the rooms are clean and simple. Like every Pueblo home they reflect the living awareness of its tenants. But an awareness of life-in-death. The individual lives, but rootless.

We cross the plaza to the adobe church. Its great, wooden doors are locked and barred. The courtyard in front, enclosed by a high wall, is overgrown with weeds. Here even the new Christ has not been a Redeemer.

Still in the blazing sun, from the top of the fresh, stripped pole, hangs the squash, the dirty flour sack of groceries and the sheep with its throat cut open for the flies.

By now there are many to stare at it: perhaps a hundred or more. The Pueblos squat patiently on benches or on the ground around the plaza. A few women file sedately down the trail, cross the upper creek and settle down in their petticoats like setting hens. A few cars and wagons have driven in to stop in the shade of a gnarled apple tree. The Anglos are already bored and restless, the Spanish-Americans still sit their horses. There is even an Indian trader with a gaudy new blanket to sell.

Suddenly into the late apathetic afternoon, into this deadness, there comes a loud, high-pitched yell.

Howling and shrieking, four Picurís dash down the trail, jump the stream and the squealing pig, and leap into the plaza. Each is naked save for clout and moccasins. Their faces and bodies are painted black, with daubs of white clay.

They are the fun makers, the *Koshares,* the *Chiffonetas,* the Black Eyes ever present at most Pueblo ceremonials. The *Koshares,* according to Keres ceremonialism, were created by Iatiku and were painted white with black stripes. They live with the sun and are not afraid of anything. They regard nothing as sacred. Hence they are clowns, and elsewhere very clever. Horribly grotesque they dash around pantomiming Anglos and Spanish-Americans, tooting imaginary automobile horns, forever drawing out imaginary watches and strutting insolently like tourists into doorways. The Pueblo is invariably patient and hospitable to summer visitors. Only in the antics of the sacred fun makers one sees revealed his acute perception and sly humor.

But here their humor has grown brittle and malicious. They dash into doorways, yelling, screeching. Perhaps one has a grudge against a neighbor. He tears open the door, cavorts through the rooms overturning benches, pans, and pots, jerking down a calendar print. Another squats down in front of a year old child, yells and makes faces until it sets up a terrified howl.

It is a great deal of fun; it rattles with the brittle deadness of a skeleton.

They see the crowd. We visitors are in for it now.

The fun makers cavort around a rancher smoking his pipe. They grab it from his mouth, take a puff each, throw it into the air, kick it into a pool of dust. Another stops and yells in front of a Peñasco boy with fresh shined shoes.

Oh yes! They know all about shining shoes! They kneel down—so!—grab the shoe and hold it on a knee. Swish! Swish! An imaginary cloth slides back and forth. But all the time, they spit, spit at the shoe until ankle and trouser leg are covered too. The owner is embarrassed and angry by turns. No use; two clowns hold him like a vise.

A little wind stirs through the pines and kicks up a cloud of dust. Wonderful idea! Right from nature! The bedaubed four grab up handfuls of the talcum dust and throw it high to drift into the faces and cars of the whites. A sedan window rolls up. The Indians splatter sand against the glass. Fun! Real Picurís fun! The tourist Whites look very proud to be thus singled out. They'll do their fancy cussing later. And now a young lady loses her pink straw picture hat. It is pancaked on the head of the leading *Koshare.* He and it might go anywhere, with the others in pursuit. But luckily it only races round the plaza, falls to the ground a time or two, and then sails—quite grandly—back into the crowd.

And at the bottom of all this mimicry is the hard corrosive sediment of hate and frustration that lies in the pit of the Picurís soul. The bitter ashes of the deep, esoteric beauty which has risen to a flame, withered, and died.

Now the fun is over. You can dig the dust out of your eyes and see what is going on.

One of the grotesquely painted clowns has discovered something. Beyond the plaza, and down the road behind the church. Something in the dust. He yells. The others come running. They squat around it, point, yell, talk, then scatter like hounds to the four directions.

One of them lopes into the plaza. He is bent almost double. The muscles of his black daubed thighs stand out like ropes. Every few yards he stops and sniffs the wind. His contorted gargoyle face peers around. His eyes are intent, alive. He is no longer the jeering fun maker. He is wonderfully aware. And this intent awareness is the one moment of true aliveness.

The silence too comes tautly alive. The heavy deadness lightens, dissipates. Even the enclosing black mud walls fall away to let the great pine hills march in, and the fading summer sun, and the wind, which gently sways the brown dry grass down the slope. And for that moment an unseen past gives up a flashing vision.

He is a strange beast of prey, this fellow, intent, aware. He leaps away, making queer animal sounds, and stops again. This is mimicry, but of a different kind. Pure life, not the life-in-death.

And all the while he is studying the ground, the unseen trail.

One sees what he is really doing. Unobtrusively, furtively almost, his closed right hand with forefingers protruding presses into the dust regularly spaced deer tracks. He is making a trail for the others to follow.

Soon they come yelping behind him. Very slowly, bent double, too. The leader returns. All four together come now, sniffing, prowling, whirling away and returning at a shout. One of them has found another deer track. They leap into the air, howling, then slide relentlessly forward once more. Wonderful creatures, really.

The trail leads them to the pole, the tall, stripped green pine pole. And hanging from its top the quarry: the slaughtered sheep with its gaping, red-slashed throat. Ten feet away they see it for the first time. In an ecstasy of discovery they shriek and dash forward, surround it.

The pole is perhaps forty feet high, almost too big at the base to reach around, and stripped by hand to an unbelievable slickness. One of the Picurís straddles it and yanks backward. How queer it doesn't pull down, says his ludicrous, painted face peering around.

Another hurls himself against it time and again. This is

very funny to the silent watching crowd. A puny, five foot clown trying to butt down a pine tree.

Hai! Watch the mighty hunters now!

Out come their bows and arrows: the bows of bent green twigs perhaps a foot long, the arrows little yellow straws which dart up the great smooth pole, break, and waft away on the wind.

The fun lasts perhaps a half hour. The four *Chiffonetas* giving their best painted grimaces of heroic endeavor and ludicrous disappointment, and the spectators patient and tolerantly amused.

Now they get down to business: to shinny up the pole after the squash, the flour sack of bread and beans, and the sheep before it is eaten up by flies. One after another wraps his arms about it, lays his daubed cheek against the smooth pine, and heaves up mightily with strong bare legs. Thigh muscles stand out, corded in the sunlight. Faces drip sweat. The moccasined feet scrape and squeak on the shiny wood. And each in turn slips down leaving a smear of grey paint to mark his three-foot rise. They gather in a group, arch backs and boost a climber from their hips to shoulders. Their hands under his heaving buttocks, he goes up another foot or two, hangs panting, and then limply slides back down.

Defeated, the four stand ludicrously disconsolate at the bottom of the pole, rubbing sweaty hands on slimy thighs. No longer fun makers, the jeering *Chiffonetas.* No longer hunters intensely aware. Just four thwarted men who can't get up a pole.

A murmur creeps round the plaza from the patient throng. Then come, from behind an adobe, a group of men carrying a long spruce ladder. This is better! When placed against the pole it reaches almost half way up. A shout. Up goes a climber. The pole is a bit smaller now: his arms go all around. But still he can't get up. And the sheep, head down, hangs staring from sticky filmed eyes at the powerless men below. And the dead, oppressive silence fills up the dreary square again, tincturing the fading afternoon. The deadness which has swallowed the flicker of life. . . .

It is San Lorenzo, Picurís' big day. Everybody is invited. The clowns will go through their funny antics. One of them will climb the pole. It is slick and shiny. It will sway a little in the wind with his weight. He creeps to windward, left leg hooked in front, right leg bent under him. His black head sticks out, he looks like a monkey. It is really a devil of a job.

Then suddenly, after so long a time, a saturnalia: shouts, yells, shrieks, hand claps, whistles, and auto hoots. The climber's left hand reaches and clings to the top of the pole.

A harder job remains: to duck his head under the squash, to squeeze up between the ropes securing the filled flour sack and the hanging sheep, and to perch on top the slightly swaying pole. He works hard with one hand. The knots are untied. A rope end flutters to the ground. Carefully the men at the bottom lower first the sheep, then the flour sack and the squash by means of a small pulley on top.

Now, to the noisy acclaim from the people in the plaza below, the climber sits on top the swaying pole. His black, windblown head towers above the squalid, mud-black adobes, above the mountain horizon. His naked sweaty body gleams more redly still in the setting sun. He is forty feet, over forty feet, high.

He hooks his legs tighter. He raises his tiny, hawk-like face to the turquoise sky, and stares fixedly out over valley and mountain. Then he lifts both arms high and wide, secure as an eagle perched on a lofty crag. He yells a high peal of triumph; sings in a mocking falsetto a song which contains all the faith and courage, the unshaken assurance of a people lifted by the high tide of destiny to the topside of its hour. Finally in a deep hush he slides back down. Afterward there will be a brief dance in the plaza. And that night a big feast for all. . . .

That is the way it is in Taos every year on San Geronimo. And that is how it has been immemorially here in Picurís on San Lorenzo.

The pueblo has had a long and proud tradition. The eastern-most of all pueblos, it sent buffalo parties out on the Great Plains as far as the Quartelejo trading post in western Kansas. It resisted Comanche attacks, received Kiowa visitors. Always close to the Jicarilla Apaches, its ceremonials bear traces of theirs; its ceremonial color system corresponds with that of the Navahos. Its scalp ceremonies were famous; tufts of human hair still hang boldly in its scalp house.

The people themselves derive from the same root branch as Isleta, Sandía, and Taos just over the mountain wall. The changing life of Isleta is still impregnated with rich ceremonialism. Taos, hemmed in by Anglos and Spanish-Americans alike, and a focal point for tourists, stubbornly maintains its strength of faith within an unbroken form. But Picurís, isolate and left alone, the reasonable pueblo to flourish without hindrance—what has happened to Picurís?

Did the legendary Great Snake of Picurís swallow all the best men children deposited at the mouth of its cave for sacrifice?

Intermarriage with Apaches? With Peñasco? Did too many young people wander away to form the settlement of El Alto de las Herreras in the blue valley of L' Eau du Mort, near Mora?

All this has occurred everywhere. But no tribe, no people impregnated with a sense of destiny, direction, time, is ever retarded thus. They keep on climbing their pole and carrying everything with them. Until, like Pecos, like Piro, like all the other now abandoned pueblo ruins, they lose their invisible spark of life.

"Mebbe lose its medicine, this place. Mebbe sold it to the White men's museums."

So today the men here at Picurís can't get up the pole. Even with a ladder. The catastrophe has struck. And they stand there coagulating in sun and dust and weeds and flies, overwhelmed by the heavy oppressive silence of defeat.

To climb ever upward or to sink back down: there is no alternative of standing still. So an automobile is driven up beside the pole. The top is too slick to support the ladder, and the sedan is driven away.

The visiting Anglos, bored to distraction, begin tooting their automobile horns. The Peñasco neighbors sit grinning derisively, staring coldly from their black reptilian eyes. The Picurís are in a proper stew. The old men congregate, mutter, point with their chins. A serious thing this. Somebody has got to shinny up the pole. Anybody! But tightening their own belts about their colored shirts hanging tail out over their ragged trousers won't help at all.

Off to the side a group of visiting Taos men rise and wrap their blankets closer. They stalk slowly across the plaza. They are older men. They too are deeply concerned. True, they cannot climb the pole. But at home there is that young man, that excellent climber who never fails even on the first attempt. Shall they send for him?

Not by car. It would be too late. The sun is already setting in a saddle of the hills. The pine slopes of the Sangre de Cristos flush blood red and then turn damson blue. Only the tall stripped pole still gleams yellow in the crowded plaza.

Perhaps he will come. He knows it is San Lorenzo in Picurís . . . Perhaps our power, our medicine, our good thoughts will bring him . . . They sit quietly on the ground, heads bent, unspeaking.

But there is no power left in Picurís, no good medicine, no strong thoughts. It has all been sold to the white man's museums, it has all gone, or something. And the visitors no longer wait. The Anglos' hooting motorcars rumble away across the creaking bridge. The Peñasco horsemen clatter back over the ridge. And the people of Picurís, afraid and ashamed, slip back into their cracked, mud-black pueblo. A moment later one of them returns with an axe.

And now as the black shadows of night and the heavy oppressive silence draw down from the pine slopes, we turn back to hear a new and dreadful sound. The sharp blows of the axe severing Picurís from its ancient traditions, its withered roots. Cutting down the pole that once climbed may never be climbed again. The Pole of Picurís.

Pilgrimage to Blue Lake

At the other end of the pole (if you will pardon the pun) stands Taos.

We here like to think of Taos as the aristocrat of the pueblos. There is little tangible evidence for this assumption of its superiority. Taos is not spectacular like Ácoma, on its lofty cliff rock. It is not as large as Zuñi. Its kivas are less beautiful than those of San Ildefonso. Only three miles from a town now swarming with tourists, it lacks the inimical aloofness of Santo Domingo and the remote Hopi pueblos.

But somehow once the beauty of its classic, terraced, twin pyramids catches the eye the heart forever retains it. Rising against the blue sacred mountain, its purity and timeless serenity suggest a mystical and other-dimensional life that is immune to the changing world around it. The people bear it out. They move slowly, shrouded in white sheets, against the blue. They speak softly. An air of mystery surrounds their simplest daily chores. Drawing water from the stream, bringing in firewood, husking corn—all seem rituals embodied in a great, never-ending ceremonial which includes every act, every moment of every day. Thus they observe life. As a ceremonial forever impregnated with the daily commonplace, just as their formal observance of it has the simplicity, the lucid clearness of life itself.

The whole calendar year is marked by formal ceremonials: the spring and fall races; the great winter dances—the Deer Dance, Turtle Dance, and Buffalo Dance—the San Geronimo pole climb; the Time for Staying Still; the annual kiva retreat and initiation ceremony; and the midsummer pilgrimage to Blue Lake. Yet none of these have the strict stylization observed elsewhere, neither the awesome kachinas of Zuñi nor the intricate ritualism of the Hopi. They all have an easy going familiarity with the daily known that masks their intensity. Simply because here the two components of life, the visible and invisible, the mystical and the practical, merge in a feather edge difficult to distinguish.

Taos is an old pueblo and it has been a traditionally strong and influential one. It has "power." Its influence extended among the Great Plains tribes as far east as Kansas, and among the Navahos as far west as Grand Canyon. It is imbedded in the origin legend of the Navaho Enemy Way with its Squaw or War Dance; and singers still send here for meal and seeds for ceremonial use.

Among the Whites of historic times Taos has been known as a stubborn and conservative pueblo since 1540, when Coronado found it "the most populous village of all that country," though doubtlessly overestimating its population at 15,000.

Here was planned the Pueblo Revolt of 1680, when all the Spaniards were killed or driven back to Mexico! [1] Here took place the Rebellion of 1765, when forty-seven medicine-men were tried as sorcerers; also the Taos Rebellion of 1847 against the incoming Anglo-Americans, when the pueblo was stormed and its old church destroyed.[2] In 1922, it was a leader in uniting all the pueblos through the formation of the All Pueblo Council for the purpose of defeating the Fall-Bursum bill.[3] In 1926, when governmental pressure was exerted to break pueblo ceremonialism, the council went to jail in defiance of the order forbidding the withholding of pueblo boys from school for kiva initiation.[4] Out of this evolved the Blue Lake Controversy of 1933.[5] Again, in 1936, Taos incited a revolt against the dominance of pueblo affairs by the influence of a woman Indian agent; and still again, in 1949, it revolted against demands for a new "democratic" government to supplant the old council system.[6]

[1] P. 42. [2] Pp. 74-75. [3] P. 130. [4] P. 371. [5] P. 371 [6] P. 376.

Always its power, extroverted or ceremonially introverted, has been exercised under its idyllic, soft-spoken mask. This genial secrecy, its close-knit solidarity, and above all its strong religious ceremonialism so deeply rooted in its everyday secular life—all these combine in the character of Taos to make it the most aristocratically conservative of pueblos, a leader in revolt against outside influence. Its feather edge is sharp and cutting as flint. And all this power stems from and is constantly renewed by the annual pilgrimage to Blue Lake in mid-August, the climax of the ceremonial year.

The trip is long and difficult: a steep ascent of over six thousand feet in twenty miles, and it is one of the most beautiful ever to be found. The route leads from the pueblo up along the Glorieta wagon road under the great interlocking cottonwoods, then turns off on a narrow trail. Up the dark forested canyon around the sacred mountain. Over the high ridge. Through groves of aspen already so yellow that one seems to be plodding through a golden cloud. There is a tiny spring oozing from beneath a boulder, where one can rest the sweating, heaving horses. Then the trail starts climbing again along a foot wide trail cut into the cliff wall extending far above and below.

Squirrels chatter in the lofty pines. Heavy mountain grouse flutter noisily through the dark spruce. Far below a band of wild mares race wildly away, the stallion poised on a crag like a mountain sheep to snort defiance. It rains, soaking one to the skin. The sun comes out to steam one dry. Then it showers again. In the clouds appear a tiny sapphire star set in a mounting of dark onyx. Star Lake. Then one really begins to climb.

Above timber line. Up the steep, bare, frost-shattered granite slope of Wheeler's Peak, over thirteen thousand feet high. It may well be the top of the world. All around below spreads a pristine wilderness of heaving mountain ranges, dark forests, deep chasms, cliffs. To the north the Rockies of Colorado. To the east the great eastern plains. To the south and west the plateau of the far Rio Grande. But suddenly as you cross the slope of the peak just below its summit, you see it below. Way down below the tortuous slope of loose gravel, set deep in the forest, indescribably blue. The clear turquoise of the sky above. The dark purplish blue of the forest in its depths. The light blue of the edges washing on its shores. All these blues merging into one blue, whose stainless purity seems instead to color sky and earth with its pulsing vibrancy.

This is Blue Lake which feeds the little stream that trickles down the dark canyons, pours fresh and full through the pueblo to separate its dual halves, and empties at last in the Rio Grande. The blue lake of life that ever nourishes field, beast, and man below. The ancient sacred lake beneath which live the *thlatsinas,* the spirits of the dead, the elements, the inner forms of all the outer forms visible to man.

The pilgrimage is tribal. Almost everybody goes. Men, women, all boys who have successfully endured their eighteen months kiva training, all girls who have reached puberty, and babes in arms. They go afoot or on horseback. Slowly. Singing. Wearing garlands of dark blue Flowers of the Night and shining yellow Flowers of the Sun . . . Always this idyllic, soft, joyful mask over the strong welling power underneath.

Around the lake spring up hundreds of lean-tos built of great logs and aspen poles, canvas tents, a few of the old tepees covered with buckskin and treasured old buffalo hides. A thousand fires glow, the sparkling flames reflecting in the lake.

What happens?

No one knows. All the trails have been blocked and are carefully guarded. Forest Service Rangers by government edict have posted notice that the whole area is closed for two weeks to all Anglos, Spanish-Americans, and other Indians. No white man has ever witnessed the ceremonies. John Collier, during the government threat to throw open the National Forest, was permitted to go half way, to the first of the two ceremonial grounds, before he was turned back. In his brief account, in *Indians of the Americas,* of the simple mass singing and dancing that took place he strikes the perceptive chord which vibrates with the meaning of the whole.

> . . . a displacement of human and mystical factors . . . a strange release of energies took place . . . the dynamic potentiality of ancient beliefs was realized . . . a partnership in an eternal effort whereby, from some remote place of finding and communion, the human and the mechanical universes alike are sustained.

It is strange indeed to pick up Vincent Sheean's recent *Lead, Kindly Light* and read almost the identical phrases describing the *darshan* experienced by the Hindu pilgrim "when after the long journey up through the green forests of the foothills, he comes to an open space and the snowy Himalayan peak of Shiva's Trident rises before him."

The blessing, benediction, or beneficent spiritual influence by which we incompletely understand the meaning of the word in English, Sheean explains as the reason for the "will of the individual to join in the immensity of his fellows" in the constant immense crowds of illiterate Hindus, who form pilgrimages to visit sacred shrines, temples, rivers, or peaks. Once there, they cannot understand the speech of a holy man or even see him, so great is the crowd. Often no speaker is there. Nothing outward takes place.

We cannot understand such pilgrimages undertaken without the specific purposes for which they are undertaken in Christendom. "But I have never seen the glow of happiness, the *darshan* glow, on any face which has come under my observation in Rome or Jerusalem at the times of pilgrimage." Yet *darshan* is not bestowed or conferred; it is neither given nor received. Nor is it the specific reward of pilgrimage. It occurs. What then is its great significance?

> Darshan in practice is a form of happiness induced among Hindus by being in the presence of some great manifestation of their collective consciousness. It may be person, place or thing, and represent past, present or future, so long as it sets up the definite recognizable glow of suprapersonal happiness.

This is the same "rejoicing" which "was not only a human rejoicing" that Collier observed in "that marvellous ever-renewed, ever-increasing, ever-changing leap and rush of song." It is that simple and sublime feeling that comes to a people who submerge for a moment their individualities in the collective unconscious which is not only tribal but universal; the simple sacred ecstasy of spiritual communion whose obverse or perverted duality is the hysteria of mob violence.

Such may be the simple joyful secret of the Taos pilgrimage to Blue Lake. As it is of the simple silent pilgrimage of the Yaquis to Magdalena, Sonora, on October 4th; and the great intertribal, all-Indian pilgrimage to the ancient hill of Tepeyac, on Guadalupe Day.*

Here then are the two poles of Indian ceremonialism in the Four Corners.

Picurís still for a little while maintaining its old ritual forms. But with a strength that has weakened, a faith that has died. An empty, meaningless, ethnological shell, devoid of life.

* Described on p. 49.

And Taos superseding all ceremonialism with its intricate, complex ritual. Achieving at last that pure exchange of energy between the microcosmic universe of the individual and the great self of the macrocosmic universe; not as individuals, but with a complete obliteration of self that merges at last into one flowing, living whole; a whole that has been, that will be, fused in the ever-living, indestructible now.

This is the secret core of all Navaho and Pueblo ceremonialism. The great Navaho sings, Pueblo dances, Zuñi kachinas, and Hopi ceremonialism are but means to the end. It is the invisible rock to which they have clung. No outline of their intellectual meanings, no perception of their intuitive truths, is possible without the ultimate recognition of Elie Faure that "The modeler of gods, at bottom, is the spiritual universe hastening unceasingly in pursuit of its center of gravity."

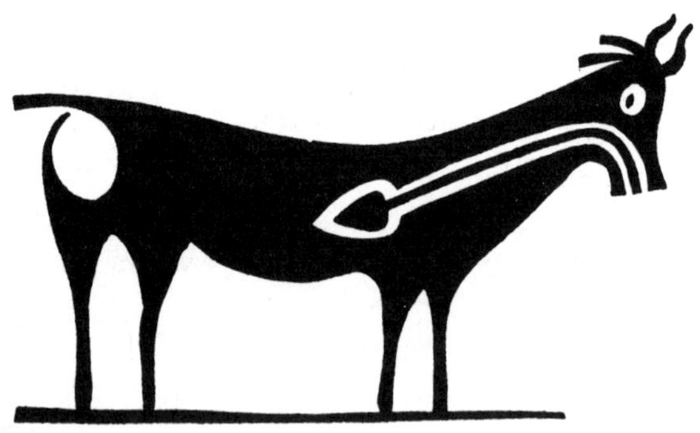

Part Three: Man-Mask and God

For what is man but the root and the flower, the image and the substance of the universe itself? . . . .

MASKED GODS

CONTENTS OF PART THREE

1 The Pueblo City-State

IT IS OVER NOW. He had fasted, remained continent, done his duties in the kiva. He had painted his body, done up his hair, and when the time came he had hurled himself forward, running with the everlasting mystery of creation.

The wonder of it all still shows in his eyes. But he is no longer part of it. He is again a mere man, coming home heavy and tired. We watch him plod across the plaza. He limps, having bruised his bare feet. Sweat and paint drip off his broad heaving chest. His eagle down has come unstuck.

"That man! He is a mess!" laughs Maria, his wife, throwing open the screen door.

Filadelfio does not deny it as he stalks in—a little majestically now as he sees his friend inside. But the majesty doesn't last long. He plops in a chair.

"Good races," says his friend. "Strong, beautiful. The best in years!"

"We seen Mondragon. That foolish old man. He is too old to race. He ran on his skinny legs like a stick!" Maria's laugh fills the shabby room with its patch of linoleum on the floor and its plaster saint and cowboy calendar on the wall.

Filadelfio nods. "A good day. A fine spring. Everything will be good this year. Now I must get that seed of mine planted, as you know."

He is not interested, really. He sits suspended between two worlds, unable to make the transition back to his wife, to his friend. The smell in the other room helps.

"Meat!" he sniffs.

"Of course! What did you expect for fiesta? After all this time in a stuffy kiva? Your guest here. He brought it. Some chiles too. And a pink store cake besides."

"I saw him throwing cigarettes from the housetop when we danced," says Filadelfio somberly. "Everybody got some but me. No. I did not get any from my friend."

His friend tosses him his pack with a scowl. He is a spoiled child, this big hulk of an Indian dripping sweat and paint. A darling of the gods. Just because he has run in paint and feathers and hopped around in the plaza he thinks everything should be handed him on a silver platter.

Maria doesn't. "What do you expect? Cigarettes cost money. Is he to supply everybody? And for what?"

Filadelfio coughs and splutters. He smokes very seldom. But always when somebody gives him a pack, whether he enjoys it or not.

"I'm hungry," nags Maria. "That meat has been cooking all day. And you haven't washed your hair with that *amole* I pounded all morning. You haven't washed your dirty feet. These old men keep you away from your wife, your home, your fields! Those Hitlers!"

"My duties. My kiva duties. Every man must do his duties," protests Filadelfio with a show of dignity.

But it doesn't last. Maria is on a tear. "You invited your friend. We are going to make fiesta. We will have some meat and some pink cake. Then maybe I will go into town and see those moving pictures. Maybe I will have an ice-cream cone afterward. I am sick of being neglected by a lazy husband! I am sick of these duties that leave me alone!"

It looks like a family row. The transition from the abstract to the concrete is difficult. Filadelfio, bested by his wife in front of his friend, is surly. He stalks into the kitchen, dips out a cup of water from the bucket.

"There is your *amole* suds. For your hair, your dirty feet!" yells Maria. "Do it yourself if it pleases you."

But as she brushes against him, he lays a hand on her hip. It is a simple gesture but a powerful one. Maria catches her breath. Filadelfio's broad chest heaves. The whole room fills with an electric tension.

Their friend can barely glimpse them in the other room. It is enough. He stands up. Filadelfio, a strong young man who has fasted and remained continent so long, has come back to earth. There won't be any picture show tonight!

But the tension is suddenly broken when they see him hat in hand. They come running out of the kitchen. Filadelfio has changed completely. He has come all the way back at last.

"My friend!" It spurts out with his usual warm gush of feeling. "Are you not invited for fiesta? As are Jesus and his young wife also? My wife will wash my hair. I will put on clean clothes. Then I will be ready. We will not go to that smelly picture house. It is spring. It is warm. The moon shines. We will go to our little summer house in the fields. We will sing and beat the drum and smell the fresh spring air. That will be better. That will be fiesta!"

"A picnic!" cries Maria. "Of course! Look. Just as I said, the meat is not done. We will take the pot and put it on a fire to finish. We will pick the wild plum blossoms. We will have fun."

"When you have washed your hair," assents their friend. "Then I will be back. In an hour, before the sun sets. No? Just like last year and the year before that."

"Why not?" says Filadelfio, smiling. "What is better than to have good friends and smell the good air and feel the good life on a fine spring night?"

Yes. It is a well-known fact that every person, regardless of race, is physically reducible to the same amount of water, carbon, and chemical salts. This process, continually practiced on a universal scale and conveniently called war, gives scientific support to the theological tenet of the Brotherhood of Man.

Everybody belongs to the Brotherhood: Social Man and Economic Man, Parsee and Pharisee, doctor, lawyer, merchant, thief, and Indian Chief. Despite their financial standing, political party, church membership, complexion, or hair-do, there is no real difference between men—neither in bone structure nor blood analysis. Not in physical man, the only scientifically proved man there is.

The only difference between men lies in that intangible kachina quality which goes in but which miraculously doesn't come out when man is reduced to his physical components. Where it vanishes to nobody knows. Perhaps it doesn't exist. But our speculations about it constitute the only difference between us.

So of course we've got to take a look at it if we are to differentiate our Indian neighbors from ourselves.

Frank H. Cushing states that in Zuñi there are five words meaning "to know." One is used for geographic knowledge of rivers, mountains, places. One for knowledge of acquaintances, of persons, animals, objects. One for methodic knowledge of how to act, speak, think. And one for acquired knowledge or understanding. All these first four methods of knowledge enable man to know life as we all know it. They are rational processes of development from childhood. And the life they reveal differs as each man differs according to where he lives, what and whom he knows, how he is taught to act and think, and what understanding he rationally acquires. By these four means Sausage Man is stuffed with most everything he knows and understands—and loses when he is moved somewhere else, taught something different, or dies.

But the Zuñis have a fifth: one for abstract understanding or intuitive self-evident knowledge. Man never acquires this. It is born in him. It may lie dormant, unused and atrophied. Or it may be awakened and strengthened—as by kiva training. Then intuitively, not rationally, it grasps cognizance of the ordered universes of within and without, their relationship to one another, and its own enduring place in the whole. It perceives its relationship to Sausage Man—that other part of him which also has an important role to fill in his life, though a transient one.

Man thus finds himself in a devil of a fix. There are two parts of him. One binding him to his concrete, factual little world with a nagging wife, a scrubby corn patch that doesn't get enough rain, no money in the tomato can, and a lot of nuisances as well as a lot of pleasures and enjoyable fiestas. The other attesting a greater world in which everything he sees has an invisible counterpart, an inner form, all ordered by laws which he feels somehow constrained to obey.

In reaction to these two gravitational pulls, the Anglos as a people traditionally bend their efforts towards stifling the intuitive, the abstract, and emphasizing the concrete, the factual. With the exception of a few rheumy-eyed preachers, philosophers, and scientists, we are almost wholly concerned with the pragmatic, the tangible, material, and transient life around us. We live toward social ends. Like well filled, cosmetically beautiful, hermetically sealed sausages.

Whereas, in order to reconcile these components, the Pueblo puts on a mask and in it plays his role as Kachina Man. Then he takes it off and plays his worldly role as mere man, Sausage Man. But gradually one role usurps the other, in his case too. Until nine-tenths of his life is taken up with his ceremonialism; he is predominantly a Kachina Man.

How then does the Pueblo's ceremonialism reflect itself in his secular life?

The Root

Each pueblo is a city-state, self-isolated and self-sufficient. For all its complexities and differences in organization, it conforms to a general pattern. Taos is a fair example.

At the head of the secular government is the Governor, elected annually by the Council. He allots living space within the pueblo, determines new building sites, orders punishment for failure to comply with the laws, and in general is the pueblo's spokesman. Literally. For when there is no Town Crier or Crier Chief appointed, he calls out in a sonorous voice from the housetops the decisions of the Council, and the names of those to dance, clean irrigation ditches, and do other communal work.

The Lieutenant Governor—the *Teniente*—carries out the Governor's edicts. He fixes up marital quarrels, assigns water rights to families, and is responsible for all happenings within the pueblo.

Two War Captains and their assistants are appointed as "Outside Chiefs," responsible for happenings outside. To them must report all returning travellers and visitors—Navahos seeking ceremonial meal or water, and tourists wishing photographs or guides. They allot use of communal pasture and give permission for trips.

The *Fiscal* and his assistants are go-betweens. One of them may be the interpreter accompanying the Governor or translating fluently in three tongues—English, Spanish, and Indian—during Council meetings. Another is the *Sacristan.* Another the *Bocal,* or mouthpiece for the *cura,* the Spanish Catholic priest.

Outside and above all these annual, secular officers is the *Cacique,* the ceremonial head of the pueblo. The *Cacique's* office is hereditary and he holds it for life. It is he who nominates two men each year for Governor, one to be elected by the Council; he who hands over the ceremonial canes of office. The *Cacique* makes solar observations from the highest housetop, determining the solstices, the times for planting and harvesting, and the dates for the ceremonials. A field is given him for life, and young men till it for him.

Associated with him in ceremonial work are the Kiva Chiefs—one for each of the six kivas corresponding in number to the directions including Zenith and Nadir—with an assistant each. Associated with the kivas are six branches or societies. Each of the kivas and its society is named, has its appropriate functions, dances, and ceremonials. These attributes are known and are described in certain ethnological reports. That they are not detailed here is consistent with the effort throughout the present book not to violate the general rule of secrecy as to ceremonial names; to interpret meanings rather than to label sacred things specifically where such information is not sanctioned, not necessary, and would offend the writer's neighbors. In the preceding section the functions of the kivas have been made apparent. And when we recall that every boy is given to a kiva and must undergo eighteen months' instruction, the importance of the Kiva Chiefs is emphasized.

All of the authorities—the Governor, *Teniente,* the War Captains or Outside Chiefs, the *Fiscal, Cacique,* and Kiva Chiefs, together with their assistants—comprise the Council. This body of thirty to forty old men, sometimes called the *principals,* rules the pueblo with an iron hand.

There is honor attached to office, but little to the man. Seeing an old man puttering about in his shabby clothes, you would never know him for a high officer. There is much work involved and no reward. The classic tale illustrating the attitude toward office was told by Charles Lummis of a respected old man chosen to be Governor of Isleta. Courteously he refused the honor three times. On the fourth refusal he was gently but firmly set astride a rail in the plaza, his feet tied underneath him and his hands tied behind him. Before long he graciously accepted the call to office and, as Lummis records, served with faithful severity.

The Council meets as often and deliberates as long as required. The procedure is painful to a visitor. The members sit with their bowed heads covered by their blankets, so as not to interrupt nor embarrass the speaker. When he is finished they weigh his words, crushing out their truth in prolonged silence. No one is in haste to "put out his face" before the others. The night drags on. The silence mounts. The silence of an inquisition.

With one of these Taos statesmen I once attended a session of Congress. The perpetual hammering of the gavel trying vainly to evoke order, the angry shouting, the empty posturings, the casual strolling in and out—all this, with the greed for office which had preceded it, was incomprehensible to my companion.

In Council every trivial aspect of the subject is presented; it is looked at "from all directions." Not only from practical viewpoints—and these are uncannily shrewd, but from a ceremonial viewpoint. How will it affect the pueblo as a whole in the long run? This is the keystone to every question posed. And toward its answer they pray, "Let us move evenly together."

Homogeneity, a close-knit solidarity, is the distinguishing mark of secular government as it is of pueblo ceremonialism.

"We are all in one nest." This old saying expresses it perfectly. Stock, both horses and burros, are herded communally. The reservation land is held communally, but allotted to individual families. As long as a man works his field it is his under the communal title; he is free to bequeath it to his son, to sell it to his neighbor although not to an outsider. But if he neglects it, it is taken back and redistributed. Some of the fields lie some distance from the pueblo. During the growing season families may live there in summer homes. But in winter when the Time for Staying Still begins, all must return to their nest.

The worst evil that can come upon a pueblo is a schism that sunders its solidarity. When such occurs the pueblo is doomed. It loses its power and swiftly decays. For the "roots of the town" are the prayer-sticks buried in the plaza, and he who forsakes them cuts himself off from his roots.

Years ago a group of conservatives departed from Laguna, taking their kivas and masks, and established a settlement at Mesita. Today neither town has much vitality and they are doomed to extinction. People from Ácoma, agreeing to the Government's sheep reduction program, moved down to Ácomita and McCarty's. Ácoma will soon be only a ruin for tourists, and the new settlements are being depopulated as men leave to find work on the railroad. The split at Oraibi likewise resulted in the new Hopi settlement of Moencopi. Today Oraibi is swiftly withering away, and Moencopi is not yet regarded as an established township because it does not have its own winter solstice ceremony. The split at San Ildefonso is still so terrible a thing that its cause is shrouded in mystery and the people are forbidden to speak of it. It has resulted in two groups, two plazas, each with its own officers and kivas. In Taos a similar split over the introduction of peyote, was narrowly averted by a combination of utmost patience and drastic public whippings.

The greatest menace to the pueblo, then, is an innovation from outside which may create a serious difference of opinion between the older conservatives and the younger liberals.

Intermarriage with other pueblos is frowned upon. "No good can come of it." It has long been the tradition that if a Pueblo marries a Spanish-American or an Anglo he must renounce his rights and leave the pueblo. This tradition has been broken by many dramatic exceptions which prove the rule. There is one uproarious story of a recent World War II veteran who was allowed to bring home his bride. She was an Irish girl of staunch peasant stock who adapted herself quickly to pueblo dress and manner. One day a group of tourists boldly entered the house and began poking around the furnishings for a souvenir. "I wonder what language these people use?" a lady inquired loudly of her companions. Whereupon her hostess instantly answered, "Sure and be-Jazis if it ain't the King's English itself you'd be hearing!"

Up until a few years ago one of the chief problems confronting the Council at Taos was the attempted introduction of manufactured goods. Iron stoves, "white" dishes, clocks, and glass window frames were all forbidden. But today not only are these in use but a communal threshing machine supplements the biblical manner of threshing by horses' hoofs.

There is a small government hospital located on the Taos reservation, occasionally visited by a doctor from town on yearly contract to the Indian Service. For years it was a sore spot erupting frequently into cankerous scandal. Finally the Council's patience was exhausted. The Governor loudly proclaimed from the housetop that no one was to go to that place any more. "Let the women have their babies at home. Our Mother Earth will look after them as she always has. She will not forget them."

Traditional dress is still insisted upon. Paradoxically the style in Taos is an ancient adaptation from visiting Plains Tribes, notably the Kiowa. The men are required to wear their hair in two long braids. As on the Plains, colored ribbons or bits of fur may be braided in the strands and the part chalked with red clay. Only during ceremonials is it worn loose or gathered in a chignon at the back, true Pueblo style. If men insist on "American" trousers the seat must be cut out, necessitating the wearing of a blanket wrapped around the middle. This resembles somewhat the old deerskin leggings worn up to the thigh, and the breech clout. When store shoes are worn in preference to moccasins the heels must be cut off, though moccasins are obligatory during ceremonials. A blanket in winter and a white sheet in summer is always required. Girls wear their hair down the back until the first menstruation, then put it up around the ears, tied in back and banged in front. A shawl or blanket is always worn by women; and high pleated boots of buckskin whitened with clay are still worn on all festive occasions.

Together with all these restrictions in dress and custom the most dogged efforts have been expended to preserve Pueblo ceremonialism. The removal of children to Government boarding schools, at the very age when boys were traditionally placed in the kivas for eighteen months training, has been bitterly fought. Children have been hidden in the pueblo, secreted away in the mountains. If they were caught and sent to school every effort was made to make them conform to Pueblo custom when they came back. For refusing to let their hair grow long again, or for persisting in wearing "American" clothes, a fine of from one to five dollars was imposed. For refusing to dance they were given the alternative of a ten-dollar fine or a dollar-a-stroke whipping in the plaza.

The Anglo point of view regarding this stubborn Pueblo conservatism is well given in testimony presented to the Supreme Court of the United States during the Sandoval Case of 1913.

In the opinion of the court:

> Until the old customs and Indian practices are broken among this people we cannot hope for a great amount of progress. The secret dance, from which all whites are excluded, is perhaps one of the greatest evils. What goes on at this time I will not attempt to say, but I firmly believe it is little better than a ribald system of debauchery. The Catholic clergy is unable to put a stop to this evil, and know as little of the same as the others. The U. S. mails are not permitted to pass through the streets of the pueblos when one of these dances is in session; travellers are met on the outskirts of the pueblo and escorted at a safe distance around. The time must come when the Pueblos must give up these old pagan customs and become citizens in fact.

It was further brought out that:

> There is a greater desire among the Pueblos to live apart and be independent and have nothing to do with the white race than among any

other Indians . . . They really care nothing for schools . . . The returned student going back to the pueblo has a harder task than any other class of returned students. It is easier to go back to the Sioux tepee, and lead a white man's life, than to go back to the pueblo and retain the customs and manners taught in school.

In pueblo life the one-man domination—the fear of the wrath of the Governor of the pueblo—is what holds this people down. The rules of the pueblo are so strict that the individual cannot sow his wheat, plant his corn, or harvest same in the autumn without permission of the authorities. The pueblos under my jurisdiction that adhere religiously to old customs and rules are Taos, Picuris, Santo Domingo and Jemez, and none of them have made much progress away from the ancient and pagan rites.

The consensus was:

As long as they are permitted to live a communal life and exercise their ancient form of government, just so long will there be ignorant and wild Indians to civilize.

As a result the Court decided that henceforth the Indians were to be considered wards of the federal government. In a following chapter we discuss the basis and effect of this ruling.

We cannot, however, accept our Anglo culture as the norm from which we pass judgment on that of the Pueblo. As Ruth Benedict writes * with reference to Puritan standards:

In our own generation extreme forms of ego-gratification are culturally supported in a similar fashion. Arrogant and unbridled egoists as family men, as officers of the law, and in business . . . are familiar in every community. Like the behavior of Puritan divines their courses of action are often more asocial than those of the inmates of penitentiaries. In terms of the suffering and frustration they spread about there is probably no comparison. There is at least as great a degree of mental warping. Yet they are entrusted with positions of great influence and importance . . . They are not described in our manuals of psychiatry because they are supported by every tenet of our civilization.

The jutting characteristics of the pueblo city-state, then, are its traditional aloofness and solidarity. When these are broken, as we have seen in many pueblos, the pueblo disintegrates. There is always slow adaptation of innovations from outside. But in its cohesive immuration the pueblo still seeks to prevent the dissipation of power by obstructing all cultural interchange with the outside world.

**Patterns of Culture,* Houghton Mifflin Co., Boston.

The Pueblo sees no need for horizontal contact with the alien world without. The Anglo compulsion for lateral expansion—for more land, more wealth, influence, and power over his neighbors—is incomprehensible to him. He is rooted to a pin-prick of earth in immeasurable space. But that pin-prick is the whole universe in miniature. Nothing outside can add to what he has here; expansion can only detract from its meaning.

Hence his contact with life is purely vertical. That is to say, his strength to live, his power to enjoy and understand life, derives from constant contact with its invisible forces. Only when this fails will the springs dry up, the air grow stale, and life in man wither at its root.

The Stalk

The Spanish word "pueblo" literally means "village." It designates either the townsite proper or the people of the community. But the cohesive relationship of the two meanings stems back into the prehistoric American past.

Among the early nomadic Navahos, sedentary groupings formed as the people gathered near springs and water-holes, good pastures, and protective cliffs. The structure of the tribe still is comprised of forty-three clans whose names are largely place-names: Bitter-Water, Red House, Close-to-Water, Yucca Blossom Patch, Horizontal Water Under Rocks, and Bend in the Canyon. The clan system is still matriarchal, reflecting their primary dependence upon the earth-mother.

Among the ancient Aztecs *calpulli* designated such a clan. As the wandering clans became sedentary the word came to be associated with locality and meant district or village. The land about it was called *atlepetlalli* or *calpullali. Atlepetlalli* from *atl* meaning water, *tepetl,* uninhabited hill, and *tlalli,* land: "irrigated lands rising" about the community. And *calpullali* because the land belonged in common to the *calpulli* or village. Like the land of our pueblos today it could not be alienated from the community, though its use was directly heritable by individuals, and if one moved away he lost his rights.

Upon their arrival in Mexico the Spaniards confirmed this Aztec communal system of land tenure. They sanctified by law the Aztec code of water rights, and granted to each village a townsite of twelve-hundred *varas* square which they rechristened the *fundo legal,* surrounded by a league square of communal land for joint agricultural and pastoral use which they named the *ejido*—"the way out."

The whole of this they termed a "pueblo," an Indian village, in order to distinguish it from a "villa," a settlement laid out and originally peopled by Spaniards, and from an "hacienda," "rancho," or "estancia," which were estates or subdivisions of grants made to Spaniards by the Crown.

Marching north in 1540, the Spaniards found a similar structure in the pueblos of the Four Corners country. Hernando de Alvarado remarked of Taos: "It has eighteen divisions (*barrios,* or clan districts); each one has a situation as if for two ground plots." These divisions, of course, were the present six kiva groups, plus an ancient, secret, seventh kiva with twelve associated society groups, which all added up to eighteen.

The Spaniards did not disrupt the social structure, and followed the same procedure among the Pueblos as they had among the Aztecs. They founded their own new settlements like the Villa Real de la Santa Fe, and gave the already established pueblos titles from the Spanish Crown to the communal land around them. This confirmation of the communal land did not destroy the old pattern of the communal land system or that of the ceremonialism behind it. And so the pueblos were enabled to persist through the next three centuries.

In Mexico the pueblos did not survive the conquistadores' increasing greed for land. Rich and powerful *hacendados* gradually absorbed the *ejidos* into their own vast estates, and the people with them as slaves. Conceded to Cortez was a veritable kingdom of 25,000 square miles, embracing the valleys of Oaxaca, Toluca, Cuernavaca, half of the Tehuantepec Isthmus and a third of the present state of Vera Cruz, and including 157 pueblos and a total population of more than 150,000 souls. As late as 1910 vast private *haciendas* of 100,000 *hectares* were the rule; scarcely two per cent of all rural families owned land.

Mexico's continuous revolution since 1910 has been aimed at restoring this land—and up to 1938, 23,000,000 *hectares,* one-third of the crop land, had been restored to 13,000 Indian pueblos. The *ejido*—"the way out"—is thus the most ironic jest politically current in America. It means simply to "give the country back to the Indians," to restore the *calpullali* to the people. "The inalienable communal ownership combined with personal usufruct," states Ernest Gruening. "Its restoration is therefore conservative—of one of the oldest patrimonies of the race. It is radical in that it goes to the root of Mexican tradition—to the ethnic heritage that will not down, to the primitive yearning of the race, unsatisfied until now . . . The agrarian reform has implications far beyond the economic, supremely important as these are." *

The contemporary rural village throughout Mexico is still predominantly an Indian pueblo, and the modern *ejido* is still the *calpullali* of the Aztecs. Riding horseback from one to another you will not find a guide to take you beyond the next. For he is rooted to his own *tierra*. It is his *matria chica*, his motherland. And even in the large cities he identifies himself by his *barrio*, his clan district.

It was the political genius for organization of the Aztecs that enabled them to weld an empire of these countless *capullis*. The land was held as clan property and was inviolable by the state. Yet a portion of its wealth was devoted as tribute to the state and the priesthood. Each *calpulli* maintained a *telpuchcalli* or "house of youth" for training children in war, arts and crafts, and commerce, and a special school or *calmecac* for training in priestcraft. But the gradual accentuation of ceremonialism over secularism proved its downfall. With the growing need for more and more priests for the pyramid temples, and for more and more victims for human sacrifice, the whole system became distorted and top-heavy, as we have already learned. From the remote *calpulli* to the top of the Pyramid of the Sun it was predominantly from first to last, a vertical system.

As the semi-nomadic Navaho tribe is founded upon the clan, the pueblos of the Four Corners are composed of moieties and phratries or the various clan, society, and kiva groups, and the Aztec empire was built upon the *calpulli* or clan district, so the governmental system of the Incas was constructed on the unit called the *ayllu*. The Incas' was an empire whose religious, political, and economic ramifications spanned thirteen generations and 380,000 square miles throughout Peru, Ecuador, and Bolivia—one of the most remarkable that has ever existed.

* *Mexico and Its Heritage*, by Ernest Gruening. Appleton-Century-Crofts, Inc., New York, 1928.

No dead earth exists. Places live. Hence the *ayllu* was not merely the community of people nor the land they lived upon, but land and people wedded through a mystical bond. Like the pueblos today, as John Collier points out in his résumé of the Inca technology, "no land of the *ayllu* could be alienated, and each of its household heads was vested with a right to the land. This had been the Pre-Inca system." Under Inca dominion several of these household groupings, each governed by a *curaca* whose office like that of the pueblo *cacique* was hereditary, were combined into a small state, and these into still larger confederacies up to forty thousand households governed by the *Tucuiricue-cunas,* "they who see all." Above these were four *Apa-cunas,* each in charge of one of the four directional quarters of the empire. Over these was the supreme Inca, the Son of the Sun.

This was the democratic structure of the collective absolutism. But it was economically communistic. For no money existed; no power and prestige through accumulation of wealth; no accumulation. There was only labor and the land. By law one-third of it was devoted to the Sun for the maintenance of religious ceremonialism. One-third went to the Inca for maintenance of government, including the phenomenal road system with its paved highways running from jungle to ocean, its suspension bridges swaying above dizzying mountain chasms, and its commodious inns for travellers. The remaining one-third was retained by the local households. None of the nobility, no soldiers, no priests of the Sun, no males under 25 or over 50 years, no women, and no sick persons were required to give tribute. Tribute from the rest consisted solely of labor and skill as a workman or artisan. And for this every worker and his family was assured tools, land, clothing, food.

Perhaps in all history no other such a purely communistic state has ever existed. Even the similar Aztec Empire became distorted and was beginning to crumble when the Spaniards arrived, because its energies were being devoted to war for the express purpose of securing sacrificial victims. Modern Soviet Russia cannot be compared to the Aztec Empire as a communistic state. Russia's ideology admits of no religious sanction to be distorted; in practice it is but a barbaric despotism built purely upon temporal force and material gain and power. To the long successful, wholly dominating, and peaceful Inca Empire it has no resemblance whatever.

For primarily—above its democratic social structure, its

communistic economic structure—the Inca Empire was a religious structure. As we now have learned, no horizontal interrelation of officials existed; there was no contact between officials of equal rank. The current of absolute authority, and with it the flow of security and plentitude, flowed ever downwards from the source of all earthly power. And ever upward flowed the sacrificial return, rather than tribute, of labor and the fruits of the land to the symbolized source of all life, the Sun.

Thus the Inca Empire at the arrival of Pizarro—when the Spaniards, by murdering the welcoming Inca, not only destroyed the secular head of the government but cut the flow of subsistence and faith.

So perished one of the greatest and least known empires in the world, perhaps the greatest autocracy motivated by religion, and certainly the purest communist state known. But as in Mexico, its ideals and necessities, forced underground, are slowly emerging again. The modern cooperative movement now sweeping the Western economic world has springs in America's ancient past.

There has been much useless speculation whether the ninety pueblos in the Four Corners might ever have fused into a northern Pueblo Empire if left alone. It is quite possible that the marauding, powerful, and adaptative Navahos might in time have served here the same function of the Aztecs who welded together the remnants of the Toltec culture. Yet even this seems a little far fetched. More to the point are indications that the great prehistoric pueblos of Pueblo Bonito, Chetro Ketl, Pueblo Colorado, and the like may have been the roots from which sprang the empire-stalk of the Aztec nation.* For psychologically they were all of a piece. From the ancient pueblos of the Four Corners, up through the Aztec empire to the empire of the Incas, it was a stalk rooted in the prayer-sticks buried in the humblest plazas and rising to the summits of the lofty pyramid-temples of the Sun. A vertical social structure that duplicated the vertical ceremonial structure of their common faith.

The faults of the system are now clearly apparent. The Inca empire bred a mass dependency upon the superiority of the nobility and priesthood. The Spaniards had only to cut off the single person of the Inca to render the whole people powerless. The Aztecs by similar over-emphasis upon ceremonial sacrifice had drained

* Pp. 31-32.

their whole empire of its strength. The three successive Maya empires perished before America was discovered because of the same absorption in religion. They developed a calendar more accurate than the one we use now, but they failed to develop a simple plow and evidently perished for lack of corn to feed the growing populations. The Toltec civilization with its equally wonderful pyramids, its astronomical accuracy and geometric precision of thought, went into a haze of abstraction and fell prey to barbarians. The Pueblos and Navahos in the Four Corners were doomed to extinction not only because of our ruthless treatment of them, but because they too from the very start failed to meet the challenge of modern rational demands.

All in common because they were socially communistic show a complete lack of "rugged" individualism; because they were principally agrarian, a lack of economic enterprise essential to the accumulation of material wealth and power necessary for protection; because they shared a smug insularity which prevented expansion and adaptation; and above all, because they were chiefly religious, an absorption with the abstract rather than the practical.

But this is the judgment, from a secular point of view, of a materialistic civilization diametrically opposed in ideology to their common basis. What is the personality of the Pueblo as he still reflects the compulsions of his own life, as he differs from us who reflects our own values?

The Flower

The Pueblo, curiously enough, has not been oppressed by the insularity and rigid conservatism he suffers. He is not frustrated by a dreary sense of futility, inadequacy, economic insecurity, and psychological maladjustment to the world around him.

He is more free of inward tension and conflict with society and nature than any man we know.

His family life is traditionally peaceful. His long immuration in the kiva at the age of twelve to fourteen completely breaks his mother's hold upon him; no Pueblo has an Oedipus complex. Taken in hand by his mother's brothers, his ceremonial fathers, he never develops a father complex. Undistorted by the conceptual illusion of romantic love, he marries early and stays married. Divorces are extremely rare. Sex is a natural function rather than a sin or gratification of appetite. Yet uninhibited sex is restrained by frequent periods of continence during ceremonials; and the taboo is psychological as well as physical; he is constantly enjoined to "keep good thoughts." Collectively minded, the Pueblo does not lay stress on the life of the individual. The important events are the marriages, births, and deaths, for these affect the life of the tribe.

His social life is likewise communal. There are no incentives to wealth, social prestige, and personal power—to keep up with the Joneses. The pueblo has no locked doors. Occasional theft, conjugal infelicity, and violence are misdemeanors easily atoned for by proper payments to the injured party. Murder is almost unheard of. Suicide is incomprehensible. That he is a member of a national racial minority seldom enters the Pueblo's head. He does not have the abject defeatism of the Negro in the South, the wildly passionate repudiation of the Spanish-American in the West, the polite timidity of the Asiatic on the west coast. And unlike the Anglo he does not see himself as the ordained master of the universe. He remains always the resolute, proudly humble Pueblo. The most completely restricted, he is at once the most free—a citizen of the universe.

The world simply is. Without a compulsion to change it, he simply fits into his place in the whole as an individual whose sole aim appears to be a resolute self-effacement. His religion is communal. He has no conception of personal prayer for personal gain to a personalized, all-powerful deity envisaged in his own image. Ever in touch with the mystery, he acknowledges the spiritual essence in all things—the forests and the fields, the clouds and mountains, the young corn, the eagle, and the deer. Like him they exist to play their parts in the cosmic whole. Free of terror, the Pueblo does not battle with them nor abjectly make obeisance. Respectfully but unafraid, he secures their assistance by esoteric ceremonials that acknowledge his kinship with them.

This calm acceptance of life under the mask of tranquillity hides a profound intensity, a deep tragic awareness. It is betrayed by a joyful spontaneity as he sings while hoeing corn and hauling wood—a constant outpouring joyfulness. And by a humor so sharp and subtle that it cuts without pain. Poverty stricken, uneducated, facing barehanded the basic verities of life—disease, storm, drought, privation, childbirth, and death—he has transformed his external insecurity into an inward security. He has attained that priceless jewel of psychological maturity which we desperately seek under the slogan of "Peace of Mind."

Little wonder that the Pueblo has been a chief object of study by anthropologists, ethnologists, sociologists, and psychologists the world over. Or that he holds for us all an inexpressible fascination that betrays itself even in our vehement denials and angry protestations. For by his strange otherness and his refutation of all we hold dear, he speaks to that hidden part of us which still seeks what he has found—the flower of individual self-fulfillment within his own social frame. . . .

"Hey!" shouts the Queen of the Bandits, interrupting. "'*Se non e vero e ben' trovato!*' Every time you start singing that panegyric to Those Indians, Panchillo comes. Here's one of your Nature's Noblemen now!"

Sure enough. Here he comes. Drunken Panchillo, staggering already at ten o'clock of the morning. He falls through the gate, tearing another snag in his begrimed, pink checkered, Montgomery Ward blanket. He totters up the driveway like a ropewalker in sloppy, muddy moccasins. Stuck in his blowsy hair is a red feather. With ludicrous dignity he pounds on the side door, then on the back. When the Bandit Queen opens it, he pulls a couple of ears of corn from under his blanket.

"Indian corn, Pretty. You hang on wall. Fifty censes."

"No!" says the Bandit Queen.

He yanks out a beaded Cheyenne moccasin. "Indian moccasin. You buy, huh? Cheap!"

"Why didn't you steal the other one?" she demands.

Panchillo does not blink a bleary eye. He offers a piece of specular iron ore after smearing it across his besotted face. "Indian paint. Secret."

"Hells bells!" shouts the Bandit Queen. "What are you, a walking museum?"

"I sing Indian song. Eagle Song. Five dollars? Fifty censes, maybe?"

"Look here," says the Bandit Queen. "I'll buy that scrubby corn. For one cup of black coffee. Throw it to the birds."

"I wash my hands in bathroom!" offers Panchillo quickly.

"And smear up all my clean towels? And pee all over the seat and the floor? No!"

No. Whenever we want to show off the sterling Pueblo there's poor drunken old Panchillo to make a fool of us. He's the one Indian everybody knows. Are you a fisherman? A hunter? He is the best Indian guide in the pueblo. Are you a tourist? Come with Panchillo. He has the best souvenirs, can sing the best songs, dance the best dances. Are you an ethnologist? Ah! winks Panchillo. Where is your hotel? He is the best informant available—and the cheapest. His lies and his tall tales have indeed filled volumes.

Many years ago Panchillo was one of the finest boys in the pueblo. He was simple, strong, with classic features and a tall muscular body whose satin skin was tinged copperish brown. Early painters here began to use him as a model. Panchillo established their reputations. Year after year he appeared on beautiful Indian calendars. You remember him now! Panchillo reclining like a Greek god beside a waterfall; crouching over a fire; bending over a piece of glowing Hopi pottery, an Apache basket, a Navaho rug. To a whole generation he was the beautiful Child of Nature, the unspoiled Hiawatha-Indian, the Romantic Redskin.

No dirty levis for Panchillo; his were the finest Sioux headdresses and beaded Cheyenne moccasins. No work in the fields or dancing for him; he was busy posing. Rain or shine he had meat, good coffee. Between times he could afford a fling at this new Indian peyote, Mexican marihuana, and Anglo whiskey.

But gradually, inevitably, he got older and fatter, and there was no one to paint him. Panchillo died with the legend he had created. A new Panchillo remained. He still remains. Contemptuous of those who betrayed him, yet unable to forsake those whom he betrayed. The obverse side of the Pueblo most of us know. An Indian who has learned to adapt perfectly to conditions outside his own frame.

But we cannot quite laugh him off. He poses for us today the problem of a minority race whose traditional ideology is swiftly crumbling and whom we have not prepared to accept another; the problem of all Latin America and the Far East whose massed populations confront the inroads of American industrialization unaccompanied by a faith to substantiate it.

2 Pride and Prejudice

SEVERAL YEARS AGO an old friend of mine, a trader, wrote me one of his treasured scrawls:

> . . . Everything is O K here, but the March doldrums are on us again. The dirty old town is swamped in mud and bad tempers. The pueblo pile is still standing as it probably will till the end of time. I figured on getting out some moccasins. You'll probably need another pair so I'll send some. Sunday I went out to the pueblo to get deerskins. — the ex-governor took me down into the old abandoned rooms far underneath the main pile. I'd heard they existed for these forty years but hadn't seen them. You know how these people are. I suppose they ran all the way across and under the old wall so they could carry food and bows and arrows and live down there in case of attack. Just pull up the ladders first. Well they must have been comfortable enough and not without picturesqueness in their day. But dark as hell and breathing was difficult in the stifling dead air. Generations of dust covered earthen pots, medling bins and all sorts of things that could be wooden pack saddles, rope harness, rude furniture and in the dim light even skeletons. One could picture the sleeping and eating places, the old people with strange powers, the children and lovers all parading back through God knows how many centuries. I was glad to get out again in the sun and leave that eerie dew to its own doom . . .

It is a perfect picture not only of the pyramid "pile", but of the Pueblo himself. Like an iceberg, only a small part of him is visible to the casual observer.

Secrecy

Pueblo secretiveness is almost too obvious a trait of character to need comment.

Clara's husband Albert is getting ready for a ceremonial. Or her little boy is practicing for his first dance.

"When is the dance to be, Clara?"

"Who knows?"

It is a scrubby public Corn Dance not worth seeing. Every tourist in town will soon know the date. Clara herself is not too devout about this ceremonial stuff when it interferes with her work. But secretiveness, evasiveness, is all we get.

Never ask an Indian a direct question.

All Pueblos have names in their own language: Sun Elk, Mountain Raining, Good Singing, Sun Corn, Antelope All Colors, Water Leaf Road. They are kiva names, Indian names, not spoken to outsiders. They also have Spanish names, and by these they are generally known even among themselves. Only rarely an aberrant individual like my old friend Joe Sandoval is known in town as Joe Sun Hawk. And sometimes the aversion to speaking a person's name extends to even the common Spanish name.

Last year we went camping. A young Pueblo boy on vacation from school came along. "What the deuce was his name, Felipe? You remember, Santiago's son?"

But Felipe doesn't like to speak a person's name. So he pretends he doesn't remember.

To detract attention from the individual: that is the rule in conversation. Hence the well known custom of interexchanging masculine and feminine pronouns. "He (my wife) is a good cook." . . . "She is the new governor." . . .

Never must one point to a person or object.

In one of his books Lummis tells the story of an Isleta youth who entered a contest to name a new movie theater in Albuquerque. His winning name was "Kimo," the Tiwa name for mountain lion. The sign was duly posted. Weeks later an old Isleta man happened to see it when he was in town. A Council meeting was called. The origin of the name's use was tracked down to the youth and he was sent for to be severely punished. Kimo, the mountain lion, was of course the sacred animal of the north in the ceremonial direction-system.

Strict secrecy about ceremonialism is the traditional law. One cannot attend a public dance with a camera lest it might be smashed with a club. Artists have wailed for years about the restriction on sketching. But words on paper are worst.

In the late twenties Miss Ruth Bunzel lived in Zuñi for five years. Her expressed purpose was to learn to make Zuñi pottery. This art she thoroughly mastered along with the language. Meanwhile she secretly carried on the anthropological research for her now basic report of the creation myth, the kachinas and ritual poetry. The Zuñis have never forgiven this betrayal. Today, nearly thirty years later, after innumerable other anthropologists have been put out of the pueblo and their books and notes destroyed, there is a movement to refuse all Whites permission to attend the ceremonials. Antagonism toward the traditional visiting Navahos is also growing. And these are consistent with the Zuñi ban on Spanish-Americans since Estevan's time.

Back in the early thirties Mrs. Elsie Clews Parsons came to Taos. In the usual manner she hired some informants and gathered preliminary notes for an anthropological study on Taos. She was unable to secure the creation legend; to my knowledge, the complete emergence myth has not yet been fully recorded. But she did obtain the names of all the six kivas, their associated societies, family groups and other pertinent information. The notes, later incorporated in a book, were published in Menasha, Wisconsin. The anthropological pamphlet was purely technical, of no interest to a casual reader, and its small circulation was probably limited to universities and libraries.

How the Taos Pueblos ever ran into a copy remains a mystery. But a Council meeting was called. Night after night an interpreter translated the pamphlet to the outraged old *principales.* Who had betrayed them? One after another every person Mrs. Parsons had talked to was traced down. A woman who had served as her maid. A man who confessed to having told her some old Spanish superstitions which he alleged were Indian. Finally they discovered the informant. He had died a year or two before. But they punished his son by taking away some of his land.

Against this background I wrote in 1940 and 1941 my own *The Man Who Killed The Deer,* a novel of Pueblo life and ceremonialism. The richness and meaning of the ceremonial forms was written fully, but as in this present book the specific names of the kivas and their ritual functions were omitted as unnecessary violations. Nevertheless I was apprehensive lest all my best friends would be accused of having contributed information. This uneasiness was enhanced by the necessity for my leaving New Mexico just before publication. I therefore sent back the first advance copy to a Pueblo friend who was in close contact with the officers of the pueblo. I suggested he read it, tell the Council members about it, and if they thought it violated any ceremonial matters, I would be glad to appear before the Council. A letter soon came back with his approbation which meant more to me than all the reviews.

This secrecy is attributed largely to Spanish and Anglo persecution. Much of Pueblo ceremonialism has been forced underground. Like similar Buddhist and Chinese teachings it is an "ear-whispered doctrine" lest it be misunderstood and distorted; it is esoteric to us as our exoteric Christianity is esoteric in Russia today.

But Pueblo secrecy, above this enforced need, derives directly from the ceremonialism itself. Power is residual in mask and rattle, the ritual and the dry painting. Hence the sand painting is destroyed after use. The mask is hidden away to isolate its power when it is not under religious control. The rattle must not be touched except by him who uses it on specific occasions to evoke power for the common good. Believing that all these outward physical forms have inner psychical forms, how can a man allow them to be photographed or painted? The reproductions will also carry away a part of the psychical entity. Nor does one speak of this power in empty words, for "power talked about is power lost." Men have died soon after betraying information to anthropologists; they "gave away their power" and there was none left to support them.

Conversely the publicizing of the Christian doctrine by missionaries is looked upon with amused contempt. "They throw away their religion as if it weren't worth anything and expect us to believe it!" The same requirement of secrecy, however, was insisted upon in the early Christian Church. It was not based on the fear of persecution, as is now generally thought, but on the tradition of esoteric schools with which the Christian Church was undoubtedly connected in the beginning.

This reluctance to specific terminology has given rise to an abstruse reference to things which is pure poetry, and a habit of thinking by analogy which is one of the chief characteristics of the Pueblo.

But also in those pueblos where ceremonialism has broken down, the trait of secretiveness still persists as a compulsive habit. It results in a minority people deeply inhibited and withdrawn into themselves, the ghost of a collective and religious personality without means of full expression.

Stubbornness

Not long ago there came from the "Jicarilla Indian Tribes" to "Dear Friend ——, General Business Man" the following letter:

> Yes Sir. I hope this my kind following letter will be fine enjoyable your kindness heart okay by this time. Indeed not long ago I been visiting to your place. Since now I would try respecting request about those which I tell you how my Indian service indirected new for like to know how you decide for help us wrong bad business. Because that you are promise will like to help us. That is the reason I would try write to you now. And sorrow I do not know your post office or number box. But I just would try ask you tell me your box number if you return answer my kind regards letter well. Best friend I think about all this time. Glad welcome answer instantly.

My dear friend "General Business Man," a Pueblo, asked me to answer it. "O.K. Tell them people to come on. I help."

They came. A group of aged Jicarilla Apaches from their reservation to visit their old tribal home in the Cimarron valley. Many of them had been born there. They knew every spot. On that cliff one of them had killed his first deer. By this waterfall another had camped with his bride. Now they wanted to try once more to get their homeland back from the Gov'ment. "General Business Man" was an influential Pueblo man. He would know how to go about it.

After war, defeat, removal to reservations and the onrush of a new civilization with its roads, auto camps and villages, tribe after tribe, group after group, are still trying to get back their ancient motherlands. The confederated Utes recently won a suit against the United States for some $31,000,000 representing payment for 6,000,000 acres of land in Colorado and Utah taken from them in 1880 and never paid for. The Navahos through Norman M. Littell, former Assistant U.S. Attorney General, are also preparing to sue the government for between $30,000,000 and $50,000,000 for alleged violations of their treaty of 1868.

Their success seems likely. A precedent has been set by the U.S. Court of Claims which in 1950 awarded $16,500,000 to the survivors of four Oregon tribes whose land was taken from them in 1855 and never paid for, though payment was promised by treaty.

Both amusing and significant was the visit of the Chiefs of the Six Nations to the United Nations meeting at Lake Success in 1950. Claiming that they were the first United Nations, the Indians had come to protest a violation by the Canadian government of a 1784 treaty, and to complain that the United States had bought up millions of acres of Indian land in violation of the treaty of 1794 by George Washington.

Hell nor High Water, nothing will sway an Indian from his rightful claim. He has the phenomenal memory of a people who do not read and commit their memories to paper. And his indomitable stubbornness is reflected in his lack of cooperation and sense of time.

Lack of cooperation among the Navahos, Apaches, Utes and Pueblos of the Four Corners always has been the rule rather than the exception.

I remember a few years ago a devil of a fuss in Taos pueblo—smoke signals, old men congregating in the plaza, young men scurrying up the trails into the mountains. What had happened? There was a severe, extended drought throughout the Navaho reservation. In a last desperate hope, Navaho singers agreed to give the rare Rain Ceremony. Runners were dispatched to bring back waters from the four sacred mountains. The runners to the East appeared before the Taos Council, requesting permission to obtain a bowl of water from Blue Lake near Wheeler Peak. Despite the gravity of the situation the Council refused the request. The Navahos obediently trudged back toward home. But suddenly they vanished. Of course they had doubled back and were stealing their way up into the mountains! Hence the rush to stop them before they reached Blue Lake. The following year the drought struck the Taos area. Naturally. Those Navahos had stolen the water!

Cooperation even among the various pueblos is rare. The All Pueblo Council is a travesty. No two pueblos can agree on an issue; delegates are always stalking out.

The lack of cooperation extends notably to the Anglos. A recent town meeting in Taos was held to secure the cooperation of Indian-Americans, Spanish-Americans and Anglo-Americans in effecting a Bigger and Better San Geronimo Fiesta. It was pointed out that so many automobiles were choking the pueblo plaza there was hardly room for the pole climb and the dance. Why didn't the Governor throw open the communal pasture for parking during that day? Tourists could be charged twenty-five cents admission apiece instead of fifty-cents a car, and the plaza wouldn't be such a tangle of cars. But no. Let the cars pile up.

Due to serious flood conditions along the Rio Grande in 1942, Army Engineers proposed to study various sites with a view of erecting a dam on pueblo land. There was a greater danger in this proposal. Such a dam would result in its backed up waters flooding the communal corn *milpas* of Cochiti, Santo Domingo, San Felipe, Santa Clara and San Ildefonso. Governor Don Sanchez of San Felipe solved the difficulty. He refused to let the preliminary surveyors set foot on the pueblo grant . . .

A cartoon of mine portrays a ragged Indian stretched out on a sofa in a psychiatrist's office. The doctor is nervously pacing back and forth saying, "I think we're getting somewhere, Mr. Great Cloud Shadow. Your neurosis apparently stems from a submerged resentment against your ancestors for disposing of Manhattan Island for only twenty-four dollars."

The deep-rooted, implacable Indian resentment against the White must be taken for granted, all evidence to the contrary. Deeply submerged, perhaps unconscious, it betrays itself subtly.

One night just after a particularly enjoyable party which ended with a mixed circle dance, the Northern Lights, so rare here, stained the sky red. "War," commented an old Pueblo. "It will color the whole world red with blood—white man's blood. We have none left to spill." Next day we heard of Hitler's march into Poland.

When the United States declared war on Germany the Mohawks and Senecas in New York, comprising the Iroquis Nation, came out with an amusing announcement:

"Under our treaties with the United States of America we are a distinct race, nation and people, owning, occupying and governing the lands of our ancestors, under the protection of the federal government in recognition for our friendship". . . . In short, they did not consider themselves at war with Germany until they had declared war!

We must hasten to affirm enthusiastically that the war

participation of the Iroquois Nation and all Indian tribes was given freely and without stint to the United States. No group of men achieved a better record than the Pueblos and Navahos.

Yet at the same time they were fighting so courageously for their country, an old Pueblo was sitting with us. One of the group on the porch happened to be reading a published letter, famous at the moment, from an English boy to his mother. With a premonition of his death the next day, he wrote beautifully of the horrors of war and the eventual brotherhood of all men. When it was read the old Pueblo broke the silence with a snort.

"Him fine soldier! Chicken heart! Those enemies kill him sure. He got nothing to fight for. . . . Them Japs they not 'fraid. They know how to die!"

He was referring of course to the suicidal *kamikaze* attacks of Japs who perished in belief of the glorified immortality insured them by their Emperor, Son-of-Heaven.

One of the group sarcastically reminded him of his own two grandsons fighting these same Japs.

He gave another stubborn snort. "Huh. They not get hurt. They same. All same. They not white."

A woman friend of mine tells this story with great relish. It happened on July 15, 1945. A pueblo *cacique* had a strange dream. Out on the desolate desert he saw a flower grow swiftly before his eyes. From no taller than a cactus it sprouted high as a tree, then higher than the highest mountain, till like a miraculous dust-devil it spanned earth and heaven. Narrow at the base. But mushrooming at the top into a great cloud that was colored all the colors of the directions and more besides; violet, blue, green, yellow, reds, whites, all the vivid tints and shades and hues. Upon waking up the old man was greatly disturbed. What was the meaning of this strange, great flower? Such dreams often have great portent. He related it to the Council.

Next day my friend happened to meet him in the plaza and hear of the dream.

"What did you do about it in the meeting?" she asked.

"Do nothing," he answered shortly.

"Well, what do you suppose it meant?"

The old man shrugged. "Who knows? Mebbe that flower like a bad weed. He choke off all plants in world. Indian peoples already choke off. Now mebbe he choke off white peoples."

That evening, on July 16, 1945, the world heard of the explosion of the first atomic bomb near Alamogordo, and of its queer shape; a shape much stressed later when descriptions were made public. "There came shooting out of the top a giant mushroom that increased the height of the pillar to 45,000 feet. . . . As it floated off . . . it changed its shape into a flowerlike form, its giant petals curving downward." . . . So wrote William A. Laurence in his report on the Nagasaki bomb release.

It is little wonder that clocks were long forbidden within pueblo walls. Or that the Koshare, to make fun of the White, ran around the plaza pointing to an alarm clock strapped to his arm, and shouting, "Time to be hungry!"

The Pueblo has no sense of time.

Unlike the Anglo, his life does not run on a railroad time schedule. Or between two fixed points. Sunrise and sunset, summer and winter, birth and death; within these arbitrary limits life slowly revolves in a repetitive, timeless circle. The future does not exist. The ancient past is constantly alive. Everything is contained within the everliving now. The Pueblo's intense awareness of this is a valid reality. Obsessed with the internal and eternal rather than the external and transient, he lives in the core of time.

He is not "going anywhere." Hence his seeming *dolce far' niente*. Personal excellence is not success. Excess in all things is to be avoided. Power, wealth and position are nothing. Maria, the famous potter of San Ildefonso, stumbled upon the prehistoric way of glazing pottery. With proper personal ambition and competitiveness she might have kept the process secret and grown wealthy. Instead, she taught her neighbors. Despite her present excellence and fame, and her renaissance of the art, she is still living in comparative poverty a rich and integrated life.

It is these traits of character—secretiveness, stubbornness, uncooperativeness, a lack of competitiveness and no sense of time—that have validated for centuries the Pueblo way of life, and make difficult the acceptance of a culture predicated on their opposite principles.

3 The Rattle and the Cane

KNOWING THAT the character and secular life of the Pueblos is modelled from and wholly dependent upon the religious, and having learned a little of their ceremonialism, we may now suspect that the whole course of history in the Four Corners can be viewed most properly as the result of antagonism against and sympathy toward Indian ceremonialism by the Spaniards and Anglos.

From our point of view the factors have been primarily geographic expansion, industrial and agricultural development, political and economic expediency.

To the Indian it has been basically a religious war.

Consistent with our ignorance of his ceremonialism and our inherent minimizing of the religious factor in our own life, we have seldom known how we transgressed or conformed. But the results bear ample testimony.

The Rattle

Once Mabel and Tony Luhan and I were stuck in a small remote auto camp deep in the *tierra caliente* of Mexico. A stretch of road and a slimy, soap-green river running through a clearing. A cluster of thatched-roof huts. And all around, the fetid, lush tropical jungle.

With night the clammy velvet heat. Swarms of mosquitos. *Zopilotes* swooping down with a sound like tearing paper from their great wings. And at dawn a jaguar slipping furtively across the road.

By day the blinding, brassy heat. Butterflies. Parakeets. Boredom. Especially for Mabel. "Why can't we get ON!" And the car still stuck, awaiting a new part sometime from somewhere.

Tony of course kept busy. From a squalid pueblo downriver he had obtained gourds. Big, perfectly shaped *guajes,* just right for rattles. So now all day he sat peeling off the thin dried skin, tediously poking loose the pulp and seeds inside with a piece of wire. Back home they would be fitted with wooden handles, painted and decorated with feathers. Dance rattles. Such fine rattles for the young men. His sweaty face beamed pride.

Since time immemorial rattles have been one of the most important ritual accessories. Gourd rattles, deer-hoof rattles, turtle shell rattles. Where they are obtained, how they are prepared, the manner of using them—all these are rituals in themselves. Haile goes so far as to assert that only Navaho ceremonials in which the songs are accompanied with a rattle are properly called "chants." Even the major Flint Way or Life Way is often referred to as Hoof Way because it specifies the use of a hoof rattle. In all Pueblo dances the sweeping upward motion of the right hand, the rattle hand, designates a katchina dance. Parsons observed that in Walpi, Chakevena Woman's rattle hangs with her mask as the kiva standard, for "her heart was in her rattle."

Power is residual in the rattle. Every chief, clan and pueblo has its distinctive rattle. No one else dares touch it. So it was before the white man came.

The first "white" man who came into the Four Corners, we remember, was a "black" man: Estevan, the giant slave who preceded Fray Marcos. All the way from Mexico he pushed ahead alone, gathering retinues of servants from the Pimas, Papagos and Tarahumares, collecting tribute, turquoise, women. Suddenly in the Seven Cities of Cibola, at Hawikuh, he vanished—cut up into small bits by the Zuñis. Nobody knows why.

But several historians, including F. W. Hodge, recall that in the old records Estevan posed as a medicine-man, a black katchina, and that he learned to send ahead to each village a token of his power. A gourd rattle decorated with one red feather and one white.

It came to Hawikuh. Closely examined, its structure and

symbolism did not pass the inspection of those traditional masters of the ritual form. For the first time Estevan's masquerade was questioned. He went no farther. So on the rattle began the history of the next four centuries, the conflict of races.

The Cane

In contrast to this is the cane.

The cane, the stick, the staff has many variations. Upon his initiation a feathered stick is given to every Hopi boy to keep for life. The Cochiti War Chief carries a staff adorned with eagle feathers as his emblem of office, and from this he is often known as the Cane Chief. So also did the Town Chief of Isleta del Sur carry a black cane. In all history the cane has been an emblem of esoteric significance. Entwined with serpents it is the *caduceus,* the staff of Mercury, the winged messenger of the Greek gods. It is the spinal column joining the sexual and the brain centers, the upper and lower selves of man. Up it from the underworld crawls the snake, the serpent power; hence the Hopi stick is also carved with the water serpent. Elongated, hung with foxskins and decorated at the top with parrot feathers, it is the ancient Aztec flag, the *huitziton,* still carried at Santo Domingo during the great Corn Dances.

Once the Spaniards had conquered the pueblos, they gave each one title to the communal land around it—five-thousand *varas* measured in the four directions from the central cross in the cemetery. This measurement according to the ceremonial direction system was a happy coincidence. But by an unconscious stroke of genius the Spaniards did something else. They gave each governor a cane to designate him an officer of the Crown!—a confirmation in his own ceremonial symbolism of his own power.

Centuries later, after Mexico had won her independence from Spain and the United States in turn had usurped the land, the later nations followed suit. In 1859 Congress confirmed the Pueblos' titles to their lands granted them in 1551 by Charles V. And in 1863 President Abraham Lincoln called the Governors of the pueblos to Washington and presented them with silver-headed canes of office.

Still today each elected governor upon taking office is presented the cane by the *cacique,* the ceremonial head of the pueblo. During all council meetings the governor holds it, and he carries it proudly into the plaza during all public functions. It is at once a secular cane of office confirmed by three conquering nations, and a religious symbol confirming a faith that reaches back into immeasurable antiquity.

Unavoidably contrasted is the local democratic self-government allowed the Navahos. The tribe is likewise governed by a council of seventy-two tribal delegates. The council was arbitrarily formed about 1921 by order of the Department of the Interior, through the Indian Commissioner, in order to facilitate matters pertaining to the discovery and probable development of oil on the reservation. Its spokesman was designated by the Chairman, and each member was given a nickel badge to wear. The People among themselves still derisively call them the "Oil Chiefs."

As we recall, Secretary of the Interior, Albert B. Fall, was driven from office as a result of the contemporary Sinclair, Doheny and Teapot Dome oil scandals; and the Fall-Bursum bill, which would have robbed the Navaho tribe of its oil, was killed.

Oil in quantity was not struck, but the government-instituted council remained. Thus Navaho self-government, based on no traditional pattern and utterly devoid of religious significance, is largely ineffective. The reservation is divided into eighteen administrative districts and The People are governed by the Indian Service from its seat of government at Window Rock.

Between these two symbols of our unconscious transgression and confirmation to the indigenous ceremonialism—the rattle and the cane, the course of history in the Four Corners has followed its turbulent course.

Spanish usurpation of territory, the enslavement of the people, tribute and taxes, whippings, death—all these the Pueblos endured as long as they were still allowed retention of their communal pueblo lands. But always it was a violation of their ceremonialism which aroused revolt.

With the advent of American domination there was little change in Indian attitudes. Pueblo adherence to ceremonialism lay behind every other issue.

We have already noted the Supreme Court's testimony in the Sandoval case, objecting to pueblo conservatism in local government: "As long as they are permitted to live a communal life and exercise their ancient form of government, just so long will there be ignorant and wild Indians to civilize."

This despite the confirmation of Pueblo autonomy by Lincoln's canes of office.

The federal government made no attempt to interfere with the Catholic missions already established. It allowed Protestant sects to establish other missions and to conduct Indian schools under contract. When abuses developed, government schools were established on a non-sectarian basis. The Pueblo refusal to send children to school was not based, as supposed, upon a stubborn refusal to be educated or to learn new customs, trades and crafts. Boys were secreted in kivas and hid in the mountains precisely because the age at which they were taken away to school coincided with the time during which they were supposed to be immured in the kivas for religious instruction in tribal ceremonialism.

When this became apparent in 1926 the Indian Commissioner attended a Taos Council meeting. He informed the members that their religion made them "half animals," and forbade the withdrawal of Pueblo boys from school for kiva instruction. When the old men refused to comply, the whole body was thrown into jail for violating the religious crimes code—only to be released by the Federal District Court of New Mexico under press of publicity.

But meanwhile there had come up an issue which threw into relief the whole Indian problem in the Four Corners. From our point of view it involved the issues of land, economics, governmental administration and the commonwealth of 20,000 people of three races. From the Pueblo viewpoint it was simply ceremonialism as always.

Blue Lake Controversy

To recapitulate briefly the basis of the controversy, the communal land of the pueblos was founded upon the same ancient premise as the Aztec *calpullali* and Inca *ayllu.*

When the Spaniards came up the Rio Grande, they confirmed the pueblos' ownership to their land by granting them titles under the King of Spain, Charles V, in 1551.

Mexico, upon winning her independence from Spain, recognized the titles of the Pueblos.

When ownership of New Granada passed to the United States, this nation in turn recognized the titles in the treaty between Mexico and the United States in 1848, and they were confirmed by the Congress in 1859. And in 1864 when President Lincoln called the tribal heads of seventeen pueblos to Washington, he presented them patents to the original grants of land from the Crown of Spain together with silver-headed canes of office as symbols of their right to local jurisdiction.

But meanwhile something else had been happening.

Settlers had been pouring in—first Spanish Colonials from Mexico, then Anglos from the east. They built up new settlements near the pueblos and gradually began to encroach on pueblo land and water-rights.

Often this encroachment was in good faith, for boundary lines to the pueblo grants were not definitely marked. More often the land and irrigation systems were usurped by force and the persuasive power of a quart of whiskey.

The federal government did nothing to prevent this continual encroachment, for the Supreme Court in 1871 had ruled that the Pueblos were not wards of the United States, and hence their land was not under government guardianship.

Then in 1913 when the Sandoval versus the United States Case came up, the Supreme Court reversed itself. It ruled that the Pueblos were wards of the government and could not dispose of their property without consent of the government. This was tantamount to saying that the pueblos' titles to their lands was unimpaired; and that all encroachments, at least since 1848, were illegal.

The decision created a turmoil. The settlers found after being in possession of their property for some sixty-five years or more, that they did not have titles. They appealed to Congress for protection.

There was soon introduced the Fall-Bursum Bill which sought to transfer the pueblo titles to the Anglo-American and Spanish-American squatters. For once at least the traditional aloofness of the pueblos was broken. They united in 1922 to form the All-Pueblo Council. With outside help they succeeded in getting the bill recalled.

A Pueblo Lands Bill was passed in 1924. One of the Statutes provided for a Pueblo Lands Board of three men: one to represent the President, one the Department of Justice, and one the Department of the Interior. The Board came to New Mexico and began an investigation of some 5,545 claims.

The investigation lasted seven years and touched off the powder keg. The Institute of Public Affairs of Washington instituted a private inquiry and published *The Problem of Indian Administration.* A Senate investigation was made. Both the Indian Commissioner and his assistant resigned. And then the Taos Council, released from jail, filed quietly home to throw a monkey wrench in the whole proceedings.

What was the picture here? It was no different than in the other pueblos. And yet it was intensified by a strange, growing obsession.

The pueblo of Taos, meaning Red Willow Canyon, was located at the mouth of a canyon marked by clumps of red willows growing along its stream. This sparkling Pueblo Creek was the physical and psychical life-stream of the town. It originated, as we remember, high in Blue Lake—the sacred tribal home of the kachinas. Trickling down the mountains it fed the dark spruce and pine forests which supplied vigas and firewood to the people, provided green mountain meadows for grazing horses, and cover for wild turkey, grouse, deer and bear. Flowing through the pueblo it divided the town's pyramidal halves and supplied the people with drinking water. Spreading out upon the mesa before flowing into the Rio Grande it watered the communal fields through the ancient irrigation system.

Just three miles from the pueblo of Taos was the old Spanish town of Don Fernando de Taos. Farther away was the community of Ranchos de Taos. And surrounding the pueblo were little villages like Arroyo Hondo, Arroyo Seco, Cordova, Talpa, and Llano Quemado. Almost half of the original Taos Grant of 27½ square miles supporting these communities were occupied by Spanish-Americans who originally had been encouraged to settle in order to protect Taos against nomadic Indian attacks. There was no ill-feeling between the Pueblos and the Spanish-Americans, for the latter had sided with the Indians against the oncoming Anglos during the revolt of 1848. But now the Spanish-Americans had preempted great sections of land and encroached upon the water rights. And they in turn were now being supplanted by Anglos. The peripheral villages were still Spanish-American in appearance and character. But Don Fernando de Taos had turned Anglo, and it was pushing out rapidly with American initiative and greed. It demanded land, water and protection of the watershed, the whole mountain area behind, as a

National Forest. The problem boiled down to the old simple question of to whom did the area belong?

In 1933 the Pueblo Lands Board reported, and hearings began in Congress. One simple statement posed the whole problem.

"You can go to the city of Taos, New Mexico, a town of about 3,000 people, and there is not a single town lot or business lot where the legal title is in the white man, though he and his predecessors may have occupied the land for many years."

Did Congress intend to give the whole town back to the Indians? "The U.S. Government has been humane with the Indians—it never fails to respond charitably to its wards," wailed Mr. Jenkins to the 73rd Congress in its first session. "The white people pay taxes and exercise all right of ownership. Are we going to pay them for their property and give it to the Indians? If someone owns a lot that belongs to the Pueblo tribe, let him pay for it. . . . The U. S. Government has a fully equipped Department of Justice. . . . Let a judge and a jury say who shall pay and is responsible."

Mr. Peavy of Wisconsin did not agree in passing the buck. "The white man is there, able to hire lawyers. The Indian is destitute. . . . The government of the United States took over guardianship of those Indians without their wish and consent, and have held it since 1848, and I maintain the government owes the Indian that duty—to protect him in land taken up by whites."

During all this hue and cry the Anglo residents of Taos had uneasy dreams at night. In them they gave up their businesses, moved out of their homes. Spanish-Americans hunted vainly in old leather trunks and carved chests for pieces of paper that might protect their little adobes and corn *milpas.*

But the old Council members at the pueblo sat pat, night after night. To the investigating Pueblo Lands Board, Senate committee, visiting lawyers and Indian agents alike, they had only one surprising statement. "We do not want that town. We do not want those houses. We do not want any money," they said, moving evenly together. "We want our lake, our church. From it flows all the blessings of life. All the good things we get."

Church? Lake? What lake? That little Blue Lake high up in the mountains, the site of some pagan ceremony or other.

A bill was prepared for Congress. It provided for the authorization of appropriations to compensate fourteen Indian pueblos for land and water rights taken from them, to the total amount of $761,954; and an additional $232,086 to compensate all Anglo and Spanish-American settlers for land in their possession and on which they had paid taxes, but for which they did not have legal titles.

This was carefully explained to the Taos Council. "Look. The government will pay $14,064 to those people who are living on your pueblo land. They will move off and you will get back your land. Now the government will also buy that Tenorio Grant which was also yours and on which you still have your rabbit hunts. It will cost the government $43,165 more, and it also will be given back to you. Now something more. The government will give you $84,707 besides, for all that land in Taos so the white people, your good neighbors, won't have to move. It will be put in the bank for you. You will be a rich people! You will have land and money both. . . . Now sign here."

But the old men would not sign. They stood evenly together. "What about our lake, our church? Our Blue Lake from which flows all the blessings of life, all the good things we get?"

The devil and damnation! What they wanted was the world by the tail. Control of Blue Lake and the mountains around it which constituted the Carson National Forest and the watershed of the whole area. For what? Merely to perpetuate some ancient, pagan ceremony held up there every year.

The whites pleaded vociferously; they had to secure a Taos agreement to insure passing the bill for the benefit of the other pueblos and all their enfringing whites: Jemez, Nambe, Santa Ana, Santo Domingo, Sandia, San Felipe, Isleta, Picurís, San Ildefonso, San Juan, Santa Clara, Cochiti, and Pojoaque.

The Taos Council members were adamant. They had just been imprisoned for violating the so-called religious crimes code, and they were taking no chances on being deprived of their right to make their annual pilgrimage to Blue Lake.

So there came up to vote one of the most extraordinary bills ever presented to the Congress. The offer of a small Indian pueblo to surrender forever its ancient rights to land legally confirmed them by three successive sovereign nations, and to forego all compensation for its preemption, in exchange for undisputed possession of a small mountain lake—their "church." What other group of some 600 half-starved people in America would surrender $142,000 to clear the title of their church?

On May 31, 1933 the 73rd Congress of the United States passed the act. It authorized the appropriations for all fourteen pueblos and non-Indian settlers as provided. It also safeguarded "the interests and welfare of the tribe of Indians known as the Pueblo of Taos" by setting aside for a period of fifty years the area in question—"upon which lands said Indians depend for water supply, forage for their domestic livestock, wood and timber for their personal use, and as the scene of certain of their religious ceremonials."

So the Supervisor of the Carson National Forest closes the Blue Lake area each August to all whites, and is permitted in turn to patrol it during the rest of the year for protection against fire, over-grazing and timber-cutting. The strip of land rising upward to the mountains past our own thirty acres is cleared of a straggle of Spanish-American adobes and is again Pueblo land. From Blue Lake, down Lucero Canyon, pours the little Arroyo Seco river past the front of the house—the symbolic life-stream of a people's indomitable faith.

Centennial Revolt

In contrast, the present squabble, just one hundred years since the Taos Rebellion against the first encroaching Anglo-Americans, reveals the final breakdown of the pueblo.

On August 3, 1948 the Indians of all the 19 pueblos in New Mexico were given the vote. Immediately newspaper agitation against it began; for here in this sparsely populated state where politics are as devious as the goosenecks of the Rio Grande, it was feared that the Indian vote would upset the balance of power between the Republicans and Democrats. The difference in opinion was reflected in Taos pueblo. Some tribal elders were reluctant to see register the 600 people of voting age among the 1,000 population, still fearing that their lands would be taxed. Other younger men hailed the privilege.

As a result, the incumbent governor resigned, leaving the pueblo without a head—the first time in the history of the pueblo that such a thing had happened. Immediately an acting governor was installed, but in the November elections the Pueblos refused to vote.

E. T. Hagberg, general superintendent of the United

Pueblos agency, and William Brophy, former U.S. Indian Commissioner and now a Bureau attorney, then announced that they would conduct a general election in all pueblos to determine whether the Indians should continue under the old council system or establish "democratic procedure" in the handling of their community affairs.

Isleta was one of the first pueblos to assent to the change. A new constitution was written. The Indian Bureau supervised the plebiscite, and personally transferred the canes of authority to the new Governor.

To all Pueblo conservatives this was an ominous portent of disaster. For traditionally the cane had been handed the new Governor by the *Cacique*, as a confirmation of secular power by the religious power which supersedes it. Now handed the Governor by the Superintendent of the Indian Bureau, it marked only the approval of secular authority by a stronger, dominating secular authority. The validation of its ceremonial meaning, its religious significance, was broken.

The Isleta action set a precedent for the younger faction at Taos. They clamored for a change in local government that would permit the pueblo to be wired for electricity, wells drilled, water piped in, and a community loan fund established so that they could be eligible in town stores for installment buying.

With all this the Indian Bureau agreed. On May 4, 1949, Superintendent Hagberg drove up to the pueblo to call a similar election meeting. He and his Indian Service employees were met outside the pueblo by the Governor and his Council members.

"Go back to Albuquerque—don't go one foot closer to the pueblo," the Governor warned them. "You have no business here. The Constitution of the United States does not apply here. We have our own laws, our own way."

The pueblo was now split wide open by a schism as disastrous as those which had occurred at San Ildefonso, Ácoma and others in the past. It was natural that returned war veterans clamored for a change—just as returned boarding school students in the past had clamored for previous changes. Until by slow reorientation to their own values they were drawn back by greater forces than the superficial influences of the outside world.

Their quarrel was taken up by neighboring Whites—politicians anxious to win Indian votes, storekeepers eager for Indian installment buying, and newspapers ready to exploit the squabble. It was ridiculous, they claimed, that Taos Pueblo citizens could vote for the President of the United States but not for their own Governor. Why should only the Council have authority? Where was freedom of religion when men were compelled to take part in Corn Dances?

Such publicity unfortunately generated more heat than light, clouding with unnecessary steam the issues involved. In an attempt to reconcile the two factions, the pueblo Council stated calmly but publicly the *Old People's Answer:*

> We have seen lots of big words written about us oldtime Indians and we are sorry that there has been so much fuss. We have heard the young men call us tyrants and dictators, but we think it is the young men who are trying to dictate to us, especially one young man who should be named Young-Man-Who-Wants-to-be-Boss. He and his committee have told their side of the story many times. Now we tell our side just once.
>
> The trouble began when Young-Man-Who-Wants-to-be-Boss got mad because we asked his friend to resign as governor. He is a good man, that governor, but he was influenced by Young-Man-Who-Wants-to-be-Boss . . . He sold our community equipment. He tried to turn the young people against us. He shot two cows and would not pay damages because Young-Man-Who-Wants-to-be-Boss told him he did not have to. He tried to make us vote. We do not want to vote because we know all kinds of politicians would come into the pueblo and make our people take sides against each other. Also we know that when we vote we sooner or later will have to pay taxes . . . We are Indians and Americans first regardless of Democrat or Republican peoples.
>
> So that's how the trouble started. It has gone on and on, worse and worse . . . We have asked Young-Man-Who-Wants-to-be-Boss to stop meddling. He does not do any community work. He does not take part in our ceremonies. And yet he is trying to tell us what to do!
>
> We are proud of our young people. We are not against them but for them . . . We never prevent anybody from using modern equipment . . . We are not against "progress", but we have our own kind of "progress" and there are some things that might interfere with us and make our people look as unhappy as the people in the big cities.
>
> So now we ask our Spanish and Anglo friends to understand us. We do not complain of the way we live . . . If a few of the young people want to go to the cities and drink water out of a pipe, if they want to build big houses and pay big taxes and big water bills and big gas and electric bills, let them go. But we do not want to do that at the pueblo. We want to live our own way without all those big worries. We are good Christians too. There is not much difference between our old Indian religion and the Christian religion. We all want to do what is right.

This local squabble in one small pueblo has grown into a national issue since the announcement of a member of Congress that he will demand a Congressional investigation of the Taos Council. Claiming that it denies individuals the right of assembly, takes children out of school to perform religious duties, interferes with the right to vote, refuses freedom of worship, and does not permit home improvements, he will also introduce in Congress a "Bill of Rights" for the Indians of Taos Pueblo. If successfully introduced and passed, this "freedom" by compulsion of Congress will be extended to all the pueblos, and will result in their final breakdown as self-governing groups. In any event, serious harm has been done.

During the heat of the controversy a peculiar thing happened. An upper-section room of the five-storied pyramidal pueblo collapsed for the first time in its seven-century history. Such breaks are difficult to repair.

4 Words on the Wordless

THERE IS NO WORD in Navaho for "religion." Among the Pueblos too it is inseparable from all the functions of life. Upon it is built the secular social system and the character of the individual. From the Indian point of view religion is the way of life.

To us religion is a distinct phase of life separate from and often contradictory to our economic and social phases. It is divided into innumerable creeds to which complete devotion is restricted to a professional few, and whose tenets are casually observed by the mass only on Sunday morning.

Hence from our viewpoint Indian religion to be understood must first be narrowed to its formal expression in ceremonialism. Then its guiding principles must be intellectually translated in terms of other faiths and creeds. By the time we have thus rationalized it we have utterly lost all sense of what Indian religion is.

The mystical, the intuitive, can never be so rationally apprehended. It cannot be fitted into any of our categories. Something wonderful, indescribable and vibrant with a living awareness of all we know of the best and deepest in us, it cannot be told. As soon as it is told in some terrific effort of the will something dies. And we are left bandying words about the wordless—the everlasting mystery that forever escapes us when we reach forth a tongue, a hand, to pin it down.

If secularly, the Anglos and Indians in the Four Corners have been in irreconcilable conflict, what has been the relationship between Indian ceremonialism and the many formalized creeds with which it has come in contact?

Catholicism

Despite its record of ruthless exploitation throughout Indo-America, perhaps no other organization in the Four Corners has done more for the people than the Roman Catholic Church. Through four centuries of assiduous cultivation it has established churches, schools and hospitals, fought off other ruthless exploiters and opposed discriminatory government edicts. Its martyred priests have been supplanted by others to continue baptising, marrying, and burying their flocks under the sign of the cross.

Today the Pueblos are nominally Roman Catholics. Each pueblo is named after its designated patron saint. A church and a resident priest is established in almost every pueblo. And they are supported in most cases by a docile and devout congregation.

In these days of religious tolerance and greater understanding, it is not amiss to grant the origin of many of the forms and doctrines of Christianity in the so-called pagan cults of the Babylonians, Egyptians, Syrians, Cretans, Essenes, Greeks, Romans, Hebrews, Celts, and Druids. If we are to believe qualified historians, baptism originated through St. John from the Hemero-baptists, a Hebrew branch of the Pythagorean Essenes. The Holy Communion, in which Jesus Christ's blood and flesh are eaten, is identified with the Hercules-Dionysus-Mithras bull whose living flesh the Orphic ascetics tore and ate in their initiation ceremony. Eleusis, where the most famous mysteries took place, means "advent," and the word was adopted in the early Christian mysteries to signify the arrival of the divine Child. The story of Moses and the Ark in the Pentateuch was the old familiar story of the Canopic Hercules who was cradled in an ark on the river Nile, died mysteriously on a mountain top, and became a hero and a judge.

Indeed, the whole strength and universality of the Christian Mother Church owed its validity to the countless and ceaseless adaptations from the past. Even the sacrifice of the Mass, as Toynbee points out, was but a mature form of the most ancient and universal religious rite of the worship of the fertility of the earth and her fruits by the earliest tillers of the soil.

Hence there was no reason against the ready acceptance of Christianity by the Indians of the Four Corners from the start. The Christian worship of the Mother and her dying and rising Son, deriving from Cybele-Isis and Attis-Osiris, was echoed here in the Navahos' Changing Woman and Monster Slayer, and the corresponding Pueblo forms. And just as, in Greece and in Italy, Venus became St. Venere, Artemis became St. Artemidos, Mercury became St. Mercourios, and the sun-god Helios became St. Elias, so was Tonantzin, ancient mother of the Aztec gods, renamed Guadalupe, sanctified by the Church, and brought here as the dark, earth-brown Madonna to be confused with the Virgin Mother Mary. Jesus and all the Saints in their images of wood and clay were regarded as simply more *kachinas.*

Yet it was all but a patina of religious conquest by the Church Militant armed with "the spear of the Mass, the shield of the Hierarchy and the helmet of the Papacy." Pueblo and Navaho ceremonialism continued unchanged.

A few years ago the resident Padre at Santo Domingo forbade any more dances under threat of going away and leaving the people unbaptised, unmarried, and unshriven. They continued dancing. A year or two later the padre came back. The people dutifully attended Mass on their Saint's Day. Then they filed out into the plaza for their usual dance; while the padre, a sadder and wiser man, but still unable to countenance pagan rites, shut himself up behind closed shutters.

The general principles of Christianity the Pueblos accepted. But curiously enough they rejected its earliest and most dramatic application. The Hermanos Penitentes—Penitent Brothers, or Los Hermanos de la Luz—Brothers of Light, derive from the Third Order of St. Francis. Their rites were brought to New Mexico in 1598 by the colonists under Don Juan de Oñate. Soon outlawed as a sect by the Catholic Church, the order perished elsewhere, even in Old Mexico. Only here it persisted.

Today the remote little Spanish-American villages of northern New Mexico and southern Colorado are almost wholly Penitente, and the last stronghold of the sect in the world. Their secret moradas hidden in the canyons are almost equivalent to pueblo kivas. Every Pueblo is familiar with their secret rites of Holy Week—the procession of flagellants lashing their naked backs with cactus scourges, and the raising of a bloody Cristo to a cross. Part pagan, with the primitive acceptance of death as a part of life, they reach back to the ancient sacrifice of blood. As a sect the Penitentes are persecuted almost as avidly as the Pueblos, and the Indians are wholly in sympathy with their rites and secrecy. But curiously none of them are Penitentes. The idea of personal sin and damnation, of self-abnegation and self-torture—this is incomprehensible.

One may write a complete, warm and truthful biography of any Pueblo as a simple peasant and devout Catholic, and yet completely omit everything essentially Indian—as has the ethnologist Alice Marriott in *Maria, The Potter of San Ildefonso.*

But behind and beyond the aspect of the Pueblo's simple secular life with its patina of accepted Catholicism lies hidden his own faith which he has never given up—that intense living and wordless awareness, that mystical component of his character, which alone distinguishes him as an Indian.

The great, nominal success of the Catholic Church lies precisely in the fact that it has learned here to accept solely this nominal allegiance.

Protestantism

Protestantism came in slowly with the advancing Anglos. Not until 1891 was the first mission established within the 25,000 square-mile homeland of the Navahos; the Navaho Methodist Mission at Hogback on the San Juan, as we remember.

The new movement made little headway against the domination of Catholicism which claimed the territory its exclusive domain by right of a four-century-old priority. Its chief impetus came from government support. The Indian Bureau declared that all churches had equal rights in the field. Then its own government school-system failing, the Bureau subsidized Protestant missions from Indian-owned funds to carry on the work. Grants of reservation land were made, and missionaries encouraged to enforce proselytizing. During the turbulent Twenties when the effort was made to break Pueblo self-government and to abolish ceremonialism, the Catholic Franciscan Order declared itself in sympathy with the pueblos. But the Protestant Home Mission Boards rallied to the support of the Indian Bureau in return for its patronage.

Today, paradoxically, in a predominantly Protestant country, and supported by government sanction, Protestantism is still comparatively weak throughout the Four Corners. In the pueblos it is practically negligible, as it is in the small Spanish-American villages. Among the Navahos there are only a few Protestant missions, and most of them are still predominantly secular schools rather than religious missions.

The answer to this paradox lies in Protestantism itself.

Not in Christianity, for which it is an equal spokesman with Catholicism, and all other creeds and sects. But in its approach to the Navahos.

The facade of Catholicism was a majestic, nobly inspired cathedral like the sublimely beautiful old church of Ácoma, an impressive native-stone Navaho Franciscan Mission of St. Michael's, or the simple adobe chapel found in most of the pueblos. Whatever its size it was aesthetic in form, warm in tone. It was built in the local tradition, of native material, and largely shaped by Indian workmen. It conformed in texture, color and outline to the landscape. The lofty room inside with its great hand-hewn vigas, its ornate altar and rich *retablos* was matched by the impressive ceremonialism of the Mass. The priests themselves wore the long, flowing robes of office that gave them their name of "Long Coats."

In contrast to this was the stark, frigid facade of Protestantism. At worst the mission church was a plank shanty with a tin roof and a fake steeple-tower. At best a formidable granite prison of dressed stone. Nothing about it appealed to the innate appreciation of beauty of a race ever reminded of the structural harmony of the universe by their own hogans, their highly developed color sense, their feeling for ceremonialism. There were no *retablos, bultos, santos*—no saints—no Christian kachinas. No candles, incense, vestments. No show at all. A preacher—a "Short Coat" in an ordinary suit coat and a choking celluloid collar—merely thundered at them from a chopping-block pulpit in hardly intelligible English (not even Spanish) a frightening, frigid doctrine of sin and damnation.

If this facade was forbidding, the actual presentation of its teachings was frightening and incomprehensible.

Why was the world round, when according to Navaho tradition it was four-cornered? In Christianity everything ran in threes, like the Trinity. In Navaho ceremonialism it ran in fours. What became of the other component? The Bible spoke only of a male deity, like the sun-father. Where was His female counterpart corresponding to Changing Woman, the earth-mother? Everything in nature reflected these cosmic dualities—plants, animals, men, the rivers, the rain, all the forces of life. If the essence of life impenetrated all creation, why did these White people deny life to the stones and mountains? Heaven and Hell. How could a man be condemned to burn for all eternity or be granted the joys of Paradise merely on the testimony of his one short span of existence here now?

What about the Road of Life, the ceaseless evolutionary process of all forms of life? And sin. The Navahos had no conception of sin. "Evil" was but the mortal component of earthly man which returned to the north, whereas the "good" continued to travel the Road toward eventual union with the sun-father. But if the Short-Coat said there was sin, and that their Father had died to save all men, why was it necessary for him to save them now? Why did he get angry at such questions? And why couldn't he answer them? No. This Jesus Way was not the Navaho way. It was too limited in its scope . . .

In contrast to Catholicism which merely accepts nominal conversion without interfering with the native tribal ceremonialism, Protestantism is characterized by an indomitable, intolerant aggressiveness. As in the days of the first Pilgrims, it still avows the complete obliteration of all vestiges of Indian faith as a corollary to salvation.

Nowhere today is this more evidenced than in the Presbyterian Mission at Ganado, the largest and most famous Indian Mission in the United States. With its large sign and guiding motto, "Tradition is the Enemy of Progress," it is unalterably opposed to all Navaho tradition.

Ironically enough, Ganado's own conservatism is firmly rooted in the Presbyterian tradition.

Its great leader, John Calvin, was one of the first protestants against the ceremonialism of the Catholic Mother Church who broke away in the Protestant revolution of 1536. Its strict discipline is fully expressive of these early Presbyterians who derived their name from their system of government: Presbyters, from a Greek word in the Bible, meaning the elders who ruled the congregation. The emphasis on discipline, thrift, and aggressiveness has made the church one of the largest, strictest and the most businesslike in the United States today.

Little wonder that Ganado, rooted in such a tradition, could not but be unalterably and aggressively opposed to a people whose even longer tradition was rooted in the faith of man's constant evolutionary growth through four successive stages of existence.

What then is the reason for the phenomenal success of the Presbyterian Mission at Ganado?

It is important to seek it without fear or prejudice for it

may give us a clue as to how we can reconcile the basic difference not only between the Jesus Way and the Blessing Way, but between two races which represent the opposite viewpoints of world society.

It is not to be found solely in the remarkable personality and humanitarianism of its director, Dr. Clarence Salsbury. We are coming close to it when we consider his superlative skill as a surgeon. But in the essential nature of Navaho ceremonialism we find the answer.

Dr. Salsbury himself expressed it in saying, "Health and religion are inseparably tied up"—though not to the point as held by either Christian Science or Navaho ceremonialism.

Healing is the primary function, as we know now, of all Navaho sings. Hence the Big White Doctor, locating in 1927 among the Navahos and knowing nothing of their language, culture and ceremonialism, yet offered an immediate and effective parallel to the singers or medicine-men with his own medicine and surgery. But even with his medical genius and administrative skill, he had trouble at first.

According to the story, his first break came when he brought in a little girl for an operation. The child took the anaesthetic beautifully. Then suddenly a thrombosis, a blood clot formation, set in. Despite his skill he could not save her.

Swiftly the news of her death spread. A mob of angry Navahos swarmed in upon the hospital, threatening to run him out or kill him. Then Red Point, a venerated old singer, stepped out and addressed the crowd.

"For many years I have been your singer. But I have not always succeeded. Did you talk of killing me, of running me away? This Big White Doctor is trying to help the Dinneh, too. But what man has the power to always preserve life? So what is this empty talk of killing him, of running him away? Let him alone. Go home. I have said it!"

In return the Big White Doctor invited Red Point into the hospital to see how his medicine worked. Red Point was impressed; and when the typhoid epidemic struck in 1930, it was largely due to his efforts that The People were induced to receive inoculation.

In 1933 the first class of two nurses was graduated from the school of nursing. Both of the girls were Navahos: Ruth Henderson and Charlotte Adela Slivers or Naglinyil Nazbah, "Peace

Army," the daughter of Da-Ha-Na-Hez, another singer. Red Point gave the commencement address.

Red Point, we must note, was as famous among his people as Dr. Salsbury is among his. His family settlement was at White Sands, only six miles from the Mission at Ganado. He was a pupil of the celebrated singer, Gray Eyes, of the Male Shooting Chant Holy. Becoming in turn a singer of this important chant, Red Point in 1924 painted forty-eight sandpaintings of the Shooting Chants and dictated their explanations for the collection of the late John Frederick Huckel of the Fred Harvey system. It was with Red Point also, before he died in 1936, that Gladys A. Reichard studied while gathering material for her two-volume study of *Navaho Religion.*

There was nothing incongruous then in Red Point's sponsorship of Dr. Salsbury; he was one of those rare, broad-minded Navahos who bent every effort to bridge the gap in understanding between their own ceremonialism and that of modern science.

Nor is it a paradox that today many practising singers themselves, as well as their patients, come to Ganado for medical treatment. At the mission hospital this is often interpreted as an admission of defeat in the efficacy of their own healing sings. Indeed, there may seem something pathetic and ludicrous to us in the efforts of a ragged old singer trying to cure a case of measles or a cracked skull by dancing, singing and shaking a rattle in front of the suffering patient. So of course The People straggle in to receive the boon of modern medical treatment.

But curiously enough, if it were known at Ganado, almost all these Navaho patients have a protective ritual before they come and another sing afterward. And this, from the Navaho point of view, is no more incongruous than from a Christian Science viewpoint.

For "health and religion are inseparably tied up." The white doctor's shiny machines, his good medicines, remedy the effect. He has learned better than any other how to cure the disease.

But the patient still remains to be treated. The underlying cause is still to be removed. For this the singer is necessary. Only he understands that every material image has its corresponding inner form, that every physical ailment has its accompanying psychical distortion.

So to the Navaho there seems something vastly pathetic and ludicrous in the assumption of the White that they can cure a patient only by administering to his fleshly ill. Indeed, we ourselves are beginning to glimpse this truth in the ever increasing hordes of alcoholics, neurotics and mentally unfit dismissed as cured who return to fill our overcrowded hospitals and overflowing insane asylums. In Jung's statement that every nervous breakdown can be traced to the lack of a sustaining faith, we are being forced to the admission that health and religion are indeed closely related as in Navaho belief.

The success of Ganado, then, seems to have been more dependent upon its superlative surgery and hospitalization rather than upon the secular or Presbyterian teachings offered. But we cannot deny the great and truly Christian humanitarianism which motivated both the mission and its founder.

The New and the Old

No words on the wordless, superfluous as they are, would be complete without briefly indicating the striking resemblance between the oldest and the newest native religions evolved in America. For there are some basic parallels between Indian ceremonialism and Christian Science that have not been generally noticed. They are both not only religions, but ways of life.

The Eternal Mind—synonymous with God or the Sun-Father—created man as extensions of His own Mind, as microcosmic images of the eternal macrocosmic mind. There is, however, the illusion known as the mortal mind. Mortal illness, evil and death are part of that illusion. The Christian Scientist, then, strives to understand the relationship between the true Eternal Mind and his own false and illusionary mortal mind. If he becomes ill, an occurrence that shows the lack of accord, he calls in a practitioner who helps him to achieve this understanding. A medical doctor is not forbidden. But he is relied upon only in extreme cases. It is recognized that he administers only to the mortal flesh with mortal means; that he may temporarily cure the effect, but not the cause of illness which is a lack of understanding. And when a member dies it is only the assertion of the false mortal mind; hence no burial services. The "Science" of this "Christian" concept is the understanding of these truths: "Christian Science."

This is identical with Navaho belief. Man is inflicted with illness of the body or evil of the mind only when the harmony between him and the universe is broken. The whole aim of Navaho ceremonialism, through the psychosomatic sings, is to cure these illnesses by restoring the harmony between the microcosmic patient and the macrocosmic universe. The practitioner is the singer, the "medicine-man." Healing in both cases is not set apart as a functional profession; it lies within the domain of religion. The patient is treated rather than the disease. And death to the Navaho is much the same as to the Christian Scientist. The mortal component goes to the north where it perishes as an illusion. The true, eternal component returns to become part of the cosmic living whole. No burial is given the body. It is left in the hogan which may be burned over it, or buried by outsiders.

It is not difficult to understand why Christian Science as a religious sect is unknown among the Navahos or Pueblos, though it has spread through seventeen languages to all continents. The Church was not formed until 1879. There are no missions, no mission schools, no preachers to proselytize. No pageantry, no evangelism. Smoking and drinking are prohibited. It concentrates upon affirmation rather than upon petition. And with its reading rooms, it presupposes a literacy that does not yet exist among Indians.

Yet it is strange indeed that between the oldest and newest religious systems truly indigenous to America there is so close a resemblance.

5 Morals and Movies

TO WHAT do all these Anglo attitudes toward the Indian add up in the opinion of the American public? And what does it mean to the Navaho or Pueblo in his relationship to society today?

The answer, trivial as it may first appear, seems completely embodied in the strange adventures of:

The Turquoise Bride

What she was and where she came from nobody knows. But somewhere in that fantastic, nebulous world of Donald Duck, Snow White and the Seven Dwarfs she began to take form. John Rose heard her knocking on that gold-plated door to fame and fortune we mortals know as Hollywood, and rushed to me for help in finding the key to let her in.

Before the war John had been Walt Disney's Story Editor and Research Director. Under his supervision had been produced those remarkable celluloid fantasies such as *Pinocchio, Fantasia, Dumbo, The Ugly Duckling* and *Ferdinand the Bull.*

During the war he was chosen to head the Disney Field Survey party through Latin America which produced *Saludos Amigos, Three Caballeros* and many propaganda shorts for the State Department. Later, in charge of motion pictures for the Army Education Program, he produced a series of documentary films including *It's Your America, Don't Be a Sucker* and *Why We Fight.*

Now as an independent producer he was planning a series of films portraying some of the great Christian leaders in the history of the United States. The current flood of publicity in national magazines about Dr. Clarence Salsbury, director of the Ganado Mission, gave him his first lead. Why not start off with a movie on the famous Sagebrush Surgeon and the colorful Navaho Indians? He promptly secured an option on the use of Ganado as a background, including full rights to all its facilities; the cooperation of the Presbyterian Board of National Missions; the interest of a movie director and an agency; and he conjured a story idea: *The Turquoise Bride.*

Would I develop the story?

We finally agreed on fundamentals. No fantasy. No Turquoise Bride stuff. The story would be a mature presentation of the clash of two races, two ways of life, giving equal accentuation to the true values of Christianity and modern medicine, and the inherent moral values of Navaho tradition. All political and economic controversies were to be omitted. We would endeavor to come to grips with the underlying issue in a warm, human love-story.

Then we went to Ganado. Dr. Salsbury opened to us the full hospitality of the mission, gave us unstintingly of his time and good company. We ate catfish with Miss Elma Smith on his teaching staff, the first Navaho woman to receive a degree from a university. We went riding with Harriet, a nurse and interpreter, eager to go to Hollywood again. We talked with Lottie and Peggy, Navaho student nurses. Reverend Douthitt, the minister, and his assistant, Mr. Woods, took us out on their field trips.

Clearly, there was no clash of red and white values here—no contemporary story. A blanketed Navaho seemed an oddity from a remote past. We would have to get out of the Mission's 2,000 square mile sphere of influence.

So we went on a medical field trip to Tselani where the Navahos rode in from their remote canyons and mesas to be innoculated. This was better. It was as it was in the old days. Here we met

Al Lee, grandson of the Mormon John D. Lee, who had established the trading post; his son, Art, who now ran the post; another son, Hugh, who ran the post at Ganado. We ran into several medicine-men, Bet-nitni, the Winker, Red Point's Son, Standing Rock.

Now the story and characters began to take shape.

There is the Big White Doctor, epitomizing the modern white world with its Christian teachings and scientific surgery. And opposing him, the singer Standing Medicine, representing the traditional Navaho way with its great psychosomatic sings. These are the two opposite polarities, each stubbornly confirmed to his own tradition.

The clash, the fusion, would be expressed in our story, as in actuality, by the present generation. A boy, Young Singer, who had been trained as a child as a Singer; but who had been away to war and had thus received training in the white world. Disillusioned, unable to find work, he is contemptuous of the Jesus Way and wishes to revert back to his profession under Standing Medicine. Of course he falls in love with Carol. Carol is a Navaho girl, the daughter of Standing Medicine, who had allowed her as a child to attend school at Ganado. Here she has stayed, studying to become a nurse under the Big White Doctor. Like so many, she has become slightly contemptuous of the ways of her own poverty-stricken people.

Most of the action would take place around the heart-breakingly beautiful white cliffs of Tselani. Here the Sage Brush Surgeon is attempting to establish an outpost station to extend his sphere of influence. Carol is selected to be the field nurse. Her only neighbors are the old trader, Cuff Simmons, and his visiting niece, Iris. This Iris is a charming stinker. A bored Eastern tourist, contemptuous of both Christian and Navaho values, she attempts to lure Young Singer into her net of glamour.

Supporting characters are the young hero's mother, the matriarchal clan leader, Nezbah; a simple young Navaho girl, Many Goats; and her dowager mother, the richest woman in the tribe.

Thus the conflict between the old and the new, and finally the fusion. Young Singer in his bitterness is won over to an admission that he, as the whole Navaho nation, must adapt to modern civilization. And Carol is finally made to realize the real values in her own people's long tradition. Hence they can live happily ever after, working together for the common good of all . . .

It is really the immortal conflict and reconciliation of the cosmic dualities inherent in the individual psyche and in mankind as a whole, the basic motif of Navaho ceremonialism.

But what are the factors that influence our characters? That would make their story at once human, plausible and appealing to a Brooklyn audience, say?

John and I struck off into the back country. The car broke down in a sandy wash seventy miles from the nearest garage. Luckily a passing motorist picked us up and carried us to Moencopi. Here we found Milo, a Hopi elder, who could repair it. Our motoring angel proved to be John Weakland, an anthropologist from Columbia University, living at Shanto for research. Together we joined forces to hunt—no less!—the secret of the Indian soul.

What factual, visible factors induce a Navaho to give up his traditional belief for Christianity?

We ran into Bob Young, linguist for the United States Indian Bureau, at the government settlement of Tuba City. The chief thing that was breaking down Navaho tradition, he said, was The People's growing realization of the great world beyond their legendary homeland defined by the four sacred mountains. Returned veterans especially were conscious of a larger world.

We talked to I. G. Bennett, the missionary working out of Tuba City, and Andrew McGaffin, the missionary at Kayenta. Here were solitary men far removed from the spheres of influence of the resplendent great missions. Devout, humble, ill-paid men armed with no more than their Bibles and their indomitable faith, they were trying to solve the same basic problem. Here were the stark ancient verities of life—disease, poverty, ignorance, impassable roads struggling through all kinds of weather, past majestic red cliffs and unmapped canyons, across a vast naked land that remains the last unchartered wilderness in America.

How was a Navaho up here converted to Christianity?

There was an interpreter who lived by his smattering of English. He had spent all his money for bootleg beer, leaving his wife and children in want. He became a Christian because the missionary paid his wages to his wife. Then he couldn't get drunk on beer he really didn't want. He was happier being a Christian.

Another new convert embraced Christianity because the old Navaho religion was dying out and did not give him what he needed. Still another in his public testimonial stated, "At one time I went to a hotel in Flagstaff and couldn't get a room because I was an Indian. A white man followed me and got the room. The church didn't turn me away because I was an Indian."

It was quite evident that neither the Christian nor the Navaho religion was to be separated from the differing cultures in which they were imbedded. If one accepted Christianity he accepted everything that went with it.

John Rose, strange to the country, was frightened by the rough, unmarked roads that crawled from nowhere to anywhere. His illusions about the colorful, romantic Navahos were utterly dispelled. We fled back to the glittering, resplendent reality of Hollywood . . . where I prepared a short synopsis of the story.

But now more stern realities set in.

The Presbyterian National Board of Missions refused to approve the outline. Categorically it struck out lines, paragraphs, scenes. Objections were made to our grizzled old trader who had said "Damn!" The character Iris must come out; she was a pernicious influence to the Christian work of the Mission. Above all, nothing good was to be said about those pagan rites, the Navaho sings. The Board definitely ordered that "the resolution of the plot must bring out strongly the idea that what remains in the 'Navaho culture' is the art, not the religion or the medicine."

At the same time Ataloa reported on the synopsis for the National Congress of American Indians. We had sold her people down the river! Was it necessary for every Navaho character in the story to give up his birthright, refute his traditions, and be baptised at the end? She sent over a copy of my *The Man Who Killed the Deer* with 97 marginal notes: "This is the quality you need!"

Now the motion picture agency reported with comments from a major studio. "Look here!" shouted the agent. "In the whole history of the industry we have used Indians as the prototypes of the villains. Cowboy and Indian! Hero and villain! Now you want to make heroes out of them. Nobody will believe it. What are you trying to do—ruin our reputation?"

Poor Producer John! None knew better than he, with his long experience, that conflict was the basis of drama. But it was in his contract to satisfy the Presbyterian Board of Missions. His story must pass the inspection of the Protestant Film Commission. He could not antagonize the National Congress of American Indians. And still his story had to have popular appeal to obtain financial backing, technical camera crews, and a release through a studio.

For his confused writer one thing was clear. As an employee a writer cannot work under three diverse directives. It was obvious that a definite approach to the subject must be formulated and approved before he could develop his treatment.

At last report John is still trying to juggle his three ideological balls, but I am not sanguine about the future of *The Turquoise Bride*. It seems a pity too. For if the differences between Carol and Young Singer cannot be adjusted soon, they will be too old to marry and settle down into an integrated life. . . .

Cowboy vs. Indian: The American Morality Play

The trivial incident throws into relief that American racial prejudice we now recognize as a tragic national psychosis.

There has never been a successful American opera based on our Indian tradition. Like Charles Wakefield Cadman's *Shanewis* they all have been notable failures. Our dance forms, despite the attempts of the early Denishawn group and others, derive nothing from one of the oldest and greatest dance traditions in the world. It is a well-proven contention among publishers that any book about American Indians is almost certain to be a dud. Even the notable exceptions like our old neighbor's *Ramona* and the sentimental *Laughing Boy* are transient successes which prove the general rule. More significantly, there never has been a valid motion picture of Indian life.

In the farthest tail-ends of the world Hollywood has feverishly sought out the bizarre and the unusual. We have had movies of the head-hunters of Borneo, the pygmies of darkest Africa, of heathen Chinese peasants galore. The camera has brought us life on the Congo and the Amazon, ancient Hungary, modern India, Persia, and the frozen steppes of Siberia. Gary Cooper has been the hero of a score of races and creeds; Clark Gable has spanned all time and space. But this celluloid cosmopolitanism has steadfastly ignored the legendary hunting ground of romantic Hiawatha. To the omnivorous maw of the movies the Indian does not exist as a palatable realism any more than as a romantic illusion. So that today, in the old pueblos of San Ildefonso and Ácoma, we are making the same million-dollar travesties of Pueblo Indians scalping Whites and getting their just desserts.

This is not the fault of the movies. More than any other national industry the motion picture most truly reflects in its products the taste and temper, the immature ideals and frantic escapism of its consumers. The corner movie-house whether we like to admit it or not is America's mouthpiece. Our every paid admission is a vote of approval upon its reflection of our sentiments.

We don't want any truck with Indians on celluloid. Any more than in person. Why?

Unlike English drama, the motion picture is a wholly American medium of expression. As a technical process it was invented and developed by Americans. Only America's great wealth and free enterprise could have ballooned it in little more than forty years into the Big Business it now is. As an art it reflects our frantic speed, our love of the shocking spectacular, our lack of subtlety, and the capricious cruelty with which we raise a favorite to the status of a star in the firmament only to claw him down overnight.

Little wonder that with this new, national medium of expression we have developed a basic art form as formal and fundamental to America as the symphony or ballet. It is grounded on our earliest moral code. The "Western," the "Horse Opera," the "Oater," as it is variously known, is essentially our American Morality Play.

Tom Mix or Roy Rogers thundering over the Tonto Rim every Saturday afternoon. Hoot Gibson or Gene Autry stalking into Dead Man's Gulch alone with drawn guns. . . .What in these unbelievable travesties can constantly evoke from our children that insane, orgiastic storm of yells, whistles, hand-claps, foot-stamps and thrown Good Humor sticks—if it is not the same secret approbation that clamps us to our seats when we watch John Wayne or Gregory Peck commit murder in a still more glorified version?

The formula is as set as concrete. Be it a three-day quickie or a three-million-dollar colossal, the Western is a compound of extroverted fast action and the triumph of quick-shooting good over evil. It stems back unchanged to the earliest Cowboy-and-Indian one-reelers of our's and the industry's childhood.

Holy Gee! How wonderful they were. Cripes!

Those fast riding, ghostly forces of evil springing up out of the ever inimical American landscape. Forming around the wagon train in a long loping crescent of Cheyennes. Then thundering inward on their spotted ponies, naked bodies streaked with war paint, feather head-bonnets streaming in the wind, their high pitched yells and arrows tearing through the wagon sheets. . . . But Bill Hart and his Cowboys arrive in the nick of time. They beat off the attack. Now watch them deal out retribution and justice! Pursuing the Indians back to their camp. Riding in upon the smoke-grey tepees clustered upon the plain. Rifles spattering. Six-guns blazing. Savage yells and screams. Lodges going up in smoke. . . . An orgy of lust and violence. In the name of law and justice. Under the motto, "The only good Indian is a dead Indian."

Why, scarcely twenty years before, this had been still a living reality. This was no make-believe! It was a drama embodied in our nerve centers and blood stream, our very guts. The Winning of the West. The American Dream.

From the arrival of the Mayflower, we had believed it was "the design of Providence to extirpate those savages in order to make room for the cultivators of the earth." Year after year, mile after mile westward, this idea became more fixed.

As early as 1641 New Netherlands began offering bounties for Indian scalps. This practice was adopted in 1704 by Connecticut, and then by Massachusetts, where Reverend Solomon Stoddard of Northhampton urged settlers to hunt Indians with dogs as they did bears. Virginia and Pennsylvania followed suit. On July 7, 1764, Governor Penn announced the following rewards: for every captured Indian more than 10 years old, $150; for every scalp of a killed Indian, $134; for every captured woman or boy under ten years of age and belonging to inimical tribes, $130; and for every scalp of a slain squaw, $50.

In 1814 a $50 reward for Indian scalps was proclaimed by the Territory of Indiana. Indian men, like deer, were called "bucks." From this they became "varmints" like cougars, "pesky critters," "game to be shot" or "vermin to be exterminated."

In Colorado, legislation was offered placing bounties for the "destruction of Indians and skunks." In 1867 a Denver citizen offered $10 apiece for Indian scalps; and residents of Central City raised $5,000 for buying scalps at $25 apiece. By 1876, in Deadwood, Dakota Territory, the price jumped to $200.

In Oregon a bounty was placed on Indians like coyotes. They were trailed with hounds, their springs were poisoned. Women were clubbed to death and children had their brains knocked out against trees to save the expense of lead and powder. The appetite of the Whites for Indian blood was whetted by Indian agents, the legislature and even the clergy which sanctioned such practices against these dangerous "seeds of increase."

So mile by mile for three thousand miles we had fought our way westward. Year by year for two hundred and sixty-six years we had justified our divine right of conquest. Now as Cotton Mather had prophecied, "the woods were almost cleared of those pernicious creatures to make room for a better growth." But the idea had grown into an obsession, a national psychosis. And now here it was drawn out of our subconscious, recapitulated in memory, portrayed before our very eyes. The conquest of good over evil. The American Morality Play.

"Yippee! Get 'em, Cowboy!" Bill Hart never misses. And another Redskin bites the dust.

They are still biting the dust. They may be bank robbers, cattle thieves, Chicago gangsters or greedy misers contriving to steal the widow's mite, but they are still Indians. The formula is still the same. . . .

We may still be waiting to see a movie of Indians as real people. But I wonder if, after all, it will be as satisfying as those early thrillers of childhood. One sat there in the little Odeon utterly transfixed, and stumbled out into the clear Colorado night still under its spell. One timidly grasped father's hand.

"Daddy, did you ever kill Indians?"

Father did not answer. Under the pale street-lamp his swarthy brown face set. His big Indian nose jutted out like Pike's Peak. His large black eyes, usually so soft and compassionate and sick with some strange sadness, seemed hard and shiny as flint. He strode to the buckboard with that sinewy lithe walk so seldom seen now.

"Get in."

He drove silently out of town to the encampment along the creek where Mother never liked him to go. The smoke-grey lodges loomed up palely in the moonlight. Somewhere there sounded the soft beat of a drum. A dog barked. At the end of the lane a fire was burning. Some dirty Utes were sitting around it, wrapped in torn blankets. A big man pushed open the flap of the nearest tepee and stalked out. The boy recognized Buckskin Charley, the old Chief.

They sat down. Father cross-legged as they on his equally small feet. He took off his bowler hat, smoothed back his coarse, straight black hair with a delicate brown hand. They smoked.

"This our last Shan Kive," said Buckskin Charley. "We don't come back no more summers. Gover'ment say no." He spoke like a man. With no bitterness, no anger, no sadness, no regret. He simply stated a fact.

"The reservation will be a good home," said Father. "Maybe it's good land. Maybe you can live like you want."

"Mebbe."

The old Chief scratched his chest. He had on a red shirt with some colored porcupine quills worked on it. His fingernail made a loud noise in the silence.

These were Indians the boy long had been familiar with as they came, summer after summer, to pitch their lodges in their old tribal hunting grounds around the sacred springs. There was nothing at all remarkable about them—these dark and inscrutable faces that could break into a shout of laughter or a grimace of rage whenever a kid stole a ride on one of their scrawny ponies. They seemed to be just plain people.

But when the boy left and looked back at their sprawl of lodges and the dying red gleam of fires and the passing blanketed shapes, it all suddenly took on that other reality he had seen an hour before in the Odeon. The dying red fires leaped into flame. The lodges crumpled and fell with a crash of tepee poles. The blanketed figures screamed and yelled. Ran hither and thither. Pulling knives from their breech clouts. Stringing bows and emptying quivers. And as the brave Cowboys rode in shooting and yelling, and the scene became a phantasmagoria of sight and sound and smell, he too could feel himself impelled by some powerful compulsion to rush in and kill and maim and destroy these Savage Redskins in an orgasm of righteous lust and violence.

He was ten years old. He did not know yet that in his own heritage he reflected the duality which is the common heritage of us all—the tragic national psychosis through which we feel the Indian to be the embodiment of all evil, and the lurking racial conscience which torments us unceasingly with a subconscious fear of his ghost.

This is the conflict that rages in America today. That in future generations will be recognized as the historical drama of our time.

6 Death—

AND SO AT LAST, through the history of the Spanish and Anglo conquests of Indo-America, and an interpretation of Navaho and Pueblo ceremonialism in modern terms, we reach the meaning of the conflict that is the major issue of our era.

In his slow but ceaseless evolution from mere bodily perceptions and autoerotic desires, man develops a naive consciousness. Controlled by emotional and instinctive impulses, he then develops an ego, a personal or self-consciousness dominated by rational thought.

Mankind everywhere has perceived these two components of his nature, symbolized in Navaho and Pueblo ceremonialism as the conflicting cosmic dualities. They were expressed in the ancient Chinese doctrine of Yin and Yang, and in the Yun-Yab doctrine of Hindu Lamaism. The Greeks recognized them as the two "ground principles" of Plato who postulated a rational, male principle and a feminine, intuitive principle. We today accept these fundamental approaches to the meaning of life, these components of life itself, under such recent names as F. S. C. Northrkop's "undifferentiated aesthetic component" and "determinate theoretical component," while modern psychology describes them further in the functions of the anima and animus of the individual psyche.

During his composite development, man gives successive allegiance to each of these principles, opposite and irreconcilable as they seem. So at this stage of his evolutionary growth, man is torn by a psychological conflict between instinct and reason, the non-personal and the personal, the unconscious and the conscious. And the reconciliation of these two components of his psyche is the major problem of the individual today.

Primarily we feel, believe, divine.

Or we think, know, prove.

So quite naturally mankind, like individual man, gives allegiance to each of these dualities. Peoples, cultures, whole civilizations are dominated by one principle or the other during long periods. Again and again an Age of Reason has supplanted an Age of Faith during the evolution of mankind.

The ancient civilizations of America, the Inca, Maya and Aztec, as well as the ancient civilizations of Asia, of India and China, were built upon the instinctual or intuitional approach. So too were their remnants and successors: the modern civilizations of the Orient, Mexico and the countries of Latin America, and our surviving little city-states of the Pueblos.

Modern Euro-American civilization, conversely, stands upon the rationalistic approach. Heraclitus declared the very air was full of reason for man to breathe. Socrates as early as 399 B.C. believed in the rational control of all impulses and feelings. The great Roman Empire was founded upon a passion for the orderly arrangement of facts, and its far-flung provinces were maintained by Roman Law which still dominates modern juridical thought as the most enduring product of classical rationalization. In 1793 when the tide of world dominance had swept westward, there was inaugurated in Paris a festival of the "Goddess of Reason" in Notre Dame Cathedral. Man had begun to reason even in religion.

The civilizations of ancient Greece and Rome have perished. Europe has crumbled. And today our America is their successor to the mantle of Western civilization. Anglo-America, a peculiarly modern country without roots in its own continental past, with all its cultural traditions brought from Europe, now dominates the world.

And yet there is a growing, deep-rooted fear that America in her hour of triumph has struck the knell of failure; that somehow she has lost her sense of direction. Where is she going now?

We do not need the statistical evidence marshalled by P. A. Sorokin to prove our increasing paucity of qualititative creativeness in the fields of art, philosophy and social science; nor the warning of Arnold J. Toynbee that we show the symptoms of a civilization on the threshold of disintegration. The proof is manifest everywhere. Our insane asylums are becoming increasingly overcrowded. We are a people ill with an anxiety neurosis.

The problem of individual man, torn by a psychological conflict between instinct and reason, thus coincides with the problem of a world humanity split by allegiance to the same opposing principles. In this shrinking one world on the threshold of the Atomic Age, America finds herself obligated to leadership over peoples whose cultures, civilizations and guiding principles of life she does not understand at all. And at the same time she feels incapable of understanding them.

How can we understand these teeming dark multitudes of Indo-America, Africa, and Asia, with our tragic psychosis against our own Indian, Spanish-American, Negro, Asiatic, and Jewish minorities—against all human beings with colored skins? How can we understand with our rational concepts the values of these millions of people polarized to the emotional and intuitive verities of life rather than to the rational and mechanistic with their monstrous transient materialism?

In art, politics, religion, economics, science, in every field we are constricted within the rational limits of demonstrable theory and practical use. And all else outside constitutes a vast realm of the unknowable which we have dismissed with the arrogant assumption that it has no validity whatever.

In the relationship of vast Anglo-America to the dwindling little tribes of Pueblos and Navahos in the Four Corners, then, we find duplicated in basic essentials the relationship, on a larger scale, of the comparatively tiny United States to the vast dark populations of the continents that comprise most of the world.

Thus the wheel has turned full circle. The introversive city-states of the Pueblos, like the ancient civilizations of the Maya, Aztecs and Incas, have given way to the rationally extroverted civilization of Euro-America. And we in turn have reached the summit of our mechanistic-material-mental advance. Like Indo-America, Euro-America has completed this phase of its destiny.

The struggle is over. We each have died a death whose causes were inherent in our very natures from the beginning. A rebirth is necessary.

To what? And how?

The cultists in part have helped us to reach an answer.

The Cultists

The great function today of our surviving Navahos and Pueblos of the Four Corners—that little island of instinct, as it were, within our national, rational boundaries—is that of relating us not only to the vast world of instinctive peoples outside, but also to that pre-Columbian America which is our own submerged past and the common past in which is rooted the whole history of mankind.

That many people have realized this is attested by our recent deep interest in the Indians and their ceremonials. But in searching them for a way out of our own dilemma, we have had posed for us two alternatives. Shall we continue to advance horizontally outward across the world with our rational values? Or should we return vertically, as it were, to the instinctive values of the past?

Unfortunately it has not been clear that we cannot confuse values. We cannot intellectualize blind faith. Nor can we impute emotionality to a mathematical equation. When we do we create cults.

And that is precisely what we have done in glorifying the Indian during our valid attempt to regain our inhibited instinctual component. It was natural that the movement began here in the Four Corners among painters, sculptors, and writers drawn by the spectacularly dramatic landscape, the colorful Pueblos and Navahos, and the restful slow tempo of the small Spanish-American villages.

Polarized to the "undifferentiated aesthetic component," as politicians and businessmen as a class are polarized to the "determinate theoretic component," the artists were not only seeking escape from the rational material life of large cities, but they found here the instinctive values they needed for expression.

On their heels trooped in a horde of pseudo-artists, escapists of every description. So here in America's last wilderness grew up America's most famous Greenwich Village. In the tiny plaza of Taos, as in the arty suburbs of Santa Fe, strutted the newest European immigrants rubbing shoulders with the oldest residents of the continent; the most fabulously rich with the abject poorest; the highly intellectual with the illiterate; the most complex, neurotic, and faithless, with the most simple, sound and devout.

Among all these, aesthetic and aesthete alike, there

inevitably developed a group of *Indianistas* who championed the Indian cause. They courageously proclaimed the inherent soundness, aesthetic beauty and psychological maturity of the Indian against the howling madness of the materialistic-mechanistic age of exploitation. No group has been less understood and more maligned, and no group has done more to help the Indians.

The larger cult of Indianism was cut from coarser cloth. It was woven on an Anglo loom. It proclaimed Indian values only to enable the cultists to set their market price. Many little reputations have been made writing romantic poems and sentimental books about Indians. Many little fortunes have been made selling Indian handicrafts. The cultists have imitated Indian jewelry, pottery, blankets; have painted Indian pictures; instituted fads in dress and wallpaper; garnered votes, and gained political influence, all without benefiting the Indians a whit.

What a mess it all has been! But what colorful figures it has thrust forward from the Four Corners!

Georgia O'Keefe, whose painting of a cow's skull made her famous, and whose painting of two blue lines, Abstraction No. 11, was selected as the frontispiece for Northrop's *The Meeting Of East And West* as the perfect expression of "The Aesthetic and Theoretic Components in Their Unity." Still painting away up near the great red cliffs of Abiquiu. . . . Becky James, whose father was the manager of Buffalo Bill's European tour, and whose flower paintings on glass are still better than O'Keefe's. . . . John Young-Hunter, society portrait painter, who saw Buffalo Bill's performance in England, was fatally fascinated by Indians and came to paint them in Taos. . . . Nicolai Fechin, graduate portrait painter of the Imperial Art Academy of Russia, who has done the finest portraits of Indians yet achieved. . . . John Marin, Andrew Dasburg, Frank Hoffman, Ernest Blumenschein, Howard Cook, painters galore. . . . Sculptors like Maurice Sterne. . . . Musicians like Natalie Curtis. . . . There was Mary Austin whose sensitive prose echoed the pulse of the landscape as few have ever felt it since. Who wound up in her home on the Camino del Monte Sol, near Santa Fe, writing her convictions that the vibrating beat of an Indian drum was necessary to carry the words of spoken prayer aloft. . . . There was Ernest Thompson Seton, the supreme writer of wild animal stories for boys of my generation, a master of Indian woodcraft, and a founder of the Boy Scout movement. Who built a village near Santa Fe and instituted a cult of Indian thought. . . . Mary C. Wheelwright whose great munificence and interest in Navaho dry paintings founded the Museum of Navajo Ceremonial Art. . . .

These and a hundred other Indianophiles were the supporting characters of a legend which still clings to our coat tails. The legend of an American Bohemia making its last stand in the wilderness heart of America. A rugged individualism echoing the last beat of an Indian drum against the approaching din of industrial materialism. . . . Listen! Remember while you can these days of our youth! Our membership is running out. Brett's solitary adobe has become the thriving Brett Junction at the crossroads. Frieda's little rancho is Lawrenceville now. The Big House of Mabletown is abandoned in favor of the quiet little River House. The old Harwood Hovels are now transformed into the Harwood Foundation of the University. Our soft adobe floors are decently covered with hardwood planks. Even the pueblo is lit with electric lights, and the sweet smell of butane gas fumes replaces that of pungent piñon. The fun is all gone. But when we pick up the nineteenth edition of D. H. Lawrence it all comes back—and the tragedy too.

What a strange, red-whiskered, self-tortured man of genius was this Lorenzo of Taos! You can ridicule his thinking. But you can't deny his feeling. The quick of life was in him, the divine sense of mystery and the nobleness of simple endeavor.

How he excoriated those who proclaimed the universe a well-oiled machine! How he damned our abject slavery to the iron monster! His vituperation was magnificent. His anger echoed like thunderclaps against the peaks. He shook us up all right!

Why, he even had that supreme rationalist, Aldous Huxley, riding on his coat tails in a cloud of dusty mysticism. We couldn't collect our wits enough to realize, like another countryman of his, J. B. Priestly, that there was something fatuous about a man who condemned the machine yet depended upon it to print and distribute his magnificent condemnations. We were all too busy asking timorously how we could escape this deadening constriction of life in the machine-age.

Why, go back to the old magic, said Lawrence. Back to the instinctual, the intuitive. Back to the deep, dark wisdom of the blood.

So here in the hinterland of New Mexico, on the high

pine slope of Lobo Mountain, Lawrence began his fight to reawaken in man the joy and quick of life, a sense of the everlasting mystery and magic. He worked on his ranch. He milked his cow, Susan. He baked his own bread. And sitting under a pine, writing in that neat calligraphy we know so well, he gave us some of the most vivid pictures ever written of our homeland.

But gradually he turns back to this more ancient America, this dark realm of the blood. *The Dance of the Sprouting Corn, The Hopi Snake Dance.* He goes down into Mexico for his supremely descriptive *Walk to Huayapa* and *Market Day* in Oaxaca.

Back to it! Back into *Mornings in Mexico.* Back with *The Woman Who Rode Away* into the instinctive, the intuitional. Back even to human sacrifice. The scene is deep in the unknown Sierre Madre of Mexico. But we recognize its wonderful portrayal. The hidden Indian village is the pueblo of Taos. The mysterious, sacrificial cave is the still sacred cave in the mountains behind our back pasture at Arroyo Seco. One day each year, on the winter solstice, the sun strikes squarely the mouth of the cave. Through its curtain of ice it shines with a pale brilliance. Now upon the waiting victim. She is Frieda, Brett, Mabel, all the Anglo women of our senseless machine-age who have ridden away to a new destiny. It is the winter solstice of our civilization. And so she waits the sacrificial knife with a deep proud affirmation, a profound expectancy.

Lawrence was a wonderful artist, one of the best this land has known. But he had reached the last oubliette; and he was writing the obituary of his own misguided faith.

The Plumed Serpent * is one of his least known and greatest books. It is a strange and powerful novel. And one of the most horrible prophecies ever written.

The scene is modern Mexico, mostly on the shore of Lake Chapala. But really, inside, it springs from New Mexico like *The Woman Who Rode Away.* Like everything he ever wrote of America. The dark, somber, *serape*-clad *Indios* have the same magic of the Red Indians of the North. The drumbeats echo the rhythm of Pueblo drums. And the stark fear of white superiority, of *gringo* industrialism sweeping Mexico, is Lawrence's own hate of American mechanization.

Pues. He starts an ideological revolution in Mexico. That

* Alfred A. Knopf, Inc., New York, 1926.

is, the main characters do. Don Ramon, a handsome, intelligent Mexican graduated from Columbia University. And Cipriano, a small bandy-legged Indian, an army officer. They will overthrow the corrupt government, kick out the greedy *gringo,* nullify the dominating power of the corrupt Catholic Church, and combat the stultifying rationalization and mechanization of life.

But what, asks Kate, an American visitor, the omnipresent doubter, shall take their place?

Why, the people shall go back to the old magic. To the instinctual, intuitional way of life. To their ancient Aztec Gods.

So from the muddy bottom of Lake Chapala old idols appear. Leaflets circulate in the villages, imprinted with the Hymns of Quetzalcoatl, the Eternal Snake of the Cosmos, the feathered-serpent god of Aztec Mexico. In the plazas at night people begin to gather. To talk. To dance softly, with measured tread, the old Round Dance of the Red Indians of the North, as danced in the pueblo of Taos.

Swiftly momentum gathers. Don Ramon submerges his identity in the First Man of Quetzalcoatl. His insignia of the new order is a blue and white *serape*—the traditional Hopi blanket colors—containing the snake and eagle symbol of the Aztec empire. Cipriano in his red *serape* is the First Man of Huitzilopochtli, the Aztec God of War. He begins forming his legions of the Men of Quetzalcoatl, teaching them to dance with knife and spear and shield. Dancing to gain power, "power over the *living* forces or potencies of the earth." But they are supplied modern rifles too.

And Kate, the omnipresent doubter, she too cannot resist the old magic, the dark forces of the blood. She becomes the First Woman of Itzpapalotl, the obsidian butterfly god of the Aztecs.

It is done! The government is overthrown. The Catholic Church is condemned, the Archbishop deported. The armies of Huitzilpochtli swarm over the country. The banners of Quetzalcoatl rise triumphant over a people who have obliterated four hundred years of progress.

Says Lawrence, through Don Ramon:

So if I want Mexicans to learn the name of Quetzalcoatl, it is because I want them to speak with the tongues of their own blood. I wish the Teutonic world would once more think in terms of Thor and Wotan, and the tree Igdrasil . . . And a new Hermes should come back to the Mediterranean, and a new Ashtaroth to Tunis; and Mithras again to Persia. . . .

Yes. *The Plumed Serpent* is a literary *tour de force.* A fictional wish-fulfillment. And a ghastly prophecy. Published in 1926, it came true in 1933. But not in Mexico.

In that year Don Ramon, alias Adolph Hitler, came very much to life. Proclaiming himself Chancellor of the Third Reich, he shouted stridently to the world that Germany once more would indeed think in terms of Thor and Wotan and the tree Igdrasil.

Back to the dark, instinctual realm of the blood! Back to the purifying force of pure feeling! "Strength Through Joy." Up from the past the whole pantheon of ancient Teutonic gods, to the tune of Wagner's Ring. Out with the Christian Church. Down with foreigners. Kill Jews. *Lebensraum. Geopolitik. Heil,* Fuehrer!

It was the identical pattern prescribed in *The Plumed Serpent.* But with the accent on the blood-feeling of the Aryan instead of the Indian. The symbol of the swastika instead of the feathered serpent.

As a pattern for one of the greatest holocausts in history *The Plumed Serpent* has no parallel.

But we saw what happened. World War II. The German *Gotterdammerung.* And a dazed world crawling out of another blood-bath. All to prove perhaps that no people can go back to the old magic of their ancient past. Not even here on a high pine mountain in magical New Mexico.

There was only one thing wrong with Lawrence's evocation. He did not know enough about Indian ceremonialism. It would have taught him that the Road of Life is a one-way road.

No. We cannot minimize the tragic falsity of the Lawrencian cult which urges us, even individually, to regress to the impulses of instinct. For when we do, we disintegrate morally and psychologically.

Yet neither can we allow the conscious ego to totally repress the instincts, impoverishing our life to sterility.

So the conflict continues between instinct and reason, the non-personal and personal, the unconscious and conscious. But as we grope desperately for a way out of it, we know that man dare not give up an inch of the ground he has gained through millennia of constant struggle on the upward path of continuous development. He cannot go back. He must go on, and find anew that faith in mankind's ceaseless evolution toward a divine destiny which alone assures him of the right to survival.

How are we to find that faith?

And how can it resolve the conflict between the deep-rooted, opposite and irreconcilable dualities of man's nature?

Why simply by enduring the conflict without seeking to escape it by repressing either the instincts or the conscious ego, affirms modern psychiatry. Then, when our pain and suffering seems too great to be borne, a solution will develop spontaneously in the depths of the unconscious. "Such a solution," explains Dr. M. Esther Harding in her superb *Psychic Energy,** "will not appear in the form of an intellectual conclusion or thought-out-plan, but will arise in dream or fantasy in the form of an image or symbol, so unexpected and yet so apt that its appearance will seem like a miracle. Such a symbol has the effect of breaking the deadlock. It has power to bring the opposing demands of the psyche together in a newly created form through which the life energies can flow in a new creative effort."

C. G. Jung called this the reconciling symbol. It comes, he explained, from two sources: the unconscious, which spontaneously produces such fantasies; or life, which if lived with complete devotion, brings an intuition of the self. In the first case the unconscious, through the symbol it produces, enforces an acceptance of life. In the second case, when one becomes aware of the self, it is expressed in a symbol.

These reconciling symbols of the patients of modern psychiatry, we have learned, are synonymous with the *mandalas* of Chinese and Tibetan Buddhism, and the sand-paintings of Pueblo and Navaho ceremonialism. They are archetypal symbols common to all time and mankind. "Things reaching so far back in human history," says Jung, "naturally touch upon the deepest layers of the unconscious, and make it possible to grasp the latter where conscious speech shows itself to be quite impotent." All react upon their makers, bringing them back to that inner domain containing the unity of life which has been lost and must now be found again.

This is the meaning and function of the reconciling symbol as it applies to the individual. But humanity is made up of individuals, and the psychic forces that impel nations to war and civilizations to growth are forces stemming from the collective

* Bollingen Foundation, Inc., New York, 1947.

unconscious of individual psyches. The problem of humanity at various stages of its development is the same as for the individual during his growth to maturity: relief from the ruthless tyranny of the instincts, or from the exclusive domination of the conscious ego. And in the past such reconciling symbols have arisen from the collective unconscious of mankind to lead whole races, nations, and civilizations in great bursts of creative energy to another Emergence, a new stage of consciousness.

We recognize these reconciling symbols in most of the great emblems of historical movements. They conform to a pattern usually with four as a basis of structure: a circle circumscribing a square, a cross, a flower, a star or sometimes a triangle.

The circle, complete, perfect, without beginning or end, is the cosmos, the absolute, the divine. It is man's psyche with all its component parts.

The square is our earth, four-cornered, the "four-square" reality of limited human consciousness, the rational principle.

Hence the attempt of ancient Greek mathematicians to "square the circle," by finding a square whose area would be commensurate with that of a circle, was no more than a search to find the relationship between the two principles of man's psyche, or between the macrocosmic universe and microcosmic man. Mathematically, the problem was solved only by means of the reconciling symbol π whose value is unknowable.

In the field of religion the pattern is even more evident. During the early Christian era the figure of Christ was represented within a circle, surrounded by a bull, eagle, lion, and angel, the four manifestations of the divinity, the symbols of the four evangelists, Mathew, Mark, Luke, John. In ancient Egyptian burial rites they corresponded to the four sons of Horus who stood as funerary figures at the corners of the catafalque. In modern times the symbology persists in the image of a child's simple prayer: "Matthew, Mark, Luke, John, bless the bed I lie upon."

Often in the center of the circle it was Mary who was enthroned, with God the Father, and His Son crowned on her lap. Again the universal significance is plain. The divine Father, the human Mother, and the Son who is the reconciling symbol linking the human with the divine.

The later symbol of an eye enclosed within a triangle, and the Masonic emblem of the letter G for God within a triangle composed of rational measuring devices, express the same meaning —the all-seeing or illimitable divine consciousness embodied within the Trinity.

The difference between the Western Christian triangular pattern symbolized by the Trinity, and the symbolic square common to Eastern Buddhism and Taoism as well as to Navaho and Pueblo ceremonialism, offers no discrepancy in basic meaning. We disregard the fourth manifestation of divinity, which is the underworld realm of "hell" or the repressed unconscious, simply because of our over-emphasis upon the conscious ego in this stage of our development.

The four-petalled Lotus of Buddhism, the Golden Flower of Taoism; the Palace of Jade, the Garden of Eden, New Jerusalem with its four gates; the Round Table and Holy Grail of Arthurian legends; the mighty symbol of the Cross of the West, and the dorje, or scepter of the gods, of the East;—all these have been reconciling symbols that have arisen out of the depths of mankind's collective unconscious, created the great religions and movements of history, and so transformed the dynamic forces of millions of people to flow into new channels of collective ethics and morality toward a new Emergence.

Today most of these symbols have become outworn and have lost their ancient meanings and potencies. The world is crying for a new symbol, a new faith, to reconcile modern rational man with the same immortal, non-personal forces of the universe. Despite the threatened cataclysm of war, insanity, and criminality, there seem indications that new symbols are arising—transforming symbols created in the idiom of our new technologies, but cast in the same basic patterns of the old, of Pueblo and Navaho ceremonialism.

7 And Transfiguration

If there is anything "more fun than a picnic" we here haven't found it.

Fiestas are dreary holidays. They occur year after year on the same day with monotonous regularity, as if ordained by Fate or scheduled by the Chamber of Commerce. The same excruciating wait in the broiling plaza. The same bedraggled parade. *Tio Vivo, dulces* and hot dogs, speeches in Spanish. Bravo! What a fizzle!

But a picnic. There is something spontaneous and warming to the blood! Instigated by versatility and chance, it stops the clock and dams the rushing torrent of time into a placid and deathless pool of pure enjoyment.

One minute you're scrounging down in your chair for a

dull day's work. The next you're rattling over the rutted road under a clear turquois sky. There's Mabel carrying Meriam in her Cape Cod britches. Or Frieda in a Bavarian blouse with Tinka in a Russian scarf. There's Tony with a couple of Indians. Angelino, Bobby and Victor in Levis. Who's coming behind? Brett with Tobie, her tin ear trumpet, and a feather in her hat. Then Betty and Catherine.

Á donde? Whither away? Up the steep slope to the old ghost mining camp of Twining. Over Palo Flechado or U. S. Hill. Down into Cimmaron Canyon. But usually down the deep gorge of the Rio Grande. Across the weathered plank bridge from San Ildefonso. But first Tony has to stop in the plaza. Indian business!

"Come ON! Really!" demands Mabel. The road crawls on. Here's Otowi, Miss Edith Warner's tasteful little tea room that once was a railroad lunch room when the Chile Line meandered down this way. And there's the great shaggy cottonwoods on the high piñon slopes overlooking the valley. The road climbs up past the ancient cliff dwellings of the Rito de los Frijoles. Good enough! Here we are.

The view's superb. But who wants to sit and look at a view we know so well? Or poke into dusty old ruins with Indians?

No dry lifeless sandwiches, please. A fire to give life, then some thick twenty-five-cent T-bone steaks of mountain-pastured beef broiled on the coals. Meanwhile the men and the Indian boys investigate the possibilities of trout. The pools are small and clear. You lie on your belly and lower a line tied into a loop. When the trout noses inside, you jerk. That is the old Indian way. Lots of patience. Little fish—for us anyway.

It is better to lie lazily around the fire. Gorging food. Stretching out lazily again. Frieda talks of Germany. Angelino of Italy. Tinka of Russia. Brett of London. Victor of Vienna. It is all very vague. Like the cloud shapes drifting overhead, breaking up into new patterns already. Ja! agrees Frieda. But still talk, talk, talk as Mabel always says. Tony will put a stop to that! And sure enough after a time he begins softly tapping on a drum. One of the boys begins singing the Eagle Song.

Lying on our backs we can see the bird circling far up in the blue. Dipping. Wheeling. Soaring aloft again, the sun glinting from his pinions. Borne up, it seems, by that gentle rush of song from below. . . .

When suddenly the eagle screeches and shoots out of sight like an arrow. Just as a tremor shakes the mountains. The peaks seem jarred out of their sockets. The brown plain below ripples like a blanket. The whole earth and we upon it, the moaning trees, the weeping stream, the crying stones, shudder with a nameless fear, a black foreboding. It is over instantly. An hallucination. Nothing has happened,

Yet something has. It is July 16, 1945. The first atomic bomb has been exploded on the desolate White Sands to the south. It is the end of thick twenty-five-cent T-bone steaks. The end of our picnics. The end of an era. The Four Corners, America, the whole world has been set on the threshold of the Atomic Age.

Clementine, Los Alamos

We know that five-mile-long and one-mile-wide plateau now as The Hill. The world's atomic bomb center and greatest nuclear physics laboratory. The Forbidden City of Atomic Research. The hush-hush bastion of the future.

But we don't know it very well. Its 69,000 acres are surrounded by a nine-foot-high wire fence with only two gates, and guarded by an 800-man Security Service force. Day and night, watchtowers and pill boxes keep vigil. Thirty-five tanks patrol the canyons. It is perhaps the most closely guarded area in the world.

But one thing is certain. Los Alamos has the finest doctors and surgeons in the world. We found it out some time ago when the Bandit Queen needed an emergency operation. Special arrangements were made to receive her on The Hill. So up we went.

Up a narrow dirt road blasted out of the cliffsides, crowded with trucks, tractors and tanks. Past armed M.P.'s. Through the guarded gate. Into a roaring settlement that was at once a frontier town, a boom mining camp, a construction camp and an army post. Dusty streets lined with auto-trailers, plank shanties and army barracks. No sidewalks, no hotels nor restaurants, no shops. But a drug store in a log cabin, an army commissary, a combination church and movie-house with a tin roof. And the army style hospital with its eleven doctors and fifty nurses waiting to receive the Bandit Queen.

She was just in time. Two hours later she went on the table. It was done! Now there was nothing for an anxious husband to do but wait. He was given a badge with a code number on it indicating where he could or could not go. Assigned a bed in a barracks. And given a pass allowing him to eat, family style, with scientists and approved visitors in—yes!—that huge Edward Fuller dining lodge of weathered logs that he had known as Los Alamos Ranch School.

It was unbelievable. Yet here it was. The birthplace of the Hiroshima and Nagasaki bombs, the strangest city in the world.

Already $500,000,000 had been spent carving it out of the wilderness. Then in 1947 it was beginning a new $100,000,000 program to modernize it into the present city of tidy buildings prefabricated by every means and materials known to man, with recreational areas for golf, tennis, baseball, football, skiing, skating, swimming and riding. To expand it to the "upper pasture" and to another mesa across the canyon on a 93-foot fill. And to increase its boom-population of 9,000 to a permanent 14,000.

Yet somehow it all gave the impression of a Japanese water-flower. You know, the little paper pellets which, when we children dropped them into water, swiftly expanded into beautiful colored blossoms. But without roots.

A city of people without permanent homes. Occupying government-owned houses only for the duration of their government-approved jobs. Opening businesses only on a concession percentage basis. Organized into 80 community groups with an elective town-council, but subject to the manager of the Santa Fe Operations Area of the Atomic Energy Commission. A city without a cemetery; when anyone died, he was shipped "home" and his family forfeited residence. Nearly one out of seven people were under the age of four—children who were learning to play hopscotch over squares they called "contaminated"; more than one-fourth of the population was under nineteen; and the average age of Los Alamos was only thirty.

This was a young people's world. A city without roots. A vast modern reservation operated under three divisions of segregated labor:

A private construction agency, the Zia Corporation, organized by government contract to maintain the industrial plant—water, gas, electricity, streets and shops—and do all construction work.

A second division of employees engaged to operate the city administration, schools and courts under the authority of the Atomic Energy Commission.

And in the third, over 1600 scientists, nuclear physicists and technical engineers proper, employed by the University of California under a non-profit contract to operate the laboratories and conduct the experiments in atomic fission. All these great laboratories and experimental sites were enclosed by a second and higher wire fence within the Tech Area itself. One could not approach it. One only glimpsed again across the wooded picnic canyons the high white cliffs which now provided a radiation shield and lateral bracing for the huge main laboratory.

So an anxious husband waiting for a wife to recover, walked the crowded, dusty streets, and thought of the pueblos of San Ildefonso and Santa Clara in their similar reservations below. There too the citizens were wards of the government. They too nominally governed themselves through an elective council subject to the federal government. But their roots were planted deep in the soil.

Through countless generations they had handed down their corn *milpas* from father to son. Their adobe homes reflected the contours of the land, and bore the imprint of their mothers' hands. And their bodies in turn nourished and sanctified their prehistoric homeland for their children. With the prayer-feathers buried in the plaza, their faith, their homes, their bodies, were rooted to the land.

Today this concept of the original American Way seemed distinctly old fashioned. For now these Pueblo men were giving up their fields for road right of ways and an air strip, and the women were deserting their homes to work as menial servants on The Hill above. Gradually they were abandoning their faith for the new and nebulous illusion of hard cash. San Ildefonso already had bought a new harvester, a community truck, a movie projector for the school, and had given each member a forty dollar bonus from funds coming into the pueblo treasury as a result of renting land to a construction camp. Los Alamos spelled the death of the old pueblos. But would the people be any happier?

He thought of Hiroshima with its 66,000 people killed, 69,000 injured and 60,000 destroyed buildings; of the 39,000 persons killed, 25,000 injured and 14,000 buildings destroyed at Nagasaki.

The first installments on the price of progress. . . . Toward what?

Yet despite the strangeness of his surroundings, Los Alamos gave him a sense of annoying familiarity. It was as if somewhere, sometime, he had known it all before. . . . The insigna of streaked lightning worn by members of the Security Service. . . . The construction company, Zia, named after the ancient pueblo of Zia; and whose emblem was the Pueblo symbol for the sun, a variation of the encircled cross. . . . The code name of "Trinity" given to the project which exploded the world's first atomic bomb in the desert to the south. . . . And "Clementine."

Clementine, it seemed, was the only fast atomic reactor in the world utilizing fissionable material. It was named for the famous miner's daughter of song and legend because it utilized plutonium, designated during the war by the code-name "Forty-Nine." Clementine with a 12,000,000-electron volt electrostatic accelerator costing $2,000,000 and being built in a high tower against the great cliffs, was dinner time and street corner conversation. The goddess of Los Alamos. People regarded her with both familiarity and respect. Every so often, to guard against her chance fickleness, they went through a community fire drill known as the Master Disaster Plan. Between times they jokingly made reservations in the ancient caves and cliff dwellings of El Rito de los Frijoles in the event of another World War.

Strangely, a parody of the old tune began ringing in his ears:

Oh my goddess,
Oh my goddess,
Oh my goddess,
Clem-en-tine!

Long before she had been a Forty-Niner's daughter, she had been a goddess indeed. The delectable scholar and truculent poet, Robert Graves, tells us all about her in *The White Goddess.*

The mystical Essenes of the first century A.D., he relates, had been an offshoot of the Therapeutae or Healers, an ascetic Jewish sect settled near Lake Mareotis in Egypt. Pliny described them as the strangest religious body in the world. Under the philosophic guidance of Pythagoras they meditated within magic circles, like that of the Zia sun symbol. And like the Pueblos they believed in the return of pure souls to the sun, whose rising they also invoked daily.

For at the Beginning, according to the Talmud, Jehovah took dust from the center of the earth (like the Sacred Middle of Zuñi) and from all the Four Quarters of the earth, and mingled it with water from all the seas to create Adam.* The angel Michael collected the dust. This angel was a feminine power, as attested by *A Discourse on Mary* by Cyril of Jerusalem, printed by Budge in his *Miscellaneous Coptic Texts:*

"It is written in the Gospel to the Hebrews (a lost gospel of the Essene Ebionites, supposedly the original of St. Matthew) that when Christ wished to come upon earth to men, the Good Father called a mighty power in the Heavens which was called Michael and committed Christ to its care. And the power descended on earth and was called Mary, and Christ was in her womb seven months, after which she gave birth to Him."

Hence the mystical Essene Ebionites of the first century A.D. believed in a female Holy Spirit. In the second century those members who embraced Christianity developed into a new sect, the Clementine gnostics. These Clementines made the Virgin Mary the vessel of the Holy Spirit, but rejected the orthodox Christian story of the Fall, asserting that the identity of true religion of all ages depends on a series of incarnations of the Wisdom of God, of which Adam, the "red man," was the first and Jesus the last.

Oh my goddess,
Clem-en-tine!

Yes, here at Los Alamos was a new vessel of faith and world power. Goddess Clementine, the only atomic reactor in the world. Giving birth to—

And suddenly, by some strange quirk, he happened to think of another lofty mesa nearby. He remembered the floor plan of the sun temple on Mesa Verde. Immediately everything rushed into focus—Los Alamos and Mesa Verde, Project Trinity and the ancient sun temple, the Essenes, the prehistoric cliff-dwellers and the laughing new Clementines strolling by him in the moonlight.

The Sun Temple, Mesa Verde

The excavated ruins of the prehistoric sun temple of Mesa Verde show it to have been a great structure roughly semi-circular in shape with a spacious inner court. In the center of this

* Compare with Zuñi Creation Myth p. 216.

were two large circular kivas, one to the east and one to the west. Around it, between the inner and outer walls surrounding the court, were fourteen partitioned chambers; quarters for those who participated in the ceremonials held in the eastern kiva. Occupying the western half of the structure were similar chambers to quarter those participating in the ceremonials of the west kiva. At the southwest corner of the temple was a sun dial; a depression in which was set a rod in front of a grooved dial. The shadow of the stick cast by the sun at a certain time of year would provide a starting point on the dial from which months and days could be calculated. The calculations were made in the summer when the sun was progressing on the southern horizon. They determined the mid-summer months when the rituals of preparing pouches and grinding medicines could be conducted, and the mid-winter months during which the kiva ceremonials could be held.

The sun, as we know, was the father of all life, the primal source. He created the first world of fire, and he still manifested his power in sun rays and lightning, in flint, in fire itself. The fire in the kivas was thus held sacred, and lighting it was a solemn ceremony.

The block and drill stick of the derivative Navaho ceremonial fire drill today are still hewed from a cottonwood which has been struck by lightning and to which a sacrificial offering has been made. In the fire ceremony a young man and a boy are placed in the east, a young woman and a girl in the west, an old man in the south and an old woman in the north. Preparation of pouches, rattles and ritual paraphernalia are finished; medicine is ground on a stone inscribed with zigzag lightning and a rainbow; and all these arranged ceremonially around the fireplace. As the fire is drilled the songs and prayers commence. Now (as translated by Berard Haile)

> The fire of darkness appears . . .
> Long life fire appears . . .
> Moon fire appears . . .
> Darkness fire appears . . .
> Dawn fire appears . . .
> Sun fire appears . . .
> Long life fire appears, happiness fire appears,
>   sunlight fire appears . . .

As the sparks leap up, cedar bark is fed from the east, oak from the south, piñon from the west, scrub oak from the north, and lightning-struck cottonwood. All members participate—the young and old of both sexes standing in their ceremonial directions.

> To the fire of Emergence Elders he added fuel . . .
> To the fire of Emergence Young Men he added fuel . . .
> To the fire of Emergence Young Women she added fuel . . .
> To the fire of Emergence Children they added fuel . . .
> Now to the fire of Tree Woman, of trees of all kinds, to this they added fuel . . .
> To the fire of long life of happiness they added fuel . . .
> Nicely they added fuel . . .

Something of tremendous importance had taken place. In lighting this fire man had shifted the electrons from their orbits within the atom, and combustion had taken place with a consequent release of energy. But it was the spiritual energy of life evoked by the ceremonial that was more significant.

The prehistoric sun-worshippers of Mesa Verde knew it. And so now out of the great kiva and the fourteen ritual chambers to the east, and out of the other great kiva and its chambers to the west, they came filing into the open inner court. Naked and painted. Singing and dancing. To begin the great ceremonial from which have been derived two major ceremonials of the Navaho.s

According to Father Berard Haile and his informant Navaho singers, this ancient Sun Temple is the original Flint Home; the west kiva being identified with the female branch of the Flint Way ceremonial, and the east kiva with the male branch of Shooting Way; and each of their corresponding fourteen chambers where the ritual flints were ground and ritual preparations made, corresponding with the traditional fourteen groups of Navaho singers, exhibitors and performers with their specialties.

We are already familiar with the meanings of the ceremonials. In their background myth dramas Changing Woman is impregnated by the masculine sun force or fire force and the feminine moon force or water force. She thus becomes the vessel of the Holy Spirit, the "power descended on earth" of the gospel of the Essene Ebionites and the Navaho parallel to the Virgin Mary. She gives birth to Monster Slayer. He too appears in dual form as the hero brothers, the masucline sun child, and his feminine counterpart, the moon child. The ceremonials which they leave for their race after they destroy the monsters are the "incarnations of the

Wisdom of God," the Sun Father. In Flint Way the adulterous hero, the singer Gila Monster, and his "living pouch" each in turn becomes the Holy Vessel of Life. All the ritualism of both ceremonials observe the duality: the flint arrowheads are male and female, the cranebills, the canes. And stemming back to the Sun Temple where they originated, the kivas themselves are masculine and feminine; the fire invoked is both sun fire and moon fire.

All the ceremonials take place within a "holy vessel" whose wall is prescribed in symbolism as the magic circle. In the prehistoric Pueblo ceremonials the vessel was the Sun Temple with its circular kivas, known in the derivative Navaho ceremonials as the Flint Home or Flint Corral. This has its parallels in still other ceremonials such as the Spruce Corral or Dark Circle of Boughs within which the Mountain Top Way is held. In modern ceremonies the circle around the fireplace is made of flint arrowheads laid so as to point to the opening at the east, and stepping is in the traditional sunwise direction.

The circle of Pueblo and Navaho ceremonialism, the *mandala* of Eastern mysticism, and the hermetic vessel of the alchemistic philosophers of the Middle Ages, are thus synonymous. They all symbolize the cosmos and the psyche of man in which the reconciliation of the opposites take place.

On the biological plane the irreconcilable elements combine within the egg or the womb, and are reconciled in the issue of a new birth. In religious symbolism Christ thus reconciles in His own person the divinity of His father and the humanity of His mother. In alchemistic philosophy the *vas Hermetis* or Hermetic vase was prescribed for fusing the elements into the mysterious *aurum nostrum* or philosopher's stone. The vase, of course, symbolized both the cosmos and man, each containing the four elements: fire, air, water, earth, from which the fifth element or "quintessence" would arise when heated. The heat applied is synonymous with the yogic meditation of Eastern Buddhism and the "creative introversion" of Western psychology.

The parallel, then, between the Sun Temple of Mesa Verde and the atomic reactor, Clementine, of Los Alamos is not as far fetched as might be supposed. It is found in their ultimate meanings. They are both allegories. For the large part of physical energy is locked inside the atom, and the large part of psychic energy is locked within the psyche. And both the transformation of matter into energy, and the transfiguration of instinctual forces into creative energy, depend upon the reconciliation of the primal dual forces of all life. With the fusion a tremendous conflict takes place, and from it is released a new birth of energy.

This new form may be a Monster Slayer or a Monster Bomb, a new faith or a new fear. Only the guiding philosophy determines whether it be constructive or destructive.

As Roger Bacon, contemporary to the culminating days of Mesa Verde ceremonialism, 1214–1292, wrote in *De Secretis Operibus Artis et Naturae* (On the Secret Works of Art and Nature):

> A fifth part of experimental science concerns the fabrication of instruments of wonderfully excellent usefulness, such as machines for flying, or for moving vehicles without animals . . . or of navigating without oarsmen . . . Also machines can be made for walking in the sea and rivers . . . Important arts have been discovered . . . From the force of the salt called saltpeter so horrible a sound is produced at the bursting of so small a thing . . . that it exceeds the roar of sharp thunder, and the flash exceeds the greatest brilliancy of the lightning . . .

He continues in *Opus Maius:*

> All these foregoing (physical) sciences are, properly speaking, speculative. There is indeed in every science a practical side . . . Nevertheless of moral philosophy alone can it be said that it is essentially practical, for it deals with human conduct, with virture and vice, happiness and misery . . . Other sciences are of no account except as they help forward right action.

The Unified Field Theory

Despite our preoccupation with the mere industrial applications of modern Western Science, there is every indication that we are awakening to the philosophical meanings behind the technology of the Twentieth Century.

As Lincoln Barnett points out in his excellent *The Universe and Dr. Einstein,* all the phenomena of nature are produced by two primordial forces, gravitation and electromagnetism. These are modern physicists' names for the cosmic dualities as they manifest themselves in the physical universe. Electrons swirl in the electro-magnetic field of the atomic nucleus. Planets spin in the gravitational field of the sun. From the study of these phenomena have been developed the two theories, the two mathematical formulae by which we define the universe.

Max Planck in 1900 discovered that the radiant energy

of the sun was emitted, not in an unbroken stream of light waves, but in discontinuous bits of energy or quanta. By this Quantum Theory he developed the equation E over $Y = h$; that is, that in any process of radiation, either by the sun or radioactive substances, the amount of emitted energy divided by the frequency of radiation is always the same, a factor named for him Planck's Constant. Energy then is simply the product of the frequency of its radiation and the factor, Planck's Constant, $E = hY$.

In this relationship between the unknown and the known, Planck's Constant serves mathematically as a reconciling symbol. By its use the Quantum Theory thus defines the inner limits of man's knowledge of the microcosmic universe—of the invisible atom, the basic units of matter and force, all the realities of nature too small to be perceived.

Proceeding from this, Albert Einstein developed the Relativity Theory which defines the outer limits of man's knowledge of the macrocosmic universe—of interstellar space, immeasurable time, gravitation, all the realities of nature too vast and remote to be perceived. In one of the most important and famous equations in history, $E = MC^2$, he stated that energy is but mass multiplied by the square of the velocity of light. Or simply that mass is merely condensed energy—light, heat, sound, motion.

Again, in his use of the velocity of light, the superlative constant acts as a reconciling symbol between immeasurable energy and measurable mass. For like the area of a circle, the infinite and boundless energy of life is unknown and unknowable. And as the mathematicians of ancient Greece and the philosophers of the Middle Ages could only express it by means of the constant π in their attempts to reconcile the areas of a circle and a square, so do our modern physicists utilize Planck's Constant and the speed of light in their attempts to reconcile energy with mass and its frequency of radiation in both the microcosmic atom and the macrocosmic universe.

But though we were blind to its metaphysical meaning—and for forty years blind to the practical significance of Einstein's Mass-Energy equation, we finally awoke to its military application. With the explosion of the first atomic bomb, we knew that every pound of any kind of matter contains as much energy as is given off by the explosion of twenty million tons of TNT. And under the expedient of war, we first applied the principle to the destruction of life at Hiroshima and Nagasaki. Hence the modern West first looked at the synonymity of matter and energy in terms of the destruction of life and matter, rather than regarding the newly defined process as a possibility of transforming matter into the supreme life-energy for purposes beneficent to mankind.

Today we are developing the hydrogen bomb, a super H-bomb one thousand times more powerful than the first A-bomb. But concurrently we are continuing to develop our understanding of the philosophic meanings implicit in nuclear fission and fusion.

We have defined the cosmic dualities as they manifest themselves in the physical universe as gravitation and electromagnetism, and we have found a relationship between matter and energy. By the Quantum Theory we have defined the inner limits of the invisible atom, and by the Relativity Theory the outer limits of interstellar space. But like man, the macrocosmic image of the atom and the microcosmic duplicate of the universe, the electron bridges both, and plays a dual role as a unit of matter and a unit of energy. The two primordial forces of the universe perpetually perform a Deer Dance within the electromagnetic field of the atomic nucleus and the gravitational field of the sun.

So in the physical realm, as in the psychological, we need one theory, one equation, to set forth the common law that governs both the infinitesimally small and the infinitesimally large, and reconciles both the fundamental forces of the universe. This "Unified Field Theory" has now been completed by Dr. Albert Einstein after thirty years of work. He has not yet verified it by experiments, and few other physicists understand it.

Yet in it and the work to follow, lies the hope that through our Western physics, as through our Western psychology, we will reach, as Einstein says, that core of metaphysics which alone validates all our approaches to the ultimate truth: *

> The most beautiful and most profound emotion we can experience is the sensation of the mystical. It is the source of all true science. He to whom this emotion is a stranger, who can no longer wonder and stand rapt in awe, is as good as dead. To know that what is impenetrable to us really exists, manifesting itself as the highest wisdom and the most radiant beauty which our dull faculties can comprehend only in their most primitive forms—this knowledge, this feeling is at the center of true religiousness.

* *The Universe and Dr. Einstein,* by Lincoln Barnett. William Sloane Associates, Inc., New York, 1949.

8 The Crucible of Conflict

FROM OUR BACK PASTURE, a meadow among the pines on the high slope of the Sangre de Cristos, we stare down upon a corner of one of the most beautiful, paradoxical and significant panoramas in the world today. In its entirety we know it as the Four Corners, the immemorial domain of the Rock and the Canyon, the center of gravity of the continental Colorado Pyramid, the wilderness heartland of America.

Perhaps in no other comparable area on earth are condensed so many contradictions, or manifested so clearly the opposite polarities of all life. The oldest forms of life discovered in this hemisphere, and the newest agent of mass death. The oldest cities in America and the newest. The Sun Temple of Mesa Verde and the nuclear fission laboratories of the Pajarito Plateau. The Indian drum and the atom smasher. Men flying like birds seeding the clouds for rain, while others below them, naked and painted, dancing with rattlesnakes in their mouths. Everywhere the future stumbles upon the jutting past, the invisible gives shape to the visible, blind instinct points the way for reason.

There is no describing it. But it has been symbolized for us in the sand-paintings of Navaho ceremonialism: the plateau-square of the Four Corners inscribed within a circle. We recognize it now as both the crucible of conflict and the *mandala* of reconciliation of the cosmic dualities.

For here as nowhere else has the confiict been fought so bitterly, and have the opposing principles approached so closely a fusion. At that fusion there will arise the new faith for which we are crying so desperately. A faith big enough to embrace all of mankind's experiences of the past, all our religious creeds, and all our scientific concepts.

It would not be too great a coincidence if the new symbols of that faith rose out of those of the past, just as mankind itself has risen to successive stages of evolution through the supreme symbol of the *sipapu* epitomized as the Grand Canyon.

An Historical Perspective

Myself, I can't account for the inexpressible fascination that this Hopi *sipapu* holds for me. Whenever things go out of focus, money runs short and the temper rises like a barometer, I always take a squint at Grand Canyon as a down payment on another lease of equanimity.

J. B. Priestly, a noted Englishman, recommends it to us even more extravagantly. "If I were an American," he advises, "I should make my remembrance of it the final test of men, art, and policies. I should ask myself: is this good enough to exist in the same country as the Canon? How would I feel about this man, this kind of art, these political measures, if I were near that Rim? Every member or officer of the Federal Government ought to remind himself, with triumphant pride, that he is on the staff of the Grand Canon."

The Hopi, I think, would pass this test. Their art, social science and government, the kiva ceremonialism which includes their cosmology and cosmogenesis, their very lives are patterned on it. Some of the rest of us fall a little short. And there are other noted Englishmen who do not seem aware of its existence.

As a matter of fact it is sunset here on the Rim now, an excellent moment to appraise Arnold J. Toynbee's colossal *A Study of History* by the Canyon's own colossal dimensions. We don't need to read the whole first seven volumes, nor even D. C. Somervell's excellent one-volume abridgement. A *Life* artist has recently illustrated his metaphor for us.

Here is the deep, shadowy Canyon itself—the *sipapu* of all life. Up its steep sides come crawling from the depths of subhumanity the twenty-one human figures representing the major civilizations of history. Most of them didn't get very far. Like the

Egyptiac, Sumeric, Babylonic, Hellenic, Maya, and Andean, they are lying dead on a low ledge. Stretched out and dying are the primitive societies like the Hopi. Stranded on minor peaks, still alive but unable to climb higher, are five "arrested" civilizations like the Ottoman and Polynesian. Five civilizations are still climbing. Four of them are short of breath and weakening in this altitude: the Islamic, Hindu, Chinese-Japanese, and the Russian. Only one is strong and healthy and has far out-climbed the others: our own Euro-American civilization.

The picture, the metaphor, is apt indeed up here. But at just this instant, in actuality, there comes striding up the Bright Angel Trail from the bottom of the Canyon a grinning broad-faced Hopi. The very same Hopi seen in the picture stretched out and dying as a "Primitive Society." Much later, far behind him, comes "Western Civilization" in the dejected persons of a group of Euro-American tourists astraddle some burros which (in our imagination) are labelled "Machine."

What is wrong with the picture?

It seems strange as we read Toynbee with the care his study warrants, that never, on any page, do we get the sense of surging uplift, of tumultuous upheavals from dark depths, that mark the history of mankind as they do the geologic history of the earth. One doubts that he has ever experienced the tremendous, psychical impact of the upflung Himalayas, the lofty Andes, the rugged Rockies, or this greatest chasm on the face of the earth. He gives the impression of a historian who sees everything from the perspective of a flat Aegean plain washed by the placid Mediterranean.

That indeed is his forte: the Hellenic civilization. It is the keystone by which he measures the structures of all the others. The basis of our own Western civilization, founded on the same rational principle or determinate theoretic component. And so all the great movements of history take place on this comparatively horizontal plane. One after another the ancient civilizations rise like gentle prominences, flower, congeal, and slide forward into the next with a kind of undulatory movement like that of a snake.

There are never any mysterious up-surges of unknown forces from deep in the soul of mankind, no strange cataclysmic plunges into obscurity, comparable to earthquakes, the rise and fall of continents which reflect the same upheavals within the earth. Yet each in some way is related to the other and dependent upon it;

both are the sheer utterance of life itself. A life stemming from a common source, whose motion and direction is unpredictable, whose logic is still not deducible. And so in Toynbee's work the great vertical, secular systems of mankind founded upon the intuitional principle or undifferentiated aesthetic component—the Hindu, Chinese, Andean, Maya and Mexic—are sketchily portrayed at best.

The reason for the successive rise and decline of all the twenty-one civilizations is embodied in Toynbee's theme of "Challenge and Response." Society is challenged by environment, war and various other rationalized pressures. As long as it successfully responds to these challenges it continues to expand; when at last it fails to respond, it perishes. But all these expansions are progressively outward, horizontally. Eastward. Southward. Mostly Westward to Europe, to Euro-America. Until now Western civilization has spread around the world. The expansive culmination of the basic Graeco-Roman civilization.

Consistently enough all the four world-religious systems —and all religions are vertical by their very nature—Toynbee sees as products of the merging of the various secular systems. Islam results from the merging of the ancient civilization of Israel and Iran with the modern civilization of the Near and Middle East. Hinduism bridges the ancient culture of the Aryans in India and the modern Hindu culture. Mahayana Buddhism links the history of ancient China with the modern history of the Far East. Christianity rises from the encounter between the Syrian and Graeco-Roman civilizations. . . . All being responses of the various civilizations to the challenge of Graeco-Roman penetration over a period of some 1,600 years.

It is no coincidence that 4004 B.C., the date set by the Christian Church for the creation of the world, is also the approximate date at which began the twenty-one major civilizations. Thus, concomitant with the horizontal spread of Western civilization has been the spread of Christianity. Until now the Christian-Western civilization reigns supreme.

So here too in Toynbee the greatest vertical religions of mankind are but shallowly plumbed. Nowhere do we find in it anything like the intuitive appraisal of Mahayana Buddhism made by F. S. C. Northrop in his penetrative *The Meeting of East and West.* Nor anything to compare with the remarkable exposition of Chinese Taoism made by Richard Wilhelm and C. G. Jung. There is scarcely a mention of the basic mytho-religious patterns that still hold sway in Africa and America. In it no continents rise and sink, leaving their vestiges of vanished civilizations engraven on the heart of land and man. The tiny, helpless, prehistoric mammal does not meet the challenge of the great armored dinosaur with the divine biological response attested by the great French biologist, Lecomte du Nouy, in his *Human Destiny*. Mankind has no record of its continuous evolutionary climb through four previous worlds to its present state of existence as attested by Buddhism, Taoism, all ancient mystics, modern psychologists, and the Hopi coming up the trail. That man has a divine destiny which will continue to guide him in his climb, which basic intuitional truth is the core of all valid religions, is not suggested. . . .

Without wishing to seem derogatory about Toynbee's work, a study so comprehensive and erudite as to be a classic of its kind, we must yet consider it here on the Rim as a study in two dimensions with little vertical depth.

There is an indication that its writer himself has some misgivings about its thinness. In his later *Civilization on Trial* Toynbee questions his own earlier assumption that these relatively modern civilizations are the "intelligible field" of historical study, the religions serving only as links between them. He now suggests that religion itself may be the "intelligible field," and that the purpose of civilizations is but to spread it among mankind.

This extreme and abrupt volte-face prompts us to ask: But which religion, which civilization's concept of a Divine Plan? The answer is even more surprising. . . .

> "There will be no reason to suppose that Christianity itself will be superseded by some distinct, separate and higher religion which will serve as a chrysalis between the death of the present Western civilization and the birth of its children. . . . So far from that, if our secular Western civilization perishes, Christianity may be expected not only to endure but to grow in wisdom and stature as the result of a fresh experience of secular catastrophe." *

Q. E. D.

But just at this moment, reassured as we are of the divine impregnability of our Christian-Western ideology, a gust of wind whips down from the Rockies. *A Study of History* is blown from our

* *Civilization on Trial,* by Arnold J. Toynbee. Oxford University Press, New York, 1947.

hands. It hits a gnarled old piñon on the Rim. The ripped off cover tumbles down into a pack-rat's nest lodged in the roots. We peer down. What an excellent roof it makes that sub-human little family, bent in the middle to keep out wind and snow; its jacket title printing vaguely reminiscent of the letters painted on the tin roof of an old barn.

But we aren't concerned about the mere binding. Where is the text? One would suppose that the history of six-thousand years would be quite visible against the background of time. Yes. There they are at last! Twenty-one paper-thin pages hovering in the blue and purple depths of a time 217 miles long, twelve miles wide and a mile deep carven out of eternity. Twenty-one civilizations floating against the six-thousand year top layer of an historical record of 2,000 million years. Convoluting like dry leaves in the air, rubbing together with a dry, brittle rustle. Catching the bright rays of the sun from above, enveloped by the dark shadows from below. How small and light they are! Seemingly impervious to the invisible laws of nature.

"Long live the Pharaoh!" echoes one of the pages. Then a down-draft catches the Egyptiac civilization and sucks it down into obscurity.

"Hail Caesar!" And Pax Romana swoops downward.

"Heil, Fuehrer!" But invisibly the law of gravity reaches up a long arm and snatches the Third Reich too.

There they go, twenty of them, lost in space, engulfed in time, sinking to rest with the fossilized remains of the brute-animal civilizations of the prehistoric past.

One remains still ballooned aloft above the Canyon. He can't read it, the Hopi beside me; he can't read. But we know what it is: the Christian-Western civilization. It sails quite grandly too. But somehow, for all the up-drafts, the invisible gravitational field draws it down too. Or maybe it lodges somewhere down there on an undiscovered ledge to serve as nesting material for a magpie, the bird of augury.

"I go home now," says the Hopi, and a shabby primitive home it is. "I got those work to do. Them kiva duties."

And one remains on the Rim alone. Staring down into the Canyon's sublime depths: at Cheop's Pyramid and the Tower of Ra; at Zoroaster's Temple, Confucius' Temple, and the Krishna Shrine; at the Valhalla Plateau and Woton's Throne; King Arthur's

Castle, Gawain Abyss and Lancelot's Point; at Solomon's Temple, Aztec Amphitheater, Toltec Point, Cardenas Butte, and Alarcon Terrace. Washed by seas of glowing color, changing shape in light and shadow, it sees a realm of the fantastic unreal. A world of illusion.

What if Buddhism is right in its assumption that the material world of the senses is nonexistent? That all physical matter, as Western Science now proclaims, is but a manifestation of that primordial energy constituting the electron? What if the Hopi is right in persisting to climb through all the successive worlds of his existence by adhering to his kiva ceremonialism in preference to the transient beliefs and material riches of his conquerors? Is the Rock that we shall cling to now the Mountain Around Which Moving Was Done, invisible to us as to the Navahos because its reality lies only within us?

We are beginning to realize, like the ancients, that time is not a linear progression of the past, present, and future. It is a complete circle enclosing the imperishable fullness of divine creation, linking the Beginning and the End. The Uroboric serpent eating its own tail. So it is with human history. It does not comprise a straight-line evolution from prehistoric societies up through primitive cultures to the proud apogee of twentieth-century Western civilizations. Previous civilizations, we know, achieved heights of conception and accomplishment we have not attained. Nor can we measure their achievements on our scale of materialistic values.

Navaho and Pueblo ceremonialism, like the religious rituals of all ancient Indian America, has never succumbed to our modern assumption that the world is wholly material. It asserts the belief in the inherent wholeness of man and his harmonious relationship with stone and star, with all the living presences in the earth and sky. Strange as this metaphysical belief may seem to us today, its ages-old truth still carries an oddly familiar ring of the ultimate meaning of life for all mankind. Toward realization of this, mythology, astronomy, nuclear physics, religion, and metaphysics are all traveling their different paths.

It is to this end purpose of human existence that Navaho and Pueblo ceremonialism, which is so uniquely American in sinew, blood, and thought, and yet which is so universally the property of all mankind, has so greatly contributed in the idiom of those mountains and rivers, those masked gods of our childhood, whose familiar and loved outlines have shaped our lives and thoughts.

* * * *

MASKED GODS was designed and decorated by Ralph Douglass, Professor of Art at The University of New Mexico. The jacket design is based on the Hopi helmet mask worn by Kipok Kachina, the four feathers symbolizing the Four Directions. The case stamping is from a Hopi pottery design. The end sheets are from an Ácoma pottery design symbolizing clouds and rain. The title page drawing is adapted from a Navaho sand-painting. The drawing on page 10 is from a Hopi pottery design; that on page 161 is from a Santo Domingo pottery design; that on page 336 is from a Zuñi pottery design; and that on page 438 is a personified rainbow figure from a Navaho sand-painting. The decorations for the chapter initials are from similar Navaho, Pueblo, and other Indian sources.